DETERRENCE IN THE 21ST CENTURY

BEYOND BOUNDARIES: CANADIAN DEFENCE AND STRATEGIC STUDIES SERIES

Rob Huebert, Series Editor

ISSN 1716-2645 (Print) ISSN 1925-2919 (Online)

Canada's role in international military and strategic studies ranges from peacebuilding and Arctic sovereignty to unconventional warfare and domestic security. This series provides narratives and analyses of the Canadian military from both an historical and a contemporary perspective.

No. 1 · *The Generals: The Canadian Army's Senior Commanders in the Second World War*
J. L. Granatstein

No. 2 · *Art and Memorial: The Forgotten History of Canada's War Art*
Laura Brandon

No. 3 · *In the National Interest: Canadian Foreign Policy and the Department of Foreign Affairs and International Trade, 1909–2009*
Greg Donaghy and Michael K. Carroll

No. 4 · *Long Night of the Tankers: Hitler's War Against Caribbean Oil*
David J. Bercuson and Holger H. Herwig

No. 5 · *Fishing for a Solution: Canada's Fisheries Relations with the European Union, 1977–2013*
Donald Barry, Bob Applebaum, and Earl Wiseman

No. 6 · *From Kinshasa to Kandahar: Canada and Fragile States in Historical Perspective*
Michael K. Carroll and Greg Donaghy

No. 7 · *The Frontier of Patriotism: Alberta and the First World War*
Adriana A. Davies and Jeff Keshen

No. 8 · *China's Arctic Ambitions and What They Mean for Canada*
P. Whitney Lackenbauer, Adam Lajeunesse, James Manicom, and Frédéric Lasserre

No. 9 · *Scattering Chaff: Canadian Air Power and Censorship during the Kosovo War*
Bob Bergen

No. 10 · *A Samaritan State Revisited: Historical Perspectives on Canadian Foreign Aid*
Greg Donaghy and David Webster

No. 11 · *Working for Canada: A Pilgrimage in Foreign Affairs from the New World Order to the Rise of Populism*
Geoff White

No. 12 · *Polar Cousins: Comparing Antarctic and Arctic Geostrategic Futures*
Edited by Christian Leuprecht with Douglas Causey

No. 13 · *Deterrence in the 21st Century: Statecraft in the Information Age*
Edited by Eric Ouellet, Madeleine D'Agata, and Keith Stewart

UNIVERSITY OF CALGARY
Press

DETERRENCE
IN THE 21ST CENTURY

STATECRAFT IN THE INFORMATION AGE

EDITED BY

**Eric Ouellet, Madeleine D'Agata,
and Keith Stewart**

Beyond Boundaries:
Canadian Defence and Strategic Studies Series
ISSN 1716-2645 (Print) ISSN 1925-2919 (Online)

University of Calgary Press
2500 University Drive NW
Calgary, Alberta
Canada T2N 1N4
press.ucalgary.ca

LIBRARY AND ARCHIVES CANADA CATALOGUING IN PUBLICATION

Title: Deterrence in the 21st century : statecraft in the information age / edited by Eric Ouellet, Madeleine D'Agata, and Keith Stewart.
Names: Ouellet, Eric, 1968- editor. | D'Agata, Madeleine, editor. | Stewart, Keith (Defence scientist), editor.
Series: Beyond boundaries series ; no. 13.
Description: Series statement: Beyond boundaries : Canadian defence and strategic studies series, 1716-2645 ; no. 13 | Includes bibliographical references and index.
Identifiers: Canadiana (print) 20230556248 | Canadiana (ebook) 20230556361 | ISBN 9781773854038 (softcover) | ISBN 9781773854809 (hardcover) | ISBN 9781773854052 (PDF) | ISBN 9781773854069 (EPUB) | ISBN 9781773854045 (Open Access PDF)
Subjects: LCSH: Deterrence (Strategy) | LCSH: Disinformation—Prevention. | LCSH: Information warfare.
Classification: LCC U162.6 .D48 2024 | DDC 355.02—dc23

The University of Calgary Press acknowledges the support of the Government of Alberta through the Alberta Media Fund for our publications. We acknowledge the financial support of the Government of Canada. We acknowledge the financial support of the Canada Council for the Arts for our publishing program.

Support for this book has been provided by Defence Research and Development Canada.

Alberta Government Canada Canada Council for the Arts Conseil des Arts du Canada

Copyediting by Ryan Perks
Cover image: Colourbox 10679220
Cover design, page design, and typesetting by Melina Cusano

CONTENTS

FOREWORD

Twenty-first-century communication technologies offer many opportunities for economic growth and social development but present also many challenges and threats to democratic nations like Canada. Among those threats, Internet-powered disinformation is a potent one that is becoming increasingly worrisome. Individual reputations can be ruined rapidly, discord and manipulation among various groups can be easily planted, and institutions like the Canadian Armed Forces (CAF) and the Government of Canada are certainly not immune to the destabilizing effect of lies, exaggerations, and twisted truths conveyed through communication technologies by organized malign actors.

Our troops deployed in support of building a peaceful and democratic world in countries such as Latvia, Ukraine, or Mali have faced various forms of disinformation campaigns. Domestically, the COVID-19 pandemic has shown how much we need to be ever vigilant against foreign and internal actors seeking to undermine our democratic foundations. This is indeed a very real challenge.

The CAF has been proactive in developing strategies and action plans to contain and protect Canada against disinformation. Yet, this is a dynamic phenomenon fuelled by ongoing technological and social change, and it requires constant update to our knowledge and approaches to remain effective in dealing with such threats. It is in this context that this timely book introduces an in-depth discussion on whether dissuasion would be an effective policy to fight back. This book brings together many experts from Canada and abroad to provide answers to central questions useful for future policy formulations and implementation, military doctrines, and procedures.

A range of important questions are addressed here, such as whether the fight against disinformation should follow the more classical approach of using both deterrence by denial and punishment; how lessons from nuclear deterrence can be distilled and applied to today's challenges; how well is Canada prepared in dealing with the new disinformation strategies emerging from anti-democratic adversaries; what can be learned from other democracies; what kind of existing and emerging approaches show promises; and many more.

Disinformation presents a complex and dynamic challenge that will be with us for quite some time. Well-informed policies and military doctrines regarding the information environment are needed more than ever. The ideas, knowledge, and recommendations found in this book represent a strong step in the right direction. Hence, I recommend to anyone interested in combatting disinformation, either in uniform or not, to read this book and push ever further our collective efforts to defeat disinformation.

VICE-ADMIRAL B. AUCHTERLONIE
Commander, Canadian Joint Operations Command

PREFACE

The last few years have seen an incredible increase in the proliferation of false or deceptive information through the information environment—especially through the communication channels provided by social media platforms. While not all false information is promulgated with malicious intent, state and non-state adversaries are actively exploiting the information environment to engage Canada's military, government, public, and institutions to influence their will, attitudes, and behaviours. Several key factors have contributed to the increased importance of the information environment as an "area of operations" for our adversaries. First, engaging with target audiences is made easy when the cyber domain is leveraged to spread false information. Not only is adversaries' reach enhanced by the high level of connectedness Western democracies have to the cyber domain, the generation and sharing of deceptive content can be done quickly and cheaply thanks to algorithms designed to create disinformation intended for online distribution (i.e., "bots"). Second, Canada and its closest allies are democracies that value and promote free speech—a quality that reduces the extent to which access to information within the cyber domain will be put under the control of governments in an effort to reduce exposures to disinformation or even hateful content. The way we use and treat the technologies designed to connect with others not only makes us vulnerable to adversary actions, it has served as an enabler for adversaries and made their operations in the information environment almost inevitable.

This book is about gathering the information Canada needs to begin the development of a framework for devising methods that discourage adversaries' engagement with Canada's institutions and its public. In our view, to successfully deter an actor from engaging us in the information domain, we must have adequate awareness and control of the information environment so that we can shape adversaries' understanding of Canada's readiness and capability to defend itself against psychological and social attempts to manipulate its various institutions.

The first step in creating this book was to hold group sessions in which the critical knowledge gaps were identified in our understanding of the factors that must be considered to discourage adversary attacks in the information environment. The gaps were translated into key issues to be addressed by the chapters. In the next step, we reached out to internationally respected experts across multiple fields to provide us with their perspectives on one or more of the key issues. The editorial team spent long hours over the past year poring over (and chasing after) proposals and manuscripts to create this book. We anticipate that it will have been worth the effort, and that this will serve as an important reference to inform the development and validation of methods and techniques to mitigate the impact of attacks in the cyber domain.

Peter Kwantes, PhD
Chief Scientist, Defence and Research and Development Canada,
Toronto Research Centre

Introduction

Eric Ouellet[1]

It is no secret that Western democracies are facing significant challenges from Internet-based campaigns of disinformation conducted by various adversaries since the early 2000s. The People's Republic of China, Russia, and Iran have been pointed out on numerous occasions as key agents of disinformation, but we should also note that in North America, anti-liberal and anti-democratic domestic non-state actors are increasingly involved in active disinformation. These acts of disinformation have taken different forms such as spreading rumours about the origins of the COVID-19 virus or the war situation in Ukraine, revealing publically compromising private emails without context, organizing character-assassination campaigns against certain individuals, posting confusing information about electoral procedures, etc.

Such aggressions are not new, and in the past have been committed through various means of communication. They were quite common during the Cold War, when both official and secretive propaganda and rumour-spreading activities were organized by the West and the East. However, given the information technology revolution of the last few decades, the potential harm that disinformation could cause has reached unprecedented levels. As any society is ultimately built on trust in its institutions, and, given our greater reliance on information sharing through easily accessible technology, we find our economic, social, and political structures more vulnerable than ever to those who seek to sow confusion and discord. Furthermore, such vulnerabilities are increasingly becoming an arena for great power rivalry, where a political and strategic fracture between liberal democracies and non-liberal regimes is widening and becoming more apparent.

It is in this context that the Canada's Department of National Defence (DND) has been tasked with exploring new avenues to protect Canada, and more generally North America, against disinformation. As an agency of DND, Defence Research and Development Canada (DRDC) launched a substantive research project seeking to evaluate if and how disinformation can be deterred in the twenty-first century. Hence, the title of this book, *Deterrence in the 21st Century: Statecraft in the Information Environment*. This book constitutes a first step in this research effort by providing the latest knowledge and thinking about how deterrence as a posture and disinformation as a threat can both conceptually and pragmatically inform policy, doctrine, and capability use and acquisition. This volume is the outcome of a call for papers sent in 2020 and 2021 that reached out broadly to academics, experts, and practitioners in Canada and abroad who have worked on new and emergent notions involving deterrence and disinformation to guide how we can fight back against disinformation and its consequences.

At the core of this book is the argument that the posture taken so far by the Canadian government and other Western states is mostly guided by inward-looking approaches, and that this is not sufficient to counter disinformation effectively. Concepts such as societal resilience build on reinforcing social justice, cohesion, and trust in key institutions through transparent and fair laws, policies, and programs, or information inoculation based on improving digital literacy and general civic education; each of these concepts focus on our societies' own vulnerabilities. Yet, disinformation involves adversaries who deliberately plan and implement activities in the information environment with malign intentions. Understanding their approaches and goals, and more importantly how their world views, prejudices, and deeply held preconceptions regarding Western societies frame their actions is equally important if one wants to be proactive in defeating disinformation. In other words, an outward-looking posture is also necessary.

This is where the concept of deterrence assumes its greatest importance. Any form of deterrence is built on understanding adversaries' strategies, tactics, goals, preferred approaches, and their assessment of their own strengths and of our own weak points, etc., so that we can pre-empt them from attacking by changing their calculus. In a deterrence posture, the other's mental world is the central focus. And yet, finer forms of deterrence require reflexivity. To this end, we must be critical of our own thinking about how our adversaries are construing us in order to avoid building our own preconceived notions into our assessment of these adversaries' world views. With this perspective in mind, this book aims to shape the contours of what a deterrence posture against disinformation may look like.

Before presenting the various chapters of this book and their unique contributions to the understanding of disinformation deterrence in the contemporary world, it is useful to provide some conceptual definitions and clarifications, as research on deterrence and disinformation is still evolving in many different directions.

What Is Disinformation?

A first issue about disinformation that often leads to some confusion is that even if most of the twenty-first-century disinformation activities, as well as their countermeasures, are conducted using Internet-based information and communication technologies, they are not simply reducible to matters of technology. Automated computerized systems that create social media accounts and disseminate false information, or complex systems that identify narratives originally coming from dubious sources, for instance, are all part of the world of disinformation. Yet, what is actually believed by flesh-and-blood people and their actual behaviours that might ensue, the actual impact on policies and decision making, as examples, are the true stakes of disinformation and counter-disinformation. In other words, the cyber domain is a key enabler of today's world of disinformation, but it needs to be understood as a socio-political issue rather than a purely technological one. Disinformation, such as spreading rumours, is as old as humanity, and does not need advanced technology to be effective. The Soviet KGB of old is well-known to have developed disinformation almost to an art form, often referred to as "active measures" (Cull et al., 2017), which included activities such as creating front organizations to disseminate certain messages, recruiting and cultivating agents of influence in foreign countries, spreading fake stories in foreign media, and producing high-quality forgeries to sow confusion. Many of these types of activities are still seen today, but they are leveraging Internet-based technologies for dissemination.

Another issue is a matter of definition, as multiple terms, such as "fake news," "post-truth era," "information pollution," "alternative facts," "misinformation," or "disinformation," have been used to describe these new threats, which also creates some confusion. Recently, there seems to be some sort of consensus around "disinformation" being the most accurate one (Kapantai et al., 2020). One useful definition that incorporates both the notion of a wilful attempt to create confusion and today's technological reality is "the purposeful distribution of fake, misleading, fabricated or manipulated content. These actors rely on 'computational propaganda'—or the use of automation, algorithms, and big data analytics—in order to influence or deceive social media users" (Bradshaw & Howard, 2021).

There are various techniques employed in putting forward disinformation campaigns, and some emerging typologies can be useful as well, especially in identifying and assessing how to respond to such disinformation (Kapantai et al., 2020). For instance, they include entirely fabricated stories and hoaxes, conspiracy theories built on existing beliefs, pseudo-scientific statements or even complete studies but with somewhat altered research results, partially true rumours, trolling (implanting incendiary comments) and posting excessively positive or negative reviews, biased analyses that may appear genuine, etc. Each of these generic forms of disinformation requires different countermeasures at the tactical level, but taken collectively they can be part of a larger strategic effort. Hence, another important distinction to keep in mind when discussing disinformation is the level of analysis, and whether it is approached from a tactical or strategic viewpoint.

The disinformation of today is also framed by the political, social, and economic constructs of the Internet-based realm. In particular, the increased use of privately owned web platforms, which are responding first and foremost to market logic rather than societal norms, has a number of quite negative consequences on matters such as data protection and privacy; controlling content for lies, hate speech, and subversive narratives; allowing foreign states and their proxies to use them for their own purposes, as well as local actors pursuing political objectives seeking to undermine democratic institutions (Salter et al., 2019). This particular context is probably the most challenging part of Western democracies' responses to disinformation, as regulating market-based firms on matters of social and political narrative content is essentially anathema to liberalism (Freelon & Wells, 2020). Not only does regulation find itself lagging behind new forms and techniques of disinformation, but many of the countermeasures, to remain within the rule of law, are also reactive and require painstaking analysis and research to prove lies, hoaxes, or true authorship. Furthermore, given the scope and amount of disinformation, countermeasures such as "reality checks" and "fact checking" put forward by legitimate news media outlets and various organizations in civil society simply cannot keep up with the pace (Tsfati et al., 2020, p. 158).

These ongoing twenty-first-century disinformation campaigns are often done or sponsored by states and politicized non-state actors aiming to undermine liberal democracies. When it comes to state actors, they see such a goal as being in their interest in achieving international dominance, while Western non-state actors consider liberal democracy bankrupt. Those two generic groups of actors can be seen as "objective allies" in disinformation, even if it appears that active collaboration between states and Western non-state actors seems to be quite limited, and usually driven by other factors like vague ideological sympathies, or mercenary purposes. Many of those disinformation attacks are opportunistic in nature and leverage short-term legitimate concerns, yet they can have a longer-term strategic impact through the ongoing erosion of trust. A recent example is the active disinformation on short-term issues such as the campaign put forward by the People's Republic of China and Russia to undermine public confidence in COVID-19 vaccines, as formally noted by the European Union (Emmott, 2021). However, there are greater concerns about the compounding and longer-lasting corroding effects of disinformation campaigns against democratic institutions with regards to the management of public health, protection of privacy, protection of basic freedom and liberties, etc. Trust in the liberal state and its various agencies could suffer a host of damages that are difficult to repair (Rini, 2019). Years of active disinformation certainly played an important role in the lead-up to the 2021 Capitol riot in the United States, an event that came dangerously close to a far-right attempt at a coup d'état. This example alone illustrates how much Canada has a vested interest in fighting disinformation from a wider North American perspective.

On the brighter side, however, several analysts note that resilience to disinformation within Western democracies is greater than it is often presented by various authors and think tanks (Humprecht et al., 2020). The most salient disinformation events are often short-lived and can be corrected by sound public communications. As well, some have also highlighted that the greatest threat might be in "distrusting trust." An exaggerated belief in the vulnerability of Western audiences could lead Western states to become less liberal over time in order to protect "truth" from their citizenries. In other words, according to some analysts the majority of citizens are in fact a lot less gullible than some experts and politicians believe, but in reacting by implementing state measures limiting freedom of expression these same citizens might become less trusting of their governments (Dobber et al., 2020). This can be a dangerous vicious circle that ironically supports the objectives sought by anti-liberal disinformation actors.

Disinformation in Canada

In light of this broader context, Canada finds itself in a situation not that much different from that of other smaller democratic states. Academic research about disinformation against Canada is still limited at the present time. A search of the available literature using the terms "disinformation" and "Canada" yields less than fifty academic articles at the time of writing. Most research and publically released information tends to be events driven, with some notable exceptions (Jackson, 2018). In the wake of revelations about foreign interference in the 2016 US presidential election, several publications focusing on prevention and post-factum assessment of disinformation during the Canadian election of 2019 were produced from various sources: academia, government, think tanks, and news media (Dubois & McKelvey, 2019; Tenove, 2020; Tenove & Tworek, 2019). More recently, with revelations of the People's Republic of China's sustained disinformation activities regarding the origin of the SARS-CoV-2 pathogen, the focus once again moved, this time toward COVID-19-related disinformation (MacDonald et al., 2020).

Information about disinformation in Canada remains mostly in publications from governmental agencies, and essentially from the Canadian Security Intelligence Service's (CSIS) open publications. These documents present disinformation in Canada in general terms and offer limited material to work with. The *CSIS Public Report 2020*, for instance, states that

> While foreign interference conducted by hostile state actors and their proxies most often occurs in the form of human interaction, the manipulative activities of foreign entities on a range of online social media platforms are increasingly of concern. Most recently, such state-sponsored manipulation, including through disinformation, has sought to reshape or undermine certain narratives to sow doubt about the origins of the coronavirus and pandemic as well as the means required to counter it; discredit democratic responses to COVID-19 while casting their own responses as superior; and erode confidence in Canada's values of democracy and human rights. Russia and Russian Intelligence Services have, for example, been actively engaged

> in disinformation campaigns since March 2020 in an effort to blame the West for the COVID-19 pandemic. This is part of a broader campaign to discredit and create divisions in the West, promote Russia's influence abroad, and push for an end to Western sanctions (CSIS, 2020, p. 23).

This longer quote constitutes, in fact, all this report has to say about disinformation. This particular example shows that for the time being the Canadian government has not engaged its population to a significant degree on the risks and dangers that disinformation represents to the country's democratic and liberal institutions. If experts and bureaucrats inside the Canadian state are well aware of the issues at stake, monitor closely new developments, and propose measures built on constructive counter-narratives, a wider dialogue on where the country stands in this brave new world remains to be initiated.

The greater source of open information about disinformation in Canada remains for the time being in mainstream news media, and a few civilian organizations such as the University of Toronto's Citizen Lab. Most of the reporting in news media tends to emphasize particular disinformation attempts, such as the claim that Canada has opened quarantine concentration camps (Tasker, 2020), that a Quebec-based professor is an active agent of disinformation for Russia (Daigle, 2020), that India is engaged in disinformation against Canadians Sikhs ("WSO's report alleges," 2021), etc. In other cases, there are general concerns raised about disinformation in Canada (Andersen, 2021; Farber & Fishman, 2021; "Half of Canadians," 2021) or general comments about the annual publication of the CSIS report, with an emphasis on disinformation. The public message, however limited it might be, is that disinformation attempts in Canada are real and actively spread by both foreign and domestic agents of influence, but the overall impact remains unstated and un-assessed.

Civil organizations such as the University of Toronto Citizen Lab offer more elaborate analyses, and on a wide set of topics ranging from privacy concerns related to certain phone or computer applications, to proposed legal changes, to the role of foreign firms in the upcoming implementation of 5G networks, to name just a few. Similarly, the NATO Association of Canada has created a Centre for Disinformation Studies presenting various research analyses on disinformation in social media, how Russia is using it, how the People's Republic of China's control over information is aligned with its disinformation campaign, etc. Although these organizations provide more in-depth research on various facets of disinformation, much of this output nonetheless fails to assess the actual scope and impact of disinformation in Canada.

A few recent studies have been published, especially in the context of the COVID-19 pandemic, that are more empirical in nature. These studies have examined beliefs in conspiracy theories in Canada, and one in particular is focused on theories about the non-natural origins of the virus, and which seem to have been embraced by a substantive number of Canadians ("Significant minority," 2021), but such results and methodologies are questionable. The Biden administration in the United States and many other governments have been questioning the World Health Organization's findings about the origins of the virus, and as noted in a detailed analysis in the *Bulletin of the Atomic Scientists*, Western journalists have uncritically swallowed dubious explanations from people linked to the Chinese regime, and by doing so have unwittingly spread disinformation. In many ways, the average Canadian seems wiser than pollsters.

Other research involved assessing whether racist acts, especially toward Asians, are on the rise in Canada (Chinese Canadian National Council Toronto Chapter, 2021), and the role of far-right disinformation has been highlighted. However, the actual causal relationship between disinformation and such racist acts is implied rather than demonstrated. As well, the possibility that Beijing-led disinformation aimed at fostering anti-Asian feelings in order to create (perversely) more sympathy for its propaganda is also not addressed. Hence, there is a general sense that Canada is indeed impacted by disinformation, and it appears to lead to reprehensible behaviours in some instances, but the overall picture is not clear. As noted before, disinformation in Canada seems mostly a tactical and opportunistic tool that exploits existing tensions and events, while the overall strategy appears to be limited to undermining social institutions in Western liberal democracies as a general and undefined goal.

In the face of such a threat, the Canadian government has not remained idle, but the response has been mostly reactive and fragmented, or kept under the wrap of secrecy. In the wake of the Canadian election of 2019, a number of initiatives were put in place by various levels of government. With respect to the federal government, awareness campaigns such as Get Cyber Safe and the Digital Citizen Initiative were launched with modest budgets. An inter-agency group, the Security and Intelligence Threats to Elections (SITE) Task Force, was also created. SITE comprised individuals from CSIS, the Royal Canadian Mounted Police, Global Affairs Canada, and the Communications Security Establishment (CSE). Several departments, such as National Defence, Global Affairs, and the Privy Council, have created informal, formal, and technical study and policy groups to deal with disinformation activities from both domestic sources and foreign, state-sponsored ones. These study and policy groups have had a renewed impetus with the disinformation campaigns that were observed since the beginning of the COVID-19 pandemic.

Canada and Defence's Reaction to Disinformation

In 2020 the federal government proposed a comprehensive umbrella policy under the name the Digital Charter, aiming at the entire Internet domain, including, among other areas, broadband access, online payment transparency and standards, the development of a digitally skilled workforce, hacking and cyber-attacks, information protection and privacy, quantum computing, and disinformation. The charter was closely associated with Bill C-11 to enact the *Consumer Privacy Protection Act* and the *Personal Information and Data Protection Tribunal Act*. The charter, although providing a global view of what the Canadian government does in the information environment, remains a patchwork of initiatives, legislation, and policies from numerous government departments and agencies. This fragmentation has also been noted by observers and academics (Bereskin, 2020; Kolga, 2021), who have highlighted that Canada lacks a clear and unified strategy to tackle disinformation, be it homegrown or from foreign powers such as the People's Republic of China, Russia, and Iran.

Within the Government of Canada, National Defence and the Canadian Armed Forces have been at the forefront of thinking about the threat that disinformation represents for many years now. However, the challenge for Defence is that although it can support other departments, such as the CSE, which is protecting the Government of Canada's information infrastructure, unless it is linked to a military or defence matter, its capacity to lead and implement solutions is limited. Defence's Public Affairs has developed various communication strategies to deal with disinformation. These strategies are not publically available, but they are not fundamentally different from similar public relations strategies found in other governmental organizations. On the more proactive side, DND found itself in a quite embarrassing, if not scandalous, situation during the COVID-19 pandemic, as it put in place a plan to fight disinformation domestically that invoked phrases like "information operations," "shaping and exploiting information," etc. (Pugliese, 2020). Using conventional military terminology, and putatively accompanied by an operational mindset, the military was seen as aiming to influence legitimate Canadian media and sources of information, something that has been construed as a potential serious breach of trust and a threat to the concept of democratic civil control over the military. Although the Canadian military's intentions were very far from being disloyal to the civilian leadership, and these were essentially actions from a few overzealous staff officers, if anything, this event highlights a substantive lack of strategic-level maturity within defence circles about the nature and risks of domestic disinformation, and how to deal with it.

On the international front, DND has performed better. The Canadian leadership and substantive deployment in the NATO Enhanced Forward Presence (EFP) in Latvia has been the target of numerous Russian attempts at discrediting the mission, especially in the eyes of Russian-speakers in Latvia. Some of those attempts were quite naive and thus easily dismissed, such as media campaigns about the "gay Canadian battalion" using file pictures of the ex-colonel and convicted rapist and murderer Russell Williams in women's underwear (Brown, 2017). Yet, other attempts are more subtle and more concerning. More recently, in 2020, there were claims that the Canadian contingent was infecting the Latvian population with COVID-19 (Brewster, 2020). Similarly, during a different mission, conducted in the summer of 2019, a Ukrainian online magazine published the names of several Canadian military trainers engaged in the Canadian assistance mission in that country, declaring them mercenaries of the United States. The names were classified to protect the individuals from personal attacks.

The Canadian military in Latvia has developed a fairly sophisticated approach to deal with disinformation that is in line with the whole-of-government philosophy, involving the Canadian embassy, Global Affairs Canada in Ottawa, governments of other nations that are part of the Latvia's EFP, the Latvian government, as well as local Latvian stakeholders. The response to disinformation is managed through a strategic communication cell within the Canadian EFP headquarters. The cell not only monitors developments in various media, but also develops a strategic outlook focusing on areas that Russian-backed disinformers are likely to target, based on various socio-demographic analyses and surveys done by the Latvian government. The cell also identifies proactive measures to build confidence and resilience against disinformation with local Latvian populations, ranging from organizing or participating in public events and fairs, organizing guest lectures in local schools about the mission, maintaining an open-minded approach with Latvian journalists, etc. Hence, in an expeditionary context at the tactical and operational levels, National Defence and the Armed Forces have shown a substantive capacity to deal with disinformation, and they continue to develop and refine ways and processes to do so.[2]

Deterrence against Disinformation as a Strategic Posture for Canada

Based on the above, it is clear that Canada is missing a strategic and comprehensive policy approach to disinformation that would help in creating synergies and greater effectiveness among disjointed capabilities and organizations. It is in this context that the notion of deterrence as a holistic posture against disinformation has emerged as a possible way forward.

DND, in conjunction with Global Affairs Canada, is now looking at deterrence as a deliberate way for Canada to address disinformation more strategically, and some internal initiatives in this regard have already begun. One such initiative is led by DRDC under the wider research portfolio of the Defence of North America, the goal of which is to explore what disinformation deterrence might mean for Canada. This initiative is looking at various questions, such as what this posture might look like, whether it is even feasible, what kind of technological requirements it would entail, DND's potential role, etc. The notion of disinformation deterrence is also being explored by some key allies of Canada, particularly the United States and several NATO countries.

A first challenge, however, is the fact that the notion of deterrence has itself been inherited from both conventional military posturing of old, and from the nuclear deterrence of the Cold War through such strategies as mutually assured destruction. Classic deterrence plays very much on the notion of fear—fear of our strengths and resilience, fear of our resolve and will; each of these support deterrence, but mostly in its retaliatory version. Another important aspect of classical thinking about deterrence is that it was understood as a dialogue of sorts, in which the various parties implicitly agree to engage. During the Cold War, each superpower made it clear where the "red lines" were, and boasted publicly of their respective nuclear capabilities should an adversary decide to cross such lines. The Cuban Missile Crisis became a crisis in part because the Soviet side hid its threatening nuclear capabilities, and so the Kennedy administration had no choice but to publicly declare a new set of "red lines" supported by a clear show of force. The so-called red phone that was implemented afterward, to avoid future misunderstandings, speaks quite eloquently to this notion of deterrence as a dialogue.

Since the end of the Cold War, debates and discussions about deterrence have evolved and new notions and concepts have emerged. The problem is that new adversaries were not interested in such a dialogue and had very little to lose, and therefore it was not possible to play on their fears. Even before the events of 9/11, there were already significant concerns that a state, and then non-state actors, would use weapons of mass destruction (WMD) based on chemical, biological, and/or radiological compounds against civilian targets, and that the old rules of nuclear deterrence between the superpowers no longer applied. Attack attribution can be very well concealed and hard to prove, and many authoritarian regimes seem not to care if their own population pays a price for their misdeeds if deterrence by retaliation or punishment is implemented. For instance, Saddam Hussein's Iraq faced a massive embargo for several years as a result of the government's WMD programs during the 1990s, and yet they did not try to come clean about their efforts, even if they eventually dismantled those programs. Then, the so-called war on terror brought to light new threats and challenges, with the fear that terrorist organizations might use various forms of attacks, including potentially nuclear bombs, and it would be even harder to determine clear or specific targets for retaliation. Accordingly, deterrence appeared at some points nearly impossible against such ghostly adversaries.

Various analysts then came up with revamped notions such as deterrence by denial, whereby an adversary, rather than be deterred by the threat of massive retaliation—fear being a key factor in such calculations—would instead be brought to the point where they would consider continued threats and attacks against their Western enemies utterly futile (Edwards, 2011; Smith & Taylor, 2008). Concretely, this meant a combination of passive measures, such as the additional security protocols introduced in airports, at borders crossings, in financial transaction tracking systems, greater surveillance capabilities, etc., and active measures such as targeted assassinations of terrorist leaders, the seizure of suspicious sea shipments, de-radicalization programs in correctional facilities and socio-economically disadvantaged neighbourhoods, etc.

Another form of deterrence discussed in the post–Cold War era was deterrence by de-legitimization (Wilner, 2011). If it is true that terrorist organizations can hide in a population and do not usually defend a particular piece of territory, they are still reliant on support from various populations and networks abroad. Such support takes many forms, such as money, equipment, transportation, intelligence, the provision of safe houses for people and caches for weapons and equipment, the recruiting of new volunteers, etc. Hence, terrorist organizations, while they cannot be engaged in a deterrence dialogue, can be cut off from their support networks, thereby significantly hampering their capacity to operate, through the de-legitimization of their goals, their policies, their methods, etc. Furthermore, by improving local governance and the socio-economic conditions of their supporters, the allure these terrorist organizations are able to exert would be undermined. In a way, this form of deterrence is about establishing a positive and constructive new deterrence dialogue with the backers, rather the adversaries themselves.

In today's world of fake news, alternative facts, and disinformation more generally, deterrence again has been assessed and discussed as a policy, strategy, and/or state posture. Some elements of deterrence show certain similarities with the effort to deter terrorists and insurgents. Many disinformers hide among the population, and they cover their tracks through various forms of technological sophistication. They have very limited assets that could be leveraged for deterrence by retaliation. The links between them and their state backers, if they do have backers, are tenuous and difficult to prove. However, they present some new aspects, or at least characteristics that are more pronounced, if compared to terrorists and insurgents.

First, contrary to foreign insurgencies, today's disinformers are acting directly on Western populations' opinions and beliefs, and yet they do so not to help their own national cause, but rather to undermine liberal state institutions in the West, an effort that is oftentimes construed as an end in itself. As well, they do have "objective allies" in the West in groups opposed to liberalism, in the Far Left but mostly in the Far Right, and in radicalized and disaffected segments of the population. If once upon a time Ho Chi Minh stated that the solution of the Indochina problem was in France's domestic opinion, we now face a quite different dynamic. It is about undermining the West from within itself, as an end in itself. In a sense, the deterrence dialogue seems to have shifted once again to focus on the West's own population rather than on adversaries or their backers.

A second aspect is that disinformers, even the ones acting directly on the behalf of a foreign state, do not depend on any particular population to support them, and hence they have little to no legitimacy or reputation to lose. Deterrence by de-legitimization therefore becomes that much harder to implement, but it is not necessarily impossible. Of course, pressures could be applied against foreign states through economic and diplomatic sanctions, and even possibly by humiliating them through public exposure, in ways comparable to the United States showing pictures of Soviet missile launch sites being prepared during the Cuban Missile Crisis of the early 1960s. The numerous and open discussions in the Western news media about the active involvement of the People's Republic of China in spreading disinformation about COVID-19 have shown that disinformation can seriously backfire if publicly exposed (Verma, 2020).

A third, somewhat ironic aspect is that nuclear deterrence is also coming back to the forefront. A number of analysts have identified the potential risk that disinformation could create so much confusion and uncertainty that a conventional attack that crosses a "red line" for nuclear retaliation would remain unpunished because of our inability to justify a robust response due to disinformation. Hence, this has the potential to nullify nuclear deterrence, as the resulting confusion would not allow for a normal deterrence dialogue. The Russian government, in its 2022 military invasion of Ukraine, has already tried this very approach, but with limited success as Western powers were able to uphold a united front. Future crises in and around Taiwan have the potential to lead to a similar scenario.

If we go back to Canada's policy in this rapidly evolving world, difficult questions are thus raised. What would disinformation deterrence look like, and what would be the effective mechanisms to play on adversaries' fears? From a technical standpoint, what new capabilities should be developed? How far should we go in developing capabilities based on a mixture of cyber technology, intelligence gathering, communication studies, and social sciences solutions? Canada could somehow copy the old Russian and Soviet playbook of developing culturally sensitive *kompromat* against adversaries' senior leadership, for instance? How realistic these options are remains to be assessed. The country has a long tradition of trying to keep its adversaries at bay by various means that do not involve direct coercion, preferring instead for others like the United States to do so while benefitting from its close relationship with its southern ally. Also, Canada's historical preference is to act only as part of a wider concerted effort when it comes to engaging in more coercive solutions. What others will do is likely to weigh heavily on our future policies. Finally, there are risks that adversaries might pay more attention to Canada. Some Canadian politicians, for instance, could possibly be seriously embarrassed if actively targeted by concerted actions from foreign actors, thereby undermining their capacity to govern. In other words, adversaries may choose to retaliate in kind against Canada more often if we implement a posture of deterrence by punishment. In the end, we may ourselves be deterred from responding to disinformation as a result of fear.

This brings us to the more practical and politically acceptable posture of deterrence by denial, but this also implies that the Canadian government will have to be much more upfront with the public by presenting the threats of disinformation with greater insistence. This also means naming our adversaries and seeking to understand and acknowledge their politically, socially, culturally, and psychologically malign inclinations toward us. The publication of the Canadian Indo-Pacific Strategy in 2022, in which the People's Republic of China is described as a "disruptive global power," constitutes a first step in that direction. Yet, powerful institutional traditions remain. For a long time, successive Canadian governments have chosen as a matter of policy mostly to keep the public in the dark with respect to the nature of the threats against the country, and their degree of intensity. This has been termed an "Alice in Wonderland" attitude (Potter, 2010). In the end, any change in Canada's strategic approach to disinformation is likely to also require a critical and self-reflexive change in its strategic culture implicitly built around the belief that we are somehow remote from the world's problems.

Structure of the Book

To provide some answers to these questions and many more, and to introduce new ideas, notions, and techniques linked to fighting disinformation, this book has been divided into four major sections. The first section, "Deterrence as an Evolving Concept," is made up of three chapters, which look deeper into the origins and the implications of deterrence as a concept to guide policy and ultimately actions against Canada's adversaries. The first chapter, from Christopher Ankersen of New York University, provides further useful definitions, and explores the assumptions implied in classical deterrence by punishment and its focus on cost-benefit analysis. The second chapter, from Stephen Cimbala and Adam Lowther, both from the US Army Staff

College, discusses the notion of time in the context of deterrence, which has been significantly compressed by the massive implementation of information technology, allowing for real-time (dis)information and thus framing how deterrence could be implemented. The last chapter in this section, by Alex Wilner of Carleton University, re-engages us in the concept of deterrence by de-legitimization, which was originally introduced in dealing with the difficult context of fighting insurgencies and terrorism.

The following section, "Wider Strategic Context and Experiences," looks into both the external origins of the disinformation threat, especially from Russia and the People's Republic of China, and the experience of Israel in dealing with the complexities of putting together a credible deterrence while dealing with disinformation. The first chapter is by Rachel Lea Heide, from Defence Research and Development Canada, and presents the more salient aspects of the disinformation techniques and approaches used by Russia. This chapter is followed by a contribution from Anthony Seaboyer and Pierre Jolicoeur of the Royal Military College of Canada discussing how the People's Republic of China is actively using disinformation to achieve its strategic pol itical objectives. Moving from adversaries to democratic nations having to deal with both deterrence and disinformation, the chapter by Ron Schleifer and Yair Ansbacher looks into the complex situation of Israel, which since its founding had to develop a credible and comprehensive deterrence posture against nation-states, but which in the last two decades has evolved in the direction of dealing with non-state adversaries such as Hamas and Hezbollah. Concluding this section, and extending the analysis from the previous chapter, Oshri Bar-Gil of the Israel Defense Forces' Applied Behavioral Science Institute presents Israel's own perspective on what constitute disinformation and how it applies to the country's situation in the Middle East. In particular, Bar-Gil highlights the challenges stemming from the asymmetric nature of disinformation and seeks to understand how deterring disinformation requires a change in mindset, away from classical deterrence, in order to be effective.

The third section, "Canada's Context," emphasizes not only the actual risks involved in being a target of disinformation, but also where our thinking and practices should focus when it comes to dealing with disinformation, and more generally where we stand in terms of our deterrence capabilities. The first chapter here comes from Nicole Jackson of Simon Fraser University. Extending the reflections emerging from the previous chapters to the particular case of Canada, Jackson proposes a refined analysis of what disinformation and deterrence could potentially mean. The second and last chapter in this section is provided by Christian Leuprecht of the Royal Military College of Canada and Joseph Szeman of Queen's University. These authors extend the reflection proposed in the previous chapter and highlight the fact that Canada has been somewhat behind the new thinking about disinformation and deterrence, which has in turn impacted our choice of policies and strategic posture, especially in light of the synergistic relationships between the cyber and informational domains.

The fourth and last section, "Emerging Tools and Approaches," is made up of three chapters that highlight and describe some emerging concepts, methodologies, and cautionary warnings to support the development of a sound deterrence posture against disinformation. The first is by Sarah Jane Meharg, of the Canadian Forces College, and explores the notion of digital tribalism. If it is clear that disinformers play on groups' feelings to motivate them to oppose liberal democratic institutions, and that older notions such as right- and left-wing populism or nationalism are becoming less useful in understanding some of the underlying dynamics of group behaviour. The next chapter, by Anne Speckhard and Molly Ellenberg of the International Center for the Study of Violent Extremism, looks into how counter-radicalization efforts can support deterrence by denial in offering credible and emotionally engaging counter-narratives tailor-made to the socio-economic and cultural realities of potential recruits. This chapter is followed by the by contribution of Ronald D. Porter (Saint Mary's University), Minqian Shen (Queen's University), Leandre R. Fabrigar (Queen's University), and Anthony Seaboyer (Royal Military College of Canada). The authors review the various methodologies available to assess indirectly how a particular audience might have been influenced by online communication, and especially disinformation.

The concluding chapter is from Keith Stewart and Madeleine D'Agata, of Defence Research and Development Canada. They propose, in light of the previous chapters, a series of reflections and some high-level conclusions from the diverse material offered throughout the book. In particular, they argue that the changing context requires a refreshing of our knowledge of, and techniques for, understanding and influencing a diversity of adversaries with an emphasis on achieving a posture based on deterrence by denial.

NOTES

1 Some portions of this chapter were previously published in Ann Fitzgerald and Craig Stone (Eds.), *Managing security and defence in the 2020s: The post-pandemic challenges*, Breakout Education, 2023.

2 This information about the Canadian EFP measures against disinformation has been provided by an expert military source who prefers to remain anonymous.

REFERENCES

Andersen, R. (2021, 26 March). Social media platforms pressured to remove accounts spreading COVID-19 disinformation. *CTV News*. https://www.ctvnews.ca/health/coronavirus/social-media-platforms-pressured-to-remove-accounts-spreading-covid-19-disinformation-1.5364495

Bereskin, C. (2021, 21 May). Should Canada adopt an anti-"fake news" law? *NATO Association of Canada*. https://natoassociation.ca/should-canada-adopt-an-anti-fake-news-law/

Bradshaw, S., & Howard P. N. (2018, 17 September). The global organization of social media disinformation campaigns. *Journal of International Affairs*. https://jia.sipa.columbia.edu/global-organization-social-media-disinformation-campaigns

Brewster, M. (2020, 24 May). Canadian-led NATO battlegroup in Latvia targeted by pandemic disinformation campaign. *CBC News*. https://www.cbc.ca/news/politics/nato-latvia-battle-group-pandemic-covid-coronavirus-disinformation-russia-1.5581248

Brown, C. (2017, 16 June). Anti-Canada propaganda greets troops in Latvia. *CBC News*. https://www.cbc.ca/news/world/latvia-propaganda-1.4162612

Chinese Canadian National Council Toronto Chapter. (2021). *A year of racist attacks: Anti-Asian racism across Canada: One year into the Covid-19 pandemic*. Chinese Canadian National Council Toronto Chapter.

Cull, N. J., Gatov, V., Pomerantsev, P., Applebaum, A., & Shawcross, A. (2017). Soviet subversion, disinformation and propaganda: How the West fought against it: An analytic history, with lessons for the present. *LSE Consulting Report*. LSE School of Global Affairs.

CSIS (Canadian Security Intelligence Service). (2020). *CSIS Public Report 2020*. Government of Canada.

Daigle, T. (2020, 21 October). Canadian professor's website helps Russia spread disinformation, says U.S. State Department. *CBC News*. https://www.cbc.ca/news/science/russian-disinformation-global-research-website-1.5767208

Dobber, T., Metoui, N., Trilling, D., Helberger, N., & de Vreese, C. (2021). Do (microtargeted) deepfakes have real effects on political attitudes? *International Journal of Press/Politics, 26*(1), 69–91. https://doi.org/10.1177/1940161220944364

Dubois, E., & McKelvey, F. (2019). Political bots: Disrupting Canada's democracy. *Canadian Journal of Communication Policy Portal, 44*, 27–33. http://doi.org/10.22230/cjc.2019v42n2a3511

Edwards, A. (2011). Deterrence, coercion and brute force in asymmetric conflict: The role of the military instrument in resolving the Northern Ireland "Troubles." *Dynamics of Asymmetric Conflict, 4*(3), 226–41.

Emmott, R. (2021, 29 April). Russia, China sow disinformation to undermine trust in Western vaccines: EU. *Reuters*. https://www.reuters.com/world/china/russia-china-sow-disinformation-undermine-trust-western-vaccines-eu-report-says-2021-04-28/

Farber, B., & Fisman, D. (2021, 14 May). The overlap between lockdown agitators and hate groups is a threat to us all. *Globe and Mail*. https://www.theglobeandmail.com/opinion/article-the-overlap-between-lockdown-agitators-and-hate-groups-is-a-threat-to/

Freelon, D., Wells, C. (2020). Disinformation as political communication. *Political Communication, 37*(2), 145–56. https://doi.org/10.1080/10584609.2020.1723755

Half of Canadians regularly receive fake news through private messaging apps. (2021, 11 May). *The Suburban*. https://www.thesuburban.com/life/lifestyles/half-of-canadians-regularly-receive-fake-news-through-private-messaging-apps/article_ded65b20-b289-11eb-983d-6b1c0dfd30a1.html

Humprecht, E., Esser, F., & Van Aelst, P. (2020). Resilience to online disinformation: A framework for cross-national comparative research. *International Journal of Press/Politics, 25*(3), 493–516. https://doi.org/10.1177/1940161219900126

Jackson, N. J. (2018). Canada, NATO, and global Russia. *International Journal, 73*(2), 317–25. https://doi.org/10.1177/0020702018786080

Kapantai, E., Christopoulou, A., Berberidis, C., & Peristeras, V. (2020). A systematic literature review on disinformation: Toward a unified taxonomical framework. *New Media & Society, 23*(5), 1–26. https://doi.org/10.1177/1461444820959296

Kolga, M. (2021, February). Taiwan demonstrates how we can defend Canadian democracy against information warfare. *Policy Perspective Calgary*. Canadian Global Affairs Institute. https://www.cgai.ca/taiwan_demonstrates_how_we_can_defend_canadian_democracy_against_information_warfare

MacDonald, N. E., Comeau, J., Dubé, E., Bucci, L., & Graham, J. E. (2020). A public health timeline to prepare for COVID-19 vaccines in Canada. *Canadian Journal of Public Health, 111*(6), 945–52. https://doi.org/10.17269/s41997-020-00423-1

Potter, M. (2010, 29 November). Canada has "Alice in Wonderland" attitude on terrorism: Wikileaks. *Toronto Star*. https://www.thestar.com/news/world/2010/11/29/canada_has_alice_in_wonderland_attitude_on_terrorism_wikileaks.html

Pugliese, D. (2020, 21 July). Canadian Forces "information operations" pandemic campaign quashed after details revealed to top general. *Ottawa Citizen*. https://ottawacitizen.com/news/national/defence-watch/canadian-forces-information-operations-pandemic-campaign-squashed-after-details-revealed-to-top-general

Rini, R. (2019). Social media disinformation and the security threat to democratic legitimacy. In Joseph McQuade (Ed.), *Disinformation and digital democracies in the 21st century* (pp. 10–14). NATO Association of Canada.

Salter, L., Kuehn, K., Berentson-Shaw, J., & Elliot, M. (2019). Literature review part 1: Threats and opportunities. *Digital threats to democracy..* https://static1.squarespace.com/static/5cbe92fcaf4683f10f6c8de5/t/5cd11bb67817f7493acb89be/1557207991882/3.DD-background-paper-lit-review-1-WEB.pdf

Significant minority of Canadians believe COVID-19 misinformation, rivalling long-established conspiracy theories. (2021, 30 April) *InsightWest.* Retrieved 10 May 2021 from https://www.insightswest.com/news/conspiracy-april-2021/

Smith, J., & Talbot, B. (2008). Terrorism and deterrence by denial. In P. Viotti, M. Opheim, & N. Bowen (Eds.), *Terrorism and homeland security: Thinking strategically about policy* (pp. 53–68). CRC Press.

Tasker, J. P. (2020, 20 October). PM, health officials warn Canadians against believing COVID-19 "internment camps" disinformation. *CBC News.* https://www.cbc.ca/news/politics/covid-19-internment-camps-disinformation-1.5769592

Tenove, C. (2020). Protecting democracy from disinformation: Normative threats and policy responses. *International Journal of Press/Politics, 25*(3), 517–37. https://doi.org/10.1177/1940161220918740

Tenove, C., & Tworek, H. J. S. (2019). Online disinformation and harmful speech: Dangers for democratic participation and possible policy responses. *Journal of Parliamentary & Political Law, 13*, 215–32. https://papers.ssrn.com/sol3/papers.cfm?abstract_id=3613166

Tsfati, Y., Boomgaarden, H. G., Strömbäck, J., Vliegenthart, R., Damstra, A., & Lindgren, E. Causes and consequences of mainstream media dissemination of fake news: Literature review and synthesis. *Annals of the International Communication Association, 44*(2), 157–73. https://doi.org/10.1080/23808985.2020.1759443

Verma, R. (2020). China's diplomacy and changing the COVID-19 narrative. *International Journal, 75*(2), 248–58. https://doi.org/10.1177/0020702020930054

Wilner, A. S. (2011). Deterring the undeterrable: Coercion, denial, and delegitimization in counterterrorism. *Journal of Strategic Studies, 34*(1), 3–37. https://doi.org/10.1080/01402390.2011.541760

WSO's report alleges Indian disinformation campaign against Canadian Sikhs. (2021, 3 February). *Online Voice.* https://voiceonline.com/wsos-report-alleges-indian-disinformation-campaign-against-canadian-sikhs/

SECTION I

DETERRENCE AS AN EVOLVING CONCEPT

1

Deterrence Is Always about Information: A New Framework for Understanding

Christopher Ankersen

Deterrence works when an adversary refrains from undertaking a particular action for fear of paying too high a price; in other words, it "means dissuading someone from doing something by making them believe that the costs to them will exceed their expected benefit" (Nye, 2017). It depends on several elements. Much focus is placed on capability (the ability of a party to effect the retaliation), giving a certain material bias to much of contemporary deterrence discourse. Do we have the right "things" (weapons systems, for instance) to be able to deter a potential aggressor? Following this material train of thought, several observers wonder if deterrence can translate from the world of nuclear and conventional statecraft into the information environment. Does deterrence, for instance, work below the threshold of armed attack in the same way it works (or at least appears to work) above that threshold? Can or does deterrence work in the domain of cyber security? If so, does it work the same way that it does in the "real world?"

This material bias, though, blinds us to the fact that deterrence actually operates—has always operated—in the information environment. In addition to, and I argue much more importantly than, the material aspects of deterrence (capability) are the ideational elements of credibility and communication.

While these dimensions are integral to deterrence, what has changed are the operant media through which and with which opponents threaten each other. What this chapter proposes is a framework that treats a variety of different attacks (across both material and ideational dimensions) and, hence, allows for some form of "valuation" to be carried out. Only once such an appraisal has occurred can any kind of "cost-benefit analysis" (the basis of deterrence) be conducted.

Where deterrence is focused on nuclear weapons, the costs are understood to be catastrophic. Based on the results of the two US atomic attacks on Japan, as well as predictions based on tests and modelling from all nuclear weapon states since then, the notion that there could be an "upside" to nuclear war was not a mainstream opinion (Blair & Wolfsthal, 2019; Waltz, 1981).[1] As Robert Jervis puts it, "the healthy fear of devastation . . . makes deterrence relatively easy" (quoted in Payne, 2011, p. 395).

Of course, deterrence has never solely been about nuclear weapons (Huntington, 1983; Paret et al., 1986). Recently the United States Department of Defense has been moved to adopt a strategy of "integrated deterrence," in which military power is not the only component. In a recent speech Secretary of Defense Austin explained that "Deterrence still rests on the same logic—but it now spans multiple realms, all of which must be mastered to ensure our security in the 21st century" (quoted in Lopez, 2021). The idea is that countries like Russia and China are waging a campaign of hybrid or grey-zone warfare, whereby they aim to disrupt and undermine the status quo, but do so "below the threshold" of armed conflict (Chivvis, 2017; Morris et al., 2019).[2] Accordingly, adversaries use "everything but" in their campaigns: propaganda, agitation, use of proxies, and cyber-attacks are the stock in trade here. The British Ministry of Defence goes so far as to claim that

> old distinctions between "peace" and "war," between "public" and "private," between "foreign" and "domestic" and between "state" and "non-state" are increasingly out of date. Our authoritarian rivals see the strategic context as a continuous struggle in which non-military and military instruments are used unconstrained by any distinction between peace and war (United Kingdom, 2021, p. 22).

By choosing to use "less kinetic" and/or "difficult to attribute" methods, thereby not setting off the tripwire of overt military action, adversaries may prod and probe freely, based on the idea that what they are doing is not worthy of large-scale retaliation. In this sense, such tactics are meant to act as a way of circumventing deterrence by inverting the usual cost-benefit analysis: the benefits accrued by an adversary operating in the "grey zone" seem too small to warrant the imposition of high costs.

The response from the West to counter and indeed deter such efforts has been, in a word, integration. Secretary Austin explains it thus:

> Integrated deterrence means all of us giving our all. . . . It means that working together is an imperative, and not an option. It means that capabilities must be shared across lines as a matter of course, and not as an exception to the rule. And it means that coordination across commands and services needs to be a reflex and not an afterthought (quoted in Lopez, 2021).

Similarly, the British approach stresses the need

> to create multiple dilemmas that unhinge a rival's understanding, decision-making and execution. This requires a different way of thinking that shifts our behaviour, processes and structures to become more dynamic and pre-emptive, information-led and selectively ambiguous. In essence, a mindset and posture of continuous campaigning in which all activity, including training and exercising, will have an operational end (United Kingdom, 2021, p. 22).

If integration is indeed the key to deterring Chinese and Russian efforts, then it is worth examining where Western thinking and acting are falling short. One such area is that of cyber security. Despite the novelty of the field, as it stands our approach to cyber is highly stovepiped—precisely the opposite of what we are aiming for. Indeed, by fragmenting cyber security we are doing our adversaries' work for them. By focusing only on some kinds of cyber activity and labelling them as attacks while dismissing others merely as hacking, we form an incomplete picture of how our adversaries use cyberspace against us. With only a partial picture, we cannot hope to achieve integrated deterrence.

In this chapter, I propose a new way of understanding cyber security, one that is more comprehensive than is currently the case. Moreover, the proposed framework concentrates not on the sources of cyber-attacks or into whose jurisdiction they might fall. Instead, it focuses on *the effects* of cyber-attacks and allows for several outcomes. Such a framing does two things. First, it lends itself to an integrated response. Second, and more importantly, it allows for the (re)establishment of deterrence, as it permits an appropriate and holistic accounting of the impact of cyber-attacks, so that a proper "cost-benefit" footing can be set.

My argument unfolds as follows. First I cover the basics of deterrence and how it applies in a world of "hybrid threats," focusing on the fact that deterrence is all about a particular frame of mind. Second, I discuss how security in, of, and from cyberspace interacts with that understanding. As mentioned above, I propose a comprehensive typology for managing cyber threats in this section. Finally, I discuss how such an approach—one centred on intended effects—leads itself to better forms of deterrence.

Deterrence Is a State of Mind

Deterrence is not only about capability. An adversary's decision not to attack is largely ideational, not material. Indeed, "deterrence is a psychological process in which subjective elements such as fear, pressure, and influence inform how calculations are made and decisions are taken. . . . Threat and fear are at the epicentre of deterrence, because deterrence as such is a state of mind" (Filippidou, 2020, p. 14). And while this is not a new observation, it is often forgotten, pushed aside in the pell-mell of calculations and preparations. "Deterrence posits a psychological relationship, so it is strange that most analyses of it have ignored decision makers' emotions, perceptions, and calculations and have instead relied on deductive logic based on the premise that people are highly rational" (Jervis et al., 1985, p. 1). Instead of concentrating on how opponents are thinking, we tend to get sucked directly into discussions of defences and countermeasures, happy to count and plan and prepare. What is more, we dismiss too quickly incidents that we regard as nothing more than vandalism, or espionage, or propaganda, waiting for our enemies to "cross the threshold," where they do "real-world harm." Only then can we conceive that some kind of retaliation is necessary, only then would deterrence be applicable.

The fact that deterrence is more ideational than material means that disinformation plays a large part in it. Convincing an adversary not to attack can be achieved as much through deceit as through defence. This is as true inside the cyber domain as it is outside of it. What is more, though, the cyber domain can be used as a powerful tool for the dissemination of disinformation in the first place. This means that disinformation in the cyber realm has a double effect. First, it can be used to confuse or deceive an adversary. Following the logic of "garbage in, garbage out," bad information injected into a decision-making process can lead to faulty conclusions on a range of aspects, from intention, to desire effect, and so on. Separately, though, disinformation can be used outside of such a rational process to generate a range of non-rational outcomes, not within the decision-making elites, but among the mass population. Such outcomes might include not only faulty conclusions, but also disbelief and, ultimately, distrust. Instead of aiming for an alternate, rational conclusion, disinformation, then, can be used to create irrational non-conclusions. This may serve to undermine legitimacy, or merely sow confusion and controversy. Either way, it is intended as a means of degrading the bases for action.

Security and Cyberspace

At first blush it may seem foolish to try and impose some form of order to activities taking place in what has been called a consensual hallucination experienced daily by billions of legitimate operators, in every nation (Gibson, 2000). While it is true that cyberspace is a virtual realm, when we analyze it as a field of security, we can and must concentrate on the effects that are generated in and because of it. In that sense, I object to referring to cyberspace as a mere domain. In my use of the term, I want to highlight its multi-dimensionality. If we regard it too narrowly, we may lose sight of what is possible. Such an overly narrow focus can mean that we lose sight of the impact that cyber-attacks have, making it harder to conceive of them as something to be deterred in the first place.

While some have envisioned cyberspace as a realm divorced entirely from the material world, the reality is less tidy. The virtual world is propped up by cables and cords; sitting beside artificial intelligences are networked toaster ovens; its population is made up of flesh-and-blood denizens as well as numeric databases. Any view of security in cyberspace must include all these elements. Only regarding "pure play" digital threats as worthy of cyber-security efforts is a strategy that leads to be being outmanoeuvred by one's opponents. The framework presented here accounts for all sources of harm that might emanate from or across cyberspace, whether they are aimed at hijacking data or tearing up fibre optics. It is this degree of comprehensiveness that allows for a holistic appreciation of the threat landscape, which in turn can enable an integrated approach to deterrence. The end goal is to reduce what Nye (2017) has labelled the "ambiguity of cyber threats." I contend that such ambiguity is often exploited and indeed exacerbated through the use of disinformation. IP masking, routing through multiple servers, the use of cut-outs, intentionally using technical markers (such as specific types of hardware or lines of code associated with a particular actor or country)—all this is deliberately done to create confusion and doubt as much as it is meant to convince an adversary of a specific, false source of cyber activity.

It is a truism to say that developments in cyberspace are constantly in flux. Future methods of attack may be difficult to predict in their precise technological dimensions. However, by focusing on the intended *effects* of cyber-attacks, this typology allows us to remain undistracted by the details. Asking ourselves, "What do our opponents attend to achieve?" forces us to concentrate on our opponents' goals, what they consider as the benefits in any cost-benefit calculation. In turn, this enables us to note that it is not necessary that a specific attack be restricted to one kind of effect. A single attack might have several different effects, either by design or as a matter of "collateral impact." Indeed, just as arson might be used as a means of disguising a murder, a cyber-attacker might choose to destroy infrastructure as a way to obfuscate the primary focus, which was data collection. Similarly, a cyber incident that appears to have been nothing more than espionage could easily have also provided an adversary with the possibility of creating a "back door" for future exploits, or even delivering a payload that could wreak havoc at a later date. Obfuscation of this kind (disguising one's true intentions) is commonplace, and if we are too quick to categorize incidents as "merely hacks" and not keep an open mind to the possibility of more serious effects, we fall prey to our adversaries' disinformation. What is better, I argue, is to regard every cyber incident as an attack in the first instance, and then proceed to rule out other possibilities based on further information. As such, I propose below a four-fold typology of cyber-attacks.

ATTACKS ON CYBER

Attacks on cyber have infrastructure as their target. Such attacks may be physical or digital, or both. Physical attacks involve the destruction of cables or other hardware. This could involve cutting wires, burning or bombing buildings, or smashing computers, servers, modems, or other physical aspects of the Internet. Digital attacks might not visibly damage or destroy materials, but they could render useless the digital capacity of physical infrastructure or media through magnetism or moisture, for example. Whether physical or digital, attacks on cyber have the same effect: the destruction of the target.

An example of such an attack on cyber could be similar to what happened to Tonga. While it has not been publicly described as an intentional event, an incident in January 2019 left the island nation without connectivity after "a boat with an anchor . . . dragged the [undersea Internet] cable, or something of this sort" (Westbrook, 2019). A satellite work-around was arranged but provided only one-tenth of the access previously provided by the cable. Repairs took about two weeks.

The impact of such relatively crude attacks is hard to downplay. According to some reports, these cables "carry global business worth more than $10 trillion a day, including from financial institutions that settle transactions on them every second. Any significant disruption would cut the flow of capital. The cables also carry more than 95 percent of daily communications" (Sanger & Schmitt, 2015). The vulnerability of submarine cables has been evident in the North Atlantic since the Russian invasion of Ukraine ("The *Irish Times* view," 2022). The destruction of the Nord Stream 2 underwater pipeline goes to show the ease with which such physical attacks can be carried out, the apparent difficulty involved in definitively determining attribution, and the disbelief that can be generated when competing accounts circulate ("Kremlin eyes object," 2023).

ATTACKS IN CYBER

Attacks in cyber focus on data, attempting to steal or corrupt it. There are myriad ways in which this might be done, ranging from unauthorized access by legitimate users to penetration of networks by outside attackers. There are two main kinds of attacks in cyber. The first seeks to gain information and exploit it. This could take the form of proprietary intellectual property (United States of America, 2021a) or other sensitive information (Sanger, 2020). The second kind of attack in cyber aims not to steal data but to corrupt or deny access to it: ransomware is an example of this kind of attack (Turton & Mehrotra, 2021).

These types of incidents are often regarded as hacks, not attacks, and are dismissed as examples of cyber espionage (Rid, 2012). By not including them as attacks, we aid our adversaries by disaggregating the effects that they are achieving. Indeed, by interfering with the confidentiality and integrity of, as well as access to, information, adversaries can, in effect, generate a form of disinformation or, alternatively, degrade our ability to counter, or disprove, other disinformation attempts. Labelling such efforts as attacks in cyber allows us to account for their effects. Of course, just as not all physical assaults are politically motivated, care must be taken when deciding whether particular cyber-attacks are the work of criminals, vandals, or state actors. However, these kinds of conclusions should be the fruit of investigations, not prima facie assumptions.

ATTACKS FROM CYBER

Attacks from cyber focus on disconnecting, damaging, or destroying devices that are connected to the Internet. Here the aim is not to steal data, but to disrupt some particular function. By 2025, it is estimated that there will be more than thirty billion connected devices in the Internet of Things (Vailshery, 2022): whether an industrial valve, an airplane, or a hospital, Web-connected devices are vulnerable to attacks from cyber.

These attacks use specially written code to interrupt the normal operations of peripheral devices, whether they are digital or mechanical in nature. The most famous such attack is the now legendary Stuxnet incident from 2011 (Kushner, 2013), which destroyed Iranian nuclear centrifuges. It is worth noting that the Stuxnet attacks involved extremely sophisticated means of generating the impression that no manipulation of the physical controllers was underway. In other words, in addition to the alteration of the intending function of the centrifuges, Stuxnet generated convincing disinformation meant to lull Iranian scientists into believing nothing was amiss. Since Stuxnet, the number of such networked systems has multiplied exponentially, meaning that the global vulnerability to such attacks has likewise ballooned. As Bruce Schneier (2018), a leading cyber-security expert, puts it, hackers can now crash your car, your pacemaker, or your city's power grid. That's catastrophic.

ATTACKS VIA CYBER

If attacks from cyber are the kinds of attacks that come to mind when we think of cyber security involving state adversaries, attacks via cyber are often regarded as "something else." Attacks from cyber do not target physical devices or stored data. Instead, their targets are us: "Disinformation is a tool commonly used by a number of states to sow discord, undermine faith in governing institutions, stoke fear and anxiety, and ultimately achieve certain policy goals" (CSIS, 2020). Given its ubiquitous presence in our lives,

Table 1.1. Effects-Based Cyber Attack Typology

Type of attack	Target	Modality	Effect	Example	Defence mechanism
On cyber	Network	Physical	Disruption/ destruction	Tonga 2019	Critical infrastructure protection (CIP)
In cyber	Data	Digital	Theft/denial/ corruption	OPM 2016	Information assurance (IA)
From *cyber*	Peripheral	Digital	Disruption/ destruction	Stuxnet 2010	CIP/IA
Via cyber	People	Information	Distrust	US election 2016	Resilience/ censorship

the Internet is a key conduit for such disinformation. Social media is particularly useful as a tool for spreading and amplifying false and/or divisive information and has been adroitly used by Russian operatives (Allyn, 2020). Some attacks via cyber have been used directly in conjunction with physical military operations (Sokol, 2019), while others have been used to "soften up" potential targets (Duszyński, 2020). In other cases, whether related to elections or COVID-19 response, the aim is to sow distrust and reduce the ability of societies to co-operate (Barnes, 2021).

Taken together, this framework allows us to better understand how malicious activities in cyberspace work. Rather than simply focusing on "whodunit" (criminals, spies, or hacktivists), it enables us to concentrate on the effects intended and, often, achieved. Such an integrated appreciation of cyber-attacks is important because, "unless statesmen [*sic*] understand the ways in which their opposite numbers see the world, their deterrence policies are likely to misfire; unless scholars understand the patterns of perceptions involved, they will misinterpret the behavior" (Jervis, 1982, p. 57). The British Ministry of Defence asserts that in today's world "our rivals employ an expanding, diverse and largely unregulated set of information tools to influence target audiences' attitudes, beliefs and behaviours. These weapons are increasingly employed above and below the threshold of war. They challenge international norms and restrict our response options. They work in the seams of our institutions, exacerbate societal divisions and prejudices, and lead people to cooperate, wittingly or unwittingly, in the undermining of democracy" (United Kingdom, 2021, p. 6).

Deterring by Defending

Deterrence relies on retaliation, or more correctly, the *threat* of some form of punishment following a transgression. As mentioned above, that clearly entails an element of capability: Is there the means available to retaliate? More so, though, deterrence hinges on the credibility of the threat: Even if means are available, is it believable that an adversary would act on their threats of retaliation? Many observers believe that deterrence is not possible in cyberspace, for this very reason: any attempt at reconstructing the norms and expectations that underpin deterrence in the physical world "fails to consider the unique characteristics of cyberspace" (Fischerkeller & Harknett, 2017). Difficulties surrounding attribution, for instance, make it hard to identify who to punish, for example.

The current approach to cyber security does not focus at all on the intended effects of its potential adversaries. It takes them for granted, labelling only certain kinds of incidents as attacks at all. Instead it proposes a "defend forward" strategy that sees American cyber assets operating persistently "over there" (United States of America, 2018). A number of other countries have also adopted similar strategies, relying on "offensive cyber operations" as a means of disrupting adversary activity, downplaying any kind of connection between that and defence or deterrence (Gold, 2020).

I contend that the notion of cyber uniqueness is often overstated. Yes, the particular details of how some attacks are carried out (through the routing of malicious code, for example) differs from what we see in the non-virtual world; by focusing on the effects of cyber-attacks we can see that, regardless of the way in which those attacks are carried out, it is possible to view them as analogous to other malicious acts, defend against them, and fit them into a deterrence framework. The aforementioned confusion surrounding the Nord Stream attacks are merely one such example.

Defence in cyberspace varies according to the particular threat. As the attack modality varies, so, too, will the means of protection. In the case of attacks on cyber, an approach that prioritizes the protection of critical infrastructure might be best: locking doors, erecting fences, and the like, as a way of preventing unauthorized entry to vulnerable network elements.[3] For attacks in and from cyber, the defences are less physical and more digital in nature, but nonetheless relatively straightforward. Maintaining "good cyber hygiene" (e.g., updating and patching programs, implementing stringent access-control procedures, eliminating known vulnerabilities, such as obsolete VPNs and the like) may sound simple, but it has proven to be effective (Such et al., 2019). Indeed, many of the largest attacks in and from cyber have hinged on basic cyber hygiene errors, leading to large and long-lasting disruptions (Carnovale & Yeniyurt, 2021; Hemsley & Fisher, 2018; Kushner, 2013). Dissuading attackers through the use of robust defences is itself a form of deterrence, deterrence by denial (Wilner & Wenger, 2021).

Beyond a denial approach, the idea of deterrence by punishment requires "threats of wider punishment that would raise the cost of an attack" (Mazarr, 2018, p. 14). However, if we are too eager to "rule out" attacks and see incidents merely as vandalism, without considering what else might be going on, we undermine our own ability to comprehend what our adversaries are attempting. I contend that without an appreciation for what the intended effects or benefits of an attack are, it is difficult to calibrate the costs necessary to dissuade an opponent from carrying it out.

Defending against or deterring attacks via cyber warrants special mention. Although other forms of attack may include elements of disinformation, these attacks rely on disinformation to generate their intended effect. Here defence is extremely difficult because access to the intended target (the population) is often very easy. Indeed, in many countries around the world, including but not restricted to those in the West, social media usage is widespread. In Canada, for instance, there are estimated to be approximately thirty-five million social media users, and that figure is set to grow by over 10 per cent per year between now and 2030 (Dixon, 2023b). What is more, the average user is on social media for over two hours each day (Dixon, 2023a). The level of susceptibility to disinformation via these sources is enormous. What, then, is the best way to guard against such attacks?

One approach, favoured by democracies, is to boost what is called "societal resilience." Sweden, for instance, has created a national Psychological Defence Agency in order to enable its population to recognize and resist propaganda (Sweden, 2023). Such an approach is regarded by some as contributing to deterrence by denial (Braw & Roberts, 2019).

However, there is another route, and that is censorship. This works in a different fashion: rather than inoculating the population to recognize and dismiss potential disinformation, censorship aims at blocking such information from reaching the population in the first place. Originally favoured in autocracies and anocracies, such as China and Thailand, respectively

(Economy, 2018; Human Rights Watch, 2016), it has become a tactic in so-called open societies too. Governments and social media providers have been accused of implementing a variety of forms of censorship, often in the name of limiting disinformation (Goldberg, 2022). As discussed elsewhere in this volume, there is a fine line between defence and paternalism in this regard.

Ultimately, any attempt at developing and deploying an integrated approach to the array of activities that countries such as Russia and China are carrying out as part of a "hybrid warfare" campaign cannot afford to be disjointed. The typology presented here allows a wide range of cyber incidents to be properly understood as attacks, permitting the development of robust defence, and the generation of a deterrent effect.

NOTES

1. It should be noted that Waltz's enthusiasm for the spread of nuclear weapons relies on the fact that states possessing them would themselves be deterred from using such weapons.
2. It is important to point out that both of these terms have a somewhat slippery, polysemic quality that renders their use imprecise. For a discussion, see Janičatová and Mlejnková (2021).
3. See, for instance, United States of America (2021b).

REFERENCES

Allyn, B. (2020, 16 June). Study exposes Russia disinformation campaign that operated in the shadows for 6 years. *NPR*. https://www.npr.org/2020/06/16/878169027/study-exposes-russia-disinformation-campaign-that-operated-in-the-shadows-for-6-

Barnes, J.E. (2021, 5 August). Russian disinformation targets vaccines and the Biden administration. *New York Times*. https://www.nytimes.com/2021/08/05/us/politics/covid-vaccines-russian-disinformation.html

Blair, B., & Wolfsthal, J. B. (2019, 1 August). We still can't "win" a nuclear war. Pretending we could is a dangerous fantasy. *Washington Post*. https://www.washingtonpost.com/outlook/2019/08/01/we-still-cant-win-nuclear-war-pretending-we-could-is-dangerous-fantasy/

Braw, E., & Roberts, P. (2019, 25 March). *Societal resilience as a deterrent*. NATO Science and Technology Organization. https://www.sto.nato.int/publications/STO%20Meeting%20Proceedings/STO-MP-SAS-141/MP-SAS-141-11.pdf

Carnovale, S., & Yeniyurt S. (Eds.). (2021). *Cyber security and supply chain management: Risks, challenges and solutions*. World Scientific.

Chivvis, C. (2017). *Understanding Russian "hybrid warfare": And what can be done about it.* RAND Corporation. http://www.rand.org/pubs/testimonies/CT468.html

CSIS. (2020, 23 September). *Countering Russian disinformation.* Centre for Strategic and International Studies. https://www.csis.org/blogs/post-soviet-post/countering-russian-disinformation

Dixon, S. (2023a, 3 March). Average time spent on social media Canada 2023. *Statista.* https://www.statista.com/statistics/1317217/time-spent-on-social-media-in-canada/

Dixon, S. (2023b, 31 March). Canada: Social media users 2019–2028. *Statista.* https://www.statista.com/statistics/260710/number-of-social-network-users-in-canada/

Duszyński, J. (2020, 11 December). Russian disinformation in Latvia. *Baltic Rim Monitor.* Warsaw Institute. https://warsawinstitute.org/russian-disinformation-latvia/

Economy, E. C. (2018, 29 June). The great firewall of China: Xi Jinping's Internet shutdown. *The Guardian.* https://www.theguardian.com/news/2018/jun/29/the-great-firewall-of-china-xi-jinpings-internet-shutdown

Filippidou, A. (Ed.). (2020). *Deterrence: Concepts and approaches for current and emerging threats.* Springer.

Fischerkeller, M. P., & Harknett, R. J. (2017). Deterrence is not a credible strategy for cyberspace. *Orbis, 61*(3), 381–93. https://linkinghub.elsevier.com/retrieve/pii/S0030438717300431

Gibson, W. (2000). *Neuromancer.* Ace Books.

Gold, J. (2020). *The Five Eyes and offensive cyber capabilities: Building a "cyber deterrence initiative."* NATO Cooperative Cyber Defence Centre of Excellence. https://ccdcoe.org/uploads/2020/10/2020-Josh-Gold-Five-Eyes-and-Offensive-Cyber-Capabilities.pdf

Goldberg, J. (2022, 16 September). Opinion: How Ottawa's Internet censorship law will affect you. *Financial Post.* https://financialpost.com/opinion/opinion-how-ottawas-internet-censorship-law-will-affect-you

Hemsley, K., & Fisher, R. (2018). A history of cyber incidents and threats involving industrial control systems. In J. Staggs & S. Shenoi (Eds.), *Critical infrastructure protection xii, IFIP advances in information and communication technology* (pp. 215–42). Springer International.

Human Rights Watch. (2016, 21 December). Thailand: Cyber crime act tightens Internet control. *Human Rights Watch.* https://www.hrw.org/news/2016/12/21/thailand-cyber-crime-act-tightens-internet-control

Huntington, S. P. (1983). Conventional deterrence and conventional retaliation in Europe. *International Security, 8*(3), 32–56. https://www.jstor.org/stable/2538699?origin=crossref

The *Irish Times* view on undersea cables: A strategic threat. (2022, 28 July). *Irish Times.* https://www.irishtimes.com/opinion/editorials/2022/07/28/the-irish-times-view-on-undersea-cables-a-strategic-threat/

Janičatová, S., & Mlejnková, P. (2021). The ambiguity of hybrid warfare: A qualitative content analysis of the United Kingdom's political-military discourse on Russia's hostile activities. *Contemporary Security Policy, 42*(3), 312–44. https://doi.org/10.1080/13523260.2021.1885921

Jervis, R. (1982). Deterrence and perception. *International Security, 7*(3), 3–30. http://www.jstor.org/stable/2538549

Jervis, R., Lebow, R. N., & Stein, J. G. (1985). *Psychology and deterrence.* Johns Hopkins University Press. https://muse.jhu.edu/book/74118

Kremlin eyes object found next to Nord Stream pipeline. (2023, 24 March). *Reuters.* https://www.reuters.com/world/europe/kremlin-important-identify-object-found-next-nord-stream-pipeline-2023-03-24/

Kushner, D. (2013, 26 February). The real story of Stuxnet: How Kaspersky Lab tracked down the malware that stymied Iran's nuclear-fuel enrichment program. *IEEE Spectrum.* https://spectrum.ieee.org/the-real-story-of-stuxnet

Lopez, C. T. (2021, 30 April). Defense secretary says "integrated deterrence" is cornerstone of U.S. defense. *DOD News.* U.S. Department of Defense. https://www.defense.gov/News/News-Stories/Article/Article/2592149/defense-secretary-says-integrated-deterrence-is-cornerstone-of-us-defense/

Mazarr, M. J. (2018). *Understanding deterrence.* RAND Corporation. https://www.rand.org/pubs/perspectives/PE295.html

Morris, L., Mazarr, M. J., Hornung, J. W., Pezard, S., Binnendijk, A., & Kepe, M. (2019). *Gaining competitive advantage in the gray zone: Response options for coercive aggression below the threshold of major war.* RAND Corporation. https://www.rand.org/pubs/research_reports/RR2942.html

Nye, J. S. (2017). Deterrence and dissuasion in cyberspace. *International Security, 41*(3), 44–71. https://direct.mit.edu/isec/article/41/3/44-71/12147

Paret, P., Craig, G. A., & Gilbert, F. (Eds.). (1986). *Makers of modern strategy: From Machiavelli to the nuclear age.* Princeton University Press.

Payne, K. B. (2011). Understanding deterrence. *Comparative Strategy, 30*(5), 393–427. https://doi.org/10.1080/01495933.2011.624814

Rid, Thomas. 2012. Cyber war will not take place. *Journal of Strategic Studies, 35*(1), 5–32. https://doi.org/10.1080/01402390.2011.608939

Sanger, D. E. (2020, 13 December). Russian hackers broke into federal agencies, U.S. officials suspect. *New York Times.* https://www.nytimes.com/2020/12/13/us/politics/russian-hackers-us-government-treasury-commerce.html

Sanger, D. E., Schmitt, E. (2015, 26 October). Russian ships near data cables are too close for U.S. comfort. *New York Times.* https://www.nytimes.com/2015/10/26/world/europe/russian-presence-near-undersea-cables-concerns-us.html

Schneier, B. (2018). *Click here to kill everybody: Security and Survival in a hyper-connected world.* W.W. Norton & Company.

Sokol, S. (2019, 2 August). Russian disinformation distorted reality in Ukraine. Americans should take note. *Foreign Policy.* http://foreignpolicy.com/2019/08/02/russian-disinformation-distorted-reality-in-ukraine-americans-should-take-note-putin-mueller-elections-antisemitism/

Such, J. M., Ciholas, P., Rashid, A., Vidler, J., & Seabrook, T. (2019). Basic cyber hygiene: Does it work? *Computer, 52*, 21–31. https://eprints.lancs.ac.uk/id/eprint/133762/1/cyber_hygiene.pdf

Sweden. (2023, 6 February). *Government taking strong action against disinformation and rumour-spreading campaign.* Government Offices of Sweden. https://www.government.se/press-releases/2023/02/government-taking-strong-action-against-disinformation-and-rumour-spreading-campaign/

Turton, W., & Mehrotra, K. (2021, 4 June). Hackers breached Colonial Pipeline using compromised password. *Bloomberg.* https://www.bloomberg.com/news/articles/2021-06-04/hackers-breached-colonial-pipeline-using-compromised-password

United Kingdom. (2021). *Integrated operating concept 2025.* Ministry of Defence. https://assets.publishing.service.gov.uk/government/uploads/system/uploads/attachment_data/file/1014659/Integrated_Operating_Concept_2025.pdf

United States of America. (2018). *Summary: Department of Defense cyber strategy 2018.* Department of Defense. https://media.defense.gov/2018/Sep/18/2002041658/-1/-1/1/CYBER_STRATEGY_ SUMMARY_FINAL.PDF

United States of America. (2021a, 19 July). Four Chinese nationals working with the Ministry of State Security charged with global computer intrusion campaign targeting intellectual property and confidential business information, including infectious disease research. *Justice News.* Department of Justice. https://www.justice.gov/opa/pr/four-chinese-nationals-working-ministry-state-security-charged-global-computer-intrusion

United States of America. (2021b, 28 July). National Security memorandum on improving cybersecurity for critical infrastructure control systems. *The White House.* https://www.whitehouse.gov/briefing-room/statements-releases/2021/07/28/national-security-memorandum-on-improving-cybersecurity-for-critical-infrastructure-control-systems/

Vailshery, L. S. (2022, 6 September). Global IoT and non-IoT connections 2010–2025. *Statista.* https://www.statista.com/statistics/1101442/iot-number-of-connected-devices-worldwide/

Waltz, K. N. (1981). The spread of nuclear weapons: More may be better: Introduction. *Adelphi Papers, 21*(171). https://doi.org/10.1080/05679328108457394

Westbrook, T. (2019, 23 January). Severed cable sends Tonga "back to beginning of the Internet." *Reuters.* https://www.reuters.com/article/us-tonga-internet-idUSKCN1PI0A8

Wilner, A. S., Wenger, A. (Eds.). (2021). *Deterrence by denial: Theory and practice.* Cambria Press.

2

Nuclear Crisis Management for the Information Age

Stephen J. Cimbala and Adam B. Lowther

The growing importance of the cyber domain to warfare requires a major rethinking of information's use during conflict. Technologies that increase the sensor-to-shooter speed in which a war fighter can find, fix, and kill a target enhance battlespace awareness, but can also pose a risk to effective target assessment and reduce understanding of an action's consequences. One case in point is the relationship between digital decision tools and the management of crises, especially crises with the inherent risk of escalation to nuclear first use or first strike. Nuclear deterrence is, at its core, an information operation that employs information, disinformation, and misinformation in order to shape the risk-reward calculation of an adversary. If the ultimate goal of deterrence is to create a perception of risk that makes changing the status quo too risky, then it should come as no surprise that this volume includes a chapter on deterrence and nuclear crisis management. The following discussion considers how the goals of nuclear crisis management might be circumscribed or even overcome by the interaction of new information technologies with command-and-control stability, communication between adversaries, and other aspects of crisis decision making. This all occurs as part of information operations where opposing sides are attempting to shape an adversary's perception of risk through information manipulation.

It is worth noting that the Cold War did not see a crisis in which states were armed with advanced cyber weapons and nuclear weapons. Employment of mis- and disinformation was a much slower process than it is today. Analog systems were state of the art for much of the Cold War, and certainly for much of the technology used in nuclear delivery systems. They were reliable and, at least for the United States, the periodic modernization effort that was due in the 1990s never took place because of the Soviet Union's collapse in 1991. Thus, the implications of cyber-based information warfare and cross-domain deterrence—using capabilities in one domain to deter action in a different domain—were far less complex than they are now. Recent advances in the cyber and space domains are changing the fundamental dynamics of deterrence and making Cold War "general deterrence" obsolete. It is worth noting that any nuclear crisis, and possible war, will likely begin with an effort to manipulate an adversary's situational awareness and create a false perception.

Today, the nuclear-cyber relationship has special significance for the United States and Russia and makes deterrence a much more complex task—particularly as the United States undertakes a digital transformation of its nuclear command, control, and communication (NC3) system (Lowther, 2020). If cyber-security experts are correct about the "D5" of cyber security, then it should come as no surprise that the United States can expect Russian and Chinese cyber warriors to focus on ways to deceive, degrade, deny, disrupt, and destroy a new digital NC3 architecture in an effort to prevent the United States from understanding what they may be doing and from commanding and controlling their nuclear forces (Reed, 2013). In such an information operation, disinformation plays a critical role because it is deception, not destruction, that is the apex of cyber conflict. Too few appreciate fully the role information and information operations play in deterrence because it is too easy to focus on the destructive capacity of nuclear weapons. Thus, in the pages that follow, it is important to keep in mind the role information operations play in crisis and escalation management. With Russia and the United States possessing approximately 90 per cent of the world's nuclear weapons and employing the most advanced offensive and defensive cyber capabilities, the real threat of employing disinformation through the cyber domain is growing (Thomas, 2015). This chapter explores the implications of this development in two steps (Futter, 2016a, 2016b; Gartzke, 2017). First, it considers the larger question of nuclear-cyber relationships in the present and near term. Second, it turns to specific issues related to nuclear crisis management.

Understanding the Nuclear-Cyber Nexus

What are the implications of potential overlap between concepts or practices for cyber war and nuclear deterrence (Arquilla, 2008; Libicki, 2009, 2017; Singer & Friedman, 2014)? Although cyber war and nuclear conflict may seem to take place at opposite ends of the conflict spectrum, they are distinctly interrelated. Cyber weapons should appeal to those who prefer a non-nuclear military-technical arc of development, but they are also the thread that ties nuclear decision making to nuclear weapons employment. War in the cyber domain offers a possible means of crippling enemy assets without the need for kinetic attack—potentially minimizing physical destruction (Koshkin, 2013; Thomas, 2005). Nuclear weapons, on the other hand, are the very epitome of "mass" destruction. Their use for deterrence—the avoidance of war by the manipulation of risk—is preferred to their actual use in conflict. Unfortunately, neither nuclear deterrence nor cyber war exist in distinct policy universes, something that was possible in the Cold War and the early post–Cold War period.

Nuclear weapons, whether held back for deterrence or fired in anger, require effective command, control, communications, computers, intelligence, surveillance, and reconnaissance (C4ISR). These weapons and their C4ISR systems must be protected from physical and cyber-attack (Lowther, 2020). Decision makers managing nuclear forces should ideally have the best possible information about the status of their own forces, adversary forces, and the probable intentions and risk acceptance of an adversary. In short, the task of managing nuclear-deterrence operations demands clear thinking and good information. Where there was a clearly defined boundary between peace and war during the Cold War, both China and Russia now employ doctrine that sees war as a constant and something that begins in the information environment (Bowen, 2020; Goode, 2008). Cyber weapons are designed to impede clear assessment of the strategic environment by achieving one or more of the "D5" effects (degrade, deny, disrupt, destroy, deceive), with a focus on deception, in the C4ISR networks of the United States (Libicki, 2007; Reed, 2013). The temptation to use cyber-attacks early against NC3 networks, for example, might make a nuclear crisis less stable rather than pre-empt a conflict altogether. In short, attempts to introduce disinformation during a nuclear crisis can lead to greater instability.

Ironically, the downsizing of American and Russian strategic nuclear arsenals since the end of the Cold War, while a positive development from the perspectives of nuclear arms control and non-proliferation, makes cyber and nuclear attack capabilities more alarming as the incentive moves toward use of both to pre-empt an adversary. The supersized deployments of missiles and bombers and expansive numbers of weapons kept by the Cold War Americans and Soviets had at least one virtue. Those arsenals provided so much redundancy against first-strike vulnerability that relatively linear systems for nuclear attack warning, command and control, and responsive launch under or after attack, sufficed. At the same time, Cold War cyber weapons were primitive compared to those available now, and it was almost impossible to penetrate command-and-control networks for the purpose of introducing disinformation. In addition, countries and their armed forces were less dependent on the fidelity of their information systems for national security. Thus, the reduction of American and Russian forces to the size of "minimum deterrents" might compromise nuclear flexibility and resilience in the face of kinetic attacks preceded or accompanied by cyber war (Forsyth, 2010; Payne, 2013). Although the mathematics of minimum deterrence would shrink the size of attackers' as well as defenders' arsenals, defenders with smaller forces might have greater fears of absolute compared to relative losses—and, therefore, be more prone to pre-emption-dependent strategies than defenders with larger forces. In other words, deception carries a much greater cost.

Offensive cyber operations are very much on the minds of American military leaders (Kaplan, 2016; Sanger, 2013). Russia is explicit about its cyber concerns. President Vladimir Putin urged the Russian Security Council in early July 2013 to improve state security against cyber-attacks, and it remains concerned about cyber-attacks on NC3 networks ("Putin calls," 2013). The war in Ukraine has only heightened this concern. Russian security expert Vladimir Batyuk, commenting favourably on a June 2013 Russo-American agreement for protection, control, and accounting of nuclear materials (a successor to the recently expired Nunn-Lugar agreement on nuclear risk reduction) warned that pledges by Presidents Putin and Obama for co-operation on cyber security were even more important: "Nuclear weapons are a legacy of the 20th century. The challenge of the 21st century is cyber security" (Earle, 2013).

On the other hand, arms control for cyber is apt to run into daunting security and technical issues—even assuming a successful navigation of political trust for matters as sensitive as these. Of special significance is whether negotiators seeking cyber arms control can certify that hackers within their own states are sufficiently under control for cyber verification and transparency. Both Russia and China reportedly use ad hoc and unofficial hackers to conduct operations to which governments would prefer to remain officially unconnected. For example, Russia's hacking into the email account of the Democratic National Committee in 2016 was attributed by some sources to

Table 2.1. Comparative Attributes of Cyber War and Nuclear Deterrence

Cyber war	**Nuclear deterrence**
The source of attack may be ambiguous—third-party intrusions masquerading as other actors are possible.	The source of attack is almost certain to be identified if the attacker is a state. Even terrorist attackers with nuclear materials are traceable.
Damage is primarily focused on data, although physical effects are possible.	Damage, even in the case of a limited nuclear war, can be large-scale destruction of property and life.
Denial of an attacker's objectives is feasible if defences are sufficiently robust and/or penetrations can be repaired in good time.	Deterrence by denial is less credible than the threat of punishment by assured retaliation.
The objective of cyber-attacks is typically disruption or confusion rather than destruction.	Nuclear deterrence rests on the credible threat of massive and prompt destruction of assets and populations.
Cyber-attacks can continue over an extended period without detection and sometimes without doing obvious or significant damage.	The first use of a nuclear weapon since 1945 by a state or non-state actor for a hostile purpose would be a game-changing event.
The price of entry for cyber war is comparatively low.	Building and operating a nuclear deterrent requires that a state spend significant time, talent, and treasure.

Sources: Gartzke, 2017; Libicki, 2017; Thomas, 2012.

"Guccifer 2.0" (an homage to the original Romanian hacker using that name). Some forensic evidence supports the hypothesis that Guccifer 2.0 was run by the FSB—the official Russian security agency—with involvement by Russian military intelligence (Lourie, 2017; Roberts, 2016; Thomas, 2012). In this case, email was exfiltrated and exposed to cause political chaos. How much worse could the consequences be of a disinformation campaign within American nuclear command-and-control networks?

On the one hand, cyber cuts across the land, sea, air, and space domains. Cyber, compared to the other domains, suffers from a lack of historical perspective. The cyber domain "has been created in a short time and has not had the same level of scrutiny as other battle domains," as one author has argued (Magee, 2013). What this might mean for the cyber-nuclear intersection is far from obvious. Table 2.1 above summarizes some of the major attributes that distinguish nuclear deterrence from cyber war according to experts, but the differences between nuclear and cyber listed here do not contradict the prior observation that cyber and nuclear operations inevitably interact in practice.

Crisis Management: Definitions and Parameters

One of the most important areas where the development of the cyber domain is reshaping nuclear deterrence is the realm of crisis management. Where Cold War nuclear crises were largely an issue of accurately judging the will of the adversary, cyber warfare, particularly attacks against NC3 systems, are certain to reshape deployed systems, the trustworthiness of information, and how data is used. Crisis management, including nuclear crisis management, is both a competitive and co-operative endeavour between adversaries. A crisis is, by definition, a time of great tension and uncertainty (George, 1991; George & Simons, 1994; Tetlock, 1990; Williams, 1976).

All crises are characterized to some extent by a high degree of threat, limited decision-making windows, and a "fog of crisis" reminiscent of Clausewitz's "fog of war" that leaves crisis participants confused as to what is happening—a particular problem in a digital-dependent world. The influence of nuclear weapons on crisis decision making is not easy to measure or document because the avoidance of war is ascribed to many causes. The presence of nuclear forces obviously influences the degree of destruction that can be done should crisis management fail. As in the past, information about an adversary's capability and will are critical elements in a decision maker's selection of a course of action. If, for example, the presidents of Russia or of the United States fear they are the victims of disinformation and do not trust the information they receive or their ability to command and control nuclear forces, they may find themselves unwilling to show the strategic patience displayed during the nuclear crises of the Cold War (Burr, 2021).

Crisis Management: The Requirements

The first requirement for successful crisis management is the ability to trust one's intelligence and effective communications that include clear signalling and undistorted messaging. *Signalling* refers to the requirement that each side must send its estimate of the situation to the other. It is not necessary for the two sides to have identical or even initially complementary interests. But a sufficient number of accurate and correctly sent and received signals are a prerequisite to effective transfer of enemy goals and objectives from one side to the other. If signals are poorly sent or misunderstood, steps taken by the sender or receiver may lead to unintended consequences, including miscalculated escalation.

Messaging also includes high-fidelity communication between adversaries, and within the respective decision-making structures of each side. High-fidelity communication in a crisis can be distorted by everything that might interfere physically, mechanically, or behaviourally with accurate transmission. As Keith B. Payne notes,

With regard to the potential for deterrence failure in the post–Cold War period:

> unfortunately, our expectations of opponents' behavior frequently are unmet, not because our opponents necessarily are irrational but because we do not understand them—their individual values, goals, determination, and commitments—in the context of the engagement, and therefore we are surprised when their "unreasonable" behavior differs from our expectations. (Payne, 1996, p. 57)

This challenge is made harder when adversaries are actively engaged in a disinformation campaign against the very systems that allow decision makers to evaluate data. Such an added challenge was not present during the Cold War and is still poorly understood by modern scholars.

A second requirement of successful crisis management is the reduction of time pressure on policy-makers and commanders so that no unintended, provocative steps are taken toward escalation mainly or solely as a result of a misperception that "time is up." Policy-makers and military planners are capable of inventing fictive worlds of perception and evaluation in which "H hour" becomes more than a useful benchmark for decision resolution. In decision pathologies possible under crisis conditions, deadlines may be confused with policy objectives themselves—ends become means and means become ends. For example, the war plans of the great powers in July 1914 contributed to a self-fulfilling prophecy shared among leaders in Berlin, St. Petersburg, and Vienna that only by prompt mobilization and attack could decisive losses be avoided in war (Tuchman, 2004). This view resulted from the inability of ruling monarchs to have accurate information concerning the capability and will of a rival. Today, a similar challenge exists in nuclear conflict, where nuclear armed adversaries possess cyber capabilities that generate a similar effect—compressing the time to decide.

One result of attack time compression, which is the shortening of response time that results from weapons reaching targets more quickly and the possible disabling of integrated tactical warning and attack assessment (ITW/AA) in a cyber-attack (introduction of disinformation), is that the likelihood of undetected attacks and falsely detected attack errors increases—a real fear in an era when an adversary may have the ability to penetrate one's NC3 system and either introduce false positives or hide inbound weapons (Erwin, 2021). During the Cold War, there was little concern that a cyber-attack would make it impossible for the United States to trust its own ITW/AA. Tactical warning and intelligence networks grow accustomed to the routine behaviour of other states' forces. However, the real possibility that an adversary can penetrate NC3 systems and deceive those networks creates greater instability and a preference for striking before NC3 systems—and trusted data—are lost to cyber-attack. Thus, stability during a crisis is certain to depend on modernized NC3 networks that assure the nuclear mission in the face of cyber-attack—no easy task.

A third attribute of successful crisis management is that each side should be able to offer the other a safety valve or a face-saving exit from a predicament that has escalated beyond its original expectations. The search for options should back neither crisis participant into a corner from which there is no graceful retreat. For example, during the Cuban Missile Crisis of 1962, President John F. Kennedy was able to offer Soviet premier Nikita Khrushchev a face-saving exit from his overextended missile deployments. Kennedy publicly committed the United States to refraining from future military aggression against Cuba and privately agreed to remove and dismantle Jupiter medium-range ballistic missiles deployed within NATO nations (Lebow & Stein, 1995). Kennedy and his inner circle recognized, after some days of deliberation and clearer focus on the Soviet view of events, that the United States would lose, not gain, by a public humiliation of Khrushchev that might, in turn, diminish Khrushchev's interest in any mutually agreed solution to the crisis. A debilitating cyber-attack, making it impossible to have situational awareness, early in a crisis/conflict could make an action untenable. Given the often unknown consequences and second- or third-order effects of a cyber-attack, reversing course may prove challenging.

A fourth attribute of successful crisis management is that each side maintains an accurate perception of the other's intentions and military capabilities—the antithesis of what disinformation seeks to achieve. This becomes difficult during a crisis because, in the heat of a partly competitive relationship and a threat-intensive environment, intentions and capabilities can change. Maintaining the confidence to wait is an important aspect of managing a crisis. This is largely dependent on each adversary's certainty that the information upon which they rely to make decisions is trustworthy. Thus, it should come as no surprise that the most dangerous of the D5 effects is deceive, not destroy. When decision makers cannot trust information, which may support holding firm over acting, Robert Jervis's admonition becomes increasingly relevant. Jervis warned that Cold War beliefs in the inevitability of war might have created a self-fulfilling prophecy:

> The superpowers' beliefs about whether or not war between them is inevitable create reality as much as they reflect it. Because pre-emption could be the only rational reason to launch an all-out war, beliefs about what the other side is about to do are of major importance and depend in large part on an estimate of the other's beliefs about what the first side will do. (Jervis, 1989, p. 183)

Intentions can change during a crisis if policy-makers become more optimistic about gains or more pessimistic about potential losses. Capabilities can change due to the management of military alerts and the deployment or other movement of military forces. Heightened states of military readiness on each side are intended to send a two-sided signal of readiness for the worst if the other side attacks and of a non-threatening steadiness of purpose in the face of enemy passivity. This mixed message is hard to send under the best of crisis-management conditions, since each state's behaviours and communications, as observed by its opponent, may not seem consistent. It is even harder when the very information used to make decisions is under attack.

Under the stress of time pressures and military threats, different parts of complex security organizations make decisions consistent with bureaucratic interests. These decisions may not coincide with a national leader's intent, or with the decisions and actions of other parts of the government. As Alexander L. George explains,

> It is important to recognize that the ability of top-level political authorities to maintain control over the moves and actions of military forces is made difficult because of the exceedingly large

number of often complex standing orders that come into effect at the onset of a crisis and as it intensifies. It is not easy for top-level political authorities to have full and timely knowledge of the multitude of existing standing orders. As a result, they may fail to coordinate some critically important standing orders with their overall crisis management strategy. (George, 1991, p. 18)

This challenge is unimaginably harder when the very NC3 system that allows a president or prime minister to communicate with forces is itself the target of an adversary.

UNCERTAINTY

Cyber warfare is certain to disrupt successful crisis management on each of the preceding attributes (Davis, 2015). For a decision maker, it is imperative that intelligence and NC3 information is trustworthy. The possibility of cyber-enabled pre-emption—to disable enemy nuclear missiles before they reach the launch pad or during the launch itself—is a real possibility that military leaders in China, Russia, and the United States all fear. Such "left-of-launch" techniques were used by the United States against North Korea (Sanger, 2017). During a nuclear crisis, would such a move be accepted by the attacked party as one of intimidation and deterrence, or, to the contrary, would offensive cyber war against missile launches prompt a nuclear first use? The answer to this question is unknown.

Cyber warfare can also destroy or disrupt communication channels necessary for successful crisis management. One way cyber warfare can do this is to disrupt communication links between policy-makers and military commanders during a period of high threat and severe time pressure. Two kinds of unanticipated problems, from the standpoint of civil-military relations, are possible under these conditions. First, political leaders may have pre-delegated limited authority for nuclear release or launch under restrictive conditions: only when these few conditions are present, according to the protocols of pre-delegation, would military commanders be authorized to employ nuclear weapons distributed within their command. Disrupted communications could prevent top leaders from understanding the perceptions of military commanders, who may see circumstances as far more desperate, and thus permissive of nuclear initiative, than the reality of the situation would warrant. For example, during the Cold War, disrupted communications between the US National Command Authority and ballistic missile submarines, once the latter came under attack, could have resulted in a decision by submarine officers to launch in the absence of contrary instructions.

Second, cyber-attacks during a crisis will almost certainly increase the time pressure under which political leaders operate. It may do this literally, or it may affect the perceived timelines within which the policy-making process results in decisions. Once either side sees parts of its nuclear command, control, and communications system being degraded, disrupted, denied, destroyed, or deceived, its sense of panic at the possible loss of military options becomes enormous. We cannot underscore enough the serious implication of disinformation efforts in nuclear crisis management. In the case of US Cold War nuclear war plans, for example, disruption of even portions of the strategic command, control, and communications system could have prevented competent execution of parts of the single integrated operational plan (SIOP). The Cold War SIOP depended upon finely orchestrated time-on-target estimates and precise damage expectancies against various classes of targets. Mis- or disinformation in the NC3 system was likely to lead to redundant attacks against the same target sets and, quite possibly, unplanned attacks on friendly military or civilian installations. Even in the post–Cold War world of flexible nuclear-response options, the potential slide toward pre-emption, based on mistaken or exaggerated fears of command-and-control vulnerability, casts a shadow over deterrence stability. As Bruce Blair warned,

> There are no widely accepted methods for calculating command and control performance under wartime conditions, and empirical validation of such an assessment cannot be done. Compared with the tight and tidy standard calculations of force vulnerability, any objective assessment of command-and-control systems would raise more questions than it answered. (Blair, 1993, p. 118)

A third potentially disruptive effect of cyber-attacks on nuclear crisis management is that such attacks may reduce the search for available alternatives to the few and desperate. Policy-makers searching for an escape from crisis denouements need flexible options and creative problem solving. Victims of information warfare may have a diminished ability to solve problems routinely, let alone creatively, once information networks are filled with flotsam and jetsam. Questions to operators will be poorly posed, and responses (if available at all) will be driven toward the least common denominator of previously programmed standard operating procedures. Retaliatory systems that depend on launch on warning instead of survival after riding out an attack are especially vulnerable to reduced time cycles and restricted alternatives:

> A well-designed warning system cannot save commanders from misjudging the situation under the constraints of time and information imposed by a posture of launch on warning. Such a posture truncates the decision process too early for iterative estimates to converge on reality. Rapid reaction is inherently unstable because it cuts short the learning time needed to match perception with reality. (Blair, 1993, p. 252)

The propensity to search for the first available alternative that meets minimum satisfactory conditions of goal attainment is strong enough under normal conditions in non-military bureaucratic organizations (March & Simon, 1958). In civil-military command-and-control systems under the stress of nuclear crisis decision making, the first available alternative may quite literally be the last—a particular challenge when an adversary is targeting the information that allows you to command and control forces. This challenge did not exist during the Cold War because the technical capacity to wage cyber war did not exist.

Accordingly, the bias toward prompt and adequate solutions is strong. During the Cuban Missile Crisis, for example, several members of the presidential advisory group continued to propound air strikes and invasion of Cuba during the entire thirteen days of deliberation (Allison & Zelikow, 1999). Had less time been available for debate, and had President Kennedy not deliberately structured the discussion in a way that forced alternatives to the surface, the air strike and invasion might well have been the chosen alternative (Lebow & Stein, 1995). As Paul K. Davis notes,

> Usual discussions of crisis stability assume that leaders are in control of their nuclear capabilities. Again, history is sobering. President Kennedy became worried in 1961 about possible unilateral actions by military leaders to prepare a pre-emptive strike against the Soviet Union. He instigated efforts to tighten the President's personal control. Soviet leadership worried about

> survivability of its forces and developed capability for launch on warning and automated response. Such systems could be the source of accidental war. (Davis, 2015, p. 14)

If the challenge for effective decision making and the fear of a mistake was this high during an era when an adversary could not achieve D5 effects against NC3 systems, it is easy to imagine how much more complex today's challenge is for a president or prime minister who faces a cyber challenge they do not fully understand.

Fourth, cyber-attacks can cause flawed images of each side's intentions and capabilities to be conveyed to the other, with potentially disastrous results. Another example from the Cuban Missile Crisis demonstrates the possible side effects of simple misunderstanding and non-communication on American crisis management. At the tensest period of the crisis, a U-2 reconnaissance aircraft strayed into Soviet airspace. American and Soviet fighters scrambled, and a possible Arctic confrontation of air forces loomed. Khrushchev later told Kennedy that Soviet air defences might have interpreted the U-2 flight as either a pre-strike reconnaissance mission or a bomber, calling for a compensatory response by Moscow (Allison & Zelikow, 1999; Lebow & Stein, 1995; Sagan, 1989). Fortunately, Moscow chose to give the United States the benefit of the doubt in this instance and to permit American fighters to escort the wayward U-2 back to Alaska. Why this scheduled U-2 mission was not scrubbed once the crisis began has never been fully revealed. This Cold War example of uncertainty generated by a lack of information is similar to the psychological affect generated by a cyber-attack, although, in this incident, neither side's ability to command, control, and communicate with nuclear forces was threatened, which gave both sides, particularly the Soviets, more breathing room to withhold action.

The preceding discussion is underscored by the assessment of Martin Libicki, who writes,

> To generalize, a situation in which there is little pressure to respond quickly, in which a temporary disadvantage or loss is tolerable, and in which there are grounds for giving the other side some benefit of the doubt is one in which there is time for crisis management to work. Conversely, if the failure to respond quickly causes a state's position to erode, a temporary

disadvantage or degree of loss is intolerable, and there are no grounds for disputing what happened, who did it, and why—then states may conclude that they must bring matters to a head quickly. (Libicki, 2012)

SCENARIOS AND RISKS

The outcome of a nuclear crisis influenced by cyber-attacks may not be favourable. Despite the best efforts of crisis participants, the dispute may degenerate into a nuclear first use or first strike by one side and retaliation by the other. In that situation, cyber-attacks by either side (or both) might make it more difficult to limit the war and bring it to a conclusion before catastrophic destruction and loss of life takes place. Although there is no such thing as a "small" nuclear war, compared to conventional war, there can be different kinds of nuclear wars, in terms of their proximate causes and consequences (Questor, 2006). Possibilities include a nuclear attack from an unknown source; an ambiguous case of possible, but not proved, nuclear first use; a nuclear "test" detonation intended to intimidate but with no immediate destruction; or a low- or very-low-yield nuclear detonation.

The prospect of a general nuclear war between the United States and the Soviet Union preoccupied Cold War policy-makers. Concerns about escalation control and war termination were swamped by apocalyptic visions of the end of days. The second nuclear age, roughly coinciding with the end of the Cold War and the demise of the Soviet Union, offered a more complicated menu of nuclear possibilities and responses and led to the creation of tailored deterrence, which suggested it was imperative to understand an adversary's history, culture, and other characteristics to design a tailored deterrence approach for that specific country (Questor, 2006). General deterrence was no longer enough. Interest in the threat or use of nuclear weapons by rogue states, by aspiring regional hegemons, or by terrorists, abetted by the possible spread of nuclear weapons among currently non–nuclear weapons states, stretched the ingenuity of military planners and fiction writers alike.

In addition to the world's worst characters engaged in nuclear threat or first use, there was also the possibility of backsliding in political conditions as between the United States and Russia, or Russia and China, or China and India (among current nuclear weapons states). The nuclear "establishment" or P-5 thus includes cases of current de-bellicization or pacification that depend upon the continuation of favourable political auguries in regional or global politics. A common susceptibility to cyber intrusion and the injection of disinformation across all critical command, control, and communication networks also creates mutual vulnerability that helps deter any nuclear power acting too aggressively. Politically unthinkable conflicts of one decade have a way of evolving into the politically unavoidable wars of another—the First World War is instructive in this regard. The war between Russia and Georgia in August 2008 was a reminder that local conflicts on regional fault lines between blocs or major powers have the potential to expand. So, too, were the Balkan wars of Yugoslav succession in the 1990s. In these cases, Russia's one-sided military advantage relative to Georgia in 2008, and NATO's military power relative to that of Bosnians of all stripes in 1995 and Serbia in 1999, contributed to war termination without further international escalation.

Escalation of a conventional war into nuclear first use remains possible where operational or tactical nuclear weapons are deployed with national or coalition armed forces. In NATO territory, the United States deploys several hundred air-delivered nuclear weapons among bases in Belgium, Germany, Italy, the Netherlands, and Turkey (Kristensen, 2005). Russia retains at least several thousand non-strategic nuclear weapons, including significant numbers deployed in western Russia (Kipp, 2010; Podvig, 2010). The New START agreement establishes notional parity between the United States and Russia in nuclear systems of intercontinental range (Cimbala, 2020; Payne, 2020). But American superiority in advanced technology and information-based conventional military power leaves Russia heavily reliant on tactical nuclear weapons as compensation for comparative weakness in non-nuclear forces. NATO's capitals breathed a sigh of relief when Russia's officially approved military doctrine of 2010 did not seem to lower the bar for nuclear first use, compared to previous editions (Pietkiewicz, 2018; Sokov, 2010). Vladimir Putin's nuclear threats in the wake of Russia's invasion of Ukraine changed that (Arnold, 2022). With Putin incorporating disinformation into his larger information operation against NATO, it is even harder to make sense of his nuclear threats.

Outside of the current conflict, Russia's military doctrine indicates a willingness to engage in nuclear first use in situations of extreme urgency for Russia, as defined by its political leadership (Giles, 2010). And, despite evident superiority in conventional forces relative to those of Russia, neither the United States nor NATO is necessarily eager to get rid of their remaining tactical nuclear weapons, deployed among NATO allies. An expert panel convened by NATO to set the stage for its 2010 review of the alliance's military doctrine was carefully ambivalent on the issue of the alliance's forward-deployed nuclear weapons. The issue of negotiating away these weapons in return for parallel concessions from Russia was left open for further discussion. On the other hand, the NATO expert report underscored the majority sentiment of governments that these weapons provided a necessary link in the chain of alliance deterrence options (NATO, 2010). As the authors were told in a 2016 visit to NATO headquarters, "NATO is a nuclear alliance" (Delegation, 2016). This last statement is even more important in the wake of Russian aggression and threats.

Imagine now the unfolding of a nuclear crisis or the taking of a decision for nuclear first use, under the conditions of both NATO and Russian campaigns employing strategic disinformation and information operations intended to disrupt opposed command, control, and communications. Disruptive cyber-attacks against enemy systems on the threshold of nuclear first use, or shortly thereafter, could increase the already substantial difficulty of bringing fighting to a halt before a European-wide conflict or a strategic nuclear war. All of the previously cited difficulties in crisis management under the shadow of nuclear deterrence, pending a decision for first use, would be compounded by additional uncertainty and friction after the nuclear threshold is crossed.

Three new kinds of frictions are posed for NATO. The cohesion of allied governments is tested under conditions of unprecedented stress and danger, doubtless aided by a confused situation on the battlefield. Second, reliable intelligence about Russian intentions following first use is essential. Third, the first use of a nuclear weapon in anger since Nagasaki establishes a new psychological, political, and moral universe within which negotiators for de-escalation and war termination somehow have to maintain their sang-froid, obtain agreed stand-downs, and return nuclear-capable launchers and weapons to secured, but transparent, locations. All of this would be taking place within the panic-spreading capabilities of 24/7 news networks, disinformation-filled social media, and the larger Internet.

Theoretically, one might finesse the issue by eliminating cyber operations that potentially conflict with de-escalation. But the political desire to do so is in conflict with the military necessity for timely information gathering, assessment, and penetration of enemy networks—in order to accomplish two necessary, but somewhat opposed, missions. First, each side wants to correctly anticipate the timing and character of the other's decision for nuclear first use—and, if possible, to throw logic bombs, Trojan Horses, electronic warfare, or other impediments in the way (or, if finesse is not at hand, bombing the relevant installations is always an option, although an obviously provocative one). Second, and somewhat opposed, is the need to communicate reliably with the other side as regards their preferences for de-escalation, a willingness to do so if reciprocity can be obtained, and an awareness of the possibility that the situation will shortly get out of hand. Consider the Russian president and general staff filtering messages while forces were fighting in Georgia, Ukraine (having been taken into NATO membership the previous year, over Russia's objections), or elsewhere.

The problem of nuanced messages and the management of de-escalation, even short of war, is illustrated by NATO's command post exercise Able Archer, conducted 7–11 November 1983. An annual exercise, Able Archer was intended to practise nuclear release procedures. Soviet intelligence routinely monitored these exercises. However, the 1983 version took place against a backdrop of rising Soviet-American political tensions and heightened suspicions within the Soviet political leadership and military high command that the United States and NATO might be preparing for a nuclear first strike. Russian sensitivities to the possibility of US or NATO nuclear first strike were high because NATO began deploying Pershing II ballistic missiles and ground-launched cruise missiles, beginning in the fall of 1983. Soviet and Warsaw Pact reactions to Able Archer 83 included an unprecedented surge of Warsaw Pact technical collection, a significant increase in reconnaissance by Soviet strategic and naval aviation, and other unusual Soviet moves that indicated increased concern about NATO and US intentions (N. Jones, 2018; Kastner, 2018). The case illustrates how mistaken interpretations of "normal" events can overvalue pessimistic assessment at just the wrong time (Andrew & Gordievsky, 1990; Gates, 1996;). As the President's Foreign Intelligence Advisory Board concluded in 1990,

> We believe that the Soviets perceived that the correlation of forces had turned against the USSR, that the US was seeking military superiority, and that the chances of the US launching a nuclear first strike—perhaps under cover of a routine training exercise—were growing. We also believe that the US intelligence community did not at the time, and for several years afterwards,

attach sufficient weight to the possibility that the war scare was real. (N. Jones, 2018)

Similar problems in coordinating the management of de-escalation and conflict termination with the conduct of cyber conflict may appear in two other situations. First, already alluded to, is the use of a bunker-busting or other advanced technology conventional weapons that the other side, during the fog of crisis or war, confused with a nuclear first use or first strike. Russia expressed this concern specifically during New START negotiations in 2010, with regard to American plans to deploy some conventionally armed ballistic missiles on nuclear-capable intercontinental or transoceanic launchers. New START counting rules will regard conventionally armed ballistic missiles as also nuclear-capable launchers and, therefore, subject to overall restrictions on the numbers of deployed launchers and weapons. American plans for prompt global strike (PGS) systems, including missiles or future space planes, were first approved during the George W. Bush administration, and carried forward under the Obama administration.

A second illustration, apart from escalation in Europe, of the problem of managing escalation control and conflict termination along with information operations is provided by the possibility of a joint NATO-Russian theatre missile defence (possibly including air defences) system. The idea has expert and highly visible political proponents on both sides of the Atlantic, and official Russian commentators do not close the door to co-operation on ballistic missile defences (BMD). NATO and Russia are facing in two political directions: (1) wariness, but also openness, toward one another; and (2) concern about possible future Iranian or other Middle Eastern nuclear weapons in the hands of leaders beyond deterrence based on the credible threat of nuclear (or other) retaliation.

However, the problems of obtaining missile defence co-operation as between NATO and Russia are not only political. Even with the best of intentions among American, European, and Russian negotiators, the military-technical problems of coordinating BMD command, control, and communications systems are considerable—even before Russia's invasion of Ukraine. Indeed, they are not strictly "military-technical" but also heavily embedded with issues of political sovereignty, classified intelligence, and trust among governments and militaries that are currently waging low-level cyber war against one another. Even NATO militaries differ in their views. For example, if a

European theatre-wide system of intelligence and missile-attack warning is established, how many capitals will host relevant servers and receive timely output? Who will decide that a missile warning is now a threat requiring activation of the European BMD system? Can a single nation do so if a missile is headed its way, or must NATO and Russia agree before responding? Perhaps most importantly, can NATO members trust that Russia will not engage in cyber-attacks against such a system?

If a political crisis between NATO and Russia erupts—and the war in Ukraine arguably is such a crisis—and both sides already deploy missile defences, will Russian or American cyber warriors attack the other's missile defences? Would it be better to reassure Russia as to the surety of its independent capabilities or share capabilities with NATO? Neither Russia nor the United States want to relinquish sovereign control over missile defences. However, it may be prudent to co-operate to establish trust and de-escalate the growing cyber conflict that is causing increasing instability in the nuclear deterrence relationship between the two countries. Although, missile defences may appear tangential to the larger issue of nuclear deterrence and cyber-attack, it is an opportunity for two countries that are clearly at war in cyberspace to co-operate in a needed and useful manner (S. Jones, 2018).

Conclusion

The United States and Russia learned to manage nuclear crises and peacetime deterrence during the Cold War and prior to the rise of the cyber domain. Advanced cyber-attacks against nuclear production facilities (e.g., Stuxnet) are well-known. Convincing American, Chinese, or Russian leaders that NC3 systems are also likely targets takes very little effort. The implications for such attacks on crisis stability are unknown in that such an event has yet to take place, leaving us to speculate about the impact of cyber-attacks and efforts to inject technical disinformation into systems responsible for nuclear crisis management. What we do know is that the decades ahead are unlikely to look like the Cold War (Ellsberg, 2017; Fursenko & Naftali, 1997; Khrushchev, 1990). As the discussion above suggests, the future is likely filled with increased risk and the possibility of imminent attack and a bias for pre-emptive action, where striking first is the last resort. Finally, it is important to emphasize that deterrence, whether it is based on the credible threat of denial or retaliation, must be successfully communicated to, and believed by, the other side. Deterrence is fundamentally an information operation that, because of technological developments, is increasingly susceptible to the injection of disinformation into nuclear command, command, and control systems (Sechser & Fuhrmann, 2017; Gray, 1996). Contrary to popular belief, deterrence and disinformation are intrinsically linked.

REFERENCES

Allison, G., & Zelikow, P. (1999). Essence of decision: Explaining the Cuban Missile Crisis. Pearson.

Andrew, C., & Gordievsky, O. (1990). KGB: The inside story of its foreign operations from Lenin to Gorbachev. Harper.

Arnold, L. (2022, 9 November). Why Russia's nuclear threats are difficult to dismiss: QuickTake. Washington Post. https://www.washingtonpost.com/business/why-russias-nuclear-threats-are-difficult-to-dismiss-quicktake/2022/11/09/2934f1b0-603d-11ed-a131-e900e4a6336b_story.html

Arquilla, J. (2008). Worst enemy: The reluctant transformation of the American military. Ivan R. Dee.

Blair, B. (1993). The logic of accidental nuclear war. Brookings Institution Press.

Bowen, A. (2020, 20 August). Russia armed forces: Military doctrine and strategy. In Focus. Congressional Research Service. https://sgp.fas.org/crs/row/IF11625.pdf

Burr, W. (2021, 26 May). Alerts, crises, and DEFCONS. National Security Archives. https://nsarchive.gwu.edu/briefing-book/nuclear-vault/2021-03-17/alerts-crises-defcons

Cimbala, S. J. (2020). The United States, Russia, and nuclear peace. Palgrave Macmillan.

Davis, P. K. (2015). Deterrence, influence, cyber-attack, and cyber War. International Law and Politics, 47(4), 327–57.

Davis, P. K., Wilson, P., Kim, J., & Park, J. (2016). Deterrence and stability for the Korean Peninsula. Korean Journal of Defense Analysis, 28(1), 1–23.

Delegation, UN. (2016, 17 May). Discussion of nuclear strategy [Interview]. Brussels.

Earle, J. (2013, 18 June). US and Russia sign new anti-proliferation deal. Moscow Times. https://www.themoscowtimes.com/2013/06/18/us-and-russia-sign-new-anti-proliferation-deal-a25070

Ellsberg, D. (2017). The doomsday machine: Confessions of a nuclear war planner. Bloombury Publishing.

Erwin, S. (2021, 2 May). Sen. Angus King: Cybersecurity a major concern in US nuclear command-and-control system. Space News. https://spacenews.com/sen-angus-king-cybersecurity-a-major-concern-in-u-s-nuclear-command-and-control-system/

Forsyth, J. W. (2010). Remembrance of things past: The enduring value of nuclear weapons. Strategic Studies Quarterly, 4(1), 74–89. https://www.jstor.org/stable/26269780

Fursenko, A., & Naftali, T. (1997). "One hell of a gamble": Khrushchev, Castro, and Kennedy, 1958–1964. W. W. Norton.

Futter, A. (2016a, 15 July). Cyber threats and nuclear weapons: New questions for command and control, security and strategy. Royal United Services Institute. https://www.rusi.org/explore-our-research/publications/occasional-papers/cyber-threats-and-nuclear-weapons-new-questions-command-and-control-security-and-strategy/

Futter, A. (2016b, 29 June). The double-edged sword: US nuclear command and control modernization. Bulletin of the Atomic Scientists. https://thebulletin.org/2016/06/the-double-edged-sword-us-nuclear-command-and-control-modernization/#:~:text=In%20the%20realm%20of%20nuclear%20command%20and%20control%2C,vulnerable%20to%20those%20seeking%20to%20interfere%20with%20them

Gartzke, E. (2017). Thermonuclear cyberwar. Journal of Cybersecurity, 3(1), 37–48. https://doi.org/10.1093/cybsec/tyw017

Gates, R. (1996). From the shadows: The ultimate insider's story of five presidents and how they won the Cold War. Simon and Schuster.

George, A. (1991). Avoiding war: Problems of crisis management. Westview Press.

Giles, K. (2010). The military doctrine of the Russian Federation 2010. Research Review. Research Division—NATO Defense College. Retrieved 20 June 2023 from https://www.academia.edu/343489/The_Military_Doctrine_of_the_Russian_Federation_2010

George, A. L., & Simons, A. G. (1994). The limits of coercive diplomacy. Westview Press.

Goode, M. (2008). Chinese national strategy of total war [Graduate research paper]. Air Force Institute of Technology. https://apps.dtic.mil/dtic/tr/fulltext/u2/a487635.pdf

Gray, C. (1996). Explorations in strategy. Greenwood Press.

Jablonsky, D. (1991). Strategic rationality is not enough: Hitler and the concept of crazy states. Progressive Management.

Jervis, R. (1989). The meaning of the nuclear revolution: Statecraft and the prospect of armageddon. Cornell University Press.

Jones, N. (2018, 5 November). The Soviet side of the 1983 war scare. National Security Archives. https://nsarchive.gwu.edu/briefing-book/aa83/2018-11-05/soviet-side-1983-war-scare

Jones, S. (2018, 1 October). Going on the offesive: A US strategy to confront US information warfare. Centre for Strategic and International Studies. https://www.csis.org/analysis/going-offensive-us-strategy-combat-russian-information-warfare

Kaplan, F. (2016). Dark territory: The secret history of cyber war. Simon and Schuster.

Kastner, J. (2018, 31 May). Standing on the brink: The secret war scare of 1983. The Nation. https://www.thenation.com/article/archive/standing-on-the-brink-the-secret-war-scare-of-1983/#:~:text=Standing%20on%20the%20Brink%3A%20The%20

Secret%20War%20Scare,November%203%2C1983%2C%20press%20briefing%20 at%20the%20White%20House

Khrushchev, N. S. (1990). Khrushchev remembers: The Glasnost tapes. Little and Brown.

Kipp, J. (2010). Russia's tactical nuclear weapons and Eurasian security. Eurasia Daily Monitor, 7(44). https://jamestown.org/program/russias-tactical-nuclear-weapons-and-eurasian-security/

Koshkin, P. (2013). Are cyber wars between great powers possible? A group of Russian security experts debate the likelihood of a cyber war involving the US, Russia, or China. Russia Direct. https://russia-direct.org/debates/are-cyberwars-between-major-powers-possible

Kristensen, H. (2005). A Review of post–Cold War policy, force levels, and war planning. Natural Resources Defense Council. https://www.nuclearinfo.org/wp-content/uploads/2021/09/NRDC_Kristensen_US_Nuclear_Weapons_in_Europe_A_Review_of_post_cold_War_Policy_Force_Levels_and_war_planning_February_2005_volume_1_of_1..pdf

Lebow, R. N., & Stein, J. G. (1995). We all lost the Cold War. Princeton University Press.

Libicki, M. C. (2007). Conquest in cyberspace: National security and information warfare. Cambridge University Press.

Libicki, M. C. (2009). Cyberdeterrence and cyber war. RAND Coprporation.

Libicki, M. C. (2012). Crisis and escalation in cyberspace. RAND Coprporation.

Libicki, M. C. (2017). The convergence of information warfare. Strategic Studies Quarterly, 11(1), 49–65. https://www.airuniversity.af.edu/Portals/10/SSQ/documents/Volume-11_Issue-1/Libicki.pdf

Lourie, R. (2017). Putin: His downfall and Russia's coming crash. St. Martins Press.

Lowther, A. (Ed.). (2020). Guide to nuclear deterrence in the age of great power competition. Louisiana Tech Research Institute.

Magee, C. (2013). Awaiting cyber 9/11. Joint Forces Quarterly, 70(3), 76–82. https://www.thefreelibrary.com/Awaiting+cyber+9/11.-a0338119401

March, J. M., & Simon, H. A. (1958). Organizations. John Wiley and Sons.

NATO. (2010, 17 May). NATO 2020: Assured security; dynamic engagement. North Atlantic Treaty Organisation. https://www.nato.int/cps/en/natolive/official_texts_63654.htm

Payne, K. (1996). Deterrence in the second nuclear age. University of Kentucky Press.

Payne, K. (2013). Minimum deterrence: Examining the evidence. Routledge.

Payne, K. (2020). Shadows on the wall: Deterrence and disarmament. National Institute of Public Policy.

Pietkiewicz, M. (2018). The military doctrine of the Russian Federation. Polish Political Science Yearbook, 47(3), 505–20.

Podvig, P. (2010, 25 February). What to do about tactical nuclear weapons. Bulletin of the Atomic Scientists. https://thebulletin.org/2010/02/what-to-do-about-tactical-nuclear-weapons/

"Putin calls to strengthen protection against cyber-attacks." (2013, 5 July). Itar-Tass. https://tass.com/russia/696603

Questor, G. (2006). Nuclear first strike: Consequences of a broken taboo. Princeton University Press.

Reed, J. (2013, 12 April). The five deadly Ds of the air force's cyber arsenal. Foreign Policy. https://foreignpolicy.com/2013/04/12/the-five-deadly-ds-of-the-air-forces-cyber-arsenal/

Roberts, B. (2016). The case for US nuclear weapons in the 21st century. Stanford University Press.

Sagan, S. (1989). Moving targets: Nuclear strategy and national security. Little and Brown.

Sanger, D. (2013, 13 August). NSA leaks make plan for cyberdefense unlikely. New York Times. https://www.nytimes.com/2013/08/13/us/nsa-leaks-make-plan-for-cyberdefense-unlikely.html#:~:text=But%20administration%20officials%20say%20the%20plan%2C%20championed%20by,over%20the%20recent%20disclosures%20about%20its%20surveillance%20programs

Sanger, D. (2017, 4 March). Trump inherits a secret cyberwar against North Korean missiles. New York Times. https://www.nytimes.com/2017/03/04/world/asia/north-korea-missile-program-sabotage.html

Sechser, T.S., & Fuhrmann, T. (2017). Nuclear weapons and coercive diplomacy. Cambridge University Press.

Singer, P. W., & Friedman, A. (2014). Cybersecurity and cyberwar: What everyone needs to know. Oxford University Press.

Sokov, N. (2010, 5 February). The new, 2010 Russian military doctrine: The nuclear angle. James Martin Center for Nonproliferation Studies. https://nonproliferation.org/new-2010-russian-military-doctrine/

Tetlock, P. E. (1990). Introduction. In P. E. Tetlock, J. L. Husbands, R. Jervis, P. C. Stern, & C. Tilly, (Eds.), Behavior, society, and nuclear war (pp. 8–84). Oxford University Press.

Thomas, T. L. (2005). Cyber silhouettes: Shadows over information operations. Foreign Military Studies Office.

Thomas, T. L. (2012). Three faces of the cyber dragon: Cyber peace activist, spook, attacker. Foreign Military Studies Office.

Thomas, T. L. (2015). Russia: Military strategy—impacting 21st century reform and geopolitics. Foreign Military Studies Office.

Tuchman, B. (2004). The guns of August. Presidio Press.

Williams, P. (1976). Crisis management. John Wiley and Sons.

3

Deterrence by De-legitimization in the Information Environment: Concept, Theory, and Practice

Alex Wilner

Deterrence theory has expanded a great deal over the past twenty years. The core, overarching logic of deterrence—manipulating an adversary's behaviour—remains the same, but the way in which manipulation might be accomplished, and the context in which deterrence might be applied, has broadened in scope and breadth. New approaches to deterrence, including the development and testing of novel frameworks and theories alongside novel empirical observation, have followed. Some scholars have concluded that deterrence scholarship has entered the "early stages of a . . . fifth wave" (Sweijs & Osinga, 2020, p. 525). The wave analogy is an apt one (Knopf, 2012; Wilner, 2018a). It helps situate deterrence theory's "classic" origins—the first wave—at the beginning of the Cold War within the context of American supremacy, emerging American-Soviet bipolarity, and nuclear weapons development. That short, vibrant period of analysis gave way to the second wave by the 1950s, with a focus on preserving the nuclear balance and great power status quo; game theory applications, scenario constructs, and some of deterrence theory's central concepts (e.g., rationality, punishment, denial, compellence) followed suit. By the mid-1970s, deterrence's third wave was marked by an emphasis on empirical study, testing the concepts and theories proposed over the past decades. New observations were added too, with an eye on the role decision making, human cognition and psychology, and conventional weaponry had on challenger-defender relations. A great flourishing of new ideas that stemmed, in part, from outside the traditional constructs of international relations theory emerged during this wave.

Without dipping into counterfactuals, third wave dynamics and scholarship might have continued had the Cold War itself not ceased. With the bipolar contest ending, the very engine driving deterrence theory also slowed to a crawl. A fallow period followed during the 1990s. The peace dividend of that era left little room for deterrence, which had proven some of its worth by having simply kept the Cold War cold, but whose primary focus on great power rivalry, high-stakes military engagement, and nuclear standoff sat uncomfortably within the emerging (and short-lived) "end of history" paradigm. Only the terrorist attacks of 11 September 2001 sparked renewed interest in deterrence. While the immediate and short-term response to al Qaeda's attack on the United States was a heavy dose of deterrence skepticism, the previous period of relative theoretical neglect gave way to an incredible renaissance (Wilner, 2015b). Deterrence's fourth wave, a golden era of creative thought that spanned the disciplines of political science, IR and security studies, criminology and psychology, terrorism and intelligence studies, and computer science and engineering, brought fresh thinking on all fronts, deterrence theory, empiricism, and policy included. As I noted in a 2015 article, the fourth wave of deterrence scholarship included applications on a

> variety of sub-state and non-state security concerns, like insurgency, terrorism, radicalization, organized transnational crime, cyber insecurity, and piracy. More traditional inter-state security dilemmas, stemming from "rogue" regimes, nuclear and missile proliferation, and recent advances in missile technology and defense, have also been added to the deterrence agenda. Coercive processes, like punishment, denial, delegitimization, dissuasion, and inducement—as well as concepts like extended deterrence and cumulative deterrence—are likewise being explored in new and exciting ways. . . . Today, we are, as a community of scholars and practitioners, thinking up new ways to expand and apply deterrence theory to emerging and evolving security environments. (Wilner, 2015a, p. 439)

This rejuvenation was welcomed by academics and practitioners alike, paving the way for new and novel research into and applications of deterrence that went well beyond the traditional and narrow boundaries of state centricity, physical domains, strategic weapons, and military engagement.

Whether, where, and exactly how deterrence skipped into a fifth wave is still up for debate. As in previous periods of transition, more research and time will tell. Certainly, today's deterrence scholarship shares hallmarks of previous waves, including a preference for all-domain observations (from space to cyberspace), an inclination toward trans-disciplinarity (from social to hard sciences), and a penchant for multi-level analysis (from supra-state to individual). But as Tim Sweijs and Frans Osinga posit, contemporary fifth wave deterrence research relies on "more general theorising based on the examination of the dynamics of particular cases." It is both exploratory and empirical in nature, they continue, crosses between civilian (i.e., safety) and military (i.e., security) applications, rests "inside and outside of war," reflects a "non-status quo orientation," and addresses the coercive impact of novel and emerging technologies (Sweijs & Osinga, 2020, p. 525).

Two further observations, both of which resonate with this volume, are warranted. First, the wave analogy as applied to deterrence scholarship from the 1950s onward captures the way in which deterrence itself has perpetually responded to its evolving external environment. Deterrence follows the times, responds to its milieu, shifts its focus as needed, and expands where it might. Deterrence has a knack for reorienting itself around what matters most, from preventing nuclear war among great states (first and second wave), to coercing a myriad of conventional (third wave) and non-state challengers (fourth wave), to manipulating behaviour across the spectrum of domains against the backdrop of novel technology (fifth wave) (Wilner & Babb, 2020). Deterrence never goes stale because it never stops moving. Second, this particular chapter, nestled as it is within this particular volume, is itself a reflection of fifth wave deterrence scholarship. The very topic contributors have been tasked to explore—deterrence in the information environment (IE)—is very much an emerging concern that emanates from the evolving structural and technological environment. Deterrence, once again, has been called up to explore whether and how coercion might be refashioned for proper application within the IE. My contribution to this volume sets out to rethink and reapply *deterrence by de-legitimization*—a theory I first developed in 2011 vis-à-vis ideologically motivated violent non-state actors—in the context of statecraft within the IE (Wilner, 2011; Wilner 2014). That exercise is speculative in nature, theoretically oriented, crosses multiple disciplines, speaks to emerging security and societal concerns, and spans two waves of deterrence research.

The chapter is presented in four sections. Having situated the chapter within the larger constructs of deterrence research in this introduction, I turn in the second section to a brisk overview of the causal building blocks of deterrence and compellence. The third section introduces the logic of de-legitimization, as it was first applied to deterring terrorism. The fourth section updates this approach, adapting and broadening the concept and framework of de-legitimization for wider application to deterrence in the IE. The fifth section, functioning as the chapter's conclusion, suggests avenues for further research on the topic of deterrence by de-legitimization in the IE.

Deterrence Theory: Foundational Principles

At its most fundamental, deterrence is ultimately about using a combination of threats to shape an adversary's behaviour in a way that meets your own objective. It entails convincing another to forgo an action you would rather they not pursue. Compellence, a related term and concept, flips this around: it entails manipulating an adversary (or ally) in order to induce it to conduct an action it might otherwise not have pursued. Deterrence avoids unwanted behaviour; compellence induces desired behaviour. In both situations at least two actors are involved: a defender deters or compels a challenger with some form of threat. In other scenarios, a third actor is also involved in the calculus. In extended (and triadic) deterrence, for instance, a threat targeting a challenger is meant to protect or induce a change in behaviour in a third party, proxy, or partner (Wilner, 2018b). In all cases of deterrence and compellence (and coercion too, which subsumes both terms), regardless of how many actors are involved, a defender attempts to change a challenger's behaviour by altering its cost-benefit calculus. All behaviour, deterrence theory speculates, is based on an actor's (near) rational calculation of the benefits of action (what might be gained or achieved), and the costs of action (what might be lost or harmed). Importantly, then, deterrence and compellence weigh on a challenger's strategic choice—they retain the option to acquiesce to a coercive threat or not, and to tailor their behaviour accordingly. Vanquishing an adversary strips a challenger of its agency: it cannot behave in a particular way because it has lost the ability and choice to do so. Defeat is not deterrence, it is the imposition of demands; it leaves a challenger with no option to behave in any other particular way. In sum, then, deterrent or compellent successes acquire a desired outcome by changing (not forcing) behaviour.

Besides these logical constructs, deterrence theory also includes several other prerequisites (Wilner, 2020). First, a challenger's level of rationality must suffice to turn some combination of threats into a change in behaviour. Second, challengers and defenders must share—to some degree and under some condition—a preference for non-violence and inaction; if a desire to hurt the other is the only shared and common attribute, then deterrence is left with little ground to function. Third, threats and behavioural expectations must be communicated to a challenger in some way, such that it can absorb information, weigh its response, and shape its behaviour. Fourth, defenders should retain a perceived capability to act as they threaten, and illustrate a resolve to do so if and when required. And fifth, coercive interactions work best against a known adversary; anonymity in either physical or digital space complicates how deterrence is communicated and carried out.

Most deterrent and compellent relationships are dictated by either a promise of a punishment or a promise of a denial. Deterrence by punishment—also referred to as deterrence by retaliation—works by threatening to harm something the challenger values. The measure, here, is to add to an adversary's perceived cost—threats of retaliation make an unwanted behaviour more costly by promising some form of pain (e.g., military retaliation, sanctions, censure) if and when the behaviour is carried out. Cold War deterrence was heavily reliant on this form of deterrence: war between the great powers was deterred by a threat of (mutual) nuclear retaliation. Besides nuclear exchanges, however, punishment strategies have been a bedrock of other, emerging deterrence-by-punishment calculations, including in deterring terrorism and deterring cyber conflict (Wenger & Wilner, 2012; Wilner, 2020). Threats of denial, the second of the two processes at hand, functions by reducing the expected (or perceived) benefits an adversary seeks to gain by its (unwanted) action (Wilner & Wenger, 2021). Deterrence by denial, long the purview of conventional deterrence scholarship but largely overshadowed by punishment strategies and nuclear threats during the Cold War, raises the cost of action by stripping away desired gains. In counterterrorism, for instance, hardening defences against violent attack raises the cost of conducting an attack by lowering the probability an adversary will accomplish what it set out to do. By raising the bar toward failure, deterrence by denial raises the perceived cost of an action. In sum, then, punishment deters through fear of pain, denial deters through promises of failure. While punishment and denial make up the bulk of the literature (and practice) of deterrence across all domains of warfare and conflict within the five waves of scholarship, a third coercive process—deterrence by de-legitimization—that weighs on an adversary's normative or ideological perspective has recently been proposed and developed. The following section provides an in-depth review of the coercive logic of de-legitimization, as it was first developed for application in deterring terrorism.

De-legitimization in Counterterrorism: Narratives, Motivations, and Behaviour

The expansion of deterrence theory beyond traditional state-centric interactions by fourth and fifth wave scholars led to a broadening of coercion to include non-kinetic deterrents and compellents that rely on inducements, rewards, and reassurance, and denial, resilience, and mitigation. These processes are particularly attuned to the unique challenges (e.g., asymmetry, non-state characteristics, and attribution dilemma) of deterring terrorists and other non-state actors, along with deterring cyber conflict. A third, particularly unique, cluster of research on non-kinetic coercion sought to explore the use of normative and narrative constraints and de-legitimization to shape and change behaviour (Bar, 2011; Brinkel, 2017; Doorn & Brinkel, 2020; Duchein et al., 2017; Jenkins, 2010; Kitzen & Kuijck, 2020; Kuijck, 2017; Lantis, 2009; Lepgold, 1998; Sawyer, 2021; Stein & Levi, 2021; Sweijs & Zilincik, 2020; Wilner, 2012).

In my award-winning 2011 article "Deterring the Undeterrable: Coercion, Denial, and Delegitimization in Counterterrorism," as well as in the 2014 article "Delegitimizing al-Qaida: Defeating an 'Army Whose Men Love Death,'" co-authored with Jerry Mark Long, I took a first stab at building a theory of deterrence by de-legitimization for counterterrorism that tackles and taps into terrorism's ideological, political, and religious rationales and motivations (Wilner, 2011; Long & Wilner, 2014). From a coercive or deterrence perspective, the objective of de-legitimization, I suggested in 2011, "is to reduce the challenger's probability of achieving his goals by attacking the legitimacy of the beliefs that inform his behavior" (Wilner, 2011, p. 26). Research on terrorism, radicalization, and political violence has found that while terrorist organizations appear to have few normative qualms regarding the use of indiscriminate (and often brutal) violence, they nonetheless base their activities, expectations, and goals on a set of principles informed by particular ideological, and in some cases socio-religious, belief structures. Terrorism is not just violence, but violence with meaning. Al Qaeda, ISIS, and other religiously inspired militant groups, for instance, may rely on suicide tactics to achieve their goals, but they also take the time and effort to legitimize suicide's use by pointing to, relying on, and interpreting religious decrees that seem to justify its use under particular conditions. Suicide is largely considered a sin by Islamic law; to employ it, terrorist organizations like al Qaeda must illustrate how and why it is nonetheless acceptable. Without this justification in place, suicide is simply illegitimate, and those supporting its use risk tarnishing their credentials as purported adherents of religious law. "Al-Qaida loses," Long and I wrote in 2014, "when its violent excesses are devoid of narratological meaning; when its behavior is deemed offensive and illegitimate by its audience; when its terrorism is judged as mere thuggery, intimidation, and baseless murder" (Long & Wilner, 2014, p. 150).

Applying coercion to this interplay of belief, justification, and action entails identifying forms of leverage that question, debate, and even ridicule the rationales, narratives, and goals informing violent behaviour. "Strengthening and disseminating opinions, positions, and information that contradicts the legitimization of terrorism," I concluded in 2011, "might deter or compel individuals contemplating and/or taking part in violence along with the socio-religious groups that facilitate terrorist efforts" (Wilner, 2011, p. 26). Without question, deterrence by de-legitimization, as described here, rests well beyond the traditional scope of deterrence, yet it nonetheless shares deterrence theory's core requisites of changing behaviour by choice and weighing on an adversary's cost-benefit calculus. The difference is that unlike punishment and denial in deterring terrorism, de-legitimization pivots on the ideas that motivate militancy. It represents an emerging third branch of deterrence scholarship: instead of defenders threating pain or denying objectives, a challenger's behaviour is manipulated by targeting the rationales that motivate and guide it.

As Long and I note in our 2014 article—which includes a deep empirical exploration of al Qaeda's reliance on meta-narratives to shape an adherent's identity, attract and recruit supporters, sanitize its violence among a larger audience, and provide a unique lens for interpreting contemporary and historical events—"the aim is to delegitimize [the group's] narrative, targeting and degrading the ideological motivation that guides support for and participation in terrorism" (Long & Wilner, 2014, p. 130). De-legitimization's causal logic holds that it should be possible to raise the costs of participating in terrorism by targeting the religious, ideological, normative, and/or cultural rationales and interpretations that groups, leaders, and individuals use to condone and participate in violence. "Stripping away that justification," Long and I argue, "by using the same logic, language, and related cultural inputs that are used to legitimize violence may resonate with individuals, groups, and communities contemplating involvement with al-Qaida" (Long & Wilner, 2014, p. 152). The organization's narrative, in other words, is exploitable. More precisely, if al Qaeda's message loses its credibility, the organization loses adherents, a cost to the group and its leadership. "Fear of narrative collapse," Long and I conclude, "or of adverse reaction among active and would-be supporters, or of popular backlash among their primary audience might manipulate some militant leaders," changing their expectations and group behaviour along the way (Long & Wilner, 2014, p. 153).

While de-legitimization was originally explored, developed, and tested with an eye to deterring terrorism, violent radicalization, and political violence, applying it to other domains of contemporary conflict is a worthy endeavour and should prove feasible. What follows, then, is a speculative account of how deterrence by de-legitimization might itself be broadened and expanded to deter unwanted behaviour by would-be challengers and aggressors in the IE.

De-legitimization in the Information Environment: Norms, Discreditation, and Resilience

Three avenues for applying the logic and theory of de-legitimization to the malicious exploitation of the IE present themselves. They each rest within a specific level of analysis, either at the international level, at the group and/or individual level, or within the ideational level (i.e., having to do with knowledge, truth, and ideas). What follows is a description of each of these distinct applications.

First, at the international and multilateral level, deterrence by de-legitimization as applied to the IE might begin with the establishment of norms of behaviour within the IE itself. Norms relate to deterrence in at least two ways: they help identify acceptable or common behaviour within a domain, delineating what is perceived as legitimate among those active within it, and (perhaps more importantly) norms help establish and communicate the behavioural bar or red lines against which subsequent threats of punishment rest. In the former case, as Tim Sweijs and Samuel Zilincik note, norms convince "potential transgressors not to engage" in certain acts by "presenting them with the prospect of social costs" (Sweijs & Zilincik, 2020, pp. 148–9). At times, norms of behaviour can eventually cultivate taboos too, which help bolster moral restraint and inform more deeply held behavioural expectations in geopolitics, as in the case of the non-use of chemical, biological, radiological, and nuclear weapons in both peace- and wartime (Tannenwald, 2017). Similar norms (and fledgling taboos) are being established for cyber conflict, especially in the realm of attacks on critical civilian infrastructure and economic cyber espionage (McKeown & Wilner, 2020; Wilner, 2020). For developing deterrence by de-legitimization in the IE, Canada should start by exploring the establishment of norms with like-minded states, allies, and traditional partners, building on already established norms of behaviour emanating from other domains, including those Canada and a variety of other nation-states already express and adhere to (e.g., against targeting civilians; limiting collateral damage; respect for human rights). Eventually enshrining these norms in some form of international agreement, accord, or statute will help solidify their widespread use and passive acceptance, and will, as described above, provide a measure against which collective threats of punishment can be used to convince the few remaining transgressors not to carry out unwanted infractions. In sum, challengers to the norm will be averse to conducting certain types of behaviour within the IE because of moral clarity and conviction (de-legitimization) and/or out of fear of international condemnation, censure, and punishment.

Second, deterrence by de-legitimization in the IE might be applied at the group and individual levels. The general idea is to discredit the individuals, leaders, or groups that use the IE maliciously. Just as al Qaeda and its leadership can be targeted with de-legitimization for their fatuous interpretation of religious texts relating to suicide, violence, and wanton bloodshed, all the while dressing themselves in religious and pious garb, those intent on leveraging the IE for harm can be the target of de-legitimization, discreditation, and ridicule. Emerging research has found, for instance, a link between the information domain, the voluntary and strategic disclosure of intelligence by state officials, and the de-legitimization (and coercion) of adversaries. Ofek Riemer's work on recent Israeli public disclosures and "performative use" of intelligence suggests that officials use the tactic to "draw global attention to violations of international regimes and norms"; the release of sensitive information and intelligence is "yet another instrument capable of inflicting damage on [an] opponent without using force or risking escalation" (Reimer, 2021, pp. 572–3).

Other scholars, like James Pamment and Henrik Agardh-Twetman, speak of "denunciation" as a form of deterrence in the information space, which involves censuring an adversary using "rhetoric, symbolism, and even humour/memes," in hopes of "damaging its reputation" (Pamment & Agardh-Twetman, 2019, p. 131). From a perspective of de-legitimization, a range of potentially embarrassing intelligence and information—collected and released by state, non-state, and non-profit organizations alike—can be publicized to help undermine and discredit a challenger bent on weaponizing aspects of the IE. As an illustration, defenders might identify, call out, and publicize embarrassing (and potentially costly) contradictions in a challenger's misuse of the IE. A semi-autocratic regime, for example, that uses democratic principles to shield itself against domestic complaints and political opposition, all the while targeting democratic principles in other countries with dis/misinformation spread through the information domain, should be openly ridiculed, loudly and often ("Repression in Putin's Russia," 2021). Hiding behind the veil of democracy domestically while undermining democracy internationally through the IE is a contradiction worth publicizing and de-legitimizing. In a similar vein, undermining an autocrat's purported support for global and domestic anti-corruption norms by showcasing their offshore misdemeanours and accumulated wealth (Hoskins & Shchelin, 2018), and glitzy domestic assets (Amos, 2017), might have a similar effect—that of de-legitimizing their claims while simultaneously punishing their actions.

Third, deterrence by de-legitimization in the IE might be applied at the level of ideas within a defender's (rather than challenger's) collective mindset. The proposition is as lofty as it sounds but nonetheless makes intuitive sense. The goal is to diminish a target society's susceptibility to certain forms of information warfare by augmenting its ideational and collective resilience, thus denying an aggressor the potency and value of the tactic and de-legitimizing its use along the way. Theo Brinkel, for instance, writes of providing Western societies with the tools they need to "mentally arm themselves against . . . ideological threats," such that a "resilient society enhances overall mental deterrence" against hybrid threats, including those stemming from the IE (Brinkel, 2017, p. 19). Opening society up to public debate about "common values and objectives," Brinkel continues, not only builds social capital and societal trust, but strengthens a society's "sense of purpose," helping it "win the hearts and minds of [its] own population" (p. 20). Brinkel, writing with Cees van Doorn, further argues that "credibility . . . veracity, consistency and respect for the truth" are the natural societal counterweights to malicious propaganda and disinformation campaigns, and work to "enhance . . . deterrence by delegitimization" (Doorn & Brinkel, 2020, p. 371). Brinkel and van Doorn go on to illustrate how the 2020 trial, held publicly in the Netherlands, of Russian and Ukrainian nationals suspected of having had a hand in the 2014 destruction of Malaysian Airlines Flight 17 (in which 193 of the 298 passengers killed were Dutch) serves "to deter by delegitimization as every single detail disclosed [during the trial] will discredit the alternative narratives that Russian actors have issued" (p. 378) about the disaster. This societal resilience, borne by doubling down on democratic ideals, principles, and values, counters and neuters the utility of malicious IE activity.

Next Steps for De-legitimization: Theory and Application

This chapter has sought to expand the notion and nature of deterrence in and through the IE by expanding de-legitimization beyond the context from which it originally stemmed (i.e., deterring terrorism) and importing it for use in the IE. That exercise has been inherently speculative. And despite making modest gains by suggesting how and where de-legitimization fits into the rubric of deterrence in the IE, much more research and thinking is needed. By way of conclusion, what follows are three avenues for further refinement of de-legitimization in terms of theory, empiricism, and practice.

First, the concept of deterrence by de-legitimization—in and outside the IE—is still rather fuzzy. It is not yet clear, for instance, whether and how de-legitimization links back to punishment and denial. My original intention (later shared with my co-author Long) when proposing the term for application in counterterrorism was to delineate a third branch of deterrence theory, one that asserted itself in the realm of ideas, emotions, and desires. Unlike punishment and denial, which threaten pain and loss in the physical and cyber domains, de-legitimization functions at a different level altogether, "targeting what terrorists believe rather than what they value or want" (Long & Wilner, 2014, p. 128). And yet several fourth and fifth wave scholars of deterrence have since made a strong case for thinking of de-legitimization as a form and function of denial, or punishment—or both. De-legitimization is not a separate branch of coercion, they argue, but an extension of existing deterrence logic.

Consider these various examples. Using social psychology, the logic of persuasion, and actor and audience analysis, Christina van Kuijck illustrates, for instance, that de-legitimization threatens an adversary by "taking away their (potential) support"—a form of denial—by preventing "friendly and neutral audiences . . . from consenting or recognising" the challenger (Kuijck, 2017, p. 200). Similarly, Brinkel's formulation surmises that social and societal resilience deters by de-legitimization by denying would-be aggressors the fertile ground upon which their malicious narratives can thrive (Brinkel, 2017). Janice Gross Stein and Ron Levi, using a criminological perspective of deterrence and a focus on "social sanctions," argue that "delegitimation . . . is increasingly important as one of the deterrence-by-denial strategies in governments' repertoires" (Stein & Levi, 2021, p. 59). Conversely, Sweijs and Zilincik's notion of "social and psychological costs" links de-legitimization to punishment (Sweijs & Zilincik, 2020). And John Sawyer's development of dissuasion by denial posits that de-legitimization is naturally Janus-faced:

> Contrary to the treatment by some scholars [Wilner included], efforts to delegitimize an ideology, key individuals or an organization fit more appropriately within [an] offensive logic rather than a distinct sub-type of deterrence. However, efforts to delegitimize a specific behavior, like targeting civilians, are well within the domain of influence. . . . For example, efforts to undermine the appeal of al Qaeda by citing its perversions of Islamic doctrine aim to restrict the recruitment pool generally, while efforts to delegitimize al Qaeda by citing the large number of Muslims killed in their attacks aim to force a behavioral change away from indiscriminate violence. Admittedly, these two forms of delegitimization may be difficult to disentangle because perceptions about actors and their actions, intentions and environments are generally not independent. (Sawyer, 2021, p.103)

I interpret these conceptual contradictions as a good sign. A healthy, constructive debate on the meaning and theory of deterrence by de-legitimization should be taken as evidence of growth, expansion, and the accumulation of knowledge. As de-legitimization acquires more attention from disparate scholars working across different domains and disciplines, including vis-à-vis the IE, conceptual delineation will continue to sharpen, paving the way for a more nuanced understanding of de-legitimization theory and a more precise approach to empirical evaluation.

Second, on this notion of empirical evaluation, a next step in bolstering and advancing research on deterrence by de-legitimization in the IE is to test it across the spectrum of conflict and warfare. Very little empirical work on the subject has yet to be pursued or published: Long and I (2014) provide a qualitative assessment of de-legitimization at the group (i.e., militant) level, using al Qaeda as a single case study; van Kuijck (2017) offers some empirical insights on deterrence by de-legitimization in countering radicalization and de-radicalization; and van Doorn and Brinkel (2021) explore de-legitimization against the case of Russian disinformation surrounding the 2014 Malaysian Airlines Flight 17 disaster. These are the rare examples. Much more hard-nosed, original, qualitative, quantitative, and interdisciplinary empirical research is needed on the subject of deterrence by de-legitimization, teasing apart how and why it works to deter behaviour across the domains of conflict. This empirical research could tap into and repurpose observations previously made in other fields of study, including from strategic culture, criminology, and terrorism studies, but it should also seek to uncover new and novel ground within information warfare and cyber security.

Third and finally, part of the reason deterrence theory has remained relevant for over seventy years is that it rarely sits irrelevantly within the ivory tower. Rather, concepts, frameworks, and theories of deterrence are regularly applied in practice, to policy, doctrine, strategy, and tactics. Deterrence's theory-to-policy transition occurred throughout the Cold War, for instance, at a time when ideas about coercive communication and extended deterrence were put into practice rather quickly and smoothly. Something similar, though in a more limited fashion, is happening today with ideas stemming from recent research on deterrence by denial, terrorism deterrence, and cyber deterrence. Scholars should eventually strive to do something similar with their work on deterrence by de-legitimization. Once concepts have been further refined and specific frameworks developed and tested across various domains of conflict, de-legitimization should be translated for real-life application, put to use for deterring unwanted behaviours within and beyond the information environment. Only then will de-legitimization truly leave its mark within the study and practice of deterrence.

REFERENCES

Amos, H. (2017, 31 August). Putin "holiday mansion" revealed by Russian opposition leader. *The Guardian*. https://www.theguardian.com/world/2017/aug/31/putin-holiday-mansion-revealed-russian-opposition-leader-alexei-navalny

Bar, S. (2011). God, nation, and deterrence: The impact of religion on deterrence. *Comparative Strategy, 30*(5), 428–52. https://doi.org/10.1080/01495933.2011.624808

Brinkel, T. (2017). The resilient mind-set and deterrence. In P. A. L. Ducheine & F. P. B. Osing (Eds.), *Winning without killing: The strategic and operational utility of non-kinetic capabilities in crises* (pp. 19–38). Asser Press.

Doorn, C., & Brinkel, T. (2021). Deterrence, resilience, and the shooting down of Flight MH17. In F. Osinga & T. Sweijs (Eds.), *NL ARMS Netherlands annual review of military studies 2020* (pp. 365–83). Asser Press. https://doi.org/10.1007/978-94-6265-419-8_19

Duchein, P., van Haaster, J., & van Harskamp, R. (2017). Manoeuvring and generating effects in the information environment. In P. A. L. Ducheine & F. P. B. Osing (Eds.), *Winning without killing: The strategic and operational utility of non-kinetic capabilities in crises* (pp. 155–79). Asser Press.

Hoskins, A., & Shchelin, P. (2018). Information war in the Russian media ecology: The case of the Panama Papers. *Continuum Journal of Media & Cultural Studies, 32*(1), 1–17. DOI:10.1080/10304312.2017.1418295

Jenkins, B. M. (2010, 26 May). Internet terror recruitment and tradecraft: How can we address an evolving tool while protecting free speech? [Testimony]. *U.S. House of Representatives Subcommittee on Intelligence, Information Sharing, and Risk Assessment of the Committee on Homeland Security*, 111th Congress, 2nd session. https://www.congress.gov/event/111th-congress/house-event/LC7021/text?s=1&r=114

Kitzen, M., & van Kuijck, C. (2020). All deterrence is local: The utility and application of localized deterrence in counterinsurgency. In F. Osinga & T. Sweijs (Eds.), *NL ARMS Netherlands annual review of military studies 2020* (pp. 287–310). Asser Press. https://link.springer.com/chapter/10.1007/978-94-6265-419-8_15?error=cookies_not_supported&code=e3550a0b-4075-4a66-a422-deac6f8d36b9

Knopf, J. (2012). Terrorism and the fourth wave in deterrence research. In A. Wenger & A. Wilner (Eds.), *Deterring terrorism: Theory and practice* (pp. 21–45). Stanford University Press.

Kuijck, C. (2017). Delegitimising the adversary: Understanding actor and audience analysis as a tool to influence and persuade. In P. A. L. Ducheine & F. P. B. Osing (Eds.), *Winning without killing: The strategic and operational utility of non-kinetic capabilities in crises* (pp. 195–220). Asser Press. https://link.springer.com/chapter/10.1007/978-94-6265-189-0_11?error=cookies_not_supported&code=55e9fbaa-10ef-4740-aeeb-c18c7ede1dbb

Lantis, J. (2009). Strategic culture and tailored deterrence: Bridging the gap between theory and practice. *Contemporary Security Policy, 30*(3), 467–85. DOI:10.1080/13523260903326677

Lepgold, J. (1998). Hypotheses on vulnerability: Are terrorists and drug dealers coercible? In L. Freedman (Ed.), *Strategic coercion: Concepts and cases* (pp. 136–45). Oxford University Press.

Long, J. M., & Wilner, A. (2014). Delegitimizing al-Qaida: Defeating an "army whose men love death." *International Security, 39*(1), 126–64. https://direct.mit.edu/isec/article-abstract/39/1/126/12287/Delegitimizing-al-Qaida-Defeating-an-Army-Whose

McKeown, R., & Wilner, A. (2020). Deterrence in space and cyberspace. In T. Juneau, P. Lagassé, & S. Vucetic (Eds.), *Canadian defence policy in theory and practice* (pp. 399–416). Palgrave.

Pamment, J., & Agardh-Twetman, H. (2019). Can there be a deterrence strategy for influence operations? *Journal of Information Warfare, 18*(3), 123–35. https://www.jstor.org/stable/26894685

Riemer, O. (2021). Politics is not everything: New perspectives on the public disclosure of intelligence by states. *Contemporary Security Policy, 42*(4), 554–83. https://doi.org/10.1080/13523260.2021.1994238

"Russia's new era of repression." (2021, 12 November). *The Economist*. https://www.economist.com/interactive/repression-in-putins-russia/

Sawyer, J. (2021). Dissuasion by denial in counterterrorism: Theoretical and empirical deficiencies. In A. Wenger & A. Wilner (Eds.), *Deterring terrorism: Theory and practice* (pp. 97–122). Cambria Press.

Stein, J. G., & Levi, R. (2021). The social psychology of denial: Deterring terrorism. In A. Wenger & A. Wilner (Eds.), *Deterring terrorism: Theory and practice* (pp. 65–96). Cambria Press.

Sweijs, T., & Osinga, F. (2020). Conclusion: Insights from theory and practice. In F. Osinga & T. Sweijs (Eds.), *NL ARMS Netherlands annual review of military studies 2020* (pp. 503–30). Asser Press. https://doi.org/10.1007/978-94-6265-419-8_26

Sweijs, T., Zilincik, S. (2020). The essence of cross-domain deterrence. In F. Osinga & T. Sweijs (Eds.), *NL ARMS Netherlands annual review of military studies 2020* (pp. 129–58). Asser Press. https://link.springer.com/chapter/10.1007/978-94-6265-419-8_8

Tannenwald, N. (2007). *The nuclear taboo*. Cambridge University Press.

Wenger, A., & Wilner, A. (Eds.). 2012. *Deterring terrorism: Theory and practice*. Stanford University Press.

Wilner, A. (2011). Deterring the undeterrable: Coercion, denial, and delegitimization in counterterrorism. *Journal of Strategic Studies, 34*(1), 3–37. https://doi.org/10.1080/01402390.2011.541760

Wilner, A. (2012). Apocalypse soon? Deterring nuclear Iran and its terrorist proxies. *Comparative Strategy, 31*(1), 18–40. https://doi.org/10.1080/01495933.2012.647539

Wilner, A. (2015a). Contemporary deterrence theory and counterterrorism: A bridge too far? *NYU Journal of Law and Politics, 47,* 439–62. https://heinonline.org/HOL/LandingPage?handle=hein.journals/nyuilp47&div=24&id=&page=

Wilner, A. (2015b). *Deterring rational fanatics.* University of Pennsylvania Press.

Wilner, A. (2018a). The dark side of extended deterrence: Thinking through the state sponsorship of terrorism. *Journal of Strategic Studies, 41*(3), 410–37. https://doi.org/10.1080/01402390.2017.1284064

Wilner, A. (2018b). Political realism and terrorism—the logic of deterrence: Using mid-range theories to save political realism from itself. In R. Schuett & M. Hollingworth (Eds.), *The Edinburgh companion to political realism* (pp. 540–53). Edinburgh University Press.

Wilner, A. (2020). US cyber deterrence: Practice guiding theory. *Journal of Strategic Studies, 43*(2), 245–80. https://doi.org/10.1080/01402390.2018.1563779

Wilner, A., & Babb, C. (2020). New technologies and deterrence: Artificial intelligence and adversarial behaviour. In F. Osinga & T. Sweijs (Eds.), *NL ARMS Netherlands annual review of military studies 2020* (pp. 401–17). https://link.springer.com/chapter/10.1007/978-94-6265-419-8_21

Wilner, A., & Wenger, A. (Eds.). (2021). *Deterrence by denial: Theory and practice.* Cambria Press.

SECTION II

WIDER STRATEGIC CONTEXT AND EXPERIENCES

4

Understanding Russia's Approaches to Information Warfare

Rachel Lea Heide

Introduction: The Russian Strategic Threat

Information operations conducted by the Russian Federation under the Vladimir Putin regime, against foreign nations considered strategic threats, have been ongoing for more than a decade. Nevertheless, information operations have been brought to the attention of the West by Russia's recent interference in the United Kingdom's 2016 Brexit vote, the United States' 2016 presidential election, and numerous 2017 European election campaigns. This chapter has researched the question "What does Russian information warfare mean for the defence and security of Canada, its allies, and the West?" and proposes a proactive way ahead for Canada and its like-minded allies and partners to counter Russia's war on information.

The current Russian government has identified the West, the North Atlantic Treaty Organization (NATO), and the United States as Russia's most significant security threats. Putin's regime blames the West for encircling Russia with democracies; militarizing and causing an arms race in the eastern European region; promulgating an image of Russia as the enemy in the eastern European region; strengthening far-right nationalist ideologies in this region; and working to destroy Russian traditional culture and values by inserting competitive foreign values into the Russian population's consciousness (Oliker, 2016; Rumer, 2017).

Russia has two strategic aims: to challenge and undermine the West, Europe, and NATO, and to promote its own national interests and great power ambitions. As a means of promoting itself as a viable alternative global leader, Russia is working to tear apart Western alliances and to tear down the West as a beacon of moral superiority. As part of the effort to challenge the idea of the West, the Russian government aims to undermine Western liberal values and democratic systems, especially in Europe, but recently also in the United States (Chivvis, 2017b; Lucas & Nimmo, 2015; Polyakova et al., 2016; ODNI, 2017). Russia is supporting the rise of right-wing extremist ideologies as a foil for Western liberal democracy (Stewart, 2017). Putin also desires to destroy Western societies from within by sowing discord and divisions within Western nations (Higgins, 2017; Watts, 2017). Additionally, Russia is exploiting Western openness and pluralism, turning these values into vulnerabilities (Polyakova et al., 2016). Russian political leaders are challenging American hegemony, influence, and morality. The intention is to reverse US global dominance, counteract its foreign policy efforts, and undermine faith in America's democratic processes and public institutions (Bugajski, n.d.; Bugajski, 2016; Lucas & Pomerantsev, 2017; ODNI, 2017). Russia is promoting multilateralism and a poly-centric world order as the preferred alternative to the Western-led international world order (Gorenburg, 2019; Russian Federation, 2015).

The Russian government's information operations activities are not random and innocuous irritants directed at strategic competitors as mere distractions. The Putin regime purposely targets chosen audiences and propagates deliberate messages to achieve specific strategic, diplomatic, and defence policy outcomes and reactions. To achieve this plethora of strategic aims, Russia disseminates strategic narratives to domestic and foreign audiences as one means of gaining support for—or at least diminishing opposition to—its goals and initiatives. These narratives paint Russia's adversaries (the West, the United States, NATO, Europe, and eastern European nations) as perpetrators of injustices while projecting an image of Russia as a desirable global leader (Iasiello, 2017; Lucas & Pomerantsev, 2016; Nimmo, 2015; Rasmussen, 2015; Rumer, 2017). As a means for justifying its foreign policy positions, Russia's leadership speaks out against what they characterize as the nefarious intentions and actions of the West.

This chapter will describe Russia's information warfare concept and methods, as well as offer a detailed case study of Russia's interference in the 2016 US presidential election. The chapter will then offer recommendations for improving the understanding, response, and coordination of Canada, its allies, and the West regarding Russia's information warfare attacks. Russia's use of information operations to challenge Western alliances, institutions, and the rules-based liberal world order will continue and expand if left unchallenged by Western nations. Russia's governing leaders have declared that their nation is in a perpetual state of information warfare against the West. Consequently, Western nations—including Canada—need to be in a perpetual state of self-defence and deterrence by methodically defending, through strategic communications, the concepts, institutions, and military missions that Russia is attacking. Canada and its Western allies also need to proactively and pre-emptively disseminate strategic narratives that decrease support for Russian aggressive policies and military actions and consequently deter the Russian government from continued attacks. The aim of this chapter's look at Russian information warfare is to convey the gravity and pervasiveness of the Russian threat and to reiterate that a reactive approach is inadequate for the security of Canada as a nation and the liberal-democratic way of life.

Russia's Information Operations: Battling for Control of the Adversary's Mind

Disinformation has become an important aspect of Russia's military doctrine, and Russian political and military leaders put a greater emphasis on information and psychological warfare than their Western counterparts (Fedyk, 2017; Lucas, 2015; MacFarquhar, 2016). For Russia, information warfare is the starting point for any operations since information superiority is imperative for future victories and should be gained as early as possible (Gilles, 2016b; Iasiello, 2017; Koshkin, 2015; Thomas, 2016). Russia considers the main battlespace to be the mind; hence, Russian officials focus on conducting war inside human consciousness through information and psychological warfare. This type of warfare is intended to lay the groundwork for victory—perhaps even without the need to start combat operations and physically invade a specific territory—by demoralizing both the adversary's population and uniformed personnel and destroying any desire to carry out resistance (Chekinov & Bogdanov, 2013; Duncan, 2017; Fedyk, 2017; Galeotti, 2014; Thomas, 2016).

The Russian government has specific objectives it wishes to achieve when attempting to influence domestic and international audiences: the Putin regime uses information operations to philosophically attack the West, specific adversaries, Western military operations, the concept of truth, and to promote Russia's agenda. The wide variety of methods to communicate carefully constructed narratives through information operations, and the advent of the Internet and social media, have increased Russia's potential reach and influence. These tools and these objectives enable and motivate the Putin regime to directly contact adversaries' populations in an attempt to influence them in favour of Russian strategic aims and security threat interpretations.

Russia's Information Operations Concept

For the objectives of attacking the West, adversaries, military operations, and the concept of truth, as well as promoting Russia's agenda, the Russian government uses carefully constructed narratives that it communicates through information operations messages to audiences around the world—foreign and domestic, decision makers and the public. Disseminating these messages is part of the Russian government's concept of information warfare. This section will describe the key elements of Russia's information operations concept, including the different types of information warfare in addition to Soviet-era practices.

Western military doctrine recognizes separate disciplines for intelligence, counter-intelligence, information warfare, psychological warfare, influence operations, strategic communications, computer network operations, electronic warfare, and military deception. In the Russian context, all these aspects are part of a unified conception of information warfare and confrontation (Gilles, 2016a; Porotsky, 2017b; Tomášek, 2015; Vowell, 2016). Russia's information space includes both the cyber and cognitive domains. In Russian military doctrine, information warfare is divided into two types: information-technical (which aims to affect any technical system that receives, collects, processes, or transmits information) and information-psychological (which aims to affect civilian populations and armed forces personnel). This means that any information source—be it the adversary's computers, smart phones, print media, television, or human minds—are targets for Russian information warfare. Russia's weaponization of information encompasses electronic warfare, cyber warfare, and psychological influence (Foxall, 2016; Gilles, 2016a; Gunzinger, 2017).

Within the information warfare concept, information operations are the starting point for engaging an adversary. The aim is to achieve strategic goals without having to resort to armed conflict by using information warfare to establish favourable political, economic, and military situations and hopefully weaken the adversary and incapacitate the enemy state before armed conflict breaks out. Targeting mass consciousness and influencing an adversary's military forces and civilian population to capitulate without armed intervention violates that state's sovereignty without the physical seizure of territory. The goal is to influence the adversary to carry out the Russian government's wishes and defeat the enemy without having to engage in costly or risky combat operations (Duncan, 2017; Fedyk, 2017; Gilles, 2016a; Gunzinger, 2017; Iasiello, 2017; Polyakova et al., 2016; Vowell, 2016).

For Russia, there is a persistent and permanent state of conflict; peacetime and the absence of information operations simply do not exist. Whether Russia and another nation are in a state of co-operation or of hostility, Russian leaders believe that enemies are using information warfare against their country. Consequently, Russia must take the offensive and perpetually and permanently conduct information operations against its rivals (Gilles, 2016a; Porotsky, 2017b; Russian Federation, 2014; Shane, 2017). Current Russian information operations use two practices from Soviet-era doctrine: reflexive control and active measures. Reflexive control is defined as the "means of conveying to a partner or opponent specially prepared information to incline him to voluntarily make the predetermined decision desired by the initiator of the action" (Thomas, 2010, p. 237). Reflexive control is the deliberate attempt by the Russian government to create a permissive environment by influencing an adversary's decision makers and population in such a way that they make a decision or carry out actions that are not only to Russia's advantage but were also predetermined by Russia's information operations efforts (Duncan, 2017; Gilles, 2016a, 2016b; Iasiello, 2017; Kepe, 2017; Lucas & Pomerantsev, 2016; Ramussen, 2015; Thomas, 2010).

The second Soviet tactic being applied by the current Russian government is active measures, which is the use of overt and covert techniques (violence, proxies, counterfeits, and information operations) to influence the actions and behaviours of a foreign government and its population. There are three avenues for shaping other nations' foreign policies: state-to-state, state-to-people, and people-to-people. Russia's active measures purposely sidestep state-to-state traditional diplomacy; instead, the Russian government directly contacts adversarial nations' populations or uses proxies such as trolls and think tanks to do so. The World Wide Web and social media have made this contact with foreign audiences extremely easy, immediate, and direct (Duncan, 2017; Gilles, 2016a; Lucas & Pomerantsev, 2016; Porotsky, 2017b; Watts, 2017; Weisburd et al., 2016).

Russia's Information Operations Methods

For the purpose of this chapter, the plethora of techniques and narratives Russia uses for information operations will be categorized as technologically focused, false information, degraded information, overwhelming quantities of information, state involvement, third-party participation, specifically targeted audiences, or the use of all available platforms. Cyber-attacks fall into the category of an information-technical approach to Russian information operations. Cyber-attacks aiding information operations are about denying information to an adversary: "all efforts to disrupt, deny, degrade, destroy the information that . . . [computers] rely upon, store, process, and generate" (Porotsky, 2017b). Russia has conducted distributed denial of service (DDOS) campaigns against its adversaries as part of conflict (e.g., Georgia, Ukraine) and non-kinetic attacks to disrupt states in peacetime, including government, media, financial institutions, and other private targets. In addition to purposely overloading websites so that they crash and cannot be accessed by any user, Russia also purposely defaces websites and replaces content with inaccurate information; corrupts data files; steals funds, intellectual property, and government secrets; shuts down commerce; or attacks critical infrastructure (Gilles, 2016a, 2016b; Iasiello, 2017; Joyal, 2016; Kepe, 2017; Lucas & Pomerantsev, 2016; Porotsky, 2017b; Waltzman, 2017).

Hacking into computer systems is a common Russian information operations activity. The most high-profile hackings recently have been of the Hillary Clinton campaign in the 2016 US presidential election and the Emmanuel Macron campaign during France's 2017 presidential election. Spear-phishing emails are sent to broad communities (campaign workers, politicians' staffers, public servants, government contractors, and related non-profit organizations) with malicious links that will download malware and allow the hackers to see and steal information stored in the compromised email account or the owner's computer. The emails encouraging people to click certain links are crafted to look legitimate. Often the scenario used by hackers is a realistic message warning recipients to log into their commercial email or social media account to reset a password after a suspicious login attempt has supposedly been identified. Another common lure is targeted news articles reflecting the user's extracurricular interests (e.g., sports or Hollywood stories). All it takes is one unsuspecting recipient to click a link to give Russian hackers access. This happened in the United States, not only to

Clinton's campaign chairman, John Podesta, the Democratic Congressional Campaign Committee, and the Democratic National Convention in 2016, but also previously to the White House, State Department, Department of Defense, and Joint Chiefs of Staff. Instead of just gathering information for future use, hackers during the 2016 US elections uploaded the Clinton-related documents they stole onto publicly available websites for the public to consume, and hackers distributed the links over social and conventional media (Calabresi, 2017; Foxall, 2016; Gilles, 2016a; Hern, 2017; Lipton et al., 2016; Shane, 2017; Weisburd et al., 2016). Russia has also hacked the social media accounts and smart phones of NATO soldiers deployed in the Baltic region; the goal is to glean intelligence regarding military operations as well as compromising information that could be used for blackmail, intimidation, or harassment against individuals or to destroy the credibility of that nation's deployed forces (Kepe, 2017).

Security and intelligence analysts have characterized Russia's manipulation of the truth as directing a "firehose of falsehoods" against the West's "squirt gun of truth" (Paul & Courtney, 2016). While ordinary citizens around the world may accidentally participate in propagating misinformation (the unintentional and inadvertent spreading of inaccurate information without malicious intent), the Russian government and its information operations apparatus create and disseminate disinformation (intentionally inaccurate or manipulated information) (Lucas & Pomerantsev, 2017; Paul & Courtney, 2016). Disinformation can take the shape of lies, hoaxes, conspiracy theories masquerading as facts, false facts, the denial of facts, fake videos and altered pictures, propaganda, and deliberate state narratives (Chen, 2015; Duncan, 2017; Gilles 2016a, 2016b; Iasiello, 2017; Joyal, 2016; Kepe, 2017; Lucas & Pomerantsev, 2016; MacFarquhar, 2016; Nimmo, 2016; Polyakova, 2016; Pomerantsev, 2014; Skaskiw, 2017; Waltzman, 2017; Watts & Weisburd, 2016). Russian information operations have invested much effort into disseminating disinformation through fabricated news, staged videos of reporters supposedly on the site of events, and fake sock-puppet websites meant to look like legitimate news sources. These are then amplified by social media posts, the sharing of these posts, and conventional Western media reporting (Chivvis, 2017b; Gilles 2016a, 2016b; Guide, 2017; Iasiello, 2017; Lucas & Pomerantsev, 2016; Vowell, 2016; Watts, 2017). Russian information operations use other means of degrading the accuracy of information that Russia distributes. Instead of completely fabricating stories, these efforts can conceal information, exaggerate, provide half-truths, destroy facts, present selective facts, misquote or falsify attribution, simplify complex topics, or change meanings or original statements by altering the context or translation (Gilles, 2016a, 2016b; Kepe, 2017; Lucas & Pomerantsev, 2017; Paul & Matthews, 2016).

Russian officials use information operations messages that attack the concept of truth. These narratives aim to pollute and degrade the information space for decision makers and populations alike. With so many versions of explanations, the goal is to make it impossible to discern fact from fiction, and to get readers to question what is purported as truth. The Putin regime wants to erode people's confidence in media, experts, and academia's objectivity, professionalism, and accuracy (Bugajski, n.d.; Calabresi, 2017; Dewey, 2016; Gilles, 2016b; Iasiello, 2017; Lucas & Pomerantsev, 2016; MacFarquhar, 2016; Porotsky, 2017c; Watts, 2017; Weisburd et al., 2016). The end goal is to create distrust and doubt in what is being communicated in the West and to cause confusion, panic, and internal conflict within Western societies (Boot, 2017; Bugajski, n.d., 2016; Gilles, 2016a, 2016b; Iasiello, 2017; Lucas & Pomerantsev, 2016; MacFarquhar, 2016; Porotsky, 2017c; Vowell, 2016; Waltzman, 2017; Watts, 2017; Weisburd et al., 2016). The Russian government does not just promulgate one consistent message with its information operations activities. Different, and sometimes conflicting, messages are disseminated: these are tailored for different audiences, and sometimes the fabricators are testing to see which themes resonate with audiences the best. Since the ultimate goal is to undermine truth, the communications are not intended to necessarily be credible or universally persuasive (Duncan, 2017; Gilles, 2016a, 2016b; Lucas & Pomerantsev, 2016; MacFarquhar, 2016; Paul & Courtney, 2016; Paul & Matthews, 2016; Waltzman, 2017). The Russian government uses a multi-channel approach so that audiences are more likely to be exposed to Russia's messages, so that an atmosphere of consensus is created, and so that recipients have the impression that the information must be true since it can be found within so many different sources (Gilles, 2016b; Paul & Matthews, 2016). The Russian government uses its multitude of narratives to change the conversation away from themes disadvantageous to its policies and prestige. Overly sophisticated arguments, presented with ample evidence (even though false), confuse people into accepting the conclusions as true, even if the recipient did not fully understand the argument. Russian information operations can elicit emotional responses of helplessness, dismay, or anger by dismissing critics, deliberately distorting facts, or appealing to fears, divisions, and discontent (Dawsey, 2017; Gilles, 2016a; Lucas & Pomerantsev, 2016; Nimmo, 2015; Raju et al., 2017; Skaskiw, 2017; Waltzman, 2017).

Identifying truth and falsehoods is made even more difficult with the existence of white, grey, and black outlets, all of which Russia uses to propagate its narratives and disinformation. White channels are overt Russian sources such as state-sponsored and pro-Russian news networks (such as RT and Sputnik News) and legitimate professional Western news networks. Russian information operations use grey outlets, such as English-language dump sites (DC Leaks and WikiLeaks) and conspiratorial websites that sensationalize fake news, hoaxes, and conspiracies. Legitimate Western news networks often report news found on grey channels, thus amplifying, disseminating, and legitimizing the disinformation among Western audiences. Grey channels can be controlled by Russia (but this is harder to trace) or promoted by "useful idiots" who chose to regurgitate Russian themes voluntarily and without any ties to Russia. Black outlets are covert operations where hecklers, hackers, and bots use fake or hacked social media accounts that appear to be those of ordinary citizens residing in Western countries. This information is even more difficult to link to official Russian direction, but these information operations efforts are deliberately sinister and purposely intend to distribute and amplify disinformation, propaganda, and Russian narratives (Lucas & Pomerantsev, 2016; MacFarquhar, 2016; Porotsky, 2017c; Watts, 2017; Weisburd et al., 2016).

The use of third parties allows the Russian government to be disconnected enough from information operations to claim plausible deniability. Russian officials use proxies—groups that are sympathetic to Russian objectives or policies—around the world to carry out information operations messaging. This can be Russian gangs and biker clubs that engage in intimidation tactics domestically; or European protest movements or far-right political parties; or Russian diasporic populations in the Baltics that perpetuate complaints of discrimination and mistreatment; or American citizens who use social media to amplify links to websites, articles, or ads created by Russian sources on divisive social issues. Local actors are easier to believe and more difficult to tie to the Russian government (Chivvis, 2017b; Duncan, 2017; Guide, 2017; Iasiello, 2017; Lauder, 2017).

Russian information operations have achieved a high impact through social media by using humans and automation to disseminate and amplify disinformation and propaganda. Russian disinformation agencies hire people to hold multiple fake social media accounts (usually under false identifies, often pretending to be from the United States or other Western countries) so that they can engage other social media users for the purpose of propagating Russia's strategic narratives, polluting the information environment with disinformation, polarizing online communities by focusing on controversial social and political issues, and diverting and suppressing actual political debate. Called "trolls," these individuals use their hacked, hijacked, or black-market social media accounts to flood news site comment sections and social media with sensational views and links to fake news stories or websites featuring stolen/hacked documents. Agencies with ties to the Russian government have hired so many of these online hecklers that they are called troll farms or factories. The Internet Research Agency (IRA), based in St. Petersburg, has been identified as such a troll factory; it operates around the clock with over a thousand employees each working twelve-hour shifts to meet individual daily quotas, such as 135 posted comments, each of 200 characters minimum, as well as 80 comments and 20 shares of internally created blogs, for propagating assigned themes and messages over Live Journal, VKontakte, Facebook, Twitter, Instagram, and various chat rooms, discussion fora, and news comment sections (Bertrand, 2017; Boot, 2017; Calabresi, 2017; Chen, 2015; Chivvis, 2017b; Fedyk, 2017; Gilles, 2016b; Iasiello, 2017; Lapowsky, 2017; MacFarquhar, 2018a; Porotsky, 2017c; Shane, 2017; Shane & Goel, 2017).

Trolls not only hold multiple identifies over numerous social media platforms to increase the quantity of disinformation each individual can push into global communications systems; they also further amplify their impact by using bot networks—groups of computers and/or social media accounts that have been automated to send out messages based on built-in instructions. Thousands of Russian-linked Twitter accounts have been automated, and they repeatedly send out the identical message, seconds apart and in alphabetical order based on the bots' account names on the automation list. Cyborg accounts are heavily automated but require some human involvement in their operation. During the 2016 US presidential election, six hundred troll and bot accounts were synchronized with news being broadcast from the RT and Sputnik News websites, further amplifying official Russian narratives. The use of humans and bots increases the proficiency with which malicious actors can flood and pollute the information space with manipulated material; in many cases, they eventually succeed in getting legitimate media sources to report on the inaccurate and false stories as if they constituted genuine breaking news

(Bertrand, 2017; Gilles, 2016b; Porotsky, 2017c; "Russian Twitter accounts," 2017; Rutenberg, 2017).

Some trolls take on a more intimate interactive role with targeted social media users—also known as the role of a honeypot. Based on the historical use of attractive female spies to lure adversaries' agents into compromising situations, the online honeypot sets up a social media profile that might feature an attractive profile picture, but more often than not, online honeypots present themselves as having common interests (e.g., hobbies, political views) so that they can befriend other online users, who have purposely been selected through social engineering to be susceptible to Russian information operations efforts. After building trust and lowering defences via these commonalities, the honeypot will start to work on the target's political views by introducing political discussions that propagate Russian influence narratives; sending links to supposed articles of interest that in reality will download malware onto the target's computer; attempting to entrap the target in a compromising situation or find embarrassing information on their electronic devices in order to blackmail them and secure their compliance; or bringing an agent of influence into the conversation, under the guise of introducing a friend, to expertly argue Russian positions regarding political and geopolitical issues. The goal is to convert this local individual into a believer of Russian positions so that they will share Russian narratives and propaganda links, shut down healthy debate among his/her own friends, or vote against politicians who oppose Russian policy positions (Porotsky, 2017c; Watts, 2017; Weisburd et al., 2016).

Although the Russian government uses proxies for hacking computers and disseminating information operations messages over social media, the state is directly involved in shaping the information sphere. Russia is able to control the messages heard by domestic audiences through censorship of anything that does not support state narratives and policies and through state ownership or state control of the television, newspapers, and radio stations that Russian citizens access. The propaganda with which domestic audiences are inundated encourages citizens to feel paranoid and to believe that their nation, culture, and way of life is under siege by the West (Pomerantsev, 2014; Skaskiw, 2017).

State-owned and state-controlled media also carry the Russian government's propaganda and narratives to international audiences as well. RT (formerly known as Russia Today) and Sputnik News are both operated by a company that is funded by the Russian government. Margarita Simonova Simonyan has been editor-in-chief of RT since 2005; on 31 December 2013, she was also made editor-in-chief of the government-owned news agency Rossiya Segodnya (which runs the Sputnik News agency, websites, and radio broadcasting services). RT, which now reaches international audiences (in English, Arabic, German, and Spanish), originally aimed at changing the world's view of Russia, but the network has rebranded itself for greater impact (and responsiveness to the Russian government's information operations efforts), such that it now questions more and purposely features stories that have not been reported by the mainstream media. Sputnik News provides an alternative to the Western media's unipolar world view and aims to tell what it claims is the untold story. This agency is anti-Western, anti-establishment, and is purposely hostile toward mainstream media; it targets disenfranchised audiences, and its gives disproportionate coverage to dissident members of European countries' governments. RT and Sputnik News propagate news stories that have been approved by the Russian government; these stories contain a mixture of truthful fact and skewed and manipulated information. These television and Internet articles are amplified over RT's and Sputnik News's social media accounts (and associated trolls and bots). The Russian government attracts non-Russian audiences in Ukraine and the Baltics because the Russian programming there tends to be more professional-looking and entertaining than local media productions. These audiences tune in to Russian television for the serials and talent shows, but viewers end up continuing to watch the news and current affairs programs, thus becoming exposed to Russian propaganda, narratives, and interpretations of world affairs (Chivvis, 2017b; Lucas & Pomerantsev, 2016; MacFarquhar, 2016; Nimmo, 2016; ODNI, 2017; Paul & Courtney, 2016; Rutenberg, 2017; Weisburd et al., 2016).

Besides controlling media messaging through its control of domestic audiences, the Russian government skews academic research by funding academic institutions and think tanks with the purpose of producing allegedly credible reports to support Russian policies, claims, and narratives. Russia also funds European politicians and protest movements that expound Russian positions and criticize the United States and other Western organizations (Chivvis, 2017b; Lucas & Pomerantsev, 2016; Stewart, 2017; Thomas, 2016; Waltzman, 2017).

By using all forms of information dissemination—state and commercial television, newspapers, radio, the Internet, social media platforms, and in-person influence agents, along with trolls, bots, and false accounts, conventional and social media synchronization;, and white/grey/black sources and outlets—Russian information operations efforts have been structured to reach as wide a range of audiences as possible. In addition to controlling the messages heard by domestic audiences and crafting propaganda to maintain domestic support for the Russian government and its actions, Russian information operations are directed at audiences in eastern Europe, western Europe, the United States, and their allies. Russian information operations target discontented groups around the world, looking for individuals who will believe and disseminate Russian narratives over social media. Information operations target journalists and politicians' staff to see who might be willing to engage in pro-Russian dialogue and to promote pro-Russian policies and narratives.

Influencing the selection of decision makers during elections requires the targeting of an adversarial nation's domestic population. Information operations are used to influence public opinion, affect mass consciousness, manipulate popular perceptions, and perhaps even destabilize a nation from within or suppress voter segments by severely dividing opinion or causing people to lose faith in the potential/resulting mandate (Gilles, 2016a, 2016b; Gunzinger, 2017; Iasiello, 2017; Joyal, 2016; Lucas & Pomerantsev, 2016; Porotsky, 2017b; Raju et al., 2017; Thomas, 2016; Tomášek, 2015; Shane, 2017; Waltzman, 2017; Weisburd et al., 2016).

Elections offer a target-rich environment where voters turn to the Internet to get the latest news on candidates' platforms and to social media to discuss contrasting policy views. The Russian government turned the Western media's tools and practices for supporting democratic debate against European and American establishment candidates in 2015, 2016, and 2017, flooding the Internet and social media with propaganda, disinformation, and stolen private correspondence resulting from computer hackings, as well as through Russian news agencies, social media trolls and bots, and independent users convinced and confused by Russian information operations efforts. The following section will detail Russia's information operations efforts during the 2016 US presidential election and how it sowed confusion and division by offering multiple conflicting narratives and amplifying already contentious topics.

Russian Information Operations during the 2016 US Presidential Election

The Russian government has been evolving its use of hybrid warfare and information operations over the past decade. On the one hand, after the information attack on Estonia in April 2007, the Putin regime has combined information operations with conventional warfare in its near-abroad, as seen in Russia's interventions in Georgia and Ukraine (Crimea) (Chivvis, 2017b; Duncan, 2017; Fedyk, 2017; Foxall, 2016; Iasiello, 2017; Joyal, 2016; Lucas & Pomerantsev, 2016; Polyakova, 2016; Vowell, 2016). On the other hand, Russia has depended more on information operations techniques when it comes to intimidating Baltic nations, potential NATO members, and NATO missions (Brewster, 2017; Campion-Smith, 2017; Gilles, 2016a; Henderson, 2016; Kepe, 2017; Lucas & Pomerantsev, 2016; MacFarquhar, 2016; Read, 2016). More recently, the Russian government has discovered the impact it can have by systematically using the Internet and social media to interfere with democratic elections in the United Kingdom, France, Germany, Spain, and the United States (Alandete, 2017; Daniels, 2017; "France's Macron," 2017; Schwirtzsept, 2017; Stelzenmüller, 2017; Watts, 2017). All of these examples demonstrate that Russia is actively conducting information operations to support its strategic objectives against its adversaries, those from both near and abroad. The logical conclusion is that the Russian government will continue to practise and perfect these methods unless Western nations disrupt Russia's information operations capabilities. Russia has had the greatest information warfare success when countries are not prepared for Russian information operations interference. Whether the nation is a small country or one of the Western powers, Russia's ability to hack computer networks and directly reach the voting public can have serious and detrimental consequences if a government is unsuspecting or complacent in terms of technical and psychological preparations and protections. The case study of Russian interference in the 2016 United States presidential election is of relevance since it directly impacts Canada's closest ally as well as the defence of North American democracies.

EXPECTED AND UNEXPECTED ELECTION INTERFERENCE: ELECTRONIC POLL BOOKS AND EMAIL HACKING

When American officials considered how the Russian government might interfere with the 2016 presidential election, the inclination was to protect voting technology against tampering so that voting counts could not be changed. It appears that these protection efforts were successful; there has been no evidence of this type of vote tampering. Nevertheless, Russian hackers did interfere with some states' electronic poll books (laptops and tablets loaded with voter check-in software). For example, VR Systems, the electronic poll book supplier for North Carolina, was hacked by the GRU (Glavnoye Razvedyvatelnoye Upravlenie, Russia's military intelligence body) in August 2016. The hackers then sent spearphishing emails from fake VR Systems email accounts to 122 local and state election jurisdictions in the hope that some election officials would be tricked into downloading malware that would allow the hackers to take over computer systems linked to the US election process. On Election Day, the hackers manipulated electronic poll books to keep some Americans from casting their votes. At the polling stations, people were told that, according to the electronic poll books, they had already cast ballots, or were ineligible to vote, or needed to go to another polling station (where they were turned away again since this information was wrong). Some North Carolina counties experiencing electronic poll book problems reverted to paper registration lists, but this slowed the voting process so much that large numbers of voters gave up waiting and left the polling stations without casting a ballot. Electronic poll book problems often occurred in counties where the largest cities were located. Russian hackers targeted the election systems of twenty-one states during the 2016 presidential election. Russian spies had been collecting intelligence since 2014 on US election processes and technological equipment, and they determined that the most profitable course of action would be to avoid altering vote tallies and instead target Internet-based systems such as email accounts, voter databases, election websites, electronic poll book vendors, and back-end election services (Perlroth et al., 2017).

The Russian government's interference with the US political system did not just begin during the 2016 presidential election campaign. Hacking efforts and social media disinformation operations both started in 2014, and these grew more extensive the closer the election came. Hackers linked to the Russian government penetrated unclassified email systems in the State Department in November 2014, and the Joint Chiefs of Staff in July 2015, by successfully installing malware that took data out of the hacked email accounts. In March 2016, the State Department was hacked again, and in June 2016, hackers stole one hundred thousand individual tax returns from the Internal Revenue Service. Hackers have been using spearphishing emails to install malware on computers by including supposed links to stories likely to be of interest to the email account holders. During the summer of 2015, the group of Russian hackers known as Cozy Bear sent spearphishing emails to government agencies, government contractors, and non-profit organizations in Washington, DC. In 2016, messages were sent to ten thousand Department of Defense Twitter users with links, masquerading as special interest stories, that would download malware. The day after the November 2016 election, Cozy Bear hackers sent another five waves of spearphishing emails, this time to think tanks and non-profits, hoping to get access to more email accounts after the successful hacking of Democratic Party members during the 2016 election (Calabresi, 2017; Foxall, 2016; Lipton, 2016).

Russian hackers had been trying to hack into members of the Hillary Clinton election campaign more than a year before the presidential election. Cozy Bear hackers had successfully hacked into the Democratic Congressional Campaign Committee (DCCC) email system before September 2015, which is the month that an individual from the Federal Bureau of Investigation (FBI) contacted the DCCC to let them know that at least one of their computers had been compromised by Russian hackers. The DCCC contact who took the FBI's call did not believe he had really been speaking with the FBI, and hence did not follow up with the caller's information. DCCC information technology specialists did not immediately see evidence of Russian hackers in their computer systems, and thus did not hire cyber-security experts to help until April 2016. In the meantime, the hackers were gleaning information with impunity, first to simply gather intelligence; this subsequently evolved into an operation to harm Clinton's election campaign. The DCCC's realization concerning the breech came a month after Cozy Bear had hacked into the DCCC and sent spearphishing emails to Clinton campaign members. A campaign worker clicked a link to change a supposedly compromised Google email password, which resulted in campaign chairman John Podesta being hacked and sixty thousand of his emails stolen. In May 2016, a member of the GRU publicly bragged that Hillary Clinton would experience payback for her 2011 influence operation against Putin and her role in orchestrating the mass protests in Russia during Putin's 2012 election campaign. Three days before the DCCC meeting, on 22 July 2016, WikiLeaks began publishing sensitive emails stolen from the DCCC. Podesta's emails were leaked to the public on 7 October 2016, one month before the presidential election vote. Russian hackers timed these leaks to ensure that voters were inundated with the media's reports of, and reactions to, the emails' politically embarrassing contents during critical decision points (Calabresi, 2017; Lipton, 2016).

THE INTERNET RESEARCH AGENCY TROLL FARM

An additional surprise to American election officials, voters, and politicians was Russia's level of cognitive interference in the 2016 election through a deliberate disinformation campaign that used fake news, fake websites and videos, fake advertisements, fake persona, and fake accounts on social media, all of which were fed directly into American voters' Facebook, Twitter, and Instagram accounts. After the 2016 presidential election, it was discovered that false personal social media accounts and Twitter bot accounts were involved in Russian disinformation activities, and these were linked to the well-known Russian troll factory called the Internet Research Agency (IRA) (Lapowsky, 2017; Mueller, 2018; Stretch, 2018). In 2011, Russian opposition groups hostile to Putin used social media to convince Russian citizens to carry out anti-government protests. Putin reacted by taking greater control of the Internet: bloggers had to register with the government, some websites were censored, and some social media platforms experienced government pressure while Kremlin allies took control of other platforms. The government instituted purposeful posting of pro-government messages on social media to drown out opposition voices as well; one such messaging factory, the IRA, was established in 2013 as a Kremlin-backed propaganda arm for Putin. Originally, it focused on communicating with domestic audiences by flooding social media with messages that attacked opposition figure Aleksei Navalny, praised the stability of Putin's regime, criticized the chaos and moral corruption of the United States and the West, condemned the West's economic sanctions, and supported the annexation of Crimea and the separatist insurgency in eastern Ukraine. Putin aimed to spoil the Internet for Russian citizens; he wanted to cultivate an atmosphere of hate and negativity with the trolls' activities so that most people would not want to use the Internet. People were attracted to the IRA by the salaries it offered recruits—which were notably higher than typical Russian wages. By late 2014, approximately four hundred people were working twelve-hour shifts for the IRA, thus enabling the troll factory to send out messages 24/7 (Calamur, 2018; Davlashyan & Titova, 2018b; MacFarquhar, 2018a, 2018c; Mueller, 2018; Taylor, 2018).

In 2014, the Russian government decided that the approach of officially disseminating Russian narratives and denigrating adversaries could work against foreign audiences as well, so efforts began to communicate directly with Western audiences over social media. In April 2014, the IRA formed a separate department to oversee the Translator Project—disinformation activities targeted specifically against the United States, carried out over Facebook, Twitter, Instagram, and YouTube. The Translator Project was part of a larger interference operation called Project Lakhta, which included all of the IRA's disinformation targeting both domestic and foreign audiences, with the goal of solidifying Putin's support in Russia and spreading confusion and distrust of government institutions in the West. The strategy to interfere with the 2016 US presidential election was devised in May 2014. Employees at the IRA began monitoring American social media accounts focused on politics and other sources of information about the 2016 election. The goal of the IRA's trolls was to spread distrust about US candidates and the political system in general and to create discord and tensions among the electorate before the vote took place. The IRA grew to over one thousand employees by 2015. There were approximately eighty to ninety people working on the Translator Project, the majority being students from St. Petersburg University. Not only were they highly skilled in the English language, but they were also working on degrees in international relations, linguistics, or journalism. Because of this specialized expertise, their pay rates were double those of the trolls working in the domestic operations department (Apuzzo & LaFraniere, 2018; Calamur, 2018; Davlashyan & Titova, 2018a, 2018b; MacFarquhar, 2018a, 2018b, 2018c; Mueller, 2018; Scannell et al., 2018).

By early 2016, the Putin regime and the IRA purposefully began supporting the Republican Party's presidential candidate, Donald Trump, and attacking the Democratic candidate, Hillary Clinton. On 10 February 2016, officials at the IRA circulated guidance that social media posts should contain content about the US elections, including derogatory information about Clinton. Employees were encouraged to denigrate other Republican candidates as well, such as Ted Cruz and Marco Rubio, but instructions were given to be supportive of Democrat Bernie Sanders in addition to Trump. It has also been reported that Putin believed that Clinton sponsored the release of the Panama Papers (stolen documents from the legal firm Mossack Fonseca, which specializes in facilitating offshore banking). Because these documents implicated Putin and his close friends in crime and corruption related to $2 billion worth of offshore deals and loans, Putin reportedly decided in April 2016 to retaliate against Clinton by attacking her election campaign efforts (Apuzzo, 2018; Gregory, 2016; Harding, 2016; Mueller, 2018; Taylor, 2017).

By the summer of 2016, the IRA's monthly budget for Project Lakhta was US$1.25 million, which was being funded by the wealthy Russian oligarch Yevgeny Prigozhin through the entities that make up his Concord Management and Consulting group of companies. Prigozhin became a favoured business contact of Putin. Once known as Putin's chef (since Prigozhin frequently provided Putin with catering services), Prigozhin has financially benefited from being willing to conduct favours and less savoury tasks for Putin, such as recruiting soldiers to fight in Ukraine and Syria, providing soldiers to protect Syrian oil fields, and establishing an online news service that disseminates nationalist views; he is the founder and head of the private military contractor organization known as the Wagner Group. Putin rewarded Prigozhin's loyalty and work through lucrative government contracts (he has received US$3.1 billion worth in the five-year period 2012–17) and a percentage of Syria's oil revenues. Since Prigozhin not only funded the IRA's disinformation operations, but has also met and communicated frequently with the IRA's top official, General Director Mikhail Bystrov, he both controls and approves of the IRA's work against the United States and the West. Because of the Putin regime's relationship with the IRA's patron, US government officials and security analysts have determined that Putin and his government endorse the IRA's mandate and operations while enjoying the plausible deniability of working through an intermediary. According to security analysts, individuals in developed states do not launch private wars against the world's superpower; hence, the type of Russian troll attacks that were occurring throughout the US election would have needed the Russian government's approval (Calamur, 2018; Davlashyan & Titova, 2018b; MacFarquhar, 2018a, 2018b; Mueller, 2018; Scannell et al., 2018).

IRA SOCIAL MEDIA ACTIVITY IN THE US 2016 PRESIDENTIAL ELECTION

The IRA's trolls interfered with the 2016 US presidential election by opening social media accounts using false identities; these fake profiles were intended to convince other users that they belonged to Americans, ranging from ordinary citizens to politically engaged individuals to political activists (Apuzzo, 2018; Edgett, 2017; Mueller, 2018). In addition to opening accounts on Facebook and Twitter under fake identities, these IRA trolls also created Twitter bot accounts that were programmed to relay propaganda automatically without human involvement; hundreds of these automated accounts would often amplify the same message at the same time, in alphabetical order of the account names on the IRA's distribution lists. In addition to 2,752 IRA-linked Twitter accounts producing organic content (free messages and posts, as opposed to paid advertisements), Twitter was able to identify 36,746 bot accounts more widely linked to Russia (Edgett, 2017, 2018; Lapowsky, 2017; Mueller, 2018; Popken, 2017; Porotsky, 2017c; Smith, 2017; Solon & Siddiqui, 2017; Stretch, 2017).

IRA employees used stolen identities (social security numbers, addresses, and dates of birth) and illegally purchased credit cards and bank account numbers to pass verification checks when opening PayPal accounts. Such accounts were often used to purchase advertisements on multiple social media platforms. The IRA had 470 Facebook accounts involved in spending over US$100,000 to purchase 3,000 ads on Facebook. Nine Russian-linked Twitter accounts conducted ad campaigns. Two RT Twitter accounts carried out 44 ad campaigns (costing $234,600 for ads targeting US audiences), while the other seven accounts spent US$1,184 to run 50 ad campaigns in the United States. Twitter earned US$1.9 million from all of RT's advertising efforts. Google determined that Russians spent US$4,700 on advertising over its platforms, as well as eighteen YouTube channels where 1,108 videos (amounting to forty-three hours of viewing material) had been uploaded in connection with the US election (Apuzzo, 2018; Dawsey, 2017; Edgett, 2017; Guide, 2017; McCabe, 2017; Mueller, 2018; Popken, 2017; Raju et al., 2017; Seetharaman, 2017a; Solon & Siddiqui, 2017; Stretch, 2017, 2018; Walker, n.d.).

IRA trolls' social media accounts were actively posting organic messages during the election campaign. The 470 Facebook accounts identified as linked to the IRA created 80,000 pieces of organic content. Between September and November 2016, the 2,752 IRA Twitter accounts pushed out election-related tweets, half of which were automated messaging. Social media investigators discovered 170 IRA Instagram accounts that posted over 120,000 pieces of content during the election. Social media platform executives estimated that approximately 150 million Americans were exposed to Russian election propaganda (Lapowsky, 2017; Smith, 2017; Solon & Siddiqui, 2017; Stretch, 2017).

IRA employees used Facebook to help organize political events in the United States, such as protests and rallies. By January 2018, Facebook investigations determined that the IRA had set up thirteen Facebook pages through which trolls created 129 events and sent out notifications announcing these events, aims, times, and locations. These Facebook event notices were seen by 338,300 Facebook accounts, and 62,500 users indicated that they would be attending at least one of the IRA's events. With information available in October 2017, the *Wall Street Journal* found that eight IRA Facebook accounts had publicized, and even financed, 60 events; the Facebook notices for these 60 events alone were liked two million times. It has been confirmed that at least 22 of the 60 events actually took place. IRA trolls pretended they were politically engaged Americans who wanted to organize public gatherings on a variety of topics, some of which conflicted: supporting police shot in the line of duty versus protesting police shootings of civilians; wanting to make Muslim neighbourhoods safer versus opposing an Islamic centre in Houston; pro-Trump rallies versus African Americans protesting the election of Trump; anti-Clinton rallies versus rallies supporting Clinton because she supported Muslims and Islamic law. Although some events were sparsely attended, others garnered media coverage, thus increasing their legitimacy. IRA employees had impact within the United States using their Facebook pages and accounts: people attended events; there were actual confrontations between protesters and counter-protesters; Americans helped organized events on behalf of one of the IRA's fake American personas, who could not attend; and the organizing and advertising of events via Facebook got other American activists to volunteer to help with future IRA political events (Lapowsky, 2017; Mueller, 2018; O'Sullivan, 2017; Scannell et al., 2018; Seetharaman, 2017b; Shinal, 2018; Stretch, 2018).

SPECIFIC IRA MESSAGES AND GOALS IN THE US 2016 PRESIDENTIAL ELECTION

With the potentially global exposure offered by social media, the IRA had three objectives for their accounts, bots, ads, and events: to divide the American electorate with divisive messages on political issues; to support Trump and harm Clinton's campaign; and to suppress voter turnout. Russian trolls helped inflame discord among American voters during the 2016 election with their purposely anti-immigration messaging designed to appeal to supporters of Trump's hardline positions (e.g., the proposed Muslim travel ban). IRA employees promoted anti-Muslim messages in ads, organic posts, and events. Other controversial topics included ethnic and racial issues, the right to gun ownership, religion, and lesbian, gay, bisexual, and transgender rights (Apuzzo, 2018; Dawsey, 2017; Lapowsky, 2017; Mueller, 2018; O'Sullivan, 2017; Raju et al., 2017; Satter & Vasilyeva, 2018; Solon & Siddiqui, 2017; Stretch, 2017; Taylor, 2018).

In keeping with the direction given by Putin and IRA management, the IRA's social media material began in 2016 to explicitly support candidate Trump and denigrate Clinton's credibility as a potential president. Attacks on Clinton included fake stories about her having Parkinson's disease, running a pedophile ring, and being involved in murder. IRA employees used social media ads to try to convince voters that Clinton supported the institution of sharia law in the United States. Furthermore, IRA Facebook and Twitter accounts (human and bot) disseminated links to hacked email dumps on WikiLeaks and DCLeaks.com (Apuzzo, 2018; Calabresi, 2017; Dawsey, 2017; Edgett, 2017; Mueller, 2018; ODNA, 2017; O'Sullivan, 2017; Porotsky, 2017c; Shane, 2017). IRA employees, using their fake American social media personas, contacted members of the Trump campaign in Florida and New York more than once seeking co-operation during IRA rally or protest events. There is evidence that some Trump campaign workers did respond to these fake personas (e.g., a volunteer from Trump's New York campaign agreed to provide signs for a pro-Trump rally march organized by the IRA) (Mueller, 2018; Scannell et al., 2018).

Voter suppression occurred when IRA-linked Twitter accounts sent messages instructing Clinton supporters to vote online, by text, or over the phone—methods that had not been implemented by American election institutions. IRA-linked social media accounts encouraged Muslim Americans to boycott the 2016 elections, claiming that Clinton would continue the war against Muslims in the Middle East if elected. Other messages told African-American readers they were better off not voting (rejecting both Clinton and Trump) or voting for a third-party candidate such as Jill Stein. More generally, IRA-linked accounts aimed to discourage voters from taking part in the election with allegations of voter fraud by the Democratic Party (Edgett, 2017, 2018; Mueller, 2018; Satter, 2018).

With the quantity of information shared on social media about an individual's personal preferences, political views, and opinions on social issues, social media platforms (as well as outside companies such as Cambridge Analytica) have created algorithms that can segment users into subgroups, identify the hot-button issues most likely to garner reactions from certain individuals, and enable other users to target audiences with specific messages and disinformation that speak to their interests, pull emotional strings, and elicit a desired response (Brannelly, 2017; Calabresi, 2017; Porotsky, 2017a).

IRA social media accounts were known to target individuals, specific social groups, and particular geographical regions with their messages, posts, and ads. Russian information operations have targeted the social media accounts of journalists deemed to be more gullible or likely to believe conspiracy theories. These accounts are then flooded with links to false stories, with the expectation that the targeted journalist will report on these links in mainstream media and disseminate them to his or her social media followers. IRA employees used social media to identify which congressional aides might be favourable to Russia's policy objectives; these staffers would then begin to receive stories, ads, and posts about Russian policies, with the IRA operatives hoping the staffers would share their personal opinions and views with their members of Congress in an effort to gain support for the issue by an elected member of the US government. IRA trolls would target specific social groups based on the organizations that these users were following, pages they had liked, or key words that were common in their posts and profiles (e.g., "Christianity," "God," "conservatism," "family," "country," "American," "patriotic," "and military"). Russian disinformation operations over social media platforms, such as Facebook ad campaigns, were seen to have targeted three states that were key to Trump's election victory: Wisconsin, Michigan, and Pennsylvania. The goal was to reinforce pre-existing divisive views in order to get chosen users to convince friends and family to vote the same way (i.e., for Trump), to nudge other voters to solidify their pro-Trump tendencies by committing to voting for him; to persuade those who were undecided to vote for Trump on a specific issue about which the disinformation campaign informed them; and to discourage Democratic voters who were not thrilled with Clinton as a candidate from supporting her on Election Day, either by not voting at all, voting for a third-party candidate, or voting for Trump as a protest vote (Calabresi, 2017; O'Sullivan, 2017; Porotsky, 2017b, 2017c; "Presidential election results," 2017; Raju et al., 2017; Watts, 2016, 2017).

ESTIMATING THE POTENTIAL IMPACT OF IRA SOCIAL MEDIA INFORMATION OPERATIONS

Without further data identifying the number of American social media users who saw Russian ads, events, or posts, and the number of American voters who made their political choice in 2016 based on Russian-linked social media material and interactions, it will remain unknown exactly how much impact Russian information operations had on the 2016 US election in taking votes away from Clinton and increasing support for Trump: Russian influence could have been manifested by Democratic voters' choosing not to vote at all because they were turned off from supporting Clinton due to IRA social media messaging and disinformation, by potential Democratic voters casting protest votes for Trump or a third-party candidate, by persuading individual voters to choose Trump based on specific policy preferences, or by solidifying anger over divisive issues to such an extent that typically complacent individuals decided to cast ballots in order to make sure their voices were heard. There were three states where Trump won the Electoral College votes by less than 45,000 votes: in Pennsylvania (representing 20 Electoral College votes), Trump won by 44,292 votes; in Wisconsin (10 Electoral College votes), Trump won by 22,748 votes; and in Michigan (16 Electoral College votes), Trump won by 10,704 votes. Consequently, Trump won the US presidency based on a difference of 77,744 votes over three states. If Clinton had been able to garner merely 77,745 votes across these three states, she would have won 46 extra Electoral College votes and, consequently, the presidency. It is possible that Russian information operations could have changed the votes of less than 78,000 voters (which is 0.56 per cent of the electorate) in these states' total 13,940,012 votes cast—out of 4,799,284 total votes in Michigan, 2,976,150 in Wisconsin, and 6,165,478 in Pennsylvania—and hence the outcome of the 2016 election (Borchers, 2017; "Presidential election results," 2017; Raju et al., 2017; Scannell et al., 2018).

Although Facebook and Twitter executives tried to downplay the impact of Russian social media activities (e.g., by emphasizing that the quantity of Russian-linked content present on Facebook's newsfeeds was estimated to be only 0.004 per cent of all newsfeed content), the fact that 150 million Americans were exposed to Russian disinformation over social media shows that a significant portion of the American voting population was subject to the nefarious actions of a foreign power. In 2016, the US population was approximately 323.1 million people; approximately 235.3 million of these people were of voting age. This means that 63.8 per cent of the voting population could have been exposed to Russia's social media content (150 million out of 235.3 million). Among Americans old enough to vote, 65 per cent used the Internet as their leading source of election news; this translates to 152.945 million voters who were using online information to stay informed on election-related issues. This means that 98 per cent of voting Americans using the Internet for election information could have been exposed to Russian social media disinformation (150 million out of 153 million). These calculations are simply meant to demonstrate that the number of Americans exposed to Russian social media disinformation was by no means insignificant. Of course, not every American voter using the Internet for news uses social media for that purpose. Furthermore, of the 150 million Americans exposed to Russian information operations material, it is unknown how many of these users are duplicate users across multiple social media platforms. Although the current data does not allow analysts to calculate how many people were turned away from voting for Clinton, were influenced to vote for Trump, or remained uninformed by debate due to cloistering themselves in echo chambers and avoiding exposure to other opinions and points of view, former Central Intelligence Agency director John Brennan's assessment that it is "implausible that Russian actions did not influence the views and votes of at least some Americans" is nevertheless both sobering and probably true (Edgett, 2018; Scannell et al., 2018; Stretch, 2017, 2018; Walker, n.d.).

Examples of recent Russian information operations and interference should be a call to action for Western leaders to better protect citizens and governments against Russian influence narratives causing confusion and division. The following section will outline some recommended measures that the West, its allies, and Canada could take in order to counter Russian information operations and diminish adversaries' information warfare capabilities.

Recommendations: Deliberate Strategic Communications Efforts Needed

The Russian government, under the leadership of Putin, has deliberately designed an omnipresent information operations threat. Russia not only acts within a persistent state of information warfare; its use of information operations to challenge Western alliances, institutions, and the rules-based liberal world order will continue and indeed expand if left unchallenged by Western nations. By comparison, some analysts argue that the Western response to Russian information operations has been slow, reactive, piecemeal, amateurish, and inadequate (Nimmo, 2015). Unless Western nations counter Russian information operations with the same level of persistent, deliberate messaging, accompanied by their own thoughtful development of information operations concepts and methods for global audiences, Russia will continue to maintain information operations superiority and do damage to Western ideals, alliances, societies, democracies, government institutions, election processes, and the belief in truth. The failure to substantively react to election meddling and interference efforts by Russia means these activities will continue into future elections and evolve into something even more insidious (Berthiaume, 2017; Boutilier, 2018; Bronskill, 2021; Canada, 2017; Nanji, 2017; Wherry, 2017). This final section will outline recommendations for improving the West's (and Canada's) information operations capabilities.

Russia is spreading disinformation about Western nations and NATO members, which forces the attacked countries to try to undo the damage and dispel myths by sharing truthful accounts after the fact. Psychological studies have shown that it is harder to dispel people's beliefs in information they have already internalized and accepted. Western nations need to carry out strategic communications campaigns that proactively tell audiences what Western democracies represent before disinformation has been distributed by adversaries. To this end, the Government of Canada needs to develop a narrative that explains to domestic, international, allied, neutral, and adversarial audiences what defines Canada, its beliefs, and its actions. For example, Ian Schugart (deputy minister of foreign affairs at the time) articulated the following vision for Canada to a Department of National Defence/Canadian Armed Forces audience in late February 2018: Canada believes in, will work for, and will defend open trade, free navigation of the seas, multilateralism, multilateral institutions, a rules-based world order, human rights, and democratic and coalition-based solutions to international problems. Such a narrative needs to be officially created and disseminated proactively by whole-of-government strategic communications capabilities.

Government strategic communications expertise is not just needed in military theatres during combat missions; strategic communications capabilities are also needed in peacetime as a means of maintaining public support and pre-emptively deterring some adversarial information operations attempts. For each known object of Russian attack, there needs to be a deliberate and proactive Western response to deliberately defend what the Putin regime is specifically trying to destroy. Nations that support the rules-based liberal world order need to develop and disseminate narratives that promote democracy and democratic institutions, defend liberal values and the concept of truth, and protect the countries' being attacked by Russia by promoting these nations' positive contributions and right to self-determination, and by exposing Russia's aggression, hypocrisy, corruption, and detrimental actions toward neighbours and the international community (Calabresi, 2017; Fedyk,

2017; Gilles, , 2016a, 2016b; Guide, 2017; Lucas & Pomerantsev, 2016; Nimmo, 2015; Šuplata & Nič, 2016; Synovitz, 2017; Watts, 2017).

Western nations need to create and support organizations—either within government or through non-governmental organizations—that are dedicated to identifying, monitoring, tracking, studying, analyzing, and advising on Russia's (or any adversarial actors') information operations efforts. Strategic communications organizations need to be stood up that consist of expert researchers, professional writers, and technology platform operators to disseminate the necessary material across social media, the Internet, and other telecommunications platforms. Civilian and military researchers at such interdisciplinary institutions would study information attack examples to clearly identify what Russia attempts to do and actually accomplishes, what protections have worked and what capability gaps exist, and what lessons can be learned by Western nations to better enhance peacetime and home-front defences, as well as in-theatre protections and wartime information operations. The researchers would also need to focus on the regions where threats exist and counter-narratives are needed by analyzing regional adversaries, audiences, culture, linguistics, politics, allies, adversarial messaging, and Western strategic communications reception (Fried & Polyakova, 2018; Gilles, 2016a; Gould, 2017; Iasiello, 2017; Kepe, 2017; Lucas & Nimmo, 2017; Lucas & Pomerantsev, 2016; Nimmo, 2015; Polyakova, 2016; Šuplata & Nič, 2016; Tomášek, 2015; Waltzman, 2017).

There needs to be more decisive counter-information operations from the West. In addition to committing to deliberate Western narratives and proactive Western strategic communications efforts, members of NATO and the European Union need to better define critical infrastructure and harden its protection; expand cyber security; investigate Russian information operations funding and cut it off; restrict access to Western telecommunications for Russian news outlets (television, radio, and Internet) that carry out state disinformation and propaganda campaigns; educate the public and media organizations as to the nature and danger of, and how to identify, Russian information operations efforts; and rate Internet news sites to improve/ensure media quality and identify fake news and sock-puppet websites (Chivvis, 2017b; Iasiello, 2017; Lucas & Pomerantsev, 2016; McClintock, 2017; Paul & Courtney, 2016; Paul & Matthews, 2016; Polyakova et al., 2016; Šuplata & Nič, 2016; Watts, 2017).

Conclusion

The Putin regime has declared that it is in a perpetual state of conflict against the West and will consequently persist in its information operations activities. Hence, Western nations—including Canada—need to be in a perpetual state of concerted self-defence and deterrence by methodically defending, through strategic communications, the concepts, institutions, and military missions that Russia is attacking, and by proactively and pre-emptively disseminating strategic narratives that decrease support for Russia's aggressive policies and military actions and consequently deter the Russian government from continued attacks. Since Putin is carrying out a war against information, Canada and its Western allies must carry on a war against Russian deceit and disinformation. If left unchallenged, Russia will always have the advantage as long as it does not have to abide by the same rules and faces only a disjointed Western reaction after the fact rather than deliberate, proactive, and coordinated information operations and counter–information operations campaigns that come to the defence of truth, democracy, and the rules-based liberal world order that the West has enjoyed and cultivated since the end of the Second World War.

REFERENCES

Berthiaume, L. (2017, 16 June). Canada's spy agency expects cyberattacks during 2019 federal election. *CBC News*. http://www.cbc.ca/news/politics/cse-report-elections-cyber-threats-1.4163868

Bertrand, N. (2017, 2 August). A new website named after a founding father is tracking Russian propaganda in real time. *Business Insider*. http://www.businessinsider.com/russian-propaganda-website-tracker-2017-8

Boot, M. (2017, 13 October). Russia has invented social media blitzkrieg. *Foreign Policy*. http://foreignpolicy.com/2017/10/13/russia-has-invented-social-media-blitzkrieg/

Borchers, C. (2017, 1 November). Four takeaways from the Senate intelligence hearing with Facebook, Twitter and Google. *Washington Post*. https://www.washingtonpost.com/news/the-fix/wp/2017/11/01/four-takeaways-from-the-senate-intelligence-hearing-with-facebook-twitter-and-google/?utm_term=.cbe1ad21bfcd

Boutilier, A. (2017, 16 June). Canada's political parties, media vulnerable to foreign disinformation hacks: Spy agency. *Toronto Star*. https://www.thestar.com/news/canada/2017/06/16/canadas-political-parties-media-vulnerable-to-foreign-hacks-spy-agency-says.html

Boutilier, A. (2018, 8 February). Trudeau to Facebook: Fix your fake news problem—or else. *Toronto Star*. https://www.thestar.com/news/canada/trudeau-to-facebook-fix-your-fake-news-problem-or-face-stricter-regulations/article_691b0e16-1ad4-5197-9452-247acc10b428.html

Brannelly, K. (2017, 4 November). Trump campaign pays millions to overseas big data firm. *NBC News*. https://www.nbcnews.com/storyline/2016-election-day/trump-campaign-pays-millions-overseas-big-data-firm-n677321

Brewster, M. (2017, 17 February). Canadians prepare to face cyberwarriors and fake news in Latvia mission. *CBC News*. http://www.cbc.ca/news/politics/canada-latvia-deployment-1.3988719

Bronskill, J. (2021, 22 July). CSIS warns of increasingly sophisticated state-sponsored activity targeting elections. *CTV News*. https://www.ctvnews.ca/politics/csis-warns-of-increasingly-sophisticated-state-sponsored-activity-targeting-elections-1.5519606

Bugajski, J. (n.d.). The geopolitics of disinformation. *Center for European Policy Analysis*. Retrieved 4 October 2017 from http://www.infowar.cepa.org/The-geopolitics-of-disinformation

Bugajski, J. (2016, 13 September). Moscow's war on Washington. *Center for European Policy Analysis*. Retrieved 25 September 2017 from http://cepa.org/Moscows-war-on-Washington

Calabresi, M. (2017, 1 May). Inside Russia's social media war on America. *Time*. http://time.com/4783932/inside-russia-social-media-war-america/

Calamur, K. (2018, 16 February). What is the Internet Research Agency? *The Atlantic*. https://www.theatlantic.com/international/archive/2018/02/russia-troll-farm/553616/

Campion-Smith, B. (2017, 17 February). Canadian troops brace for Russian propaganda campaign. *Toronto Star*. https://www.thestar.com/news/canada/2017/02/17/canadian-troops-brace-for-russian-propaganda-campaign.html

Canada. (2017). Cyber threats to Canada's democratic process. *Communications Security Establishment*. https://publications.gc.ca/collections/collection_2017/cstc-csec/D96-2-2017-eng.pdf

Chekinov, S. G., & Bogdanov, S. A. (2013). The nature and content of a new-generation war. *Military Thought*, *4*, 12–23. https://www.usni.org/sites/default/files/inline-files/Chekinov-Bogdanov%20Miltary%20Thought%202013.pdf

Chen, A. (2015, 2 June). The agency. *New York Times*. https://www.nytimes.com/2015/06/07/magazine/the-agency.html

Chivvis, C. S. (2017a, 22 March). Addendum: Understanding Russian "hybrid warfare" and what can be done about it [Testimony]. *U.S. House Committee on Armed Services*. https://www.rand.org/content/dam/rand/pubs/testimonies/CT400/CT468z1/RAND_CT468z1.pdf

Chivvis, C. S. (2017b, 22 March). Understanding Russian "hybrid warfare" and what can be done about it [Testimony]. *U.S. House Committee on Armed Services.* https://www.rand.org/content/dam/rand/pubs/testimonies/CT400/CT468/RAND_CT468.pdf

Daniels, L. (2017, 23 April). How Russia hacked the French election. *Politico.* https://www.politico.eu/article/france-election-2017-russia-hacked-cyberattacks/

Davlashyan, N., & Titova, I. (2018a, 19 February). Ex-workers at Russian troll factory say Mueller indictments are true. *Time.* Retrieved 21 February 2018 from http://time.com/5165805/russian-troll-factory-mueller-indictments/

Davlashyan, N., & Titova, I. (2018b, 19 February). Former workers at Russian "troll factory" say US charges are well-founded. *Toronto Star.* https://www.thestar.com/news/world/2018/02/19/former-workers-at-russian-troll-factory-say-us-charges-are-well-founded.html

Dawsey, J. (2017, 26 September). Russian-funded Facebook ads backed Stein, Sanders, and Trump. *Politico.* http://www.politico.com/story/2017/09/26/facebook-russia-trump-sanders-stein-243172?lo=ap_a1

Dewey, C. (2016, 19 October). One in four debate tweets comes from a bot. Here's how to spot them. *Washington Post.* https://www.washingtonpost.com/news/the-intersect/wp/2016/10/19/one-in-four-debate-tweets-comes-from-a-bot-heres-how-to spot them/?utm_term=.6e370538b560

Duncan, A.J. (2017). New "hybrid war" or old "dirty tricks"? The Gerasimov debate and Russia's response to the contemporary operating environment. *Canadian Military Journal, 17*(3), 6–16. http://www.journal.forces.gc.ca/Vol17/no3/page6-eng.asp

Edgett, S. (2017, 31 October). Testimony of Sean J. Edgett, acting general counsel, Twitter, Inc. *US Senate Committee on the Judiciary Subcommittee on Crime and Terrorism.* https://www.judiciary.senate.gov/download/10-31-17-edgett-testimony

Edgett, S. (2018, 15 January). Questions for the record. *Senate Select Committee on Intelligence Hearing on Social Media Influence in the 2016 U.S. Elections.* https://www.intelligence.senate.gov/sites/default/files/documents/Twitter%20Response%20to%20Committee%20QFRs.pdf

Fedyk, N. (2017, 4 May). Russian "new generation" warfare: Theory, practice, and lessons for US strategists. *Small Wars Journal.* http://smallwarsjournal.com/jrnl/art/russian-%E2%80%9Cnew-generation%E2%80%9D-warfare-theory-practice-and-lessons-for-us-strategists-0

Foxall, A. (2016). Putin's cyberwar: Russia's statecraft in the fifth domain. *Henry Jackson Society Russia Studies Centre.* Retrieved 18 October 2017 from https://henryjacksonsociety.org/wp-content/uploads/2016/05/Cyber-FINAL-copy.pdf

France's Macron, alongside Putin, denounces two Russian media for election meddling. (2017, 29 May). *Reuters.* https://www.reuters.com/article/uk-france-russia-influence/frances-macron-alongside-putin-denounces-two-russian-media-for-election-meddling-idUKKBN18P1T8

Fried, D., & Polyakova, A. (2018). Democratic defense against disinformation. *Atlantic Council*. Retrieved 28 July 2013 from https://www.atlanticcouncil.org/wp-content/uploads/2018/03/Democratic_Defense_Against_Disinformation_FINAL.pdf

Galeotti, M. (2014, 6 July). The "Gerasimov Doctrine" and Russian non-linear war. *In Moscow's Shadows*. https://inmoscowsshadows.wordpress.com/2014/07/06/the-gerasimov-doctrine-and-russian-non-linear-war/

Gilles, K. (2016a). The handbook of Russian information warfare. *NATO Defense College Research Division*, Fellowship Monograph 9. http://www.ndc.nato.int/download/downloads.php?icode=506

Gilles, K. (2016b). *Russia's "new" tools for confronting the West: Continuity and innovation in Moscow's exercise of power*. Chatham House. https://www.chathamhouse.org/sites/default/files/publications/2016-03-russia-new-tools-giles.pdf

Gorenburg, D. (2019). Russian foreign policy narratives. *George C. Marshall European Center for Security Studies*. https://www.marshallcenter.org/en/publications/security-insights/russian-foreign-policy-narratives-0

Gould, J. (2017, 23 March). EUCOM commander: US needs stronger response to Russian disinformation. *Defense News*. http://www.defensenews.com/global/europe/2017/03/23/eucom-commander-us-needs-stronger-response-to-russian-disinformation/

Gregory, P. R. (2016, 5 April). Putin caught in huge Panama Papers scandal. *Forbes*. https://www.forbes.com/sites/paulroderickgregory/2016/04/05/putin-caught-in-huge-panama-papers-scandal/#3c7310ff7d31

Guide, K. (2017, 15 March). Russia's 5th column. *Center for American Progress*. https://www.americanprogress.org/issues/security/reports/2017/03/15/428074/russias-5th-column/

Gunzinger, M., Clark, B., Johnson, D., & Sloman, J. (2017). Force planning for the era of great power competition. *Center for Strategic and Budgetary Assessment*. http://csbaonline.org/uploads/documents/CSBA6302_%28Developing_the_Future_Force%29_PRINT.pdf

Harding, L. (2016, 3 April). Revealed: The $2bn offshore trail that leads to Vladimir Putin. *The Guardian*. https://www.theguardian.com/news/2016/apr/03/panama-papers-money-hidden-offshore

Henderson, N. (2016, 23 November). Russian disinformation: How U.S. information operations need to adapt. *Cornell Policy Review*. http://www.cornellpolicyreview.com/russian-disinformation-how-u-s-information-operations-need-to-adapt/

Hern, A. (2017, 8 May). Macron hackers linked to Russian-affiliated group behind US attack. *The Guardian*. https://www.theguardian.com/world/2017/may/08/macron-hackers-linked-to-russian-affiliated-group-behind-us-attack

Higgins, A. (2017, 16 February). Fake news, fake Ukrainians: How a group of Russians tilted a Dutch vote. *New York Times*. https://www.nytimes.com/2017/02/16/world/europe/russia-ukraine-fake-news-dutch-vote.html

Iasiello, E. J. (2017). Russia's improved information operations: From Georgia to Crimea. *Parameters, 47*(2), 51–63. https://press.armywarcollege.edu/cgi/viewcontent.cgi?article=2931&context=parameters

Joyal, P. (2016). Cyber threats and Russian information warfare. *Jewish Policy Center.* https://www.jewishpolicycenter.org/2015/12/31/russia-information-warfare/

Kepe, M. (2017, 7 June). NATO: Prepared for countering disinformation operations in the Baltic states? *RAND Blog.* https://www.rand.org/blog/2017/06/nato-prepared-for-countering-disinformation-operations.html

Koshkin, P. (2015, 2 April). The paradox of Kremlin propaganda: How it tries to win hearts and minds. *Russia Direct.* Retrieved 23 October 2017 from http://www.russia-direct.org/analysis/paradox-kremlin-propaganda-how-it-tries-win-hearts-and-minds

Lapowsky, I. (2017, 1 November). Eight revealing moments from the second day of Russia hearings. *Wired.* https://www.wired.com/story/six-revealing-moments-from-the-second-day-of-russia-hearings/

Lauder, M. (2017). *Leveraging proxy agents: The night wolves and other examples of Russia out-sourcing activity to criminal and grey-market enterprises* [Paper presentation]. 2017 Adversarial Intent Symposium: Putin's Russia—The Weaponization of Society, Kingston, ON, 11 October 2017.

Lipton, E., Sanger, D., & Shane, S. (2016, 13 December). The perfect weapon: How Russian cyberpower invaded the U.S. *New York Times.* https://www.nytimes.com/2016/12/13/us/politics/russia-hack-election-DCCC.html

Lucas, E., & Nimmo, B. (2015). CEPA info war paper no. 1: Information warfare—what is it and how to win it. *Center for European Policy Analysis.* Retrieved 4 October 2017 from http://cepa.org/files/?id_plik=1896

Lucas, E., & Pomerantsev, P. (2016). *Winning the information war: Techniques and counter-strategies to Russian propaganda in central and eastern Europe.* Center for European Policy Analysis. https://cepa.ecms.pl/files/?id_plik=2773

MacFarquhar, N. (2016, 28 August). A powerful Russian weapon: The spread of false stories. *New York Times.* https://www.nytimes.com/2016/08/29/world/europe/russia-sweden-disinformation.html

MacFarquhar, N. (2018a, 18 February). Inside the Russian troll factory: Zombies and a breakneck pace. *New York Times.* https://www.nytimes.com/2018/02/18/world/europe/russia-troll-factory.html

MacFarquhar, N. (2018b, 18 February). Russian trolls were sloppy, but indictment still 'points at the Kremlin." *New York Times.* https://www.nytimes.com/2018/02/17/world/europe/russia-indictment-trolls-putin.html

MacFarquhar, N. (2018c, 16 February). Yevgeny Prigozhin, Russian oligarch indicted by US, is known as "Putin's cook." *New York Times.* https://www.nytimes.com/2018/02/16/world/europe/prigozhin-russia-indictment-mueller.html

McCabe, D. (2017, 1 November). What Facebook, Google, and Twitter told the Senate Intel Committee. *Axios*. https://www.axios.com/what-facebook-google-and-twitter-told-the-senate-intel-committee-1513306593-acf2d8d6-3459-45c5-963b-482e42071d52.html

McClintock, B. (2017, 21 July). Russian information warfare: A reality that needs a response. *RAND Blog*. https://www.rand.org/blog/2017/07/russian-information-warfare-a-reality-that-needs-a.html

Mueller, R. (2018, 16 February). Grand Jury for the District of Columbia indictment against Internet Research Agency, et al. *US Department of Justice*. https://www.justice.gov/file/1035477/download

Nanji, S. (2017, 19 October). Facebook's Canadian "election integrity" plan puts much of the responsibility on political players. *Toronto Star*. https://www.thestar.com/news/gta/2017/10/19/facebooks-canadian-election-integrity-plan-puts-much-of-the-responsibility-on-political-players.html

Nimmo, B. (2015, 19 May). Anatomy of an info-war: How Russia's propaganda machine works, and how to counter it. *StopFake.org*. https://www.stopfake.org/en/anatomy-of-an-info-war-how-russia-s-propaganda-machine-works-and-how-to-counter-it/

Nimmo, B. (2016). CEPA information warfare paper no. 2: Sputnik—propaganda in a new orbit. *Center for European Policy Analysis*. Retrieved 4 October 2017 from http://cepa.org/files/?id_plik=2083

ODNI (Office of the Director of National Intelligence). (2017, 6 January). *Assessing Russian activities and intentions in recent US elections: The analytic process and cyber incident attribution*. National Intelligence Council. https://www.dni.gov/files/documents/ICA_2017_01.pdf

Oliker, O. (2016, 7 January). Unpacking Russia's new national security strategy. *Center for Strategic and International Studies*. https://www.csis.org/analysis/unpacking-russias-new-national-security-strategy

O'Sullivan, D. (2017, 2 November). Seen any of these before? You may have been targeted by Russian ads on Facebook. *CNN Money*. http://money.cnn.com/2017/11/01/media/russian-facebook-ads-release-house-intelligence-committee/index.html

Paul, C., & Matthews, M. (2016). *The Russian "firehose of falsehood" propaganda model*. RAND Corporation. https://www.rand.org/content/dam/rand/pubs/perspectives/PE100/PE198/RAND_PE198.pdf

Paul, C., & Courtney, W. (2016, 13 September). Russian propaganda is pervasive, and America is behind the power curve in countering it. *RAND Blog*. https://www.rand.org/blog/2016/09/russian-propaganda-is-pervasive-and-america-is-behind.html

Perlroth, N., Wines, M., & Rosenberg, M. (2017, 1 September). Russian election hacking efforts, wider than previously known, draw little scrutiny. *New York Times*. https://www.nytimes.com/2017/09/01/us/politics/russia-election-hacking.html?rref=collection%2Fnewseventcollection%2Frussian-election-hacking&action=click&contentCollection=politics&region=stream&module=stream_unit&version=latest&contentPlacement=5&pgtype=collection

Polyakova, A., Laruelle, M., Meister, S., & Barnett, N. (2016). *The Kremlin's Trojan Horses: Russian influence in France, Germany, and the United Kingdom*. Atlantic Council. https://www.atlanticcouncil.org/wp-content/uploads/2016/11/The_Kremlins_Trojan_Horses_web_0228_third_edition.pdf

Pomerantsev, P. (2014, 11 December). Russia's ideology: There is no truth. *New York Times*. https://www.nytimes.com/2014/12/12/opinion/russias-ideology-there-is-no-truth.html?_r=1

Popken, B. (2017, 30 October). What to expect when Facebook, Google, and Twitter testify on election meddling. *NBC News*. https://www.nbcnews.com/business/business-news/what-expect-when-facebook-google-twitter-testify-election-meddling-n815631

Porotsky, S. (2017a, 27 August). Cambridge Analytica: The darker side of big data. *Global Security*. https://globalsecurityreview.com/cambridge-analytica-darker-side-big-data/

Porotsky, S. (2017b, 27 August). Cold War 2.0: Russian information warfare. *Global Security*. https://globalsecurityreview.com/cold-war-2-0-russian-information-warfare/

Porotsky, S. (2017c, 27 August). Facebook, compromised: How Russia manipulated US voters. *Global Security*. https://globalsecurityreview.com/russia-manipulated-u-s-voters-social-media/

Presidential election results: Donald J. Trump wins. (2017, 9 August). *New York Times*. https://www.nytimes.com/elections/results/president

Raju, M., Byers, D., & Bash, D. (2017, 4 October). Russian-linked Facebook ads targeted Michigan and Wisconsin. *CNN News*. http://www.cnn.com/2017/10/03/politics/russian-facebook-ads-michigan-wisconsin/index.html

Rasmussen, R.C. (2015, 26 November). Cutting through the fog: Reflexive control and Russian STRATCOM in Ukraine. *Center for International Maritime Security*. http://cimsec.org/cutting-fog-reflexive-control-russian-stratcom-ukraine/20156

Rumer, E. (2017, 30 March). Russian active measures and influence campaigns [Testimony]. *US Senate Select Committee on Intelligence*. http://carnegieendowment.org/2017/03/30/russian-active-measures-and-influence-campaigns-pub-68438

Russian Federation. (2014). *Russian military doctrine*. Embassy of the Russian Federation to the United Kingdom of Great Britain and Northern Ireland. Retrieved 21 September 2017, from https://rusemb.org.uk/press/2029

Russian Federation. (2015). *Russian national security strategy*. Russian Federation president, edict 683. http://www.ieee.es/Galerias/fichero/OtrasPublicaciones/Internacional/2016/Russian-National-Security-Strategy-31Dec2015.pdf

Russian Twitter accounts promoted Brexit ahead of EU referendum: Times newspaper. (2017, 15 November). *Reuters*. https://www.reuters.com/article/us-britain-eu-russia/

russian-twitter-accounts-promoted-brexit-ahead-of-eu-referendum-times-newspaper-idUSKBN1DF0ZR

Rutenberg, J. (2017, 13 September). RT, Sputnik, and Russia's new theory of war. *New York Times*. https://www.nytimes.com/2017/09/13/magazine/rt-sputnik-and-russias-new-theory-of-war.html?action=click&contentCollection=Politics&module=Trending&version=Full&region=Marginalia&pgtype=article

Satter, R., & Vasilyeva, N. (2018, 20 February). Russia troll farm more strange than Mueller's indictment says, according to insiders. *Global News*. https://globalnews.ca/news/4036331/russia-troll-farm-strange-muellers-indictment/

Scannell, K., Shortell, D., & Stracqualursi, V. (2018, 17 February). Mueller indicts 13 Russian nationals over 2016 election interference. *CNN News*. https://www.cnn.com/2018/02/16/politics/mueller-russia-indictments-election-interference/index.html

Schwirtzsept, M. (2017, 21 September). German election mystery: Why no Russian meddling? *New York Times*. https://www.nytimes.com/2017/09/21/world/europe/german-election-russia.html

Seetharaman, D. (2017a, 30 October). Russian-backed Facebook accounts staged events around divisive issues. *Wall Street Journal*. https://www.wsj.com/articles/russian-backed-facebook-accounts-organized-events-on-all-sides-of-polarizing-issues-1509355801

Seetharaman, D. (2017b, 31 October). Tech executives testify in Senate hearing on Russian election activity. *Wall Street Journal*. https://www.wsj.com/livecoverage/senate-judiciary-hearing-tech-executives-russia-campaign/card/1509476733

Shane, S. (2017, 7 September). The fake Americans Russia created to influence the election. *New York Times*. https://www.nytimes.com/2017/09/07/us/politics/russia-facebook-twitter-election.html

Shane, S., & Goel, V. (2017, 6 September). Fake Russian Facebook accounts bought $100,000 in political ads. *New York Times*. https://www.nytimes.com/2017/09/06/technology/facebook-russian-political-ads.html

Shinal, J. (2018, 25 January). Facebook admits to the Senate that it recommended Russian propaganda to some users. *CNBC News*. https://www.cnbc.com/2018/01/25/facebook-tells-senate-its-software-recommended-russian-propaganda.html

Skaskiw, R. (2017, 27 March). Nine lessons of Russian propaganda. *Small Wars Journal*. http://smallwarsjournal.com/jrnl/art/nine-lessons-of-russian-propaganda

Smith, D. (2017, 31 October). Angry Al Franken hammers Facebook lawyer at hearing over Russian ads. *The Guardian*. https://www.theguardian.com/us-news/2017/oct/31/facebook-russia-ads-senate-hearing-al-franken

Solon, O., & Siddiqui, S. (2017, 31 October). Russia-backed Facebook posts "reached 126m Americans" during US election. *The Guardian*. https://www.theguardian.com/technology/2017/oct/30/facebook-russia-fake-accounts-126-million

Stelzenmüller, C. (2017, 28 June). The impact of Russian interference on Germany's 2017 elections. *Brookings Institution*. https://www.brookings.edu/testimonies/the-impact-of-russian-interference-on-germanys-2017-elections/

Stewart, B. (2017, 15 December). More than just hacks: Russia's "hybrid warfare" has been targeting western Europe for months. *CBC News*. http://www.cbc.ca/news/world/russia-cyber-warfare-election-hack-1.3896613

Stretch, C. (2017, 31 October). Testimony of Colin Stretch, general counsel, Facebook. *US Senate Committee on the Judiciary Subcommittee on Crime and Terrorism*. https://www.judiciary.senate.gov/download/10-31-17-stretch-testimony

Stretch, C. (2018, January 8). Facebook's response to US Senate Intelligence Committee [Testimony]. *U.S. Senate Select Committee on Intelligence*. https://www.intelligence.senate.gov/sites/default/files/documents/Facebook%20Response%20to%20Committee%20QFRs.pdf

Šuplata, M., & Nič, M. (2016, 31 August). Summary—Russia's information war in central Europe: New trends and counter-measures. *GlobSec*. https://www.globsec.org/publications/russias-information-war-central-europe-new-trends-counter-measures/

Synovitz, R. (2017, 17 January). Europe bracing against risk of Russian "influence operations." *Radio Free Europe/Radio Liberty*. https://www.rferl.org/a/europe-russian-influence-operations/28236212.html

Taylor, A. (2017, 28 August). Putin saw the Panama Papers as a personal attack and may have wanted revenge, Russian authors say. *Washington Post*. https://www.washingtonpost.com/news/worldviews/wp/2017/08/28/putin-saw-the-panama-papers-as-a-personal-attack-and-may-have-wanted-revenge-russian-authors-say/?utm_term=.69e78ec6cd3b

Taylor, A. (2018, 18 February). The Russian journalist who helped uncover election interference is confounded by the Mueller indictments. *Washington Post*. https://www.washingtonpost.com/news/worldviews/wp/2018/02/18/the-russian-journalist-who-helped-uncover-election-meddling-is-confounded-by-the-mueller-indictments/?utm_term=.02bb5ea6f423

Thomas, T. (2010). Russia's reflexive control theory and the military. *Journal of Slavic Military Studies, 17*(2), 237–56. http://www.tandfonline.com/doi/pdf/10.1080/13518040490450529?needAccess=true

Thomas, T. (2016). The evolution of Russian military thought: Integrating hybrid, new-generation, and new-type thinking. *Journal of Slavic Military Studies, 29*(4), 554–75. http://www.tandfonline.com/doi/pdf/10.1080/13518046.2016.1232541?needAccess=true

Tomášek, J. (2015, 13 October). Countering Kremlin's information war. *GlobSec*. https://www.globsec.org/publications/countering-kremlins-information-war/

Vowell, J. B. (2016, 30 October). Maskirovka: From Russia, with deception. *Real Clear Defense*. https://www.realcleardefense.com/articles/2016/10/31/maskirovka_from_russia_with_deception_110282.html

Walker, K. (n.d.). Responses to questions for the record for Mr. Kent Walker, senior vice president and general counsel, Google [Testimony]. *US Senate Select Committee on Intelligence.* https://www.intelligence.senate.gov/sites/default/files/documents/Google%20Response%20to%20Committee%20QFRs.pdf

Waltzman, R. (2017, 27 April). The weaponization of information: The need for cognitive security [Testimony]. *US Senate Committee on Armed Services Subcommittee on Cybersecurity.* https://www.rand.org/content/dam/rand/pubs/testimonies/CT400/CT473/RAND_CT473.pdf

Watts, C. (2017, 30 March). Disinformation: A primer in Russian active measures and influence campaigns [Statement]. *US Senate Select Committee on Intelligence.* https://www.intelligence.senate.gov/sites/default/files/documents/os-cwatts-033017.pdf

Watts, C., & Weisburd, A. (2016, 8 June). How Russia dominates your Twitter feed to promote lies (and, Trump, too). *Daily Beast.* http://www.thedailybeast.com/how-russia-dominates-your-twitter-feed-to-promote-lies-and-trump-too

Weisburd, A., Watts, C., & Berger, J. M. (2016, 6 November). Trolling for Trump: How Russia is trying to destroy our democracy. *War on the Rocks.* https://warontherocks.com/2016/11/trolling-for-trump-how-russia-is-trying-to-destroy-our-democracy/

Wherry, A. (2017, 19 October). Facebook launches "election integrity initiative" to fight hacking and fake news. *CBC News.* http://www.cbc.ca/news/politics/facebook-election-hacking-fake-news-1.4362002

5

The Evolution of China's Information Exploitation of COVID-19

Anthony B. Seaboyer and Pierre Jolicoeur

Introduction

China is the single state actor producing the greatest volume of COVID-related disinformation. The effects of this targeting became increasingly evident with more waves of outbreaks unfolding as vaccination rates were insufficient. A major factor—but not the only contributing factor for the continuation of the pandemic—was disinformation-based vaccine reluctance. Some Western governments—such as the US government under the Trump administration—have undoubtedly also contributed to the COVID disinformation that Western audiences have consumed. But in terms of the amounts of COVID-related disinformation reaching Western audiences, China is the state actor that has most targeted the Western information space.

This chapter asks how China's messaging related to COVID has evolved during the pandemic. As COVID-related exploitation of the information space is part of China's information warfare operations, the chapter first describes China's general information warfare capabilities and how they evolved to show the context in which COVID-related messaging was exploited. It then looks into the role of information exploitation in China's political system and policies and the effects China's messaging is having. Based on this background, the chapter then describes five trends that can be observed in the evolution of China's COVID exploitation in the information space. The authors argue that the evolution can be described as moving from a limited quantity of defensive, unspecific, and rather vague posts, primarily directed at domestic audiences via local sources, to strategic, widespread, and very specific and aggressive messaging increasingly targeting Western audiences through Western social media outlets.

What Are the Information Warfare Capabilities of China?

To understand the evolution of China's COVID-related exploitation of the information space, it is essential to consider the context in which these messaging operations are implemented. China's COVID messaging is part of its broader information warfare operations, which, in the early stages of the pandemic, initially primarily served the general goal of improving China's reputation both domestically and abroad. Information exploitation has played a very crucial role in China's political development in the past.

For decades China has focused on what it has described as "informationalization" by trying to catch up with Western development though information exploitation at all levels of the state—while at the same time attempting to control the very flow of all information—domestically and abroad. In an effort to simultaneously exploit information-based systems and control the flow of information, China developed a model for propaganda distribution and censorship that is unmatched in scale and, at some levels at least, such as censorship, also effectiveness.

Chinese information warfare (IW) capabilities can be divided into seven different categories: information operations (IO), cyber warfare, computer network operations (CNO), psychological operations, electronic warfare (EW), legal warfare, and space-based operations.[1]

Information Operations

The Chinese regime considers information operations to be at the core of IW, just as it considers IW to be at the core of informationalization (Anand, 2006). Chinese IO capabilities enable the implementation of the following strategies:[2] sabotaging information operation structures (Lovelace, 2015; Sabbagh, 2021); creating false situational impressions (Anand, 2006); launching surprise information attacks (Anand, 2006); weakening adversary information fighting capacity (Office of the Director of US National Intelligence, 2021; Spade, 2012); dispersing an adversary's forces, arms, and fires (Office of the Director of US National Intelligence, 2021); confusing or diverting the adversary (Ventre, 2014); information deception (Ellis, 2020; Ruwitch, 2021; Tsang, 2010); diverting an adversary's reconnaissance (Dell, 2017; Romo, 2021); targeting an adversary with false impressions or statements (Harold et al., 2021); disrupting adversarial thinking (Cheng, 2021); forcing adversaries to believe what is true is false and what is false is true (Anand, 2006); information-based attacks exploiting collected information ("Hearing on China," 2021); information reconnaissance (Stokes et al., 2011); directing political, military, academic, and media assets as agents of influence (Bronskill & Bryden, 2021; Shaffer, 2017); intellectual property theft to access capabilities and technologies (Sobiesk, 2003); intercepting adversary signals (Sahay, 2016); mapping targeting information in foreign military, government, and civil infrastructure (Wortzel, 2010); influencing foreign media broadcasting—also through foreign media acquisition (Raska, 2015); influencing foreign information dissemination—also through distributor acquisition (Tromblay, 2017); propaganda production and dissemination abroad (Swanson, 2016); influencing foreign entertainment production and distribution (Tromblay, 2017); media broadcasting (Karásková, 2020; Quing & Schiffman, 2015); and social media exploitation (Cadell, 2017; Harold et al., 2021).

How Has China's Information Warfare Capability Evolved?

INFORMATIONALIZATION

China's leadership has a long history of valuing information exploitation. The People's Liberation Army (PLA) has traditionally seen information as a key to victory (Pomerleau, 2017a, 2020)—to help improve China's standing and capabilities as a developing country, but also as a dictatorship needing to control information as a central element enabling the Chinese Communist Party (CCP) to stay in power (Cheng, 2016). As the world economy became more globalized and information more integrated with development, the CCP view of the relationship between information and power has evolved. Initially, the Chinese understanding of IW was based on Western concepts (Anand, 2006), though China soon moved toward evolving its own orientation of what Chinese analysts have named "informationalization":

> Informationalization is a comprehensive system of systems, where the broad use of information technology is the guide, where information resources are the core, where information networks are the foundation, where information industry is the support, where information talent is a key factor, where laws,

policies and standards are the safeguard. (State Council Information Office, 2002)

Accordingly, threats to China's national security (where perceived) also have become informationalized as adversaries enjoy unprecedented access to national economies, populations and decision makers: "as the long-range missile allows an opponent to directly strike a nation without having to break through ground or naval defences, so too information outflanks traditional military forces" (Cheng, 2016, p. 1)—to which we might add borders and most kinds of traditional protections against adversaries. The CCP began to perceive information itself as a threat. It is capable not only of eroding the morale of the military or reducing the population's support for a mission, but internally can also lead to much better-organized uprisings and domestic challenges to party leadership. With the increased "informationalization" of Chinese society, the CCP adapted its definition of national security interests and its military and security apparatus to lead informationalized wars and defend against informationalized attacks. At the same time, the CCP determined that security in the age of informationalization requires a response both on the civilian side and in government institutions. "An informationalized society will create an informationalized military, while an informationalized military can be produced only by an informationalized society and economy," which leads to the need to prepare for informationalized warfare (Cheng, 2016, p. 2).

INFORMATION AS THE KEY TO DEVELOPMENT

In the 1950s, as a highly disadvantaged country, China perceived that access to technical and military information could be a means to improve its standing and capabilities (Cheng, 2016). At the time, the primary target for China's information and political warfare campaigns was Taiwan (then known as Formosa, the seat of the Nationalist Chinese government-in-exile), with operations attempting to exploit political, cultural, and social frictions inside Taiwan, undermine trust between varying political-military authorities, de-legitimize Taiwan's international position, and gradually subvert public perceptions in order to "reunite" Taiwan on Beijing's terms (Chan & Thornton, 2022; Raska, 2015). Since then, China has been broadcasting propaganda toward Taiwan through the "Voice of the Strait" radio. Soon, though, added value was seen in investing in information technology as a means to improve China's economic situation. Heavy investment in information technology followed in order to improve China's standing as a developing country (Cheng, 2016). The goals then were not only to enhance communication between ground troops in the PLA and generally improve communication in China, but also to catch up to the development level of Western countries and transition toward an information economy.

INFORMATION AS A KEY TO EXPANDING NATIONAL POWER

As the leadership of China became interested in expanding its comprehensive national power, it identified that it could only do so if information technologies were incorporated and integrated into the broader society. To this end, Beijing refocused its informationalization activities from building an information economy to creating an information society (Cheng, 2016).

In 1999, the then vice-minister of science, technology, and industry for national defence, defined IW as the exploitation of information technologies to influence enemy decision-maker determination while protection China's systems (Ventre, 2016).

In 2002, the Sixteenth Party Congress formally recognized "informationalization" as essential for Chinese "comprehensive National Power" (Cheng, 2016). China's goal in using IW had by then evolved to be to "force the enemy to regard their goal as our goal, to force the opponent to give up the will to resist and end confrontation and stop fight by attacking enemy's perceptions and belief via information energy" (Anand, 2006, p. 785). Apart from defence, the Chinese leadership also identified that "modernization in all parts of society depends on the information sector" (Cheng, 2016, p. 6). Accordingly, the Tenth Five-Year Plan (2001–5) for the first time included national "informationalization" among China's top sixteen priorities (Cheng, 2016).

The 2004 "Historic Missions for the New Phase of the New Century," as introduced by the chairman of the Central Military Commission, declared that the PLA's support role in maintaining the nation's interests would, for the first time, also include the information domain. In 2005 the focus on information integration was formalized in the first "National Strategy for Informationalization Development for 2006 to 2020." The strategy requested the strengthening of information security systems and enhancing the use of information in China on all levels of society (Cheng, 2016). To enable sufficient training, an information warfare simulation centre was created for training the PLA. The centre uses high-tech simulation skills and equipment to simulate information warfare and its environment (Anand, 2006). In 2007, after the Seventeenth Party Congress, five members of the Politburo (out of twenty-four) directly focused on the informationalization of Chinese society. This reflected not only a substantial slice of Chinese political power, as well as high-level attention to the role of information, but also the increasing dominance of military and security interests in the area of information. Consequently, in 2008, most of the information technology (IT) and aerospace sectors were consolidated into the Ministry of Industry and Information Technology. This super ministry also oversees the military industrial complex (Cheng, 2016).

Since 31 December 2015, the Strategic Support Force (SSF) is responsible for the PLA's space, cyber, and electronic warfare missions (Costello, 2016). The SSF's space unit is responsible for preparation and conduct of co-orbital counter-space missions, while its cyber and EW unit is responsible for jamming satellite communications and GPS signals, as well as computer network operations against space facilities and satellites (Costello, 2016). The establishment of the SSF suggests that information warfare, including space warfare, long identified by PLA analysts as a critical element of future military operations, appears to have entered a new phase of development in the PLA (Pollpeter et al., 2016). It unifies the PLA's space, cyber, and EW capabilities for the first time (DOD, 2017). The SSF may be the PLA's first effort to combine cyber reconnaissance, attack, and defence capabilities in one organization (Pomerleau, 2017a). This of course leads to a further blurring of the distinction between peacetime and wartime capabilities in that peacetime operations now include the defence of the electromagnetic space and cyberspace (Bing, 2017). It appears there is no longer any detectable difference between wartime and peacetime information management in China, as informationalization is now all about expanding the political power of the leadership. At the same time, any flow of unauthorized information is seen as a national security threat, and China's leadership may well perceive itself to be in a constant wartime environment.

What began in the 1980s as an effort to enable the PLA to move from a loosely connected body of soldiers on the ground now extends to outer space, the electromagnetic spectrum, and the information domain. Today China is still assumed to remain behind US capabilities and is therefore improving training and domestic innovation to achieve its cyber capability development goals (Pomerleau, 2017b). It has openly appreciated the effectiveness of information and cyber warfare in recent conflicts and is continuing to make further significant investments in a more "informationalized" military. Its officially disclosed defence budget has increased on average by 8.5 per cent during the 2007–17 period, though the steady increases fell during the pandemic, due to China's economic downturn (DOD, 2017). China's focus, though, has shifted away from a primary focus on domestic interests to more global ones. Accordingly, its military modernization program has become more intent on supporting missions beyond China's periphery, including power projection through information warfare. The opening of China's first overseas military base in Djibouti is testament to the country's new ambitions (Lendon & George, 2017). There can be no doubt that China has placed a growing emphasis on cyber and information warfare, pursuits for which it is streamlining its forces (O'Connor, 2017).

China has been learning from Russia's 2014 annexation of Crimea and the reaction of the international community. Chinese policy seems to have moved away from opposing any sovereignty movements (such as in Tibet) to caring less about the perceptions of the international community and in many cases simply adopting Russian narratives and approaches (Saalman, 2016). China subscribes to the Russian treatment of the Ukraine crisis as a "great power competition" between Washington and Moscow (Saalman, 2016). China's tactics more and more seem informed by some of Russia's while often further developing them (Saalman, 2016).

HOW ARE NON-STATE ACTORS AND PROXIES USED?

In China, as in Russia, the aim of the country's leadership is to "weaponize" the whole society, both covertly and overtly. Besides the openly involved state actors like state media or individual government officials, unofficial media is forced to abide by the same strict rules regarding the handling of information and what can be published ("Complete list of blocked websites," 2021; DFRLab, 2020). Through the trust system, citizens are forced to police other citizens or face dire consequences. As such, there is hardly any meaningful differentiation between state and non-state actors among the population at large, though actual adherence to the rules varies significantly. Corruption is very widespread in all levels of society. In China, similar to Russia, there is a clear implementation of the weaponization of society, from schools to the arts, media, architecture, and science. The PLA directs, manages, or guides political, military, academic, media, and intelligence assets that either overtly or covertly serve as agents of influence of the Chinese government (Anand, 2006).

There are many examples of how China uses proxies. The PLA even uses engagements with foreign militaries in order to enhance its presence and influence abroad, to bolster its image, assuage other countries' concerns about its rise, and to communicate its positions to foreign audiences (DOD, 2017).

A more direct example of China's exploitation of proxies is its manipulation of media and journalists. Official media sources in China are considered by the public to be experts on the position of the state and in manipulating public opinion (Cheng, 2016). But non-official media is thought to report slightly more from the perspective of the public and in a less biased way (Stockman, 2011). Actually, though, the so-called non-official media is only slightly less official as it acts under almost all of the same rules with only slightly more relaxed restrictions (Cheng, 2016). China's government uses unofficial media to disseminate propaganda from seemingly non-state sources. As a result, in 2021 Reporters without Borders ranked China 177 out of 180 countries for press freedom, and in 2017 it called China the "world's leading prison for citizen journalists" (Reporters without Borders, 2021a). There is no longer any independent commercial or private media in China today (Cheng, 2016). China is also aggressively exporting its state media networks, particularly to Africa, Southeast Asia, and eastern Europe, and in this sense very much follows the Russian model of exporting RT (formerly Russia Today) and its global, multilingual apparatus (Mwakideu, 2021; Sui, 2019).

The CCP's Central Propaganda Department (CPD) exercises close oversight of all Chinese media (including cultural products). The CPD regularly issues directives on news topics, dictating which topics should and should not be covered, and which specific perspectives should be allowed, encouraged, or forbidden (McGregor, 2010). These directives come with the threat of punishment, including fines, job dismissal, jail time, or even the closure of entire news outlet. Also, any interviews with experts must be approved by both the work unit leadership and the CPD. Not only are certain stories forbidden; if incidents are intended to be covered up, stories to divert attention are suggested and encouraged (Murphy, 2011). Foreign journalists are also used—even against their will—as proxies. Journalists, as part of their "professional conduct," are not allowed to speak about any kind of information, source material, or news product (Foreign Correspondents Club of China, 2014). Any foreign journalist interviewing a Chinese journalist must either report the chosen narratives of the Chinese government or risk harming their Chinese colleague. Chinese journalists are generally not allowed to participate in any professional exchanges or co-operate in any form with foreign media. Even Chinese citizens who work for foreign media organizations are regularly harassed or arrested (Kockritz, 2015).

The Chinese government goes even further, forcing foreign journalists to report according to its agenda. To begin with, only a small number of foreign journalists are allowed to work in China (Foreign Correspondents Club of China, 2014). They are granted permission only after a very lengthy and strenuous process that effectively chills any desire to risk gaining the attention of the authorities. If a foreign journalist nevertheless publishes stories critical of the Chinese government, visas are no longer issued to journalists from that organization. For this reason, Bloomberg and the *New York Times* can no longer report from inside China. Imagine a foreign journalist, who may have had to learn Mandarin for many years, considering such critical coverage while contemplating the fact that they will subsequently never be able to work in China again. The chilling effect is obvious—as is the likely desire to maintain a good relationship with Chinese authorities—and this again enables potential proxy relationships. Furthermore, journalists applying for a visa to report on a specific story face the same challenges as they have to be invited by a China-based organization. This process effectively makes hosts responsible for the reporting of their foreign invitees and assures that visiting journalists refrain from reporting on any other topics during their stay (Cheng, 2016).

CNO grant funding is a good example of the blurred line separating the state and non-state actors with whom the Chinese government works. Government grant programs to support CNO-related research (offensive and defensive) aim at commercial IT companies as well as civilian and military universities. As Krekel et al. (2012) show, a review of PRC university technical programs, curricula, research foci, and funding for research and development in areas contributing to information warfare capabilities illustrates the breadth and complexity of the relationships between the universities, government and military organizations, and commercial high-tech industries countrywide.

In civilian academia, the government has created at least five national grant programs for information warfare research, and at the same time has also funded the PLA's informationalization programs. Fifty civilian universities conducting information security research benefit from one or more national-level grant programs, reflecting a broad technology-development plan. There is considerable debate as to the extent and effectiveness of China's influence over foreign academic institutions, particularly when those institutions become accustomed to the funding provided by the Chinese government (Krekel et al., 2012).

The PLA relies strongly on China's commercial IT sector for research and development (R&D) of dual-use and military-grade micro-electronics and telecommunications. Rather than isolate certain state-owned IT firms as exclusively "defence" in orientation, the PLA, often operating through its extensive base of R&D institutes, alternately collaborates with China's civilian IT companies and universities and benefits as a customer of nominally civilian products and R&D. The military benefits from this arrangement because it receives access to cutting-edge research. This work is often carried out by Chinese commercial firms with legitimate foreign partners supplying critical technology and often sharing the cost of the R&D (Krekel et al., 2012).

This enables the state to enjoy the latest commercial off-the-shelf telecommunications technology available through China's access to foreign joint ventures and international markets. The close relationship between some of China's—and the world's—largest telecommunications hardware manufacturers creates a potential vector for state-sponsored or state-directed penetration of international supply chains for micro-electronics (USCC Research Staff, 2011).

This has played out in the debate over Huawei's development of 5G networks, or the outright banning of Huawei's involvement in joint ventures in several countries, such as Japan, the United Kingdom, and Australia (Panettieri, 2021).

What Effect Has Been Achieved in Operations?

Domestically, the government has succeeded in eradicating any truly independent media in China. It is increasingly difficult for Chinese citizens to access "unauthorized" information—from either domestic or foreign sources. However, at least up until the recent blocking of the use of VPNs (virtual private networks), Chinese citizens have been very creatively circumventing government censorship by, for example, reading foreign media. So as to have debates on issues that are censored, citizens use code words that are very difficult for the government to censor.

After the death of Nobel laureate and famous dissident Liu Xiaobo of cancer in a state prison (due to the government's denial of medical treatment), his name became a targeted keyword, and Weibo blocked all mentions of him since 13 July 2017 (Si, 2017). Simultaneously, the "RIP" abbreviation, and even the candle emoticon, were blocked (Hernandez, 2017). Instead, citizens used the image of an empty chair, or simply the years of Liu's lifespan (1955–2017), to reference the dissident. He was also referred to by way of the phrase "someone died today," while others referred to the thunder and lightning storms that day in Beijing as a sign of "heavenly disquiet" (Mitchel et al., 2017). So while the Chinese government manages to control most communication, it is far from able to silence all dissenters in China or effectively block out ideas from other cultures.

Netizens posting videos and other content describing the most deplorable conditions in Chinese hospitals at the beginning of the pandemic represent further examples of dissidents circumventing the PRC's influence efforts (Ruan et al., 2022). The sheer number of code words and euphemisms that exist for sensitive content make it impossible for the government to achieve full censorship (Si, 2017)—unless it wishes to ban every image of a chair. It appears also that China's sensors are starting to realize, at least to some extent, that full censorship is not possible (nor particularly desirable). China's digital firewall, known as the "Golden Shield," was created to "protect" the Chinese population from the influence of unauthorized information from external and internal actors (Cheng, 2016). It appears, though—despite its efforts to drastically reduce what the general public can access—that the government is always a few steps behind when it comes to patching holes that have been found and exploited by citizens interested in real information. With some effort, it is still possible to access independent information in China. It is, however, increasingly difficult to do so—particularly without being noticed by the authorities.

China has undoubtedly succeeded in infiltrating the computer systems of foreign governments around the world to extract information from diplomats or members of the economic or defence industries. They have also successfully targeted defence contractors and succeeded in stealing proprietary information, such as plans of for high-tech military systems such as aircraft (Pomerleau, 2017b).

One of the most prominent Chinese successes in this regard was the 2015 hack of the US Office of Personnel Management database, which saw the personal data of over 22 million federal employees breached (Nakashima, 2015). This hack included the fingerprints of 5.6 million US federal employees, enabling unprecedented exploitation of personal information (Associated Press, 2015). China is clearly capable of penetrating the computers that control vital national and military infrastructure, reconnoitering them electronically, and mapping or targeting nodes in the systems for future penetration or attack and planting malicious code to facilitate future entry (Wortzel, 2014).

China has also been successful in using its economic strength to inject itself into Western media, providing the ability to directly influence Western information dissemination and thereby influence foreign government decision making. The Chinese government has purchased telecoms, media companies, movie production companies, and even video game companies, which can all be used to disseminate Chinese propaganda through Western organizations. China can effectively diminish the impact of films that it deems to be counter to its interests, such as those portraying China as an aggressor or glorifying protest and civil disobedience. Ownership of distribution and production capabilities gives China increased influence on what Western audiences see. These acquisitions not only lead to heightened Chinese influence but also to the degradation of Western interests through the production and dissemination of hostile propaganda by (for example) Hollywood companies.

In the field of video games, China has succeeded in acquiring Riot Games, Epic Games, and Cryptic Studios. Similar to movies, video games can be designed to propagate desired messages. The positive treatment of China in virtual combat settings or the incorporation of Chinese mythology into a game's narrative could make effective use of high-end technology for perception management (Tromblay, 2017).

China has also succeeded—at least initially—in forcing a highly reputable publishing house, Cambridge University Press, to remove from its Chinese website 315 articles from *China Quarterly*, a journal published by Cambridge (Link, 2017). Immediate and extensive protest from Western academics led Cambridge to reverse its decision. China's response to this decision was very telling; speaking through the state-controlled daily paper the *Global Times*, the government offered the following rejoinder:

> It's no big deal if a few barely-read *China Quarterly* articles cannot be found on China's Internet. The real issue is that the fundamental principles of the two sides are in conflict, and the

> question is: Whose principles are a better fit for today's world? This is not a matter of "each to his or her own"; it is a contest of strength. In the end time will tell who's right and who's wrong. ("China Quarterly debate," 2017)

China sees itself in a contest for information dominance—no longer just domestically, but globally as well.

The Evolution of China's COVID-19 Exploitation

From the very beginning of the pandemic, China began spreading disinformation related to the virus. As early as 31 December 2019, Chinese government officials tried to deflect attention from reports on the origin of the virus and aimed to cast doubt on claims that the source of infection was in China (Kinetz, 2021). After facing increasing criticism and scrutiny for China's response to the virus, the country's officials took the lead in spreading disinformation related to the virus. Since the beginning of the pandemic China has been the single largest state actor spreading COVID-19-related disinformation targeting Western audiences. However, the forms, style, quantity, and targeting of such messaging has evolved since the beginning of the pandemic.

Initially, the main focus of narratives spread by China were directed at creating a positive image of the country, depicting as decisive in its actions against the virus and competent in meeting the challenge presented by the emerging pandemic (DFRLab, 2020). Positive events in the PRC's dealing with the virus where also exploited for propaganda to improve China's overall image domestically and abroad ("SARS hero follows leads," 2020). This initial messaging was basically an adaption of the main pre-pandemic focus of Chinese state propaganda, which aimed to establish a highly favourable image of the country while distracting from commentary critical of the Chinese government. While some messaging initially was directed at casting doubt as to the origin of the virus, as well as distracting from growing criticism of the country's handling of the pubic health crisis, the majority represented a continuation of information operations strategies already in use, such as downplaying, undermining, and/or discrediting any narratives that seemed undesirable to the PRC's leadership. Also, when positive messaging did not seem sufficient to cover up or distract from undesired foreign criticism, PRC messaging aimed at diminishing the credibility of China's geopolitical rivals (DFRLab, 2020).

As reports about the virus became more widespread, PRC officials aimed at suppressing reports of outbreaks of the virus, which led also to large-scale muzzling of data reporting (to the World Health Organization and to inquisitive news media), and even the arrest of whistle-blowers and doctors reporting on cases of illness related to the virus.

While PRC broadcasting originally confirmed the Wuhan's Huanan Seafood Market as the place at which the virus first emerged (Pan, 2020), the main messaging soon shifted to spreading disinformation about this question (DFRLab, 2020). At the same time vast censorship efforts were introduced aiming at deleting any online content that contained keywords relating to the outbreak—particularly after doctors tried to warn the public about the then unknown virus. For example, WeChat broadly censored coronavirus-related content, including criticism of the government, rumours and speculative information on the epidemic that were deemed undesirable, and even neutral references to the Chinese government's handling the outbreak (Ruan et al., 2022). The key focus of messaging and censorship campaigns became the control of available social media content in China relating to the virus (Crete-Nishihata et al., 2020).

Messaging subsequently focused on how the West was weaponizing COVID rumours to harm China (Shi, 2020). At the same time, rumours were deliberately spread by PRC sources to deflect from undesirable information that showed, for example, the deficiencies in the PRC's pandemic response (DFRLab, 2020). Social media posts by Chinese officials at this time raised doubts about the effectiveness of the vaccines then being developed by Western-based multinational pharmaceutical companies (Shi, 2020).

PRC officials then tried to claim that independent, established sources form other countries had also identified that the United States was behind the virus. In February 2020 the *People's Daily* claimed that a "Japanese TV report sparks speculations in China that COVID-19 may have originated in US" ("Japanese TV report," 2020). Additionally, PRC sources started to disseminate the narrative that COVID was actually a bio-weapon (DFRLab, 2020). In March 2020, messaging claiming that the outbreak could have originated in the United States was being widely distributed. In much larger numbers than before, content was posted to Western social media sites by China's Foreign Ministry officials and China's foreign diplomatic mission staff. Many such posts subsequently directly asked for readers to share the original posts (Zhao, 2020).

Chinese sources started posting on Western social media more aggressively—even though these platforms were blocked in China, as was the case, for example, with Twitter[3]—trying to more effectively target Western audiences. On Twitter, China's official diplomatic user accounts more than tripled from May 2019 to May 2020, going from 40 to 135 in just one year. Narrative production doubled and turned more aggressive and conspiratorial as well (Watts, 2020). These narratives started to target US audiences directly—for example, by claiming that the "CDC was caught on the spot" and that the US Army had brought the epidemic to Wuhan (Zhao, 2020).

Chinese narratives then started to become more specific in claiming a US origin for the virus. Chinese sources even went as far as to claim that COVID was imported to China through a batch of lobsters from Maine (Solon et al., 2021).

Tying into pre-existing conspiracy theories, social media posts connected to China's government started claiming that COVID originated in Fort Detrick, in the US state of Maryland, before it was spread to China by the US military. Between May and October 2021, over a thousand tweets, videos, and articles linked to Chinese accounts claimed that Fort Detrick was the origin of the virus (Aghekyan & Shafter, 2021).

Google News searches for "Fort Detrick" in August and September of 2021 were dominated by Chinese sources. Conspiracy theory narratives related to Fort Detrick reached a peak in August 2021, when they dominated even Google's Top Stories feature as well as Bing News results, with the *Global Times* and the *China Daily* appearing in the top results (Aghekyan & Shafter, 2021). At the same time, four of the six top videos on YouTube in searches for "Fort Detrick" came from Chinese media channels, while the remaining two also promoted Beijing-friendly talking points. In a further attempt to claim that other countries were responsible COVID, in 2022 China spread narratives on social media claiming that Beijing's first Omicron case came to China from Canada (Tunney, 2022).

This domination of news feeds and search engine results hints at the extent to which China had increased its narrative output, as well as its focus on spreading content targeted at Western audiences—a markable difference in output and target audience from the beginning of the pandemic. The following six trends can be observed in China's evolution of COVID exploitation in the information space.

From Defence to Offense

Messaging related to COVID has evolved from defensive posts covering up and distracting from the deficiencies and inhuman measures employed in the PRC's COVID response to offensive narratives aggressively claiming in large, international information campaigns that the United States is responsible for the origin of the outbreak.

NON-SPECIFIC TO SPECIFIC

Initial narratives spread by China were often not specific in their claims. The goal was initially to crowd out undesirable information and generally post content that made China appear in a positive light. Over time, the posting intentionally grew more specific, such as when the virus was claimed to have originated in the United States, rather than just raising doubt about reports indicating China as the origin. More recently, Chinese sources claim to have identified the exact location in the United States at which the virus was produced, and even that it was allegedly imported to China via a delivery of Maine lobsters.

VAGUE TO AGGRESSIVE

Initial posts where comparatively vague in their claims, often merely casting doubt on unfavourable reporting. Following the declaration of a global pandemic by the World Health Organization, China's messaging became increasingly aggressive toward Western actors (the United States in particular), even demanding information from US authorities based on nothing more than claims from conspiracy theories.

LOW TO HIGH OUTPUT

The sheer volume of messaging related to COVID increased significantly over the course of the pandemic. Both due to the proliferation of international criticism of China's handling of the virus and because COVID dominated the attention of audiences, which opened up opportunities for exploitation related to other messaging agendas.

INCREASED OUTPUT IN WESTERN SOCIAL MEDIA OUTLETS

While social media posts were initially directed primarily at domestic audiences in China, the PRC's messaging soon started to target Western audiences more directly. Increasingly, Western media outlets were targeted—for example, via posts in the online comment sections of the BBC, the *Washington Post*, and other major news outlets, as well as on Western social media.

Overall, based on the above examples, China's exploitation of COVID in the information space can be described as evolving in the following general directions: from a limited quantity of defensive, unspecific, rather vague posts primarily directed at domestic audiences via local sources to strategic, very specific and aggressive messaging targeting Western audiences through Western social media outlets.

INCREASED CO-OPERATION WITH RUSSIA ON DISINFORMATION CAMPAIGNS

In the early phases of China's COVID exploitation in the information space there was little evidence of co-operation between China and Russia on disinformation campaigns. During the later phases of China's COVID information exploitation efforts, however, this changed, with the two countries showing an increasing level of co-operation in the dissemination of similar narratives and circular disinformation amplification becoming more common (Lucas et al., 2022). China and Russia started co-operating on multiplying the effects of their COVID disinformation campaigns by coordinating the distribution of narratives claiming that COVID is a biological weapon created in the United States and that China and Russia are responding more effectively to the pandemic (Jozwiak, 2020). This trend continues in other contexts today as China openly backs other Russian positions, such as narratives related to Russia's February 2022 invasion of Ukraine. Both actors co-operate on information space exploitation more than ever (Standish, 2023). Increasingly there is now evidence for the formation of a disinformation alliance between China and Russia (Bandurski, 2022).

Conclusion

This chapter asked how China's messaging related to COVID has evolved during the pandemic. After describing the role of information in the recent development of the political system in China, and the regime's general information warfare capabilities, the chapter described six trends that can be observed in the evolution of China's COVID information space exploitation. A transformation can be observed from a limited quantity of defensive, unspecific, rather vague posts, primarily directed at domestic audiences via local sources, to strategic, widespread, very specific and aggressive messaging targeting Western audiences through Western social media outlets. Finally, we have observed the emergence of a disinformation alliance with Russia. For more definitive conclusions these observations will need to be substantiated with much larger research projects that can process a far greater volume of PRC-influenced posts.

While domestic narrative distribution did lead to substantial effects in China, where many citizens have been convinced that there is little merit to Western criticism of the PRC's dealing with the virus, internationally the impact is different. Despite mass messaging on alleged Chinese successes in dealing with the virus, and China's influence growing in some regions, like the Gulf, during the pandemic (Gurol-Haller & Saggar, 2023), few among these messages' Western audience seem convinced (Pierson, 2023; "Wuhan lab leak theory," 2021). Instead, it appears that despite the increasing output and sophistication of such messages, and the more direct targeting through Western media outlets and social media, Western audiences remain largely skeptical of China's handling of the virus and seem not to have been convinced by PRC online influence campaigns. This impression has not changed with China's declaration of a "decisive victory" over COVID in February 2023. While China claims to have created "a miracle in the history of human civilization," having had the lowest COVID death rate in the world (Hawkins, 2023), many countries, as well as the World Health Organization (Rigby & Tétrault-Farber, 2023), instead believe that Chinese leaders have been under-reporting the country's COVID deaths (Orr & Munroe, 2023), and that they have exploited the COVID response to accumulate power and increasingly establish a totalitarian political infrastructure in China (Xuecun, 2023).

NOTES

1. In research debates, there is no clear agreement on which of these seven components belong to IW, or if it even makes sense to separate some of them as they have impacts in most of the other areas. This selection is based largely on China-specific perceptions of IW based on the work of Vinod Anand (2006, 2014).
2. As can be seen in the list of examples, the means of delivery have evolved since 2006 but the strategies remain mostly consistent.
3. Twitter is "officially" banned in China but is widely consumed in China via VPN access. Algorithm-based content filters are, however, used in China to prevent the trending of certain words, phrases, or hashtags, or to block access to prohibited content.

REFERENCES

Aghekyan, E., & Shafter, B. (2021). *Deep in the data void: China's COVID-19 disinformation dominates search engine results*. German Marshall Fund of the United States. https://securingdemocracy.gmfus.org/data-void-china-covid-disinformation

Anand, V. (2006). Chinese concepts and capabilities of information warfare. *Strategic Analysis, 30*(4), 781–97.

Anand, V. (2014, 21 April). PLA's information warfare capabilities on an upward trajectory. *Vivekananda International Foundation*. https://www.vifindia.org/print/2123

Associated Press. (2015, 23 September). US government hack stole fingerprints of 5.6 million federal employees. *The Guardian*. https://www.theguardian.com/technology/2015/sep/23/us-government-hack-stole-fingerprints

Bandurski, D. (2022, 11 March). China and Russia are joining forces to spread disinformation. *Brookings Institution*. https://www.brookings.edu/techstream/china-and-russia-are-joining-forces-to-spread-disinformation/

Bing, C. (2017, 22 June). How China's cyber command is being built to supersede its US military counterpart. *Cyberscoop*. https://www.cyberscoop.com/china-ssf-cyber-command-strategic-support-force-pla-nsa-dod/

Bronskill, J., & Bryden, J. (2021, 23 June). Feds ask court to keep documents related to scientists' firing under wraps. *CTV News*. https://winnipeg.ctvnews.ca/feds-ask-court-to-keep-documents-related-to-scientists-firing-under-wraps-1.5482962

Cadell, C. (2017, 11 August). China investigates top local social media sites in push to control content. *Reuters*. https://www.reuters.com/article/us-china-cyber/china-investigates-top-local-social-media-sites-in-push-to-control-content-idUSKBN1AR07K

Chan, K., & Thornton, M. (2022, 19 September). China's changing disinformation and propaganda targeting Taiwan. *The Diplomat*. https://thediplomat.com/2022/09/chinas-changing-disinformation-and-propaganda-targeting-taiwan/

Cheng, D. (2016). *Cyber dragon: Inside China's information warfare and cyber operations*. Praeger.

Cheng, D. (2021). An overview of Chinese thinking about deterrence. In F. Osinga & T. Sweijs (Eds.), *NL ARMS Netherlands annual review of military studies 2020* (pp. 177–200). Asser Press. https://doi.org/10.1007/978-94-6265-419-8_10

China Quarterly debate a matter of principle. (2017, 20 August). *Global Times*. Retrieved 31 August 2017 from http://www.globaltimes.cn/content/1062304.shtml

The complete list of blocked websites in China & how to access them. (2021, 19 October). *VPNMentor.com*. https://www.vpnmentor.com/blog/the-complete-list-of-blocked-websites-in-china-how-to-access-them/

Costello, J. (2016). *The Strategic Support Force: Update and overview*. Jamestown Foundation. https://jamestown.org/program/strategic-support-force-update-overview/

Crete-Nishihata, M., Dalek, J., Knockel, J., Lawford, N., Wesley, C., & Zhou, M. (2020, 25 August). *Censored contagion II: A timeline of information control on Chinese social media during COVID-19.* Citizen Lab. https://citizenlab.ca/2020/08/censored-contagion-ii-a-timeline-of-information-control-on-chinese-social-media-during-covid-19/

DFRLab (Digital Forensic Research Lab). (2020). *Countering Chinese disinformation reports.* Atlantic Council. https://www.atlanticcouncil.org/in-depth-research-reports/dfrlab-china-reports

DOD (Department of Defense). (2017, May 15). *Annual report to Congress: Military and security developments involving the People's Republic of China.* Office of the Secretary of Defense.

Ellis, S. (2020, 7 October). Here's what could happen if China invaded Taiwan. *Bloomberg.* https://www.bloomberg.com/news/features/2020-10-07/here-s-what-could-happen-if-china-invaded-taiwan

Foreign Correspondents Club of China. (2014, 12 September). *Position paper on working conditions for foreign journalists.* fccchina.org/2014/09/12/fccc-position-paper-2014/

Gurol-Haller, J., & Saggar, R. (2023, 17 April). China's renewed influence in the Gulf. *Chatham House.* https://www.chathamhouse.org/2023/04/chinas-renewed-influence-gulf

Harold, S. W., Beauchamp-Mustafaga, N., & Hornung J. F. (2021). *Chinese disinformation efforts on social media.* RAND Corporation. https://www.rand.org/content/dam/rand/pubs/research_reports/RR4300/RR4373z3/RAND_RR4373z3.pdf

Hawkins, A. (2023, 17 February). China claims "decisive victory" over Covid amid doubt over figures. *The Guardian.* https://www.theguardian.com/world/2023/feb/17/china-victory-covid-deaths-virus

Hearing on China and US national security. (2021, 4 August). C-Span. https://www.c-span.org/video/?513854-1/hearing-china-us-national-security

Hernandez, J. C. (2017, 14 July). Chinese citizens evade internet censors to remember Liu Xoabo. *New York Times.* https://www.nytimes.com/2017/07/14/world/asia/china-liu-xiaobo-censorship-internet.html?mcubz=3

Japanese TV report sparks speculations in China that COVID-19 may have originated in US. (2020, 23 February). *People's Daily.* http://en.people.cn/n3/2020/0223/c90000-9661026.html

Jozwiak, R. (2020, 22 April). EU monitors see coordinated COVID-19 disinformation effort by Iran, Russia, China. *Radio Free Europe/Radio Liberty.* https://www.rferl.org/a/eu-monitors-sees-coordinated-covid-19-disinformation-effort-by-iran-russia-china/30570938.html

Karásková, I. (2020, 13 November). China's evolving approach to media influence: The case of Czechia. *The Diplomat.* https://thediplomat.com/2020/11/chinas-evolving-approach-to-media-influence-the-case-of-czechia/

Kinetz, E. (2021, 15 February). Anatomy of a conspiracy: With COVID, China took a leading role. *AP News*. https://apnews.com/article/pandemics-beijing-only-on-ap-epidemics-media-122b73e134b780919cc1808f3f6f16e8

Kockritz, A. (2015, 14 January). They have Miao. *Die Zeit*. https://www.zeit.de/feature/freedom-of-press-china-zhang-miao-imprisonment?utm_referrer=https%3A%2F%2Fwww.google.com%2F

Krekel, B., Adams, P., & Bakos, G. (2012, March). *Occupying the information high ground: Chinese capabilities for computer network operations and cyber espionage*. US-China Economic and Security Review Commission. https://info.publicintelligence.net/USCC-ChinaCyberEspionage.pdf

Lendon, B., & George, S. (2017, 13 July). China sends troops to Djibouti, establishes first overseas military base. *CNN*. http://edition.cnn.com/2017/07/12/asia/china-djibouti-military-base/index.html

Link, P. (2017, 5 September). Beijing's bold new censorship. *New York Review of Books*. http://www.nybooks.com/daily/2017/09/05/beijings-bold-new-censorship/

Lovelace, D. (2015). *The cyber threat*. Oxford University Press.

Lucas, E., Dubow, B., Lamond, J., Morris, J., Rebegea, C., & Zakem, V. (2022). Post-mortem: Russian and Chinese COVID-19 information operations. *Centre for European Policy Analysis*. https://cepa.org/comprehensive-reports/post-mortem-russian-and-chinese-covid-19-information-operations/

McGregor, R. (2010). *The Party: The secret world of China's Communist rulers*. Harper.

Mitchel, T., Wildau, G., & Feng, E. (2017, 14 July). China online censors rush to erase Liu Xiaobo tributes. *Financial Times*. https://www.ft.com/content/b6d56066-6847-11e7-8526-7b38dcaef614

Murphy, Z. (2011, 28 July). China struggles to censor train crash coverage. *BBC News*. http://www.bbc.com/news/world-asia-pacific-14321787

Mwakideu, C. (2021, 29 January). Experts warn of China's growing media influence in Africa. *Deutsche Welle*. https://www.dw.com/en/experts-warn-of-chinas-growing-media-influence-in-africa/a-56385420

Nakashima, E. (2015, 2 December). Chinese government has arrested hackers it says breached OPM database. *Washington Post*. https://www.washingtonpost.com/world/national-security/chinese-government-has-arrested-hackers-suspected-of-breaching-opm-database/2015/12/02/0295b918-990c-11e5-8917-653b65c809eb_story.html?utm_term
=.3bb698ba57ee

O'Connor, T. (2017, 19 April). Chinese military prepares for new cyber focus, streamlined force. *Newsweek*. http://www.newsweek.com/chinese-military-prepares-massive-changes-new-cyber-division-586313

Office of the Director of US National Intelligence (2021, 9 April). *Annual threat assessment of the US intelligence community*. https://www.dni.gov/index.php/newsroom/reports-publications/reports-publications-2021/item/2204-2021-annual-threat-assessment-of-the-u-s-intelligence-community.

Orr, B., & Munroe, T. (2023, 16 February). China declares "decisive victory" over COVID-19. *Reuters*. https://www.reuters.com/world/china/china-declares-decisive-victory-over-covid-19-2023-02-17/

Pan, Z. (2020, 27 January). Experts confirm Wuhan seafood market was source of novel coronavirus. *CGTN*. https://news.cgtn.com/news/2020-01-27/Experts-confirm-Wuhan-seafood-market-was-source-of-novel-coronavirus--NAHPUtsPgA/index.html

Panettieri, J. (2021, 11 November). Huawei: Banned and permitted in which countries? List and FAQ. *Channel E2E*. https://www.channele2e.com/business/enterprise/huawei-banned-in-which-countries/

Pierson, D. (2023, 27 February). China dismisses latest claim that lab leak likely caused Covid. *New York Times*. https://www.nytimes.com/2023/02/27/world/asia/china-react-covid-lab-leak.html

Pollpeter, K., Chase, M., & Heginbotham, E. (2016, 2 May). *In with the old, out with the new? The creation of the Strategic Support Force and its implications for Chinese military space operations*. RAND Corporation. https://www.rand.org/paf/casi/research-topics.html

Pomerleau, M. (2017a, 22 March). Breaking down China's electronic warfare tactics. *C4ISRNET*. https://www.c4isrnet.com/c2-comms/2017/03/22/breaking-down-chinas-electronic-warfare-tactics/

Pomerleau, M. (2017b, 7 June). DoD's assessment of China's information capabilities. *C4ISRNET*. https://www.c4isrnet.com/2017/06/07/dod-s-assessment-of-china-s-information-capabilities/

Pomerleau, M. (2020, 1 September). China moves toward new "intelligentized" approach to warfare, says Pentagon. *C4ISRNET*. https://www.c4isrnet.com/battlefield-tech/2020/09/01/china-moves-toward-new-intelligentized-approach-to-warfare-says-pentagon/

Quing, K. G., & Schiffman, J. (2015, 2 November). Beijing's covert radio network airs China-friendly news across Washington, and the world. *Reuters*. http://www.reuters.com/investigates/special-report/china-radio/

Raska, M. (2015, December). China and the three warfares. *The Diplomat*. http://thediplomat.com/2015/12/hybrid-warfare-with-chinese-characteristics-2/

Reporters without Borders. (2021, 28 June). At least 22 newspapers "murdered" in the past five years. *RSF.org*. https://rsf.org/en/news/least-22-newspapers-murdered-past-five-years

Reporters without Borders. (2021). 2021 world press freedom index. *RSF.org*. https://rsf.org/en/ranking

Rigby, J., & Tétrault-Farber, G. (2023, 4 January). WHO says China data underrepresents COVID surge and deaths. *Reuters*. https://www.reuters.com/world/china/whos-tedros-concerned-by-china-covid-surge-calls-again-data-2023-01-04/

Romo, V. (2021, 24 March). Chinese hackers made fake Facebook profiles, apps to spy on Uyghur activists. *NPR*. https://www.npr.org/2021/03/24/981021257/chinese-hackers-made-fake-facebook-profiles-apps-to-spy-on-uyghur-activists.

Ruan, L., Knockel, J., & Crete-Nishihata, M. (2020, 3 March). *Censored contagion: How information on the coronavirus is managed on Chinese social media*. Citizen Lab. https://citizenlab.ca/2020/03/censored-contagion-how-information-on-the-coronavirus-is-managed-on-chinese-social-media/

Ruwitch, J. (2021, 28 October). Would the U.S. defend Taiwan if China invades? Biden said yes. But it's complicated. *NPR*. https://www.npr.org/2021/10/28/1048513474/biden-us-taiwan-china

Saalman, L. (2016). Little grey men: China and the Ukraine crisis. *Survival, 58*(6), 135–56.

Sabbagh, D. (2021, 23 September). Experts say China's low-level cyberwar is becoming severe threat. *The Guardian*. https://www.theguardian.com/world/2021/sep/23/experts-china-low-level-cyber-war-severe-threat

Sahay, R. K. (2016). *History of China's military*. Alpha Edition.

SARS hero follows leads on illness. (2020, 23 January). *China Daily*. http://en.people.cn/n3/2020/0123/c90000-9651455.html

Shaffer, L. (2017, 7 August). Pro-Beijing professor expelled from Singapore for being "agent" of foreign power. *CNBC*. https://www.cnbc.com/2017/08/07/pro-beijing-professor-expelled-from-singapore-for-being-agent-of-foreign-power.html

Shi, T. (2020, 18 February). Some in West weaponize rumors to attack China. *Global Times*. https://www.globaltimes.cn/content/1180041.shtml

Si, J. (2017, 21 July). *The Chinese language as a weapon: How China's netizens fight censorship*. Berkman Klein Center. https://medium.com/berkman-klein-center/the-chinese-language-as-a-weapon-how-chinas-netizens-fight-censorship-8389516ed1a6

Sobiesk, E. (2003, 1 March). *Redefining the role of information warfare in Chinese strategy*. SANS Institute. https://www.sans.org/white-papers/896/

Solon, O., Simmons, K., & Perrette, A. (2021, 21 October). China-linked disinformation campaign blames Covid on Maine lobsters. *NBC News*. https://www.nbcnews.com/news/china-linked-disinformation-campaign-blames-covid-maine-lobsters-rcna3236

Spade, J. (2012). *Information as power: China's cyber power and America's national security*. US Army War College.

Standish, R. (2023, 6 March). Disinformation wars: China, Russia, cooperating on propaganda more than ever, says report. *Radio Free Europe/Radio Liberty*. https://www.rferl.org/a/china-russia-cooperation-propaganda-marshall-fund/32305566.html

State Council Information Office. (2002). *Tenth five year plan for national economic and social development, informationalization key point special plan*. People's Republic of China. http://www.cia.org.cn/information/information_01_xxhgh_3.htm

Stokes, M. A., Lin, J., & Hsiao, R. L. C. (2011, 11 November). The Chinese People's Liberation Army signal intelligence and cyber reconnaissance infrastructure. *Project2049.net*. https://project2049.net/.../pla_third_department_sigint_cyber_stokes_lin_hsiao.pdf

Sui, C. (2019, 1 November). China wants state media to peddle its "soft power" in Africa, but tech platforms are a better bet. *Quartz Africa*. https://qz.com/africa/1736534/china-daily-cgtn-fight-for-influence-in-africa-vs-bbc-cnn

Swanson, A. (2016, 24 September). China's influence over Hollywood grows. *Washington Post*. https://www.washingtonpost.com/news/wonk/wp/2016/09/24/chinas-influence-over-hollywood-grows/?utm_term=.56d914bac548

Tromblay, D. E. (2017, 22 May). No more fun and games: How China's acquisition of U.S. media entities threatens America's national security. *Small Wars Journal*. https://smallwarsjournal.com/jrnl/art/no-more-fun-and-games-how-china%E2%80%99s-acquisition-of-us-media-entities-threatens-america%E2%80%99s-nati

Tsang, S. (2010). *If China attacks Taiwan: Military strategy, politics and economics*. Oxford University Press.

Tunney, C. (2022, 17 January). Doctors say claim that Beijing's 1st Omicron case came from Canada isn't based on science. *CBC News*. https://www.cbc.ca/news/politics/china-allegations-mail-1.6318115

USCC Research Staff (2011, January). *The national security implications of investments and products from the People's Republic of China in the telecommunications sector*. US-China Economic Security Review Commission.

Ventre, D. (2014). *Chinese cybersecurity and defense*. Wiley.

Ventre, D. (2016). *Information warfare*. Wiley.

Watts, C. (2020, 15 May). *Triad of disinformation: How Russia, Iran, & China ally in a messaging war against America*. Alliance for Securing Democracy. https://securingdemocracy.gmfus.org/triad-of- disinformation-how-russia-iran-china-ally-in-a-messaging-war-against-america/

Wortzel, L. (2010, 10 March). China's approach to cyber operations: Implications for the United States [Testimony]. *US House of Representatives Committee on Foreign Affairs*. https://www.uscc.gov/sites/default/files/Congressional_Testimonies/LarryWortzeltestimony-March2010.pdf

Wortzel, L. (2014, March). *The Chinese People's Liberation Army and information warfare*. US Army War College Press. https://press.armywarcollege.edu/monographs/506

Wuhan lab leak theory: How Fort Detrick became a centre for Chinese conspiracies. (2021, 23 August). *BBC News*. https://www.bbc.com/news/world-us-canada-58273322

Zhao, L. (@zlj517). (2020, 12 March). *This article is very much important to each and every one of us. Please read and retweet it. COVID-19: Further Evidence that the Virus Originated in the US* [Tweet]. Twitter. http://archive.today/2020.03.13-114631/https:/twitter.com/zlj517/status/1238269193427906560

6

Deterrence in the Gaza Conflict: Hamas Case Study Analysis

Ron Schleifer and Yair Ansbacher

Introduction

Hamas, the Palestinian branch of the international Muslim Brotherhood movement, took over the Gaza Strip in 2007. Fully cognizant of its disparity of power vis-à-vis Israel, it deployed a strategy of gradual encroachment designed to get Israel accustomed to Hamas's breaching of Israel's sovereignty in the South. It in fact utilized this strategy during the period leading up to Operation Cast Lead in 2008–9, Operation Protective Edge in 2014, and most recently in the lead-up to Operation Guardian of the Walls in May 2021.

In each instance, Hamas's approach has involved a very slow and steady increase in violence, as mortars, then Qassam rockets, and then Grads have been fired first at open territories, then at industrial zones, and finally at inhabited areas, including the central city of Tel Aviv, and even Israel's capital city, Jerusalem. Hamas's plan has been designed to psychologically wear out Israeli resilience and deter Israel from exercising its military power in the Gaza Strip.

Along with these physical attacks, Hamas has engaged in another form of deterrence, disinformation, and the combination of the two concepts is unique in the history of warfare, and most probably will be used in the future in other conflicts as well. Following the abduction of Israel Defense Forces (IDF) soldier Gilad Shalit in June 2006, Hamas warned that the Strip is lined with attack tunnels and is booby-trapped; that they possess an arsenal of superior weapons and personnel; that Israel will pay a high price in terms of the lives of civilians bordering the strip as well as those far deeper inside Israel;

that more hostages will be taken if the IDF breaks into Gaza; and that Hamas combatants are unafraid of dying and are even willing to produce their own civilian casualties, for which Israel will be blamed, as has occurred at the International Criminal Court in The Hague. These threats were a mixture of fact and fiction but were nevertheless effective. In ensuing operations (2012, 2014, 2021, 2022), Hamas used disinformation techniques extensively in order to direct blame toward Israel and cover its own failures and losses. This chapter will outline Hamas's use of deterrence and disinformation strategies over the past two decades, and how it has eroded Israeli sovereignty and resolve and interfered with and disrupted Israeli strategic objectives using a variety of tactics and techniques.

The Strategy of Deterrence

During the Cold War, a theory of nuclear deterrence evolved. At its core was the notion that nuclear war could be averted by psychologically influencing one's adversary to carefully weigh the costs of aggression. However, in order for deterrence to be effective, the theory posited, the threat should exact a cost that outweighs the benefits that the opponent hopes to achieve by his act. Deterrence, then, is an attempt to influence the opponent's strategic calculation with regard to its cost (Inbar & Sandler, 1993).

Applying that theory to conventional military deterrence—as opposed to nuclear deterrence—Israel has maintained a strategy of signalling to Gaza terror groups that Hamas will pay a very heavy cost should it and its cohorts overstep certain red lines. This was demonstrated in the case of the planned "mega" terror attack on Israel that was in the final stages of preparation by Zuhir alQaisi (also known as Abu Ibrahim), a terror chief who headed the Popular Resistance Committees in Gaza. An IDF strike on 9 March 2012 resulted in alQaisi's assassination. What followed was four days of intense rocket attacks on Israel from Gaza during Operation Returning Echo. However, notably, Hamas claimed not to have participated in the fighting *directly*, observing that escalation would "be devastating to the Palestinian people" (Brulliard, 2012).

Defiance in the Face of Kinetic Deterrence

To understand better the wider context in which Hamas uses disinformation against Israel, it is first necessary to appreciate the odd deterrence dialogue between the belligerents. Israel's kinetic-based deterrence is having only a limited impact on Hamas's willingness to fight. At the end of the March 2012 conflict, a senior IDF military officer was quoted as saying, "We taught them a lesson with a hint that they should think twice before they contemplate whether to mess with us again" (Melman, 2012). However, Hamas and its fellow-travellers failed to take that hint, considering that over 2,600 rockets and mortars were fired into Israel from the Gaza Strip during the two-year period ending December 2019 alone (Aronheim, 2019). All of which begs the question: Who is being deterred? The reality is that rather than deterring Hamas from launching rocket attacks and tunnel warfare on Israel, it is Israel that has been deterred from taking decisive—or even provisional—reprisal against Hamas. Thus, the would-be deterrer, Israel, has become the de facto object of deterrence.

Ersatz Air Force

Given the effectiveness to date of Israel's Iron Dome system in shooting down missiles, rockets, and other such conventional offensive weapons, Hamas, undeterred, has resorted to simpler, less sophisticated weapons to do the same damage. In order to bridge the power gap with Israel, Hamas deployed creative substitutes to not only cause physical harm, but also to wage psychological warfare. For example, the organization's lack of an air force capable of striking Israel's economic infrastructure has been compensated by the use of incendiary balloons and kites—airborne explosive devices that destroyed hundreds of acres of crops in southern Israel—leaving Israeli farmers defenceless as they watch their fields and livelihoods go up in flames year after year. Hundreds of fires have resulted in millions of shekels' worth of damage (Gross, 2018). Hamas's wind-carried weapons are not just intended to produce economic damage; they serve as part of its PSYOPS strategy of terrorizing citizens of the South. Balloons carrying an explosive device landed on a trampoline in a family's backyard in southern Israel. "Balloons on a trampoline in the backyard—that's a decorative play area and beckons the most innocent ones, and yet our children have lost their innocence because of this phenomenon," said Meirav Vidal, the mother of that household (Gross, 2018).

In a step-up from armed balloons and kites, Hamas and its affiliates have also developed the weaponizing of drones. In May of 2019, Hamas located an Israeli Matrice 600 drone that had been lost in Gaza in a previous operation, repaired it, took control of its systems, and attached a rocket-propelled grenade launcher to its hull. The drone was then sent into Israeli airspace, and a few minutes after it crossed over the border above Israeli territory, the drone's Hamas handler spotted tanks in a military base. The handler quickly attacked one of the manned tanks by dropping a grenade on it from the height of a hundred metres. The grenade failed to detonate (Zitun, 2020). The embarrassing incident remained shrouded in secrecy by Israel until seven months later, but the seriousness of Hamas's technological advances—as well as the damage to Israeli morale and the corresponding boost to Hamas's—could not be ignored. The message delivered thereby to Israel was, "We are creative and will use your own forces against you."

"An Army in Every Way"

As reported in 2017, Hamas is built like an army in every way, with 27,000 armed men divided into 6 regional brigades, and with 25 battalions and 106 companies. Nukhba, Hamas's elite unit, is comprised of 2,500 armed men. One-third of these troops is intended to be sent to carry out attacks inside Israeli territory. These operatives are supposed to strike from the sea (the naval commandos), from the air (using flying ATVs or motorized gliders, for example), and from the ground, mainly via cross-border tunnels, from which they would emerge to raid an Israeli residential community or army base (Issacharoff, 2017).

Hamas's Elite Nukhba Naval Commandos

In March of 2014, Hamas operative Ibrahim alAloul was killed in an explosion during what was characterized as a "training exercise." However, within days of his death, rumours circulated that he in fact had been the commander of Hamas's previously unknown naval unit. Confirming the rumours, Hamas created a commemorative video featuring members of alAloul's unit sailing on boats, patrolling Gaza's beaches and launching rockets from the coastline into Israel, and alAloul himself training with his nascent navy (Ben-Zvi, 2014). However, the broad distribution of the video represented far more than just an attempt at self-promotion both at home and abroad; rather, it again granted Hamas control of a large part of the playing field: it forced Israel into expending vast amounts of resources, both financial and military, to deal with this new seaborne threat. It also caused a sea change in Israel's strategic thinking as to where future threats would come from—now not merely from the air or via tunnels, but from beyond its coastline as well.

This new naval threat, which some sought to dismiss as a mere assemblage of swimmers and divers, proved itself as a force to be reckoned with on 8 July 2014, at the very start of the Gaza war (Operation Protective Edge): five Hamas scuba divers armed with rifles, RPGs, and explosives emerged from the sea near Kibbutz Zikim in southern Israel, intent on carrying out a massive terror attack at the kibbutz and nearby IDF bases (Israel Defense Forces, 2015). IDF observers spotted them on camera and all five terrorists were neutralized, following their attack on an IDF tank.

By 2018 Hamas had built up a formidable maritime strength, training hundreds of divers for its elite Nukhba naval commando unit. This caused Israel to employ the IDF's 916th Division, the unit responsible for the maritime sphere around the Gaza Strip and home of Israel's elite naval commando unit, Shayetet 13, focusing its operations on thwarting Hamas's continuous attempts to launch attacks on Israel via the sea. In fact, around 50 per cent of the targets attacked from the air by the Israeli Air Force (IAF) during the round of escalation that started at the beginning of June 2018 were naval targets belonging to Hamas, including naval outposts and sea vessels, according to a senior Israeli naval officer. In northern Gaza, the IAF bombed a terror tunnel intended for use by Hamas's elite Nukhba naval commandos to secretly go underwater (Zitun, 2018).

Why the focus on Hamas's "blue tunnel" strategy? One reason is because, according to Israeli naval assessments, as far back as 2013, Hamas planned to resume attempts to smuggle rocket-building materials from Sinai to Gaza via boats, following a pause in such efforts. "The sea is one big blue tunnel," stated an Israeli naval source at the time, and Egypt's continuing demolition of tunnels between Sinai and Gaza was expected to increase attempts to smuggle via the sea (Lappin, 2013). Another reason is due to the fact that Hamas received Iranian operational instructions on how to prepare swarm-like boat attacks for use in clashes with Israel: "It [Hamas] is improving its diving commando units, and creating sea forces that are much more capable than they were before. Hamas has received battle doctrines from Iran—which is also building up its sea capabilities—on how to deliver 'stings' through swarms," the source said. "They will try to attack our vessels with swarms" (Lappin, 2013).

Hamas's Terror Tunnels

Aside from Hamas's advances in aerial attacks—both with rockets and missiles as well as their crude but effective homemade flying incendiaries—and their sophisticated amphibious skills and weaponry, it is the ever-present threat of "terror tunnels" that has been highly effective in keeping Israel on guard, because of the security threat they pose to both Israeli civilians as well as IDF bases, and in deterring Israel from launching full-scale operations against Hamas. The tunnels, dubbed "the Metro" by Israeli military intelligence, due to their being constructed as an expansive underground network beneath every major urban centre in the Gaza Strip, are ubiquitous: following Hamas's takeover of the Gaza Strip in 2007, they proceeded to dig in excess of five hundred tunnels, employing seven thousand workers, and spreading out from underneath such urban areas as Khan Yunis, Jabalia, Shati, and numerous other densely populated towns and cities (Piven, 2014).

Although initially serving a commercial purpose by circumventing overland surveillance of the smuggling of goods, weapons, and other contraband from Egypt into the Gaza Strip, even before their official takeover, Hamas discovered a practical offensive value of the vast network: on 25 June 2006, a cell from Hamas's Izz ad-Din alQassam Brigades infiltrated into Israel via a tunnel originating from the Rafah area, passing under the security fence to the area between the Kerem Shalom and Sufa crossings. Under cover of mortar and anti-tank fire from within the Gaza Strip, the cell attacked an armored personnel carrier, an IDF tank, and a watchtower. Two IDF soldiers were killed, and a twenty-year-old corporal, Gilad Shalit, was wounded and abducted. His captors forced him back into Gaza via the same tunnel from which they had emerged (Israel, 2006). IDF forces subsequently uncovered the opening of the tunnel inside a Palestinian house located about 350 metres from the border fence. The length of the tunnel was about 650 metres.

The abduction of Corporal Shalit set off what was to become a five-year ordeal of not only familial anguish but of national torment as well, as Israelis felt both helpless to secure the swift release of the soldier, and a new sense of vulnerability exposing their sons to a newfound danger unrelated to the battlefield experience for which they were trained. In addition, the five-year-long ordeal was replete with messages and rumours orchestrated by Hamas regarding the whereabouts and the welfare of the kidnapped soldier. As if this was not enough of a sublime victory for Hamas, it also culminated in the successful release of over a thousand Palestinian security prisoners held in Israeli jails, among them the infamous Hamas terrorist Ahlam Tamimi, who planned and participated in the attack on Sbarro's pizzeria in Jerusalem on 9 August 2001, which left 15 civilians killed and 130 seriously injured

("Interpol said to drop warrant," 2021). The practical as well as PSYOPS value of the Shalit tunnel abduction was not lost on Hamas.

A New Front Is Opened

Having learned how effective a weapon the tunnels could be, Hamas attempted numerous additional kidnappings of IDF soldiers. On 17 July 2014, thirteen Hamas operatives emerged from an underground tunnel inside Israeli territory at Kibbutz Sufa, close to the Gaza Strip (Kershner, 2014). Although the air force neutralized most of the invaders, some escaped, and two IDF soldiers were killed in the ensuing battle. The next day, the IDF said it had already uncovered ten tunnels with twenty-two exit points and that there were dozens more "terror tunnels" spread around Gaza. In a statement, it described tunnels crossing the border from Gaza to Israel (Kershner, 2014).

But the IDF's efforts to uncover Hamas tunnels were only partially successful, and on 19 July, a group of Hamas operatives crossed under the border and emerged 700 metres from Kibbutz Ein Hashlosha. Again, IDF soldiers spotted the group in time and prevented them from attacking civilians in the village. The next day, a massive tunnel was discovered by IDF forces 170 meters inside Israel, near Kibbutz Netiv HaAsara. Residents of the village had to stay inside and lock their doors and windows until it could be confirmed that no terrorists had yet used the tunnel. On 21 July, more than ten heavily armed Hamas operatives infiltrated Israel through another tunnel. They were planning to split into two groups: one to attack Kibbutz Erez and the other Kibbutz Nir Am. They were wearing IDF uniforms to deceive civilians and Israeli security forces. Ten were killed by the IDF, but four IDF soldiers were also killed during the battle (Israel, 2014).

From Vietnam to Mosul to Gaza

During the Vietnam War, in just the first six months of 1967, booby traps killed 539 American GIs and wounded an additional 5,532. By the end of the war, of the 47,322 servicemen killed, 7,432 (15 per cent) died from such explosives (Sheehan, 1966). By the time of the West's war against ISIS, booby-trapped tunnels had become the weapon of choice by jihadis fighting Kurdish Peshmerga troops. As they fled areas being overrun, ISIS left behind a trail of destruction in the form of booby traps and secret tunnels underneath houses, thus making it difficult for Iraqi troops trying to capture and hold territory in a dense urban area like Mosul (Solomon, 2016). As civilians returned home to Mosul and other areas of northern Iraq freed from the Islamic State, homemade bombs and explosives, laid on an industrial scale by the insurgents, claimed hundreds of victims and hampered efforts to bring life back to normal. Everything from houses, schools, mosques, and streets were all booby-trapped; beyond Mosul, in villages and fields stretching from the Nineveh Plains to the Kurdish autonomous region, retreating Islamic State fighters sowed a vast area with improvised bombs and mines (MacSwan, 2017). During a two-week period in October 2020, ISIS employed a booby-trap technique in the Sinai Desert, killing more than a dozen civilians by way of explosive devices laid down in several homes (Sweilam, 2023).

It is no wonder, then, that the extensive array of booby-trapped tunnels, schools, mosques, hospitals, and other infrastructure throughout the Gaza Strip have served as a formidable deterrent to Israeli policy-makers who have become circumspect with regards to sending soldiers into the Gaza Strip. During the 2014 Operation Protective Edge conflict, exploiting a vast network of secret tunnels to snipe at enemy troops and blast their vehicles even inside Israel, Hamas killed thirty-two Israeli soldiers—almost three times as many as in the previous major ground clashes in the 2008 conflict (Browning, 2014). Describing the destruction of an armoured personnel carrier lured into a booby trap and the killing of the IDF soldiers inside, Hamas declared, "Our holy warriors detonated the minefield with such force that (the carrier) was destroyed. They advanced on it, opened its doors and finished off all left inside" (Browning, 2014). Noting that this was more than the typical Hamas bravado, an Israeli military spokesperson responded, "They have undergone extensive training, they are well supplied, well-motivated and disciplined. We have met a more formidable enemy on the battlefield. We are not surprised about it because we knew that they were preparing for this battle. They didn't just invest in the tunnels for the last two or three years" (Browning, 2014). For Hamas, the underpinning of deterrence—exacting a cost that outweighs the benefit—is a foreign concept. It thrives upon the ideology of martyrdom and suicide as a principle of warfare.

"Dual-Use" Material Diversion

Shortly after the conclusion of Operation Protective Edge, a tripartite agreement between Israel, the Palestinian Authority, and the UN was crafted with the aim of rebuilding Gaza. Known as the Gaza Reconstruction Mechanism (GRM), the heavily funded, highly ambitious mega-construction project was intended to build new housing, entire neighbourhoods, and vast infrastructure projects, including a state-of-the-art water de-salinization plant. With such humanitarian goals in mind, Israel agreed to allow dual-use material into Gaza, such as concrete and rebar (World Bank, 2018).

But despite the import safeguards that Israel insisted be included in the GRM as to cement and other construction materials—provisions that Israel and Egypt deemed crucial to the GRM—as early as December 2014, Hamas nevertheless managed to divert various quantities of cement, which had recently entered Gaza for the purpose of housing and infrastructure repair efforts, to the reinforcement of its damaged tunnel network ("Report: Hamas using Gaza reconstruction," 2014).

A year later, the Coordinator of Government Activities in the Territories reported that Hamas had seized the wood and other construction materials that Israel had permitted to be imported into the territory, thereby further delaying the reconstruction program: "Hamas operatives have forcefully taken over storage facilities for housing construction imports, and seized them for the organization's underground infrastructure," noted IDF major general Yoav Mordechai ("Hamas diverting construction materials," 2015). The problem of Hamas's misappropriation of material and Palestinian Authority recalcitrance in working with Hamas was echoed by Israel's Ministry of Foreign Affairs (2017) in an update regarding the slow pace of reconstruction in Gaza.

Hamas's eagerness to threaten Israel therefore takes precedence even over housing, sanitation, and every other quality-of-life infrastructure improvement that could benefit its own populace, and any strategy of deterrence that Israel thought it could apply in bringing about pressure from Hamas supporters for improved conditions simply has no effect upon the Hamas equation of one-sided deterrence. The bottom-line message of these deeds is to cause despair among Israeli decision makers in the face of Hamas's never-ending resolve.

Disinformation—a Further Tool

How does it come about, then, that the strongest military power in the Middle East is effectively stopped from utilizing that power to eliminate—or even deter—continuing rocket and arson attacks by the most active anti-Israel terrorist organization in the region? The answer lies in the non-military tools that Hamas has in its arsenal—whether or not these are directly under its control. One of these is disinformation.

Disinformation is different from a lie, as it uses large parts of the truth, though not all of it. For example, Hamas has been constantly disseminating information about Israel's cruelty toward the Palestinians (the siege on Gaza, war crimes, harming civilians), leaving out of its story its own violent activities. It sends out visuals of ruined buildings, without mentioning that Israel almost always warns the residents to clear out of a structure before bombing it; more than once it has staged supposed attacks on children, and although Israel proved the story to be false, the damage had already been done. The demonization of Israel was successful.

As Israel holds world opinion in high regard, in many instances it has refrained from taking full-scale action in order to minimize the negative coverage such actions might receive. In other words, in this case disinformation is being used as a method of deterrence; in fact, it is a key element in deterring Israel from using its full range of military abilities.

More directly, the above-mentioned announcement that the entire Gaza Strip is booby-trapped, as well as other pieces of disinformation, has had an effect on Israeli decision making, as the Israeli public is particularly averse to loss of life in what some might consider an unnecessary or hopeless battle.

One example where Hamas has been quite successful in using subtler forms of disinformation was in 2014, when Israeli citizen Avera Mengistu, an immigrant from Ethiopia, entered the Gaza Strip in an unknown way; he has been kept hostage by Hamas ever since. In January 2023 Hamas released a clip in which a person calls for the Israeli government to act for Mengistu's release (Martinez, 2023). The clip is unclear, raising doubts of its authenticity. The ensuing public debate discussed whether computer technology was used to produce a fake clip. Hamas never supplied another clue in authenticating the video. It presumably prefers to stoke Israeli internal disagreement and social unrest, as Ethiopian political activists accuse the government of not releasing Palestinian terrorists in exchange for a dark-skinned person (Mualem, 2015).

The Tools of Diplomatic Deterrence

Yet another tool widely used by Hamas is the diplomatic channel, which is building on general disinformation against Israel. After 11 September 2001, the European Union established a list of persons, groups, and entities involved in terrorist acts and subject to restrictive measures. Those on the "EU terrorist list" are subject to both the freezing of funds and other financial assets, as well as enhanced measures related to police and judicial co-operation in criminal matters. However, in September 2010, Hamas brought its case before the European Council's General Court, challenging its continued presence on the terrorist list, and, in December 2014, the General Court annulled (albeit on procedural grounds) the council's decision to maintain Hamas on the list. One month later, the European Council decided to appeal against the judgment of the General Court (European Council, 2021), but the threat of full engagement with and legitimization of Hamas still looms large, as underscored by the writings of Hugh Lovatt, a policy fellow with the European Council on Foreign Relations, in which he advocates that "the EU should welcome Hamas' new political platform and seize the opportunity to engage moderates within the movement" (Lovatt, 2017).

More insidious is the threat of criminal charges against Israeli officers and statesmen alike. In September 2005, as Israeli major general Doron Almog's plane landed at Heathrow Airport, an Israeli embassy attaché boarded the aircraft and warned him not to deplane. A warrant had been issued for the arrest of the general over the demolitions of terrorist operatives' houses in Gaza—a punitive measure dating, ironically, back to British Mandatory rule. He escaped being detained ("Israel slams general arrest bid," 2005), but the episode unveiled a new non-military weapon to be deployed at will by Hamas sympathizers. Threats of arrest in the United Kingdom were also faced by former Israeli military chief Moshe Yaalon, who cancelled a charitable fundraising trip to London for fear of arrest on war crimes charges, and by then Israeli chief of staff General Dan Halutz, who was also warned against travel to Britain (McGreal, 2005).

It is not only military officers who have been threatened with criminal action in the United Kingdom. In December 2009, a British court, again acting under its "universal jurisdiction" premise, issued a purported war crimes arrest warrant for Israel's former foreign minister Tzipi Livni, based solely on the fact that she was a cabinet member during the 2008 Operation Cast Lead. The warrant was only withdrawn after it was determined that she was not in fact in the United Kingdom (Black & Cobain, 2009). In January 2017, Livni was forced to cancel a speaking engagement at a European Parliament event after Belgian police confirmed that it intended to question the former Israeli foreign minister upon her arrival in Brussels in regard to "suspected war crimes" ("Tzipi Livni cancels Brussels trip," 2017).

The campaign by Israel antagonists to further besmirch the country's reputation on the world stage and to endanger the freedom of movement of its political and military leaders reached a new low on 5 February 2021, with the ruling by the pre-trial chamber of the International Criminal Court (ICC) that The Hague has jurisdiction to open a criminal investigation against Israel—and the Palestinians—for war crimes alleged to have taken place in the West Bank, Gaza Strip, and East Jerusalem (Magid, 2021). But lest anyone believe that the inclusion of "Palestinians" in the ruling signalled even-handedness, ICC chief prosecutor Fatou Bensouda had already made clear in 2019 that a criminal investigation, if approved, would focus on the 2014 Israel-Hamas conflict (Operation Protective Edge), on Israeli settlement policy, and on the Israeli response to protests at the Gaza border (Magid, 2021).

Another tool in Hamas's non-military arsenal, building on disinformation, is the United Nations High Commissioner for Refugees, which, since its inception, has issued many official condemnations of Israel (Sherman, 2015), and its evidence can be used by prosecutors of the ICC in cases brought against Israel. These and other such non-military threats have limited Israel's ability to successfully function on the battlefield.

The Numbers Game

One the very effective ways that Hamas uses disinformation is by concealing reality through the diffusion of false numbers of victims in its conflict with Israel. During Operation Guardian of the Walls (May 2021), Israel executed a deception plan (code-named "Lightning Strike") that was designed to deal a blow to the Nukhba elite force. The IDF mapped the Gaza tunnels and announced an incoming raid. Nukhba soldiers entered their underground positions and were hit by targeted and precise bombing. To conceal their casualties, Hamas announced that it suffered a minimal loss, and the dead were buried in unmarked graves or announced as deceased due to health problems. This ploy proved very effective, as it caused a bitter argument in Israeli media, involving among others former IDF officers who claimed this long-planned deception plan was wasted as a result of political reasons without bringing any significant results ("Report: IAF bombing," 2021).

On the other hand, Hamas inflated the number of civilian casualties during armed conflict (which it tries to prevent as much as possible) with Israel. Israeli intelligence noticed that a large number of these clashes involved males aged eighteen and over. Following more digging, their organizational affiliation was revealed, but by then the political damage was already done.

The Impact of Hamas's Deterrence Built on Disinformation

Hamas's successful campaign of deterrence has resulted in a trajectory change in Israel whereby the IDF and its political handlers have orbited away from the IDF's underlying mission to "preserve the State of Israel, to protect its independence, and to foil attempts by its enemies to disrupt the normal life within it" (Israel Defense Forces, n.d.). Rather, instead of engaging in first-strike, pre-emptive measures that Israel used so successfully in the Six Day War as well as in other battles—thereby taking control of the battlefield from the enemy—current policy has been relegated to a series of tit-for-tat responses to Hamas's highly aggressive disruption of normal life. This policy is now almost always reactive—coming only after rockets have been fired, acres of fields destroyed, or, in the worst case, casualties inflicted—and hardly ever proactive. After the 2008 Operation Cast Lead, then Israeli prime minister Ehud Olmert declared, "Iran and Hamas mistook the restraint Israel exercised as weakness. They were mistaken. They were surprised" (Israel, 2009). In fact, not only does Hamas always regard Israeli restraint as weakness, but they have furthermore succeeded in giving certain Israeli policy-makers pause to consider whether or not "restraint" should be incorporated as part of Israel's defence policy.

Yaakov Amidror, former IDF major general and national security adviser to former prime minister Benjamin Netanyahu, underscored the fact that Israel's military strategy has not been aimed at winning the war against Hamas for quite some time. "The purpose of all the Gaza operations over the past fifteen years has been to hurt Hamas and restore quiet to people living in the south—not to topple the terror groups or conquer the Strip," he stated during an interview with *Mishpacha* magazine. "Israel didn't embark on Operation Guardian of the Walls with the goal of winning," continued Amidror. "The goal was to inflict maximum damage on Hamas' military capabilities, in hopes of establishing deterrence" (Schulman, 2021). There is perhaps no greater proof of the failure of those deterrent hopes than the fact that, despite the fifteen-year history of that strategy, Hamas was not at all deterred from launching attacks on Israeli civilians in 2008, 2014, or even as recently as May 2021, while its capacity to influence Israeli calculus through disinformation has remained unchallenged.

Dictating Ceasefires

Israel's inability to deter Hamas's aggression has had ramifications not only as to how and when wars start, but also as to how and when they end. In each of the past three wars, Hamas chose the timing of the start date by utilizing indiscriminate rocket fire—first into Israel's southern Gaza envelope region, and then expanding as far north and east as Hamas desired—thereby drawing Israel into military engagement. And, partway through each of these wars, after gaining enough sympathy points with visuals of death and destruction across global media outlets, Hamas then complained and employed its diplomatic resources to prevent Israel from accomplishing its operational goals. In the course of Operation Guardian of the Walls, President Joe Biden called Prime Minister Netanyahu four times to express his concerns over Israel's campaign, despite initial public statements of support for Israel's right to defend itself. Finally, on 19 May 2021, the president informed the prime minister that he expected "a significant de-escalation today" in Gaza (Macias & Wilkie, 2021). But as to how long ceasefires last, Amidror expressed some resignation: "The cease-fire will last as long as Hamas wants it to. The fact that Israel is dependent on Hamas' whims is a real problem that we don't have a solution for at the moment" (Shulman, 2021).

Payouts in Lieu of Protection

A further effect of Hamas disinformation can be seen through indirect changes in Israeli policies and programs. In December 2020, Israel proudly announced the unveiling of its new LahavOr (Light Blade), a laser system designed to intercept airborne incendiary threats from Gaza (Saban et al., 2020). The Light Blade "provides a near conclusive response to everything relating to balloons and kites, and delivers a safe and effective solution to the drone threat," boasted Border Police commissioner Major General Yaakov Shabtai (Saban et al., 2020). Yet it should be remembered that LahavOr is merely another strictly defensive measure. Indeed, just ninety days later, Israel's Ministry of Agriculture and Rural Development, Ministry of Defense, and Ministry of Finance formulated a joint decision to support Israeli farmers along the Gaza Strip with up to NIS 8 million to encourage early harvesting of their crops before the arrival of "arson season" blowing in from Gaza (Savir, 2021). Dr. Nahum Itzkovich, director general of the Ministry of Agriculture, explained that "this support provides a sense of security and certainty for the surrounding farmers and improves their resilience to continue cultivating the land near the border" (Savir, 2021). Never before in Israel's history were attacks on civilians and their property responded to with "anticipatory payments" to would-be victims in place of providing real security and serenity for its citizens.

By contrast, in January 2013, the Egyptian military came up with a novel—albeit noxious—new tactic to shut down Hamas's tunnels: flooding them with sewage. Advisers to then Egyptian president Mohamed Morsi, himself a leader of the Muslim Brotherhood's political arm, responded to critics by stating that he was determined to shut the tunnels to block the destabilizing flow of weapons and militants into Sinai from Gaza (Akram & Kirkpatrick, 2013). The response from Hamas—also an offshoot of the Muslim Brotherhood—was muted, unlike when former Egyptian president Hosni Mubarak used far less effective methods to close the tunnels (Akram & Kirkpatrick, 2013).

For Israel, the notion of employing such a simple but environmentally and physically threatening offensive tactic would be unthinkable. Rather than risk global condemnation and further accusations of war crimes, Israel instead embarked on a NIS 3 billion project beginning in 2017 to erect its "anti-tunnel barrier" along the Gaza border (Harel, 2020). In the course of the construction, Israel discovered about twenty tunnels, the latest being one that was dug from a point east of Khan Yunis to near Kissufim, inside Israel; it was comparatively deep underground and penetrated a few dozen metres into Israel, but although it didn't get past the barrier, it seemed to have been "a work in progress and was discovered before it was finished," according to the IDF Spokesperson (Harel, 2020).

"The Devil You Know"

One of the most ironic elements of Hamas's deterrence against Israel is accomplished through its ongoing commitment to floating the notion that "things could be worse" in the information environment. When confronted with the possibility of regime change from one bad actor to another, one of the guiding inquiries for policy-makers has been to weigh "the devil you know versus the devil you don't know." Is it strictly deterrence by Hamas that restrains Israel from acting decisively and resolutely? Or is Israel perhaps further deterred by the prospect of "the morning after Hamas"? While the terrorist organization does pose a very real threat to the livelihoods, normalcy of life, and indeed life itself for thousands of Israelis living within the Gaza Strip region, and while it is true that Hamas's obsession with destroying Israel has only brought misery to its own populace, Hamas's continued control of Gaza might nevertheless also serve Israel's interests. Hamas is but one of the Palestinian groups opposed to Israel. Jihadist groups more akin to the Islamic State and al Qaeda also have limited followings in Gaza, as does Hamas's long-time rival, Palestine Islamic Jihad, which works closely with Iran. In addition, members of Hamas's own military wing have radical leanings. At times, Hamas has allowed these groups to operate in order to put pressure on Israel, but Hamas also cracks down on these groups, arresting some members and even killing others. Hamas fears that these radicals will precipitate an unwanted massive clash with Israel and ultimately endanger Hamas's own power (Byman, 2018).

The Ultimate Effect of Hamas Deterring Israel through the Information Environment

In the midst of Operation Guardian of the Walls, Michael Armstrong, an associate professor of operations research at Brock University in Canada, observed that unless Israel occupies Gaza, it will be impossible to disarm Hamas. Hamas has shown that it can rebuild its destroyed capacities, so unless Israelis want to stay in Gaza and occupy it, he really can't see how they would disarm it (Vohra, 2021).

However, the prospect of putting boots on the ground in Gaza has been dismissed as nothing more than an idle threat. The threat tactic worked well when, on 14 May 2021, the IDF announced that "ground troops were massing on the Gaza border," only to "clarify" the miscommunication a short while later. But after the announcement succeeded in drawing hundreds of Hamas fighters into their "Metro" tunnel network, ready to execute suicide measures against the would-be invaders, Israeli jets used the opportunity to pound the tunnels, thereby dispatching hundreds of Hamas fighters (Vohra, 2021).

But if the reality of four thousand rockets being fired into Israeli civilian population centres—including Tel Aviv and Jerusalem—was not enough to motivate Israel's military planners to dismantle Hamas's rocket industry, as Professor Armstrong noted, then it is hard to imagine that Israel will ever regain the resolve to enter Gaza, even as a limited incursion, as it did in 2009 and 2014. To actually exercise the option of sending in ground troops would entail a large-scale, long-term, bloody campaign, one for which Israel's current military planners seem hesitant to claim responsibility.

Conclusion

For how long can Israel's southern civilian population tolerate continued attacks and threats of attacks from Hamas rockets, incendiary devices, and tunnel invasions? In reality, if Israel is going to live up to its mission statement of safeguarding the security, life, and normalcy of all of its citizens, then it is time for a sea change in Israeli foreign and defence policy. Hamas will never be placated by Israeli restraint, nor will it be deterred by Israeli military hardware obstacles coupled with brief, periodic incursions. To continue along the current path means to remain in a constant state of vulnerability, and this is true not just for citizens living in the Gaza region, but—as Hamas has demonstrated repeatedly—also for those in Tel Aviv, Jerusalem, and residents of all of Israel's major population centres within range of Hamas's arsenal.

Israel's current strategy of deterrence vis-à-vis Hamas has run its course and all that remains, in all practicality, is the option of military confrontation to dismantle the military wing of Hamas and the other terrorist organizations operating in the Gaza Strip (Dekel, 2019). It is indeed a costly proposition both in terms of human sacrifice and national losses, but sometimes the Latin adage *Si vis pacem, para bellum* (If you want peace, prepare for war) offers the only practical solution. So far, Hamas has been successful in maintaining the psychological and informational notion that invading and permanently occupying the Gaza Strip is an unthinkable option.

See Postface on page 351 for reflection on current events.

REFERENCES

Akram, F., & Kirkpatrick, D. D. (2013, 20 February). To block Gaza tunnels, Egypt lets sewage flow. *New York Times*. https://www.nytimes.com/2013/02/21/world/middleeast/egypts-floods-smuggling-tunnels-to-gaza-with-sewage.html?_r=5

Aronheim, A. (2019, 1 December). Israel struck by over 2,600 rockets and mortars over past two years. *Jerusalem Post*. https://www.jpost.com/arab-israeli-conflict/gaza-news/israel-struck-by-over-2600-rockets-and-mortars-over-past-two-years-609544

Ben-Zvi, G. (2014, 20 March). Hamas navy SEALS revealed following death of jihadist commander. *The Algemeiner*. https://www.algemeiner.com/2014/03/20/hamas-navy-seals-revealed-following-death-of-jihadist

Black, I., & Cobain, I. (2009, 14 December). British court issued Gaza arrest warrant for former Israeli minister Tzipi Livni. *The Guardian*. https://www.theguardian.com/world/2009/dec/14/tzipi-livni-israel-gaza-arrest

Browning, N. (2014, 23 July). Hamas tactics exact high toll in Israeli ground thrust. *Reuters*. https://www.reuters.com/article/us-palestinians-israel-hamas/hamas-tactics-exact-high-toll-in-israeli-ground-thrust-idUSKBN0FS1X

Brulliard, K. (2012, 13 March). Egypt-mediated truce calms Israel-Gaza border. *Washington Post*. https://www.washingtonpost.com/world/middle_east/egypt-mediated-truce-calms-gaza-border/2012/03/13/gIQAnHPs8R_story.html

Byman, D. L. (2018, 19 March). Why Israel is stuck with Hamas. *Brookings Institution*. https://www.brookings.edu/blog/order-from-chaos/2018/03/19/why-israel-is-stuck-with-hamas/

Dekel, U. (2019, 19 March). Israel's exhausted strategy of deterrence vis-à-vis Hamas. *Institute for National Security Studies*. https://www.inss.org.il/publication/israels-exhausted-strategy-deterrence-vis-vis-hamas/

European Council. (2021, 8 February). EU terrorist list. *European Council*. https://www.consilium.europa.eu/en/policies/fight-against-terrorism/terrorist-list/

Gross, J. A. (2018, 20 June). Condoms, kites, birthday balloons: "Silly" Gaza weapons could lead to real war. *Times of Israel*. https://www.timesofisrael.com/condoms-kites-birthday-balloons-silly-gaza-weapons-could-lead-to-serious-war/

Hamas diverting construction materials to terror tunnels. (2015, 1 September). *Hamodia*. https://hamodia.com/2015/09/01/hamas-diverting-construction-materials-to-terror-tunnels/

Harel, A. (2020, 21 October). Israel's anti-tunnel barrier pays off, but Gaza groups are working on alternatives. *Haaretz*. https://www.haaretz.com/israel-news/.premium-israel-s-anti-tunnel-barrier-pays-off-but-gaza-groups-are-working-on-alternatives-1.9250068

Inbar, E., & Sandler, S. (1993). Israel's deterrence strategy revisited. *Security Studies, 3*(2), 330–58. https://doi.org/10.1080/09636419309347551

Interpol said to drop warrant for Sbarro pizzeria bomber Ahlam Tamimi. (2021, 12 March). *Times of Israel*. https://www.timesofisrael.com/interpol-said-to-drop-warrant-for-sbarro-pizzeria-bomber-ahlam-tamimi/

Israel. (2006, 25 June). Two soldiers killed, one missing in Kerem Shalom terror attack. *Israel Ministry of Foreign Affairs*. https://www.gov.il/en/departments/news/two-soldiers-killed-one-missing-in-kerem-shalom-terror-attack-25-jun-2006

Israel. (2009, 17 January). Israel holds its fire: Statement by PM Ehud Olmert. *Israel Ministry of Foreign Affairs*. https://www.gov.il/en/departments/news/statement-pm-ehud-olmert-17-jan-2009

Israel. (2014, 22 July). Behind the headlines: Hamas' terror tunnels. *Israel Ministry of Foreign Affairs*. https://www.gov.il/en/Departments/General/hamas-terror-tunnels#:~:text=The%20tunnels%20are%20used%20by,exit%20points%20inside%20Israeli%20territory

Israel Defense Forces. (n.d.). Our mission. Retrieved 21 July 2023 from https://www.idf.il/en/who-we-are/

Israel Defense Forces. (2015, 21 July). Watch: 5 of the scariest moments from the 2014 Israel-Gaza conflict. *Israel Defense Forces*. www.idf.il/en/articles/hamas/watch-5-of-the-scariest-moments-from-the-2014-israel-gaza-conflict/

Israel slams general arrest bid. (2005, 14 September). *BBC News*. http://news.bbc.co.uk/2/hi/uk_news/4246848.stm

Issacharoff, A. (2017, 4 June). With an army of 27,000, Hamas terror chief Deif readies Gaza for war. *Times of Israel*. http://www.timesofisrael.com/with-an-array-of-27000-hamas-terror-chief-deif-readies-gaza-for-war/

Kershner, I. (2014, 18 July). Trouble underfoot on Israeli kibbutz near the border. *New York Times*. https://www.nytimes.com/2014/07/19/world/middleeast/hamas-gaza-strip-tunnels-led-to-israels-invasion.html

Lappin, Y. (2013, 3 March). Exclusive: Hamas preparing Iranian-style swarm boat attacks for future clash. *Jerusalem Post*. https://www.jpost.com/arab-israeli-conflict/exclusive-hamas-preparing-iranian-style-swarm-boat-attacks-for-future-clash-446851

Lovatt, H. (2017, 5 May). Time to bring Hamas in from the cold. *European Council on Foreign Relations*. https://ecfr.eu/article/commentary_time_to_bring_hamas_in_from_the_7283/

Macias, A., & Wilkie, C. (2021, 19 May). Biden tells Israel's Netanyahu U.S. expects "a significant de-escalation today" in Gaza. *CNBC*. https://www.cnbc.com/2021/05/19/biden-tells-israels-netanyahu-us-expects-a-significant-de-escalation-today-in-gaza.html

MacSwan, A. (2017, 26 July). Booby-traps plague North Iraq as Islamic state targets returning civilians. *Reuters*. https://www.reuters.com/article/us-mideast-crisis-iraq-explosives-idUSKBN1AB0TS

Magid, J. (2021, 5 February). ICC has jurisdiction to probe Israel, Hamas for war crimes, pretrial judges rule. *Times of Israel*. https://www.timesofisrael.com/icc-has-jurisdiction-to-probe-israel-hamas-for-war-crimes-pretrial-judges-rule/

Martinez, S. (2023, 17 January). Hamas video of Israeli hostage Mengistu sparks talks of "deep fake" tech. *i24NEWS*. https://www.i24news.tv/en/news/middle-east/technology-science/1673978168-hamas-video-of-israeli-hostage-mengistu-sparks-talks-of-deep-fake-tech

McGreal, C. (2005, 16 September). Israeli ex-military chief cancels trip to UK over threat of war crimes arrest. *The Guardian*. https://www.theguardian.com/world/2005/sep/16/israelandthepalestinians.warcrimes

Melman, Y. (2012, 15 March). Under fire. *Tablet*. https://www.tabletmag.com/sections/israel-middle-east/articles/under-fire

Mualem, M. (2015, 13 July). Israel slow to rescue captured citizen. Is it because of his race? *Al-Monitor*. https://www.al-monitor.com/originals/2015/07/israel-mengistu-affair-discrimination-ethiopian-community.html#ixzz7wPJyLu7W

Piven, B. (2014, 23 July). Gaza's underground: A vast tunnel network that empowers Hamas. *Al Jazeera*. http://america.aljazeera.com/articles/2014/7/23/gaza-undergroundhamastunnels.html

Report: Hamas using Gaza reconstruction materials to repair infiltration tunnels. (2014, 19 December). *Jerusalem Post*. https://www.jpost.com/breaking-news/report-material-for-gaza-reconstruction-diverted-to-hamas-for-tunnel-reparations-385178

Report: IAF bombing of Hamas "metro" smashed miles of tunnels; no info on deaths. (2021, 15 May). *Times of Israel*. https://www.timesofisrael.com/report-heavy-bombing-of-hamas-metro-destroyed-miles-of-tunnels-killed-dozens/

Saban, I., Golan, G., & ILH Staff. (2020, 8 December). Israel deploys first-of-its-kind laser system to Gaza border to fight incendiary balloons. *Israel Hayom*. https://www.israelhayom.com/2020/08/12/israel-deploys-first-of-its-kind-laser-system-to-gaza-border-to-fight-incendiary-balloons/

Savir, A. (2021, 17 March). Israel urges farmers near Gaza to harvest wheat before the arson terrorism season begins. *Jewish Press*. https://www.jewishpress.com/news/israel/israel-urges-farmers-near-gaza-to-harvest-wheat-before-the-arson-terrorism-season-begins/2021/03/17/

Sheehan, N. (1966, 7 October). Casualties show how Vietnam differs from earlier wars. *New York Times*.

Sherman, E. (2015, 25 June). Report: Since inception, UNHRC condemned Israel more than rest of world's countries combined. *The Algemeiner*. https://www.algemeiner.com/2015/06/25/report-since-inception-unhrc-condemned-israel-more-than-rest-of-worlds-countries-combined/

Shulman, E. (2021, 25 May). Who won the Gaza war? *Mishpacha*. https://mishpacha.com/who-won-the-gaza-war/

Solomon, E. (2016, 18 October). Secret tunnels and booby traps hamper march on Mosul. *Financial Times*. https://www.ft.com/content/a2f86c6c-954a-11e6-a1dc-bdf38d484582

Sweilam, A. (2020, 25 October). At least 14 civilians killed by booby traps in Egypt's Sinai. *AP News*. https://apnews.com/article/egypt-africa-a1ef2bfa5fdb1744717cc90e76847af1

Tzipi Livni cancels Brussels trip amid threat of arrest. (2017, 23 January). *Al Jazeera*. https://www.aljazeera.com/news/2017/1/23/tzipi-livni-cancels-brussels-trip-amid-threat-of-arrest

Vohra, A. (2021, 17 May). Israel is bluffing about ever invading Gaza. *Foreign Policy*. https://foreignpolicy.com/2021/05/17/israel-is-bluffing-about-ever-invading-gaza/

World Bank. (2018, 13 March). Reconstructing Gaza—donor pledges. *World Bank*. https://www.un.org/unispal/document/auto-insert-209286/

Zitun, Y. (2018, 15 June). How IDF foils Hamas' naval designs. *Ynet*. https://www.ynetnews.com/articles/0,7340,L-5288030,00.html

Zitun, Y. (2020, 27 January). Hamas raises stakes with weaponized drones. *Ynet*. https://www.ynetnews.com/article/SkRfsvhb8

7

Resilience as a Framework for Deterrence in the Information Age: Lessons Learned from Israel about Information and Influence Operations

Oshri Bar-Gil

Introduction

The growing use of information and influence campaigns as part of hybrid warfare necessitates a new deterrence approach. Although such campaigns are on the rise, they are not new; since ancient times, they have been employed to defeat opponents and prevent rivals from acting. Even the writings of the ancient Chinese strategist Sun Tzu (2013) emphasized the need to obtain dominance and manage information to deter opponents. Throughout the last century, different measures have been taken to deceive the adversary, boost military morale, and motivate soldiers and leaders to battle. The purpose of indoctrination was to encourage the forces to continue fighting and to deter enemies. Propaganda, misinformation efforts, and "active measures" were employed in the struggle for narrative dominance. In this process, communication channels are utilized to influence attitudes, beliefs, and actions following the objectives of the influential sides. As part of "active measures," spies and influencers affected target audiences to reduce their motivation to act, and even increased the perceived cost of military actions to deter the adversary from fighting (Rid, 2020).

According to Mazarr (2021), deterrence is convincing one's adversary that the costs and hazards of a particular course of action outweigh its rewards.

While the search for deterrence strategies in twenty-first-century wars continues, one approach to establishing deterrence is through resilience, which can circumvent the opponent's aspirations and prevent him from achieving success in this domain.

The purpose of this chapter is to suggest ways to enhance resilience to deter adversaries from planning and implementing information operations. Looking at the Israeli case, it seeks to understand the strategies, techniques, and technologies that Israel used to detect, reduce, or minimize Iran's non-state proxy operations.

The chapter will examine the need for new forms of deterrence in the face of hybrid threats and how resilience may be one of them. It will then examine the changing context of the information battleground in the twenty-first century and the transition to hybrid warfare, which includes political, economic, and communication measures to disrupt trust and social legitimacy in Western democracies. Then it will provide an overview of global threats: first, the traditional Russian national model, followed by ISIS's operational model as a global terror organization, and then the broader international model of infodemic, which uses disorder to cause even more havoc. The last model will be the Iranian threat model, contextualizing the case presented in the chapter—Israel's efforts to deter Iran and its proxies.

The following section will cover general coping methods and responses to those threats. These involve the use of social media to acquire intelligence against those dangers, acting in a kinetic manner, and creating information inoculation tactics. Following a broad description of these strategies, it will concentrate on ways to establish national and military resilience as a means of deterrence, including ways to develop a framework or doctrine for influence campaign resilience. Based on the Israeli experience, the discussion section will determine whether resilience-enhancing tactics can truly dissuade actors from influence campaigns and other elements that should be considered when employing this strategy.

"New" Hybrid Warfare and Threats Call for New Methods of Deterrence

Deterrence can be defined as discouraging or restraining someone—in world politics, usually a nation-state—from taking unwanted actions, such as an armed nuclear attack or information campaign. It entails attempting to halt or prevent an action (Mazarr, 2021; Mazarr et al., 2018). The fundamental theme of this book is that disinformation should not be tackled solely with inward measures such as resilience development or information inoculation. The outward concept of understanding the adversary and how the adversary thinks about us is at the heart of deterrence, thereby allowing us to be significantly more proactive. While deterrence comprises the broad military dimensions (whether conventional, nuclear, or informational) and the means and capacity to respond to an external threat, resilience focuses on the preparedness that allows militaries to perform their duty. In other words, minimizing the military's and society's vulnerabilities reduces the possibility of an attack by decreasing its effectiveness and strengthening deterrence (Lasconjarias, 2017; Thiele, 2016).

In an age of hybrid warfare, cyber and information operations are intertwined to amplify enemy achievements through the information they reveal. Recently, at the Warsaw Summit in July 2016, NATO acknowledged the significance of resilience in deterring hybrid warfare as heads of state and government signed an official statement pledging to "continue to build . . . resilience against the full spectrum of threats, including hybrid" (Meyer-Minnemann, 2016; van Doorn & Brinkel, 2021).

Another hybrid aspect that can be used to guide the definition of resilience in the face of new hybrid threats is cyber resilience, which is defined by the US-based National Institute of Standards and Technology as "the ability to anticipate, cope with, adapt to, and recover from difficulties, pressures, or attacks on systems that use or are enabled by cyber resources" (Ross et al., 2019, p. 71). This resilience notion has three interconnected layers—preparation, inclusion, and adaptation—and it may provide some direction while trying to establish a resilience framework for influence campaigns.

Hybrid Warfare: From Clausewitz to the Information Battlefield of the Twenty-First Century

Born centuries before the Internet, Clausewitz argued that "war is not merely a political act but a real political instrument, a continuation of political intercourse, a carrying out of the same by other means" (Clausewitz, 1989, p. 65). Using incorrect, fake, and falsified information to undermine the fighting spirit, divide nations, and impair enemy capabilities can be seen as a continuation of policy in other ways. Military, intelligence, and operations personnel well understand "digital espionage" and its history. Nevertheless, there is still some ambiguity over the use of "disinformation," which further influences public opinion and politics through "active measures," or actions used by parties to sow mistrust and riots among the people while retaining intelligence operatives working behind the scenes.

The modern era of disinformation began in the early 1920s with the KGB's establishment of a foreign propaganda bureau. The KGB even coined the term "disinformation" in an attempt to sound French; Singer and Brooking (2018) contend that by doing so, the truth was buried alongside the term's genesis. In the meantime, the West referred to it as "political warfare." It also sought to capitalize on rumours, discrepancies, and incorrect or partial information within the adversary's political body (Goldschmidt & Wergan, 2017; Rid, 2020).

Over the last three decades, the Internet has become the primary medium for communication, messaging, and politics. This global information highway was designed in the 1960s under the sponsorship of the US Department of Defense as a conduit for communication within the United States and between it and the rest of the globe amid the threat of a nuclear strike by the Soviet Union. The Internet is now as crucial for business and social life as it is for governments, armies, and individuals. Everyone uses it to influence other people and to conduct information campaigns for economic and political benefit, as well as national and other reasons, aimed at winning not only on the Internet but also within the global mindset. Online forces' struggle alters the definition of war. Temporary battles impact the world by influencing everything from celebrity status to election results in countries around the world. Our physical senses, memories, and consciousness are all part of this war, and we are all engaged in wars of which we are unaware.

Information has become a potent weapon in international politics, and the practical tools utilized on the global battlefield have evolved in recent years. The attempt to develop new ideas of action in this area and the intensification of the national-military dialogue about it represent this transformation, as does the establishment of dedicated entities concerned with the problem. Weapons and concepts utilized in deterrence strategies have even shifted away from the military domain and toward the political, economic, humanitarian, and communicative domains, and influence campaigns play a key role in these areas (van Doorn & Brinkel, 2021).

These approaches are usually associated with the emerging concept of "hybrid warfare" (Chivvis, 2017), which includes using direct force with cautious and calculated methods, constantly weighing and adjusting the intensity of various combat efforts, and concentrating on local politics and the civilian population. In addition to cyber-attacks and influence operations, hybrid warfare employs proxies for broad impact (e.g., economic/commercial), political influence, extortion (among other things following cyber-attacks), and inflammation (Chivvis, 2017). With the introduction of new technology and the expansion of Internet culture, the global wave of disinformation is gradually building and increasing in the first decades of the twenty-first century. What was formerly a gradual, professional psychological impact is now a high-speed action that even the least competent, remote, and disassembled forces may conduct due to technological improvements (Rid, 2020). According to Schia and Gjesvik (2020), the weaponization of disinformation has been on the rise in recent years as the Internet and social media have grown in popularity (Bennett & Livingston, 2020; Rid, 2020; Singer & Brooking, 2018).

Deepfakes represent one newer technology that has recently undergone significant improvement. Its name combines deep learning, a machine learning technology used in artificial intelligence, and the notion of fakeness. The American intelligence community designated it a strategic threat to national security in 2019. It is a technology that allows the creation of synthetic video or audio, such as a video that puts words in the mouth of a leader (Hwang et al., 2021). Deepfakes symbolize, in a broader sense, the post-truth ethos, which makes the public more distrustful and calls into question the veracity of any content to which it is exposed. In other words, such technology distorts the human impression that what we see exists and thereby undermines the credibility of any movie or recording, hence lowering the value of truth (Andrejevic, 2013).

"Terrorism is theater," declared RAND Corporation analyst Brian Jenkins (1974) in an article that became one of the most recognized studies on terrorism. This mindset has guided terrorists for decades. They now have access to a new audience and battleground thanks to the Internet, online social networking, and new technological tools. Nations fight them in this terrain to defend their sense of security, prestige, and public legitimacy.

The affordances brought about by technological advancements and social transformations—the blurring of lines between attitude, opinion, and deception in the "post-truth" era—also impact national security. As conflicts no longer conclude in obvious wins, the importance of narrative struggles grows. Successes are not solely perceptual; however, the attitudes that troops and civilians have in countries worldwide significantly impacts how the success of military missions are evaluated. By building resilience against attempts to cast doubt on the military's capability and purpose, it will be possible to prevent opponents from misusing information to nefarious ends.

Overview of Threats from a Global Perspective

This section will briefly review the critical threat models discussed in the current literature: (1) the conventional Russian national model; (2) ISIS's operational model as a global terror organization; and (3) the wider global model of infodemic, which utilizes disorder to bring about further chaos, as in the case of COVID-19 disinformation campaigns. While these three models have received much attention, this chapter will focus on a fourth one, a unique model that is more pertinent to Israeli efforts to develop resilience as a form of deterrence—the so-called Iranian model.

NATIONAL INFLUENCE CAMPAIGNS COUPLED WITH ACTIVE COMBAT: THE RUSSIAN HYBRID MODEL IN CRIMEA

The actual conquest of the Crimean Peninsula was accomplished through military force, but the incursion "into the mind" of Crimean residents began far earlier. The 2014 invasion of Ukraine and annexation of Crimea were supported by a propaganda campaign conducted by Russian official media that was widely circulated on the peninsula at the time. When the Russian military offered "assistance" in annexing and safeguarding the peninsula, the local population was willing to accept this in part (Summers, 2017). Russia has undertaken cyber-attacks on Ukrainian government offices and crucial infrastructure, in addition to propagating fake news through social media (Greenberg, 2019b; Singer, 2014). These acts exacerbated societal problems and rifts while reinforcing public skepticism about the Ukrainian government's ability to safeguard its citizens. This "constant disruption of stability" contributed to the narrative that justified Russia's annexation of Crimea.

In so doing the Russian state emphasized the "Gerasimov Doctrine," named after Putin's favourite military intellectual, General Geresimov, which takes advantage of information asymmetry. Gerasimov is the creator of the Russian version of "hybrid war." Since 2014, Russia's military-strategic compass has emphasized a new focus on political, economic, and cyber warfare. Russia has committed significant resources to organizing its power through influence operations to upgrade the doctrine. It has since been conducting numerous initiatives worldwide to strengthen its positions in a way that allows it to exploit the disparity between it and Western democracies (Stengel, 2019).

INFORMATION TERRORISM IN THE MIDDLE EAST: THE ISIS DISINFORMATION MODEL

The meteoric rise of the Islamic State, or ISIS, terrorist organization demonstrates social media's enormous influence. The key to its success is its exceptional capacity to dominate social media and draw international attention, without distinctive military capabilities or a substantial cyber-attack capacity (Stengel, 2019). Its biggest weapon was the hashtag #AlleyesonISIS. During its peak, this the was the most popular hashtag on Arab Twitter, filling the screens of millions of users, including city residents and defenders. Thousands of the organization's messages terrified defence forces, prompting them to abandon helicopters, tanks, and other vehicles; the spread of terror can be matched by considering it as an unconventional weapon (Singer & Brooking, 2018).

THE USE OF COVID-19 INFODEMIC AS A BASIS FOR INFLUENCE CAMPAIGNS

One of Russia's most successful operations, Operation Infection, was triggered by an HIV outbreak. KGB agents have directed their colleagues to promote the myth that AIDS is a biological weapon created by the United States to kill Blacks and homosexuals. This information caused distrust in the US military, as seen in increased negative attitudes among Black and LGBT soldiers (Rid, 2020). Looking at the contemporary situation, we can see parallels with the COVID-19 pandemic. In early February 2020, the World Health Organization named the epidemic an "infodemic" owing to the information overload that accompanied it (Thomas, 2020). Since then, the infodemic has brought millions of people worldwide to their knees in a torrent of information as they tap WhatsApp screens and other social networks at an ever-increasing rate. This information crisis costs society dearly, resulting in uncertainty, worry, anxiety, misunderstanding, and the inability to make social judgments and engage in decision making at a critical time (Bar-Gil, 2020). In addition to the information epidemic produced by the uncertainties surrounding the new virus, some actors began influence attempts comparable to the prior exploitation of AIDS.

According to some, the coronavirus originated in Chinese biological weapons laboratories. Another report by Harvard's Freeman Center for Free

Communication claimed that Russia is trying to gain influence by promoting conspiracies surrounding the deployment of the fifth-generation communication network (5G) in the United States, claiming that the radiation it emits aggravates the disease (Bush, 2020). As nations raced to vaccinate a sizable section of their populations, there were reports that Russia was attempting to gain an advantage through hacks, data theft, and disinformation against the vaccine (Sabbagh & Roth, 2020). Russian motivations were likely to include a desire to weaken Western countries' trust in the ability of their vaccines to compete and restore the economy through widespread vaccination (Scott, 2020).

THE IRANIAN MODEL

US National Security Adviser John Bolton labelled Iran a "national security risk" in 2018. Surprisingly, it earned this status for its information efforts, which aimed to push topics and narratives in line with Iranian foreign policy, supporting "anti-Saudi, anti-Israeli, and pro-Palestinian themes, as well as support for certain US policies beneficial to Iran, such as the US-Iran nuclear deal" (Tabatabai, 2018).

Tehran is no stranger to information warfare. The Islamic Republic, like other authoritarian governments, exploited information as a form of hard political capital, and the disinformation strategies used by the Iran are as old as the Iranian revolutionaries who worked to depose the shah in the 1970s. Back then, they employed various techniques to amplify the voice of Ayatollah Ruhollah Khomeini by distributing brochures and cassette recordings with his speeches on them. The cassettes were inexpensive, quickly duplicated, and easy to hide from the shah's intelligence agency. Khomeini's voice and message acquired traction on Iranian streets thanks to the cassettes, even as he remained in exile in Paris. Khomeini's advisers, educated in the West, assisted him in marketing his messages to many audiences: Iranians at home and in exile, Shia Muslim communities in the Middle East, the broader Muslim world, and the West. Khomeini's supporters laid the groundwork for his ascension with a clandestine political strategy that combined propaganda and disinformation (Tabatabai, 2018). Nowadays, Iran employs a plethora of fake social media accounts, fake websites, and news outlets with cyber capabilities to further its policy objectives in many countries. The precise impact of these activities is unknown (ClearSky Security, 2018).

Iran, Russia, and China are active in today's regional and global information war. Iranian attitudes and experiences in such conflicts as the Iraq-Iran War and fears about foreign involvement have made information warfare a preferred tactic of the Iranian state over the years. Iran demonstrates to its adversaries that it can hurt their "soft underbelly," or the fabric of civilian life in their countries, by employing cyber and information warfare. Among other methods, Iran aims to hurt Israel through this dimension, which can bridge the significant distance between the nations.

Overview of the Israeli Case

As an introduction, it is critical to recognize that high degrees of trust and social legitimacy have evolved to play a growing role in the operations of the Israeli military and the State of Israel. In his article "The Clocks that Tapped Lazily," Guy Brooker (2011) cites several critical variables that determine the Israel Defense Forces (IDF) public legitimacy and allow it to maintain its military freedom of action: the sensitivity to social protest in democratic regimes complicates army operations, as seen during the First Lebanon War (1982), when public opposition was a primary concern in its administration (Toby & Rartner, 2007). The sense of vulnerability on the home front, as well as Operation Pillar of Cloud (2012), intensified pressure to stop the war during the Second Lebanon War (2006) and Operation Cast Lead (2009), on both the international and Israeli fronts. The Israeli public regards the IDF as a moral army, and any transgression of this paradigm may jeopardize its freedom of action and credibility at home. Globalization trends, which also exist in Israel, increase the role of the international arena in managing hostilities, and international legitimacy is primarily shaped by public opinion. This infringement was shown in Operation Grapes of Wrath (1996), which resulted in considerable internal and international pressure following a misdirected attack on a UN refugee compound.

Over the last twenty-five years, there has been a substantial practice in the battle for narrative in Israel. As part of this endeavour, the IDF Spokesperson's Unit has been bolstered, and the Prime Minister's Office now has a National Cyber Directorate. Preparations for the prospect of a negative effect on public discourse and democratic processes in Israel, particularly the Knesset elections, are essential in such attempts (Goldschmidt & Warren, 2017).

The IDF developed and published a doctrine on influence and information operations in 2017. The doctrine recognized and defined the threats to

IDF action posed by global environmental change. In particular, it recognized that "the enemy's influence effort is activated and developed via a comprehensive examination of the State of Israel's and its military power's strengths and vulnerabilities. Its underlying premise is based on the notion that the enemy will be using asymmetrical tactics to weaken the IDF's authority, affect its public image, and limit its freedom of action" (IDF, 2019, p. 3).

The more complex and advantageous a country's digital infrastructure, the more vulnerable it is to "asymmetric" information and cyber-attacks. Furthermore, the socio-cultural capital of Western democracies, whose citizens and institutions enjoy a higher level of trust, is more vulnerable than in low-trust countries (San-Akca, 2014). Compared to its adversaries, Israel has more to lose, and more "attack surface" in the form of information networks (Mazarr et al., 2022; Ross et al., 2019), and Israel's adversaries strive to compensate for this advantage through asymmetric warfare.

Some unique features distinguish the Israeli case, and while these may limit the generalizability of the research, they may also provide some insight into potential essential areas to consider when building a strategy for engaging and deterring threats. The first is the linguistic aspect. Hebrew, the most widely spoken language in Israel, is spoken by fewer than ten million people worldwide. This could present new difficulties and opportunities. It may call into question the availability of global information as well as the availability of language-based solutions to combat deception and disinformation. On the other hand, it provides superior control and the ability to discern communication trends. It is a significant barrier for those who seek to mount influence campaigns in areas where technical capabilities and English are insufficient. They must learn the language and culture to conduct credible influence operations.

Another distinguishing feature is the Israeli military's high level of trust. It is the most trusted institution in Israel (Shafran-Gittleman, 2022) and has one of the greatest confidence percentages of any of the world's militaries (Gains, 2021). With such high levels of trust, the IDF's ability to manage public dialogue may appear legendary, but this is not the reality. However, the opinions of military personnel (or ex-military personnel) are highly appreciated.

The next distinctive feature to evaluate is Israel's censorship and its connection with the institutional media. Its role is to develop the essential capacities to monitor, filter, and control content and information in order to avoid potential harm. It might be utilized as a significant coordinating and synchronization hub during times of conflict, influencing efforts conducted by other governments to weaken Israel's security and resilience. Some countries have similar bodies, such as the United States, Australia, Denmark, and Belgium (Bodine-Baron et al., 2018; Cooperwasser & Simen-Tov, 2019). They do not, however, have the communication-governance mechanisms of legislation and regulation developed in Israel. Those may be of interest and offer some insight in attempting to achieve the complex balance between public rights, the development of critical thinking, and the need to protect nations from foreign influence operations.

The main threat to Israel is the multi-layered Israeli-Iranian confrontation, which has been going on for years. Iran must find ways to bridge the physical distance between the two countries. Some of these ways include using proxies and acting in dimensions where distance is irrelevant, such as the cyber and information spheres. Iran's influence operations against Israel are part of a broader set of initiatives subordinated to the Iranian regime's top priorities. One facet of Iran's threat to Israel is the deployment of proxies, such as Hezbollah, trained and operated from Teheran, providing it with cyber deniability (Clarke, 2017; Schaefer, 2018). Iran employs three primary methods that reinforce one another in its influence campaigns against Israel: (1) the use of fake accounts to incite public dissent on social media (ClearSky Security, 2018); (2) fake news outlets portraying Israel as a weak state while delivering news favourable to Iran and its geopolitical objectives (Barel, 2021); and (3) using cyber capabilities to conduct hack-and-leak operations to undermine trust in Israeli officials and institutions and Israeli citizens' sense of security in the cyber domain (Hochberg, 2021). Former intelligence minister Eli Cohen recently cited reports about fake websites identified in the country (Cohen, 2018), claiming that Iran is not only attempting to influence public opinion in Israel but is also investing considerable resources in doing so (Halperin, 2020b). These efforts were carried out by operatives impersonating Israelis to stir social and political strife (Tony, 2020). It was revealed before the 2020 election that Iran utilized an army of bots and phony accounts to promote disinformation, bad talk, and provocation. It is also expected that the infrastructure of false accounts would be utilized for fraud to steal information and take over multiple electronic devices and user accounts (Rubinstein, 2019). Following a series of extortion operations attributed to Iranians, the media's attention has also intensified. Several such attacks have occurred recently, but the most well-known is the attack on the Shirbit insurance company.

It was announced in December 2020 that a group calling itself "Black Shadow" had targeted Shirbit. It obtained a vast array of data, including sensitive information on its policyholders and internal corporate data. The attackers later used media attention to humiliate the company and its insured customers by revealing several details and negotiating a ransom payment (Ziv, 2020).

Cyber-attacks and influence campaigns promote embarrassment, humiliation, media awareness, and trust erosion. However, Israel is not alone in the world; therefore, on the following section looks at global engagement strategies and their local implementation in Israel in a way that reinforces resilience and deterrence.

Deterrence Strategies: From Global Threat to Local Implementation

TURNING DISADVANTAGE INTO ADVANTAGE: USING SOCIAL MEDIA AS OSINT

If nations understand how to harness the asymmetry generated by the rising use of social networks, they can turn this to their advantage. Extensive information can be obtained from expanding open-source intelligence technologies (OSINT). The civic intelligence organization Bellingcat, which solved the enigma of Malaysian Airlines Flight MH17's destruction over Ukraine, gained widespread attention (Bellingcat, 2018). The group was established soon after that tragedy. Following the plane's destruction, members of the organization discovered numerous images and videos of a Buk missile launcher near the MH17 flight route on the day of the tragedy—within the separatist, Russian-supported zone (Singer & Brooking, 2018). The organization's investigators were then able to locate the unit to which the missile launcher belonged. The Bellingcat analysts' report presented compelling evidence to answer the mystery that troubled several Western intelligence organizations while relying primarily on visible sources, and they were able to expose the misinformation spread by Russia and direct the blame to specific personnel.

In Israel, the blogger "Abu Ali Express" engaged in similar actions and received institutional support. Abu Ali Express is a famous Israeli blogger who covers Arab matters on social media platforms such as Telegram and Twitter, as well as on his website. He bases his posts on gathering and evaluating open-source news and social media. He held the Telegram channel with the highest views per post in Israel as of September 2022, and his posts go viral in both social media and traditional news agencies. Despite his Arabic alias, the blog was founded by an Israeli citizen. In 2021, *Haaretz* newspaper exposed that he had been endorsed by the IDF in 2018 to administer the channel as an OSINT-based influence tool to expose disinformation and actors spreading it using his fast response and broad audience (Kubovich, 2021).

A KINETIC WAR INFLUENCED BY CYBERSPACE

Following the COVID-19 pandemic, the word "super-spreader" has become ingrained in our vocabulary. The role of these players on social media is significant. Social media can help spread a particular message in the real world. Their virtual networks allow nefarious actors to disseminate lies, hate, and other societal toxins. Some nations use kinetic power to harm these super-spreaders. Washington killed an ISIS spokesperson in 2019 to prevent ISIS from rallying people and resources against the United States via social media (Coles et al., 2019). There is no evidence that Israel had used firepower against social media influencers, but in May 2019, Hamas attempted to create cyber offensive capabilities in Israel. It acted from the Gaza Strip to attack Israeli cyberspace. The infrastructure failed to achieve its goal because all attempts and operations were identified and blocked technologically. As a result of counterterrorism operations, the IDF targeted a Hamas cyber array (Newman, 2019; Shahaf, 2019). One might consider kinetic attacks used to respond to cyberspace-based activities, such as cyber-attacks or influence campaigns, as the opposite of hybrid warfare—taking the cyber battle to a kinetic dimension to convey a message rather than simply stopping the activities in cyberspace.

Developing Military and National Resiliency to Deter Foreign Actors?

While the examples above may deter actors from conducting influence operations through social media influence or kinetic force, they do not do so by establishing resilience. The following section will illustrate various ways to develop resilience in general and as a deterrent to information operations. It begins by looking at the various ways of implementing national plans to improve critical thinking, trust, regulation, and governance processes. It then outlines how to increase the military's resilience and the role of technology products and partnerships before concluding with a concept for a resilience framework to influence campaigns.

Developing Nationwide Strategies

SUPPORTING SOCIAL CRITICAL THINKING MECHANISMS FOR SOCIAL NETWORKS

Could one of the possible solutions to our social media trust problem be a different type of social media? In many countries, social media is used to raise public awareness of how information is consumed, uncover fraud and lies, and promote civic demands (van Doorn & Brinkel, 2021).

Stanford University researchers examined information consumption behaviours among three groups: undergraduate students, history PhDs, and fact-checking specialists, and compared how they judged the accuracy of Internet content. Undergraduate and PhD students received poor grades. Despite their apparent intelligence, the study discovered that they focused on "vertical" information—evaluating only one source and assessing it from within their world view. As a result, they were susceptible to manipulation. The researchers concluded that dealing with inaccurate information requires learning the proper skills rather than being "clever" (Bergstrom & West, 2020). People should be able to identify and cross-reference sources, spot suspicious details, and use fact-checking websites to develop the requisite competencies (WHO, 2020). While these educational initiatives benefit individuals, societies can also benefit from comparable methods. Some civic organizations in Israel analyze facts and fight disinformation. For-profit news organizations even support some of these efforts, but institutionalized support can boost resilience to disinformation.

USING CHANGE AGENTS AND INFLUENCERS TO ENHANCE TRUST

Finland, Estonia, Lithuania, and Sweden, all neighbours of the former Soviet Union, developed initiatives over the years to prepare their citizens to resist Soviet influence, and these methods remain applicable to the post–Cold War context. These states' "immune systems" involve extensive initiatives for educating residents and monitoring public information for unfounded claims, deception, and foreign media involvement (Singer & Brooking, 2018). According to a World Health Organization study, persons who "doubted the extent to which they received the message," or who "did not pass on the communication," reduced their exposure to fraudulent messages by about 80 per cent (WHO, 2020).

Increasing trust and decreasing misinformation affect both individuals and societies. The well-known word "influencers" implies that the way information is consumed is influenced by virtual and traditional leaders in a given group. Influencers in various organizations can be trained to establish resilience against false and erroneous information. They can have the ability to hinder the success of information efforts. Any team member who decides not to share material they are unsure about should double-check such material or even question the distributor (Bennett & Livingston, 2020).

In Israel, one further step aims to capitalize on the high trust enjoyed by the country's military leaders by institutionalizing their role as influencers even on subjects that are not strictly military or security related.

REGULATION AND GOVERNANCE MECHANISMS

In 1933, the British Mandatory authorities decided to regulate the Jewish and Arab press through the Press Ordinance and other censorship agencies. Similarly, the British government enacted the Emergency Protection Regulations in 1945, which required all printed material—newspapers, magazine, books—to be approved by the censor before being printed. As soon as Israel was established, the Press Ordinance and Emergency Protection Regulations were written into Israeli law. Israel is the only Western democracy where censorship is enshrined in law and enforced by the military itself (Goldschmidt & Warren, 2017).

In his piece "The End of Censorship," journalist Guy Kotev (1999) argues that new media technologies have led to the demise of censorship, which only persists due to the reactive nature of the media. Digital online media necessitates a makeover of Israel's unique censorship stance and relationship with the institutional media (Altshuler & Lurie, 2016). It might help develop the tools required to monitor, filter, and control content and information in order to avert potential harm. It might be utilized as a significant coordinating and synchronization hub for foreign governments' influence operations to undermine Israel's security and resilience. Similar organizations exist in other countries, including the United States, Australia, Denmark, and Belgium (Bodine-Baron et al., 2018; Cooperwasser & Simen-Tov, 2019).

These countries do not, however, have the same rules and mechanisms as Israel. The regulations imposed elsewhere may be problematic since they impede the transparency and critical thinking required for a thriving democracy, however, adopting them can give Israel an advantage in establishing resistance to influence campaigns. On the other hand, such regulations can be why Israel's National Cyber Security Directorate[1] does not consider defence against influence operations as part of its mission, despite global trends that place a high emphasis on such efforts (Goldschmidt & Warren, 2017).

Developing Military Resilience: Train Hard to Fight Easy?

A simulated battle breaks out several times a year, forcing the media to cover the killing of uninvolved people and the foiling of potential terrorist acts in a replica of the Internet designed to mimic what happens in real-world wars in the cyber and social networking dimensions. The fabricated network comprises blogs, foreign news outlets, and social media profiles that work together to create a virtual war in response to the real one. As the units trained at this facility deploy on operations, the "people" who oppose them use social media to organize their attacks. Singer and Brookings's book *Like Wars* (2018) features an interview with a former intelligence officer involved in developing these scenarios. According to him, such exercises enable soldiers to deal with a large and complex information environment. The significance of training is found in its application. As a first step, commanders must approach this as a new and extensive operational problem. The drills give commanders a better grasp of how social media may impact fights and be utilized by the enemy to influence them. The operators also learn how their activities affect media, how information operations affect their susceptibility and the vulnerability of their peers, and so discover better ways to deal with them. This way, the units develop resilience and are better equipped to operate in the networked social media environment.

Some commanders' education includes a social media literacy component that aims to educate units to operate in a social media context and to be critical consumers of information. To complement the updating of the new online communication directive, the IDF's chief education officer created a comprehensive kit for social media usage.

Understandably, soldiers' and commanders' social networking participation is limited in Israel. During an emergency, military personnel will be bombarded with information. It will be up to their training to determine how they will contribute to the military and national resilience through crucial information consumption.

Resilience through Technology Development

This fight against disinformation does not have to be conducted by humans alone. For instance, it is possible to block information in a widely distributed environment, as seen, for example, through the technology used in the war on pedophilia. PhotoDNA is a pedophilia-fighting content-control technology. Employing a database containing over a million visual objects, it compares any image or video submitted on social media to its massive collection of pedophilic images to verify that the image posted on the Internet does not include or promote pedophilia. Any major social media platform is likely to eventually integrate this technique, drastically lowering the number of pedophilia and child pornography cases on social media (Singer & Brooking, 2018).

In reaction to the PhotoDNA system's success, Facebook has announced a similar initiative to combat the spread of revenge porn—private photographs obtained illegally or without permission and then published on social media to harm the person being photographed. Facebook encourages people to report photographs and films they suspect of falling into this category. Similarly, it is technologically feasible to create a digital "fingerprint" for incorrect or harmful visual or textual material spread on social networks in order to monitor and prevent its spread (Statt, 2017).

Disinformation is a global problem, and many technologies are available to aid in the fight. This can begin with browser extensions that can notify you when information is suspected to be fake, sites that check suspicious information among expert communities, and plug-ins that check the credibility of information sources and block the display of suspected fake sources. All these technologies might be converted to the local arena or used to inspire the development of comparable tools for soldiers and commanders to resist fabricated, inaccurate, and misleading information. New tools are always being developed and enhanced through competitions, grants, and other resources (Knight, 2020). The Israeli setting may present distinct obstacles and opportunities due to the use of the Hebrew language. Israel should encourage the use of local platforms and the formation of collaborative action teams with media platforms. Learning from other countries' and platforms' collaboration has been successfully integrated into the fight against ISIS, for example. Building partnerships between heads of state, regulators, and technological platforms is a major component of such efforts. A meeting in 2016 between US defence leaders and the heads of Facebook, Twitter, Google, and other firms to develop a coordinated plan to diminish ISIS's social dominance provides an interesting illustration of this (Wong & Yadron, 2016).

Creating a Framework for Influence Operations Resilience

The literature in international law provides several recommendations concerning cyber security, foreign influence, multinational regulation of social networks, and other broadly applicable recommendations that take a long time to execute (Bodine-Baron et al., 2018). This chapter aims to provide proposals that will help nations and militaries right now, until long-term global solutions can be established. One crucial recommendation is to develop a doctrine capable of deterring opponents from participating in information operations by building their internal resilience mechanisms. To this end, I endorse Padan and Elran's (2018, p. 7) definition of resilience: "Resilience is a system's ability to adjust flexibly to interruption and the inevitable functional degradation that ensues, then quickly recover, return to full or even increased functionality." The key proposal for developing resilience to threats in this dimension is to take a proactive strategy, which can be drawn from the concept of resilience to cyber-attacks, available in many military doctrines, and then expand it. Cyber resilience refers to the ability to foresee, cope with, adapt to, and recover from challenges, pressures, or attacks on systems that use or are facilitated by cyber resources. The expansion proposed here is based on the National Institute of Standards and Technology's ideas around cyber resilience, which contain three interconnected layers: preparation, inclusion, and adaptation (Ross et al., 2019). In this section, I will go through the changes that need to be made to cyber resilience policy and the emphases that will allow these updated measures to cope with influence operations, and possibly deter them, as well as the concrete recommendations that will result from such changes.

PLANNING, TRAINING, AND GATHERING DEDICATED INTELLIGENCE

To fully understand an opponent's abilities, it is necessary to assign sufficient intelligence resources. One type of data collection is exploiting open-source intelligence, which adversaries frequently use to coordinate attacks. This could involve identifying suspected negative influence attractors online, establishing analysis tools, and developing and exposing techniques for identifying bots, fake profiles, and coordinated influence networks.

Planning and gathering information intelligence is not enough, however. Practice makes perfect, and this is especially true when it comes to building resilience. Nations and militaries must brace themselves for influence operations that may undermine the public's faith in the military.

Monitoring and developing appropriate metrics and base rates are part of the preparation process. This should also include incorporating and enforcing the use of various monitoring technologies so that campaigns can be discovered and impacted. These tools should collect data on various parameters, such as posts produced by Israeli users versus posts published from other nations. Moreover, regularly monitoring and evaluating popular trust in the military is crucial. Such monitoring will allow for the detection of anomalous activities during ordinary operations, thereby contributing to our understanding of what works and what does not in the narrative battle over these topics, and developing methods for mitigating those impacts in emergencies and crises. Furthermore, regular monitoring will aid in detecting fake accounts influencing soldiers or preparing infrastructure for subsequent cyber activities.

DEVELOPING FAST INCLUSION AND RESPONSE

This phase is the time between the onset of an unrecognized campaign's effect and its discovery and containment to the point that it does not cause more damage. It is part of responding to an occurrence quickly and creating the resilience needed to continue functioning. Influence operations necessitate more resources, just as resources are required to cope with a significant occurrence. In a severe occurrence that undermines the credibility and legitimacy of army actions, damage must be identified and successfully addressed as well as attributed to specific causes. Specific counter-campaigns should be used to deal with such damage in order to reduce the short- and long-term harm.

Conclusion

Once the Internet became a battleground, its influence could potentially be felt by militaries and governments, civilians and operators, in the realms of politics and war alike. Identifying who might be hurt by such behaviour is critical in developing and evaluating coping mechanisms. The multiplicity of actors makes it difficult for militaries and governments to engage in initiatives in this area.

When a security organization, the IDF, or other forces monitor social media influence and messaging, a delicate balance must be struck that allows for the preservation of civil and democratic rights following legislation and regulations. While the Israeli context is unique, there is much to be learned from its experience with the threat from Iran in a systematic manner, considering the different contexts of other nations.

Can resilience deter opponents in this field? To date, resilience can be seen as a strategy to combat hybrid warfare campaigns. It can also be a potent deterrent for opponents in this arena by making it difficult for them to achieve their goals while also allowing the defender to exhibit a sense of readiness and preparedness that provides the ability to "bounce back" in the face of such campaigns and to diminish their intended impacts. Although Israel can further strengthen its resilience, the intensifying confrontation with Iran has yet to prove the role of resilience as a deterrent.

Disinformation divides societies and organizations into groups by exploiting psychological and sociological weaknesses. This is more than a scientific debate for us: How can we ensure that open access to information allows for a constant appraisal of various societal views while minimizing the potential damage caused by distorted and fraudulent information intended to weaken Western militaries and societies?

According to Paul Virilio (1991, 2005), a technology philosopher, every new technology is followed by an accident, a catastrophe caused by its unique point of failure. He asserted that the invention of the ship brought about the possibility of the shipwreck, the development of the plane brought about the possibility of the plane crash, and the discovery of the automobile brought about the possibility of the car accident. The spread of disinformation could be considered a social network accident or disaster. The greater the flow and movement of information, the more difficult it is to separate the wheat from the chaff and prevent foreign forces from being impacted via cyber or influence campaigns. As we become more dependent on digital systems, we add new risks to our lives—risks that we must strive to reduce in order to enjoy the benefits of the digital age fully. It is simply a question of seizing the opportunity before influence activities occur, as has happened worldwide.

This chapter indicates that resilience might complement deterrence in a novel way, reducing enemy achievements in this domain by action and supporting frameworks and doctrines that will bring about greater results without endangering the open and democratic society's resilience.

NOTES

1 Located within the Prime Minister's Office, the National Cyber Security Directorate is the security entity responsible for protecting the Israeli civilian cyber space. For more information, see their web site at https://www.gov.il/en/departments/israel_national_cyber_directorate/govil-landing-page.

REFERENCES

Altshuler, T. S., & Luria, G. (2016). *Censorship and security secrets in the digital age* [Hebrew]. Policy Research 113. Israel Democracy Institute.

Andrejevic, M. (2013). *Infoglut: How too much information is changing the way we think and know.* Routledge.

Bar-Gil, O. (2020). *In world media # 2: The coronavirus as an infodemia* [Internal report; Hebrew]. Applied Research Institute for Behavioral Sciences in the IDF.

Bellingcat. (2018, 20 November). Truth in a post-truth world [Dutch]. *BNNVARA.* https://joop.bnnvara.nl/videos/terugkijken-idfa-documentaire-bellingcat-truth-in-a-post-truth-world

Bennett, W. L., & Livingston, S. (2020). *The disinformation age: Politics, technology, and disruptive communication in the United States.* Cambridge University Press.

Bergstrom, C. T., & West, J. D. (2020). *calling bullshit: the art of skepticism in a data-driven world.* Random House.

Bodine-Baron, E., Helmus, T. C., Radin, A., & Treyger, E. (2018). *Countering russian social media influence* (RR-2740-RC). RAND Corporation. https://www.rand.org/pubs/research_reports/RR2740.html

Brooker, G. (2011). The clocks that ticked lazily: The army's conduct in the tension between legitimacy and the limits of the use of force [Hebrew]. *Between the Arenas,* 10, 12–33.

Bush, D. (2020, July 30). *Two faces of Russian information operations: Coronavirus coverage in Spanish.* Stanford Internet Observatory. https://fsi.stanford.edu/news/two-faces-russian-information-operations-coronavirus-coverage-spanish

Chivvis, C. (2017). *Understanding Russian "hybrid warfare": And what can be done about it.* RAND Corporation. https://doi.org/10.7249/CT468

Clarke, C. P. (2017, 19 September). How Hezbollah came to dominate information warfare. *RAND Blog.* https://www.rand.org/blog/2017/09/how-hezbollah-came-to-dominate-information-warfare.html

Clausewitz, C. von. (1989). *On war, indexed edition* (M. E. Howard & P. Paret, Trans.; Revised ed.). Princeton University Press.

Cohen, S. (2018, 6 September). This is not an Israeli site; this is Iranian propaganda [Hebrew]. *YNET.* https://www.ynet.co.il/articles/0,7340,L-5342357,00.html

Coles, I., Osseiran, N., & Donati, J. (2019, 28 October). Islamic State spokesman killed in U.S. airstrike. *Wall Street Journal.* https://www.wsj.com/articles/islamic-state-spokesman-targeted-in-u-s-airstrike-say-kurds-11572268364

Cooperwasser, J., & Siman-Tov, D. (2019). *The battle for consciousness: Strategic and intelligent aspects.* Institute for National Security Studies. https://www.inss.org.il/he/publication/the-cognitive-campaign/

Goldschmidt, R., & Wergan, J. (2017). *Dissemination of false information on the Internet and cyber-attacks to influence elections* [Hebrew]. Knesset Research and Information Center.

Greenberg, A. (2019a, 23 August). Cyberwar: The complete guide. *Wired.* https://www.wired.com/story/cyberwar-guide/

Greenberg, A. (2019b). *Sandworm: A new era of cyberwar and the hunt for the Kremlin's most dangerous hackers.* Doubleday.

Halperin, J. (2020a, 22 October). Gil Schweid: "The future of the cyber world—scary" [Hebrew]. *People and Computers.* https://www.pc.co.il/news/324292/

Halperin, J. (2020b, 25 November). Minister of intelligence: "Iran is trying to influence Israeli public opinion online" [Hebrew]. *People and Computers.* https://www.pc.co.il/featured/326648/

Hwang, Y., Ryu, J. Y., & Jeong, S.-H. (2021). Effects of disinformation using deepfake: The protective effect of media literacy education. *Cyberpsychology, Behavior, and Social Networking, 24*(3). https://doi.org/10.1089/cyber.2020.0174

IDF (2019). *Field guide for information operations* [Internal report; Hebrew].

Jenkins, B. M. (1974). *International terrorism: A new kind of warfare* (No. P5261). RAND Corporation. https://www.rand.org/content/dam/rand/pubs/papers/2008/P5261.pdf

Kotev, G. (1999, 9 September). The end of censorship. [Hebrew]. *7th Eye.* http://www.the7eye.org.il/23579

Kubovich, Y. (2021, 18 August). Israeli army employs popular blogger for psyops on social media. *Haaretz.* https://www.haaretz.com/israel-news/2021-08-18/ty-article/.premium/is-the-idf-behind-popular-arab-news-telegram-channel/0000017f-dc61-d3ff-a7ff-fde14daf0000

Mazarr, M. J. (2021). Understanding deterrence. In F. Osinga & T. Sweijs (Eds.), *NL ARMS Netherlands annual review of military studies 2020: Deterrence in the 21st century—insights from theory and practice* (pp. 13–28). Asser Press. https://doi.org/10.1007/978-94-6265-419-8_2

Mazarr, M. J., Chan, A., Demus, A., Frederick, B., Nader, A., Pezard, S., Thompson, J. A., & Treyger, E. (2018). *What deters and why: Exploring requirements for effective deterrence of interstate aggression.* Rand Corporation. https://www.rand.org/pubs/research_reports/RR2451.html

Mazarr, M. J., Rhoades, A. L., Beauchamp-Mustafaga, N., Blanc, A. A., Eaton, D., Feistel, K., Geist, E., Heath, T. R., Johnson, C., Langeland, K., Léveillé, J., Massicot, D.,

McBirney, S., Pezard, S., Reach, C., Vedula, P., & Yoder, E. (2022). *Disrupting deterrence: Examining the effects of technologies on strategic deterrence in the 21st century.* Rand Corporation. https://www.rand.org/pubs/research_reports/RRA595-1.html

Newman, L. H. (2019, 6 May). What Israel's strike on Hamas hackers means for cyberwar. *Wired.* https://www.wired.com/story/israel-hamas-cyberattack-air-strike-cyberwar/

O'Connor, C., & Weatherall, J. O. (2019). *The misinformation age: How false beliefs spread.* Yale University Press.

Padan, K., & Elran, M. (2018). *Localities in the "Gaza envelope"—a test case for social resilience in Israel (2006–2016)* [Hebrew]. Institute for National Security Studies.

Rid, T. (2020). *Active measures: The secret history of disinformation and political warfare.* Farrar, Straus and Giroux.

Ross, R., Pillitteri, V., Graubart, R., Bodeau, D., & McQuaid, R. (2019). *Developing cyber resilient systems: A systems security engineering approach* (NIST SP 800-160v2). National Institute of Standards and Technology. https://doi.org/10.6028/NIST.SP.800-160v2

Rubinstein, R. (2019, 31 January). Report: The Iranian "bot" army trying to influence the Israeli elections [Hebrew]. *YNET.* https://www.ynet.co.il/articles/0,7340,L-5455832,00.html

Sabbagh, D., & Roth, A. (2020, 16 July). Russian state-sponsored hackers target Covid-19 vaccine researchers. *The Guardian.* https://www.theguardian.com/world/2020/jul/16/russian-state-sponsored-hackers-target-covid-19-vaccine-researchers

San-Akca, B. (2014). Democracy and vulnerability: An exploitation theory of democracies by terrorists. *Journal of Conflict Resolution, 58*(7), 1285–1310.

Schaefer, B. (2018, 12 March). The cyber party of God: How Hezbollah could transform cyberterrorism. *Georgetown Security Studies Review.* https://georgetownsecuritystudiesreview.org/2018/03/11/the-cyber-party-of-god-how-hezbollah-could-transform-cyberterrorism/

Schia, N. N., & Gjesvik, L. (2020). Hacking democracy: Managing influence campaigns and disinformation in the digital age. *Journal of Cyber Policy, 5*(3), 413–428. https://doi.org/10.1080/23738871.2020.1820060

Scott, M. (2020, 19 November). In race for coronavirus vaccine, Russia turns to disinformation. *Politico.* https://www.politico.eu/article/covid-vaccine-disinformation-russia/

Shafran-Gittleman, I. (2022, 10 January). Restoring public trust in the IDF. *Israel Democracy Institute.* https://en.idi.org.il/articles/38089

Shahaf, T. (2019, 8 May). *Hamas' cyber capabilities have been fatally damaged* [Hebrew]. *YNET.* https://www.ynet.co.il/articles/0,7340,L-5506315,00.html

Singer, P. W. (2014). *Cybersecurity and cyberwar: What everyone needs to know.* Oxford University Press.

Singer, P. W., & Brooking, E. T. (2018). *Likewar: The weaponization of social media*. Eamon Dolan/Houghton Mifflin Harcourt.

Statt, N. (2017, 7 November). Facebook's unorthodox new revenge porn defense is to upload nudes to Facebook. *The Verge*. https://www.theverge.com/2017/11/7/16619690/facebook-revenge-porn-defense-strategy-test-australia

Stengel, R. (2019). *Information wars: How we lost the global battle against disinformation and what we can do about it*. Atlantic Monthly Press.

Summers, J. (2017, 25 October). *Countering disinformation: Russia's infowar in Ukraine*. Henry M. Jackson School of International Studies. https://jsis.washington.edu/news/russia-disinformation-ukraine/

Thiele, R. D. (2016). Building resilience readiness against hybrid threats—a cooperative European Union/NATO perspective. *ISPSW Strategy Series: Focus on Defense and International Security, 449*. https://css.ethz.ch/content/dam/ethz/special-interest/gess/cis/center-for-securities-studies/resources/docs/ISPSW-Building%20Resilience%20Readiness%20against%20Hybrid%20Threats.pdf

Thomas, Z. (2020, 13 February). Misinformation on coronavirus causing "infodemic." *BBC News*. https://www.bbc.com/news/technology-51497800

van Doorn, C., & Brinkel, T. (2021). Deterrence, resilience, and the shooting down of Flight MH17. In F. Osinga & T. Sweijs (Eds.), *NL ARMS Netherlands annual review of military studies 2020: Deterrence in the 21st century—insights from theory and practice* (pp. 365–83). TMC Asser Press. https://doi.org/10.1007/978-94-6265-419-8_19

Virilio, P. (1991). *Lost dimension*. Semiotext.

Virilio, P. (2005). *The information bomb*. Verso.

WHO (World Health Organization). (2020). *Immunizing the public against misinformation*. https://www.who.int/news-room/feature-stories/detail/immunizing-the-public-against-misinformation

Wong, J. C., & Yadron, D. (2016, 8 January). Silicon Valley appears open to helping US spy agencies after terrorism summit. *The Guardian*. http://www.theguardian.com/technology/2016/jan/08/technology-executives-white-house-isis-terrorism-meeting-silicon-valley-facebook-apple-twitter-microsoft

Ziv, A. (2020, 12 April). The cyber-attack on Shirbit—who is behind it and why it is worrying [Hebrew]. *The Marker*. https://www.themarker.com/technation/.premium-1.9348718

SECTION III

CANADA'S CONTEXT

8

Deterrence and Strategic Disinformation: An Overview of Canada's Responses

Nicole J. Jackson

Over the past half decade, in Canada and globally, considerable public and policy attention has focused on the question of whether and how to respond disinformation. Among Western governments, there is now a widespread understanding that strategic disinformation, especially through social media, may present serious challenges to national and societal security. A major concern is that some state and non-state actors, both foreign and domestic, are involved in organized strategic deception and/or are intentionally creating confusion by promoting divisive content that plays on pre-existing biases. There is an assumption that these actions may undermine credibility and trust in authorities, as well as in information itself, which makes it easier to manipulate societies and leaders. For the military, a particular concern is that disinformation, and other manipulations of information, may exacerbate or even create a chaotic environment in which to make decisions. Yet, despite the acknowledged need to respond urgently to disinformation, there is no academic or policy consensus about whether, when, and how to do so.

This lack of consensus is partly because the subject of disinformation is fraught with problems of definition and therefore ambiguity. A spectrum of disinformation has always existed, and specific cases have varied, but today actors and processes appear and evolve at an unprecedented rate, some almost instantaneously and with global reach. Within this context, academics and practitioners analyze and advocate for different responses to a range of "disinformation." Even when focusing more specifically, for example, on "strategic disinformation" or "*foreign*," "strategic *digital* disinformation," there is little or no consensus as to which measures, or combination of measures, are needed, are most effective, or are ethical in particular circumstances.

Currently, some experts are questioning whether the theory and practice of "deterrence" may provide some insights into possible state responses in the information environment. The traditional military understanding of deterrence is based on the idea that a potential aggressor's cost-benefit calculation might be influenced, for example, by the threat of a punitive response (deterrence by punishment) or by the realization that the defender's preparations are so advanced or effective (deterrence by denial) that the costs of carrying out the aggression would be too great (Snyder, 1961). Of course, when applied to "disinformation" or "strategic disinformation," as examined in this chapter, the traditional logic of deterrence, which is already controversial, is further complicated. In fact, many would argue that deterrence has little or no place in a discussion about (dis)information. Yet the concept has evolved, and deterrence remains at the core of US and NATO—and hence Canadian—strategy.

This chapter therefore examines whether and how both the concept and theory of deterrence have evolved in ways that make them useful to understand and assess responses to "strategic disinformation" and uncover their limits. It also provides a case study of Canadian security and foreign policy responses to specifically ask whether the "widening of deterrence" is helpful in explaining Canada's burgeoning approach. In doing so, we see how Canada's fragmented actions may be illuminated by these wider understandings, in addition to revealing certain missing actions.

The chapter first examines the contested definitions of "disinformation" and "deterrence." Both concepts have been conceptually stretched within scholarly works and in practice, creating uncertainty about "what to deter" and "how to deter." It then examines recent literature on the theory and practice of deterrence to highlight where "new" understandings have relevance and limits for considering whether and how to respond to disinformation. Next, the chapter examines whether and how Canada is attempting to "deter," that is, how it is trying to foster restraint and prevent (some) disinformation and its negative effects. It categorizes the government's major foreign and security actions since 2014 according to whether they fit within deterrence by denial (including technical and strategic denial through resilience) or "deterrence by punishment or imposing costs" (including social and psychological costs). By framing Canada's major actions through the broadened lens of deterrence, this review also highlights what is missing from Canada's fragmentary approach. The chapter concludes by suggesting that, despite the contributions of recent literature on deterrence, "democratic suasion" may be a more appropriate and holistic concept to describe and guide Canada's approach.

Of course, context matters, and the context for Canadian (and other governments') responses to disinformation is a world in which many state and non-state actors have become more proactive and increasingly global—by co-opting traditional and social media around the world for their own purposes and taking more aggressive moves to shape and suppress online *and* offline discourse at home and abroad. Adding further complexity, but also opening new opportunities for reform, this is increasingly happening through the use of new technologies at a time when Western liberal democracies are confronted with political polarization, media echo chambers, and widespread questioning of the resilience of Western democratic institutions and quality of governance.

The chapter begins by examining the definitional ambiguity and conceptual stretching of "disinformation," which is necessary to answer a question of key interest here: What is to be deterred? It then examines the conceptual stretching of "deterrence" to discover insights from recent literature that may be applied to the questions of whether and how disinformation can be deterred, and then to the case of Canada.

The Ambiguity of What to Deter: The Conceptual Stretching and "Hybridization" of "Disinformation"

Perhaps the most significant challenge in addressing disinformation is how to define it. Definitional and practical scope ambiguity have direct implications for thinking about whether we can "deter" the challenge, and how. Whether we are, or believe we are, facing "misinformation," "digital disinformation," "disinformation," "strategic narratives," "information *warfare,*" or "strategic information campaigns," the language we use can imply different sets of challenges and strategies that need to be addressed, and thus different responses.

Disinformation is not new, and neither is the study of disinformation. Yet, despite a recent proliferation of studies, the scholarly definition (and identification) of disinformation remains controversial. In practice, disinformation is often very loosely defined, reflecting its ambiguity and complexity, including the blurred line between a variety of often related activities including cyber-attacks, leaks, and corruption. Today, there is some academic consensus that "disinformation" is best defined as the deliberate dissemination of *intentionally* false or inaccurate information, as opposed to "misinformation," which is the act of spreading false information unintentionally, including when intent can not be determined (Jack, 2019; Jayakumar et al., 2021; Lanoszka, 2019; Tucker, 2018). Disinformation, it has been shown, can be disseminated through the written word and visually, by traditional means (e.g., newspapers, radio, and TV), and by newer digital technologies of social media (e.g., Facebook, Twitter, YouTube). Online and offline there are many legitimate and illegitimate actors (individuals, groups, states, and non-state entities), all manipulating and shaping, or trying to shape, public discourse in a constantly evolving process. Recent studies, for example, highlight the fact that relatively simple automated bots have been replaced by more sophisticated or blended disinformation agents that include domestic and foreign actors (Bradshaw & Howard, 2018).

In the Western context, the term "information warfare" tends to refer to disinformation that is deliberate or coordinated in a *military* context. It usually describes limited, tactical information operations carried out during hostilities by either state or non-state actors using and exploiting an open system with the *intent to do harm* (some definitions say that harm actually has to be done), through illegitimate if not illegal ways (Lucas & Pomeranzev, 2016). "Information operations" originally was a military term that referred to the strategic use of technological, operational, and psychological resources to disrupt the enemy's informational capacities and protect "friendly forces." Today, many analysts (and social networking services, most notably Facebook), have adopted the terms "information operations" or "information campaigns" to refer to a variety of actors' "deliberate and systematic attempts to steer public opinion using inauthentic accounts and/or inaccurate information" (Jack, 2019, p. 8).

Questions of how to identify, and whether and how to respond to, such a range of amorphous or "soft" phenomenon are obviously exceedingly controversial and challenging. Information operations can involve accurate information, misinformation, disinformation, or a mix of all three. What is false or misleading information can be contested. Even scientific data evolves with new information, and analyses and commentaries are shaped by cognitive biases and preferences that may stem from cultural identities and other complex factors. Whether an information campaign edges over from "persuasion" to "deliberatively manipulative" or "deceptive" can sometimes be a matter of perspective. Significantly, information is often "laundered," sources can be, and increasingly are, blurred or hidden, and the distinction between "domestic" and "foreign" appears less relevant than it once was.

To further complicate matters, it is not just the "disinformation" itself that needs to be responded to. There often are other related activities (corruption, cyber-attacks, etc.) as well the broader strategy itself. Many experts are now convinced that (some) deliberate and coordinated disinformation is a key part of a broader strategy by various actors to undermine democracy and social cohesion (Lin & Kerr, 2021; Wigell, 2019). Some highlight a broad global shift since 2014 from "outright falsification to a greater emphasis on subtle and strategic manipulation and amplification of divisive narratives"—for example, on immigration/migration, anti-religious sentiment, nationalist identity, women's health, gender-based harassment, climate change, and now COVID-19 (Jackson, 2017). Key think tanks, experts, and government agencies warn that issues and identities (anti-Semitism, anti-Muslim hate speech, misogyny, etc.) are being "weaponized" in both targeted and coordinated ways, and not only during elections. The strategies, they speculate, include undermining arguments for multilateralism, spurring polarization along "culture war" lines, eroding trust in democratic institutions, and/or sewing confusion (Institute for Strategic Dialogue, 2019). For the military, a key concern is that malicious actors may use strategic disinformation and other forms of manipulation to gain advantage in the information environment in order to create chaos for adversaries' "command and control."

In short, given the complex and ambiguous nature of disinformation, it is unsurprising that we encounter loose definitions and "hybridization" of the challenge (its rhetorical linkage with other issues) as well as ambiguity over whether and what to deter. To understand specific motives requires deep knowledge of the context (the different theatres of disinformation), as well as the actor(s) and their intentions (if any) over time. A range of disinformation exists, and it can often be debated what the underlying strategy is, and whether and when a range of responses may be needed in both the cyber/information and the psychological "domains."

Can We Deter (Strategic) Disinformation, and How? Insights and Limits from the Literature on Deterrence

Beyond the above-mentioned definitional difficulties of "what it means to deter," is it possible or even desirable to have "deterrence of disinformation"?

Do deterrence theory and practice have any relevance to countering "disinformation," or more specifically to thinking through responses to state-sponsored (and non-state-sponsored) "strategic disinformation"? Scholars point to multiple limits and problems with governmental attempts to respond, or not respond, to disinformation (Bjola & Papadakis, 2020; Gregor & Mlejnkova, 2021). For example, as mentioned above, since disinformation can be "laundered," it can be difficult to attribute sources or to have accountability. Others say that this is overstated or that this may also grant flexibility when considering various responses. Still others could argue that almost any government involvement in this area would be/is detrimental, especially if it is perceived as a state intrusion on freedom of speech or privacy. In other words, for some scholars and practitioners, disinformation (or some disinformation) may be better understood and dealt with as a social and cultural issue than as a security "threat" (Ramersad & Althiyabi, 2020; Sample et al., 2018).

Nevertheless, the question of how to deter or dissuade efforts at disinformation has some commonalities with questions about whether and how to respond to a range of asymmetrical aggressions from state and non-state actors. The latter are considered by many scholars and practitioners to be some of today's most urgent and challenging issues. To address them, a growing academic and policy literature has sought to examine the role of "deterrence" in responding to "cross-domain" (cyber, space, economic, etc.) (Adamsky, 2015; Brantly, 2018a, 2018b; Lindsay & Gartzke, 2019a, 2019b; Sweijs & Zilincik, 2020) as well "hybrid"[1] (ambiguous and blended) "threats" (Cullen & Wegge, 2019; Jackson, 2019; Stoker & Whiteside, 2020; Sweijs & Zilincik, 2019). Authors writing on these topics provide insights into how deterrence, and understandings about it, are evolving. These in turn have relevance for considering responses to disinformation.

How to Deter Disinformation? Technical and Strategic "Deterrence by Denial" and Resilience

Both the theory and practice of deterrence have evolved considerably over time. The so-called fourth wave of deterrence began at the end of the Cold War, when threats came to be perceived as more uncertain and less predictable. Many scholars have since written about a new, more complex and less state-centric environment defined by asymmetric changes. Today, some scholars argue that we are in a "fifth wave" of deterrence, defined by the need for "resilience" to address vulnerabilities through a long-term approach—for example, to build strong and adaptive infrastructure, to ensure social cohesion, and to sustain trust in government (Prior, 2018). In practice, it seems that the diffuse nature of threats is leading to more distributed responses through new or non-traditional networks and approaches.

Within this recent literature on "deterrence," "resilience" is conceptualized as an important part of both technical and strategic "deterrence by denial." The logic is that to increase resilience not only mitigates harmful effects of hostile influence, but also changes adversaries' cost-benefit analyses by denying them (technical or strategic/political) benefits. In *strategic* "deterrence by denial," the strategic or political impact is absorbed with no long-lasting result (Hartmann, 2017; Hellman, 2019), as opposed to *technical* "deterrence by denial," which denies direct impact. Applied to the case of disinformation, technical denial could then occur, for example, through the bolstering of cyber defences and technical capabilities (or shutting down/denying access to a news outlet). Strategic denial could include credible actions to deny objectives, for example, by protecting the psychological realm (e.g., through education to increase critical thinking, or in media to increase fact-checking) or by strengthening democratic institutions. If an adversary's strategy is to gain "information dominance," then showing that society can "keep going" physically and psychologically (and leaders can keep making sound decisions)—despite the disinformation and related confusion—may help to "maintain deterrence."

The literature on deterrence in the so-called grey zone between peace and war applies this logic of "deterrence by resilience" to "hybrid threats." It argues that greater resilience might be accomplished through a coordinated approach, with governments, private actors, and civilians working together at the domestic and/or global levels (Lorenz, 2017; Wilner, 2017). By extension, actions to increase technical and strategic denial to "strategic disinformation" would also include a range of efforts in different areas, including political/institutional (e.g., efforts to secure elections, or to increase trust in democratic institutions), military (e.g., efforts to improve strategic communications), infrastructure (physical or digital), social (e.g., to increase awareness), and information (e.g., to govern platforms or regulate media) at home and abroad (Monaghan, 2019). Strengthening resilience to disinformation in this way would be a "cross-domain" effort to prepare societies in a "cross-sectoral" approach in order to convince actors/adversaries of the futility of their efforts to engage in strategic disinformation (Sweijs & Zilincik, 2020).

In other words, widening the theory and concept of "deterrence" to include strengthening resilience to hybrid threats helpfully points to a range of non-traditional responses to a variety of hybrid challenges, including disinformation. Some scholars argue that this widening alters too much the traditional logic and practice of deterrence, even while others argue that it adds little in the way of new benefits (Lindsay & Gartzke, 2019a). Similarly, the concept of "resilience" significantly alters the focus of traditional deterrence responses. This can be criticized for encompassing too many activities to be analytically or practically helpful. Resilience can also be a confusing term in that it aims to represent processes that simultaneously seek to maintain status quo in the face of shocks and those that allow for transformation (Bourbeau & Ryan, 2018).

Nevertheless, in practice, and facing the rapidly evolving and increasingly global reach of some "hybrid threats" such as strategic disinformation, Western governments have called for strengthening domestic (and global) resilience as a means to "deter" activities in the "grey zone." The United Kingdom, for example, now interprets the term "deterrence" very widely to include defensive resilience measures (reasoning that capable and resilient governance raises the price of hybrid aggression and reduces its chances for success) (UK Ministry of Defence, 2019). At the same time, and seemingly paradoxically, recent calls by NATO and the European Union for "more resilience" have been critiqued both for trying to legitimize these organizations' roles in countering "hybrid threats" (including disinformation), and for abdicating or transferring responsibility to domestic actors. Below, we will see how resilience has become a cornerstone of Canada's approach to disinformation.

How to Deter? The Broadening Conceptualization of "Costs" and "Punishments"

The more traditional concepts of "deterrence by punishment" and "deterrence by increasing costs" (as well as the more proactive "compellence") (Shelling, 1966) have also been applied in the so-called cross-domain literature (Sweijs & Zilincik, 2020). In other words, just as the logic of "deterrence by denial" has been applied to other domains (e.g., cyber, economic, and outer space), so has the logic of ensuring that punishments or costs "outweigh benefits" been brought to bear in a variety of areas outside traditional military concerns. Furthermore, the traditional understanding of "costs" and "punishments" has been expanded to include, for example, the relevance of identity and belief systems to the cost-benefit analysis. For example, recent research examines the benefits of increasing the *social costs* of norms (the "calling out" of bad behaviour) and increasing the *negative costs*, through "deterrence by de-legitimization" (raising the reputational cost to motivate restraint) (Wilner, 2014, p. 449), or through "deterrence by counter-narrative" (Knopf, 2010). At the same time, scholars have examined how positive *incentives* can play a role in dissuading attacks—for example, by fostering interdependence through "deterrence by entanglement" (Brantley, 2018).

Applied to disinformation, these new understandings provide a wider range of options for how to "deter." They include not only military means (kinetic and non-kinetic), but also, for example, political (travel restrictions, expulsions of diplomats), economic (sanctions, financial penalties), civil (public blaming), information (legislation), and international law. In keeping with traditional deterrence theory, they also suggest a reactive approach. However, a more extreme version of "deterrence by punishment" also includes offensive actions aimed at disrupting or degrading an adversary's capacity for action. An example here is the US strategy of "persistent engagement" to shape the parameters of acceptable behaviour in cyberspace, including, if necessary, aggressive cyber operations (Healey, 2019). Unsurprisingly, when applied to strategic disinformation, attempts to prevent an adversary from taking further action (offensive pre-emption) are also the most controversial since they raise concerns about intervention and sovereignty and the need for secrecy versus transparency.

The Illusion and Limits of "Deterrence of Disinformation"

Recent literature on deterrence also suggests possible limits to the logic of "deterrence of disinformation," showing that creating an "illusion of deterrence" may be especially relevant in response to an ambiguous threat.

First, much of the recent literature stresses that deterrence is fundamentally the outcome of a psychological relationship (Kroenig & Pavel, 2012), meaning that capabilities are less relevant than our perception about them (Jervis, 2016). The implication is that even though strategic disinformation can never be completely countered, and our capabilities will always be limited or in need of "catching up," the "illusion of capability" (to deter) is still possible, and indeed may matter most. Nevertheless, as others have commented, this is not a new revelation, and perception has long been acknowledged as central to traditional deterrence theory and international relations (Hudson, 2014).

Second, recent literature finds that deterrence is not about absolutes, it is about making "attacks" less likely or effective over time ("cumulative" or "punctuated" deterrence) (Kello, 2017; Tor, 2015). If (an adversary's) individual activities can be rendered difficult, the greater process may be undermined. As mentioned above, the "cross-domain" literature also suggests that actions taken in adjacent areas may render the broader strategy ineffective. Thus, to deter disinformation, actions in other realms may be possible (e.g., sanctions in the economic realm), and even minor actions taken may affect an adversary's perceptions and actions. Moreover, when disinformation is understood as part of "hybrid warfare," or one of many hybrid threats, then "hybrid deterrence" (as opposed to "comprehensive deterrence") may make sense as an approach to deter (some) strategic disinformation (Monaghan, 2019). Related to this, if success can be rendered tactically difficult (e.g., through regulation of social media platforms), it may be harder to maintain coordination, and the whole effort may be undermined (i.e., "tactical denial") (Kroenig & Pavel, 2012).

Third, there is a developing consensus in the deterrence literature that more needs to be understood about actors, their motivations, aims, and limits. For example, work on deterrence and terrorism has shown the limits of deterrence while highlighting that terrorists may be deterred—we just need to find out and target what they really cherish (e.g., political motives) (Trager & Zagorcheva, 2006; Wilner, 2011, 2014). It can also be logically speculated that the same may be true in the case of disinformation, thus it is not just the processes (e.g., media, bots, culture) that we need to examine, but also the actors' key (political and other) motivations and other root causes of disinformation.

Deter How? A Case Study of Canada's Responses to Disinformation

This section provides an overview of where the Canadian case fits with the above analysis of recent literature on deterrence and how it may be applicable to disinformation.

DETERRENCE BY DENIAL: BUILDING TECHNICAL AND STRATEGIC RESILIENCE

Although strategic disinformation can obviously not be completely shut out, denial of direct access aims to make it more difficult through technical solutions and bolstering infrastructure and institutions. In Canada, attempts to deter strategic disinformation have included accelerated efforts to strengthen cyber defence and resilience and to develop legislation and norms to hamper disinformation efforts, especially during elections. More generally, there have been efforts to increase co-operation and to share more information (about disinformation) to "deny" actors (further) access at the domestic and international levels.

To give some examples, the Canadian Departments of National Defence (DND) and Public Safety, CSIS, and the Communications Security Establishment (CSE), among others, have increased their work to develop greater internal IT capacity, discover data solutions, and strengthen institutional resilience in response to an array of recent misinformation and disinformation. The CSE and CSIS joined Elections Canada to track and analyze big data to share with other G7 members and conducted simulations to identify vulnerabilities (Government of Canada, 2019; Pinkerton, 2019). There has also been a significant increase in research concerning the creation, attribution, and dissemination of (especially digital) disinformation, including, for example, research into the development of algorithms to identify and block "fake news." It is widely acknowledged that the next shift in disinformation is well underway with the artificial intelligence (AI) revolution, and this reality is informing research into how to leverage AI against AI, including how to detect coordinated activities by malicious actors. In this regard, Canada has greatly increased its co-operation with other governments and NGOs working in these fields. For example, it supports and shares technical and other research on fake online personas and images with the US Global Engagement Center. At the same time, Canada has actively supported research into the ethical implications of possible responses.

The Canadian government has also developed new legislation to counter disinformation. The 2019 *Elections Modernization Act*, for example, introduced new provisions aimed at deterring or preventing "foreign interference" (Reepschlager & Dubois, 2019). Other institutional initiatives have aimed to increase bureaucratic collaboration. For example, in advance of the October 2019 federal election, the government created a new RCMP-led task force, Security and Intelligence Threats to Elections (SITE). SITE included Global Affairs Canada, the CSE, and CSIS, to build awareness and prepare the government to prevent and respond to "covert, clandestine or criminal attempts to interfere with the electoral process." It analyzed foreign social media and coordinated responses with the G7 Rapid Response Mechanism (see below)

(Government of Canada, 2019). The government also initiated the Critical Elections Incident Public Protocol, under which five senior bureaucrats were to be informed of any potential interference during the 2019 federal election, in order to determine whether the incidents were serious enough to inform Canadians (none were) (House of Commons, 2019).

Canada's attempts to "deny through information sharing" have also taken place at the international level. They include the efforts of Global Affairs Canada (GAC) to position Canada at the centre of collective cyber defence by sharing reports, coordinating roles, and sharing best practices as network coordinator of the Rapid Response Mechanism (Government of Canada, 2019). GAC also addresses disinformation and related "foreign interference" through many partnerships—for example, with NATO and the European Union, as well as with NGOs such as the US Alliance for Securing Democracy.

However, as mentioned above, "deterrence by denial" is not just about denying or making access more difficult; it is also about denying political and cognitive "wins." Here the Canadian government has encouraged the development of individual/cognitive and societal resilience to misinformation and disinformation through programs designed to foster *awareness* of the challenges. Since 2014, Canadian government departments and security agencies have been quick to publicly explain why disinformation is a security challenge and to expose specific actors and their actions (Jackson, 2022). A series of bureaucratic and think-tank reports examine the roles allegedly played by Russia (and Russia-related actors) and China, as well as Iran, North Korea, former US president Donald Trump, right-wing extremists, etc. These reports, along with heightened political rhetoric about the dangers of disinformation from leaders such as then Canadian foreign minister Chrystia Freeland, have played an important role in raising awareness about the challenges and their (possible) negative effects (Bradshaw, 2018; Canadian Centre for Cyber Security, 2018, 2020; CSE, 2017; Greenspoon & Owen, 2018; Kolga, 2019; National Security and Intelligence Committee of Parliamentarians, 2020; Picard, 2019; Sukhankin, 2019; Tenove, 2018). Recent works on deterrence would suggest that such reports may further increase societal resilience and trust in government responses by signalling governments' respect for truth and transparency (Doorn & Brinkel, 2020). The Canadian government has also articulated its *intentions* to respond to misinformation and disinformation in official cyber-strategy documents, in Canada's defence policy, and in several other non-legal documents. These stated intentions refer to disinformation and the wider category of misinformation in relation to the challenges of "hybrid conflict" and "foreign interference," and they propose "whole of government" and "whole of society" responses. Taken together, this official and rhetorical "securitization" of disinformation (using rhetoric to refer to it as an urgent security threat) may itself function as a deterrent by signalling recognition of a challenge and implying clear intentions to act. However, it may also be criticized for being vague and not showing enough political resolve.

Other efforts to develop strategic "deterrence by denial" include a range of attempts to identify specific targeted messages and audiences and to deploy credible narratives (or counter-narratives) through strategic communications (Pamment et al., 2018). Overall, Canada's military and security agencies have increased their monitoring (in terms of aggregate data and community policing), research, and exposure of false or manipulative narratives. The latter are not generally directly responded to because such efforts can backfire and have unintended consequences. However, as mentioned above, there are different kinds of disinformation "campaigns" that have targeted Canada, and there are also examples of Canada making specific and effective small-scale responses (Potter, 2019). For example, Canada's Task Force Latvia, along with the local Canadian embassy, was adept at using various public outreach efforts in countering malicious narratives designed to impugn Canadian military personnel.

To give some other examples of broad Canadian efforts in this area, the Canadian military and the DND track trends in narratives and emerging technologies such as "deepfakes," both of which are recognized now as potentially decisive factors in future conflicts. The RCMP examines how foreign actors intersect with domestic extremism, reflecting the current concern that disinformation may be part of a broader phenomenon of violent transnational social movements, based locally, but inspired internationally (Kelshall & Dittmar, 2018). Similarly, Public Safety Canada is exploring links between communities, extremism, and disinformation.

DETERRENCE THROUGH THREATS OF PUNISHMENTS AND IMPOSING COSTS

Beyond attempts to build technical and strategic resilience, Canada has pursued some threats and attempts to impose "costs" (narrowly and widely defined) on the perpetrators of disinformation. These include attempts to impose normative costs through "public blaming," as well as legislation and international law. Such attempts are, however, limited, and it is highly questionable whether the costs imposed or threatened outweigh aggressors' perceived benefit.

First, Canada has called out the "bad behaviour" of certain actors (as seen above in Canada's bureaucratic reports and political rhetoric), and it can be argued that this "shaming and blaming" may also increase social and psychological costs. Theoretically, along with other allies' similar actions, over time they may contribute to "deterrence through de-legitimation" (*and* bolster resilience, as seen above). On the other hand, they may also contribute to perceived grievances and hinder other diplomatic efforts.

Perhaps Canada's greatest efforts thus far to impose *normative costs* and restrain behaviour have been in legislation and international law. These include Canada's engagement with allies to develop norms in response to various activities in cyberspace, including disinformation. For example, Canada has been involved in intergovernmental negotiations at the United Nations to create a new global cyber-security architecture that would protect digital information and the infrastructure on which it resides. This effort faces many obstacles, but the point here is that it is an attempt to deter "by entanglement," by increasing interdependence among states (if not among the non-state actors, or state-affiliated actors, that act independently).[2] Canada's initial efforts to regulate social media platforms are outside the scope of this chapter, but they are also examples of attempts to impose "harder" costs by regulating rules, content, and competition.

There is little public information about Canada's consideration of more offensive cyber "punishments" of actors engaged in response to strategic (digital) disinformation. Certainly, some argue for Canada to take more offensive actions to disrupt or degrade actors' capacity to spread strategic disinformation as part of a more effective "deterrence by punishment" response. (Such actions have also been framed as a pre-emptive measure to increase defensive resilience.) However, steps have been taken to revamp Canada's national security infrastructure and to give the CSE the power to defend elections if they come under cyber-attack. In June 2019, the CSE was granted wide-ranging powers to engage in "defensive cyber operations" and "active cyber operations" to "degrade, disrupt, influence, respond to or interfere with the capabilities, intentions or activities of a foreign individual, state, organization or terrorist group as they relate to Canada's defense, security or international affairs," as per the wording of the *National Security Act* of 2017. In other words, for the first time, Canada could launch its own cyber-attacks. The threat of possible Canadian counterattacks (including against the digital information environment) is meant to deter attacks and "proactively shut down the source of a possible attack against Canada" (Kolga, 2019, p. 26).

Of course, the larger context of Canada's responses to strategic disinformation includes efforts to "deter" aggressive actors and actions. For example, in the case of Canada's responses to Russia, deterrence is practised through military means to increase "costs" (by stationing troops in the Baltics), political means (through the expulsion of diplomats and travel restrictions), and economic means (economic sanctions). None of these attempts to impose costs have been used specifically for disinformation "acts" or applied specifically to those who spread disinformation. However, there may be some "spillover" in the area of disinformation. As mentioned above, actions taken in adjacent areas may render the broader strategy ineffective. Yet Canada has not yet clearly communicated any exact costs in relation to specific cases of disinformation. Imposing targeted sanctions in the information realm would narrow the focus of deterrence, but it is not clear how effective they would be. Nevertheless, they are one example of how, despite heightened rhetoric, there is more that could be done to show capacity and the political resolve to follow through.

Conclusion and Discussion: Deterrence, Delusion, or Democratic Suasion?

This chapter attempted to show that, despite many challenges, "deterrence" has relevance when considering how to respond to strategic disinformation. Recent literature expands the scope of traditional deterrence and points to a wider range of non-traditional means "to deter." Applied to strategic disinformation, these means include strengthening technical, individual, and social and institutional "resilience" and imposing a broad range of "costs" and incentives in a nuanced cost-benefit analysis. The literature further highlights the significance of the "illusion to deter," which may be especially important in responding to ambiguous threats such as disinformation. Other insights include the importance of acting in areas outside the information domain in order deter any larger strategy, as well as the need to learn more about actors' perceptions, aims, and strategies (which can be extremely difficult to ascertain).

These contributions can be used to illuminate Canada's fragmented foreign policy and security responses to disinformation. They show that Canada is attempting to deter disinformation by taking a broad yet ad hoc approach that reflects the real difficulties and uncertainty about how to respond to such a complex and ambiguous challenge. At first glance, Canada may seem to be taking a random "whack-a-mole" approach. However, overall its rhetoric and actions fit within the wider understandings of both technical and strategic "deterrence by denial." Canada's responses, including what might be termed "denial by information sharing," are attempts to increase resilience, so that society can "take the first punch" and "negate the benefits."

Examples of strategic disinformation have also been "called out" and normative costs "raised." However, these actions are limited. Specific thresholds for specific actions are not clear, and there have been few, if any, positive inducements to change behaviour (e.g., the lifting of sanctions). More generally, viewing Canada's actions through the lens of deterrence highlights the fact that assumptions, especially about actor motivations and strategies, could be further questioned and more effort made to shape the perceptions and thinking of adversaries, as well as giving more consideration to the unintended consequences of actions.

In sum, while this overview shows that deterrence in its broad conceptualization may rightly point to a range of activities in response to disinformation, it remains questionable whether it is a sufficiently accurate concept with which to describe or analyze Canada's (and other countries') actual or possible responses. In a recent study, Sweijs and Zilincik (2020) proposed "dissuasion" to describe the broader efforts that are now often encompassed under the term "deterrence." Similarly, Wiggle (2021) coined the term "democratic deterrence," which he conceives as a "whole of society approach," coordinated by the government, to build resilience.

This chapter concludes with the suggestion that "democratic suasion" is another umbrella concept worth developing. "Democratic suasion" would encompass dissuasion *and* persuasion, since disinformation is often at its core a political problem, dependent upon the type of relationship between the disinforming actor and its target. It would also capture Wiggle's stress on building *democratic* institutional and ideational resilience as a key deterrent and means of compellence. In this conceptualization, "democratic suasion" may be a better and more inclusive term than "deterrence" to capture Canada's stated policy *aspirations* to create a more holistic approach and the diverse actual and possible responses needed in response to this complex challenge. Democratic suasion would suggest strengthening technical and democratic resilience, building upon recent domestic and international collaborations, but also incentivizing "good behaviour" and "thinking ahead" to consider aggressors' motivations and how to shape their thinking. In contrast to deterrence, this would be more along the lines of a context-specific "public health approach" where more *preventative* action would be taken, but with a focus on reducing the harm from disinformation, while accepting that some kinds of disinformation will always be with us. For the military, this would mean continuing work with allies and other domestic actors and civil society to address the strategy behind disinformation, and showing that it can function despite disinformation and related manipulations, which increase confusion.

This chapter provides an overview of Canada's actions in light of new thinking about deterrence and its application to disinformation. Future studies could usefully examine the above ideas and their limits, analyze in more depth *specific* Canadian responses in *specific* theatres of disinformation, their effectiveness in different cases, and how Canada's experiences in turn may contribute to the literature on deterrence.

NOTES

1 The "hybrid warfare" paradigm perceives (some) disinformation as part of an ambiguous or blended conflict or one of multiple instruments that may be used in synchronized "attack" and tailored to specific vulnerabilities. Either way, it is understood as deliberate and strategic, but also including elements of uncertainty and deniability.

2 The 2014–15 Group of Governmental Experts outlined voluntary, non-binding peacetime norms of state behaviour in cyberspace. Subsequently, the General Assembly unanimously adopted a resolution that states should be guided by these norms. See United Nations (2015).

REFERENCES

Adamsky, D. (2015). Cross-domain Coercion: The current Russian art of strategy. Security Studies Center.

Bjola, C., & Papadakis, K. (2020). Digital propaganda, counterpublics and the disruption of the public sphere: The Finnish approach to building digital resilience. Cambridge Review of International Affairs, 33(5), 638–66.

Bourbeau, P., & Ryan, C. (2017). Resilience, resistance, infrapolitics and enmeshment. European Journal of International Relations, 24(1), 221–39.

Bradshaw, S. (2018). Securing Canadian elections: Disinformation, computational propaganda, targeted advertising and what to expect in 2019. Behind the Headlines: Research Paper Series, 66(3). https://thecic.org/research-publications/behind-the-headlines/securing-elections-2019/

Bradshaw, S., & Howard, P. N. (2018). Challenging truth and trust: A global inventory of organized social manipulation. Computational Research Project, University of Oxford.

Brantly, A. (2018a) Back to reality: Cross domain deterrence and cyberspace. Virginia Tech.

Brantly, A. (2018b). Conceptualizing cyber deterrence by entanglement. Social Science Research Network.

Canadian Centre for Cyber Security. (2018). National cyber threat assessment 2018. Retrieved 2 May 2020 from https://cyber.gc.ca/en/guidance/national-cyber-threat-assessment-2018

Canadian Centre for Cyber Security. (2020). National cyber threat assessment 2020. Retrieved 3 February 2020 from https://cyber.gc.ca/sites/default/files/publications/ncta-2020-e-web.pdf

CSE (Communications Security Establishment). (2017). Cyber threats to Canada's democratic process. Retrieved 2 May 2020 from https://cyber.gc.ca/sites/default/files/publications/cse-cyber-threat-assessment-e.pdf_

CSE (Communications Security Establishment). (2019). Cyber threats to Canada's democratic process, update 2019. Retrieved 2 May 2020 from https://cyber.gc.ca/sites/default/files/publications/tdp-2019-report_e.pdf

Cullen, P., & Wegge, N. (2019). Countering hybrid warfare. Development, Concepts and Doctrine Centre, Shrivenham.

Goodale, R. (2018). National cyber security strategy: Canada's vision for security and prosperity in the digital age. Public Safety Canada. http://epe.lac-bac.gc.ca/100/201/301/weekly_acquisitions_list-ef/2018/18-27/publications.gc.ca/collections/collection_2018/sp-ps/PS4-239-2018-eng.pdf

Government of Canada. (2019). Canada's digital charter: Trust in a digital world—innovation for a better Canada. Innovation, Science and Economic Development Canada. https://www.ic.gc.ca/eic/site/062.nsf/eng/h_00108.html

Greenspoon, E. & Owen T. (2018). Democracy divided: Countering disinformation and hate in the digital public sphere. Public Policy Forum. https://ppforum.ca/publications/social-marketing-hate-speech-disinformation-democracy/

Gregor, M., & Mlejnková, P. (2021). Challenging online propaganda and disinformation in the 21st century. Palgrave Macmillan.

Hartmann, U. (2017). The evolution of the hybrid threat, and resilience as a countermeasure. Center for Security Studies.

Healey, J. (2019). The implications of persistent (and permanent) engagement in cyberspace. Journal of Cybersecurity, 5, 1–15.

Hellman, A. (2019). How has European geostrategic thinking towards Russia shifted since 2014? European leadership Network. https://www.europeanleadershipnetwork.org/policy-brief/how-has-european-geostrategic-thinking-towards-russia-shifted-since-2014/

Hudson, V. M. (2014). Foreign policy analysis: Classic and contemporary theory. Rowman and Littlefield.

Institute for Strategic Dialogue. (2019). 2019 EU elections information operations analysis: Interim briefing paper. Institute for Strategic Dialogue.

Jack, C. (2019). Lexicon of lies: Terms for problematic information. Data and Society Research Institute. https://datasociety.net/pubs/oh/DataAndSociety_LexiconofLies.pdf

Jackson, D. (2017, 17 October). Issue brief: Distinguishing disinformation from propaganda, misinformation and "fake news." National Endowment for Democracy. https://www.ned.org/issue-brief-distinguishing-disinformation-from-propaganda-misinformation-and-fake-news/

Jackson, N. (2019). Deterrence, resilience and hybrid wars: The case of Canada and NATO. Journal of Military and Strategic Studies, 19(4), 104–25.

Jackson, N. (2022). The Canadian government's response to foreign disinformation: Rhetoric, stated policy intentions and practices. International Journal, 76(2), 544–63.

Jayakumar, S., Ang, B., & Anwar, N. D. (Eds.). (2021). Disinformation and fake news. Palgrave Macmillan.

Jervis, R. (2016). Some thoughts on deterrence in the cyber era. Journal of Information Warfare, 15, 66–73.

Jordan, D., Kiras, J., Lonsdale, D., Speller, I., Tuck, C., & Walton, C. D. (2016). Understanding modern warfare. Cambridge University Press.

Kello, L. (2017). The virtual weapon and international order. Yale University Press.

Kelshall, C., & Dittmar, V. (2018). Accidental power: How non-state actors hijacked and reshaped the international system. SFU Library and CASIS.

Knopf, J. W. (2010). The fourth wave in deterrence research. Contemporary Security Policy, 31(1), 1–33.

Kolga, M. (2019). Stemming the virus: Understanding and responding to the threat of Russian disinformation. Macdonald Laurier Institute.

Kolga, M., Jakub J., Vogel, N. (2019). Russian proofing your elections. Macdonald Laurier Institute.

Kroenig, M., & Pavel, B. (2012). How to deter terrorism. Washington Quarterly, 35, 21–36.

Lanoszka, A., (2019). Disinformation in international politics. European Journal of International Security, 4(2), 227–48.

Lindsay, J. R., Gartzke, E. A. (2019a). Cross-domain deterrence: Strategy in an era of complexity. Oxford University Press.

Lindsay, J. R., Gartzke, E. A. (2019b). Conclusion: The analytic potential of cross-domain deterrence. In J. R. Lindsay & E. A. Gartzke (Eds.), Cross-domain deterrence: Strategy in an era of complexity (pp. 335–71). Oxford University Press.

Lorenz, W. (2017). The evolution of deterrence: From Cold War to hybrid war. Polish Quarterly of International Affairs, (2), 22–37.

Lucas, E., & Pomeranzev, P. (2016). Winning the information wars. Center for European Policy Analysis.

Monaghan, S. (Ed.). (2019). MCDC Countering Hybrid Warfare Project: Countering hybrid warfare. Multinational Capability Development Campaign. https://assets.publishing.service.gov.uk/government/uploads/system/uploads/attachment_data/file/784299/concepts_mcdc_countering_hybrid_warfare.pdf

National Security and Intelligence Committee of Parliamentarians. (2020). National Security and Intelligence Committee of Parliamentarians annual report 2019. https://www.nsicop-cpsnr.ca/reports/rp-2020-03-12-ar/intro-en.html

Osinga, F., & Sweijs, T. (Eds.). (2021). NL ARMS Netherlands annual review of military studies 2020: Deterrence in the 21st century—insights from theory and practice. Springer Nature.

Pamment, J., Twetman, H., Nothhaft, H., & Fjällhed, A. (2018). The role of communicators in countering the malicious use of social media. NATO Strategic Communications Centre of Excellence.

Picard, C. (2019). Online disinformation threats in the 2019 Canadian federal election: Who is behind them and why. In J. McQuade (Ed.), Disinformation and digital democracies in the 21st century (pp. 35–40). NATO Association of Canada.

Pinkerton, C. (2019, 30 January). Government releases blueprint for protecting election from interference. iPolitics. https://www.ipolitics.ca/news/government-releases-blueprint-for-protecting-election-from-interference

Potter, E. (2019). Russia's strategy for perception management through public diplomacy and influence operations: The Canadian case. The Hague Journal of Diplomacy, 14, 402–25.

Prior, T. (2018). Resilience: The "fifth wave" in the evolution of deterrence. Center for Security Studies.

Public Safety Canada. (2019). National cyber security action plan 2019–2024: Budget 2018 investments. Public safety Canada. http://epe.lac-bac.gc.ca/100/201/301/weekly_acquisitions_list-ef/2019/19-34/publications.gc.ca/collections/collection_2019/sp-ps/PS9-1-2019-eng.pdf

Reepschlager, A., & Dubois, E. (2019, 2 January). New election laws are no match for the Internet. Policy Options. https://policyoptions.irpp.org/magazines/january-2019/new-election-laws-no-match-internet/

Sample, C., McAlaney, J., Bakdash, J., & Thackray, H. (2018). A cultural exploration of social media manipulators. Journal of Information Warfare, 17(4), 56–71.

Snyder, G. (1961). Deterrence and defense. Princeton University Press.

Stoker, D., & Whiteside. C. (2020). Blurred lines: Grey-zone conflict and hybrid war—two failures of American strategic thinking. Naval War College Review, 73, 1–37.

Sukhankin, S. (2019). The Western Alliance in the face of Russian (dis)information machine: Where does Canada stand? SPP Research Paper CGAI/School for Public Policy, 12(26). https://doi.org/10.11575/sppp.v12i0.61799

Sweijs, T., & Zilinicik S. (2019). Cross domain deterrence and hybrid conflict. The Hague Centre for Strategic Studies.

Sweijs, T. & Zilincik, S. (2020). The essence of cross-domain deterrence. In F. Osinka & T. Sweijs (Eds.), NL ARMS Netherlands annual review of military studies 2020. https://link.springer.com/content/pdf/10.1007%2F978-94-6265-419-8_8.pdf

Tenove, C. (2018). Digital threats to democratic elections: How foreign actors use digital techniques to undermine democracy. Centre for the Study of Democratic Institutions.

Tor, U. (2015). Cumulative deterrence' as a new paradigm for cyber deterrence. Journal of Strategic Studies, 40, 92–117.

Trager, R. F., & Zagorcheva, D. P. (2006). Deterring terrorism: It can be done. International Security, 30(3), 87–123.

Tucker, J. (2018). Social media, political polarization, and political disinformation: A review of the scientific literature. Hewlett Foundation.

United Nations (2015). Report of the Group of Governmental Experts on developments in the field of information and telecommunications in the context of international security. A/70/174. https://documents-dds-ny.un.org/doc/UNDOC/GEN/N15/228/35/PDF/N1522835.pdf?OpenElement_

Wigell, M. (2019). Hybrid interference as a wedge strategy. International Affairs, 95(2), 255–75.

Wilner, A. S. (2011). Deterring the undeterrable: Coercion, denial, and delegitimization in counterterrorism. Journal of Strategic Studies, 3(1), 3–37.

Wilner, A. S. (2014). Contemporary deterrence theory and counterterrorism: A bridge too far. New York University Journal of International Law and Politics, 47, 439–62.

Wilner, A. S. (2017). Cyber deterrence and critical infrastructure protection: Expectation, application and limitation. Comparative Strategy, 36(4), 309–18.

9

Exit, Voice, or Loyalty? Functional Engagement as Cyber Strategy for Middle Power Statecraft

Joseph Szeman and Christian Leuprecht[1]

Introduction

The cyberspace environment is a microcosm of deepening geopolitical competition between adversarial state actors (Valeriano et al., 2018). Since other operational domains (land, air, sea, space) and national instruments of power (diplomatic, information, military-economic, finance, intelligence, and law enforcement) are increasingly enabled by, and dependent on, cyberspace, such dependence opens opportunities for state and non-state actors to leverage cyber operations to disrupt, degrade, deny, or influence rivals' instruments of statecraft to meet objectives or jockey for strategic advantage (Fischerkeller & Harknett, 2017). Over two decades of trial and error, malicious state actors have demonstrated intent and capability to leverage cyber espionage, subversion, and sabotage operations to advance their national interests and degrade those of their rivals (Leuprecht, Szeman, & Skillicorn, 2019). Between 2005 and 2020, the Council on Foreign Relations' cyber operations tracker found that China, Iran, North Korea, and Russia sponsored 77 per cent of all suspected operations. China and Russia each carried out nearly fifty adversarial cyber campaigns between 2000 and 2016. The scale and impact of cyber operations conducted by malicious state actors to achieve strategic advantage in the international environment are growing exponentially (Maness et al., 2022).

Middle powers have high levels of digital connectivity; strong, knowledge-based economies; leading research institutions; and membership in coveted multilateral groupings and security alliances. Generally, middle powers also have limited resources with which to defend and assert themselves, and consequently represent low-risk, high-reward targets for more powerful adversarial state actors to exploit in cyberspace. Middle powers thus have strong incentives (but limited capability) to prevent the cyber-enabled degradation of their sovereignty, stability, and economic competitiveness. In essence, middle powers (and especially those aligned with the United States) are both targets of significant adversarial cyber activity, yet are too resource-constrained to engage shield and spear persistently. Absent a cyber doctrine tailored to the unique geopolitical characteristics and resource realities of middle powers, state actors—and not only Russia and China, but also Iran—have the initiative.

How should middle powers respond to their strategic deficit in cyberspace? Albert Hirschman's (1970) classic book *Exit, Voice, and Loyalty* posits a framework for describing how an individual or group will react to a deleterious change in their environment. Hirschman identifies three possible responses: the actor can *exit*, use *voice*, or demonstrate *loyalty* (Hischman, 1970). By choosing to *exit*, an actor accepts the undesirable change in their environment and alters their behaviour to adapt to the new situation. For example, a middle power could respond to the deleterious changes in their environment resulting from a weakened rules-based international order and unrestricted cyber activity targeting their interests and instruments of national power by abandoning its status and role as a middle power. Choosing *voice* means taking forms of direct action to change the environment back to its original condition. For example, a middle power could attempt to reverse changes to its environment, asserting itself in and through cyberspace by devising strategies to uphold the international order, advance its interests, and protect its sovereignty. Finally, choosing *loyalty* means the actor accepts the undesirable change in their environment but does not change their behaviour. This response means a middle power accepts the changes to its environment and the resulting threats to their interests and the rules-based international order by not altering its response, and instead choosing to draft behind the activities and responses of more powerful allies. This chapter contends that a *loyalty* response, which characterizes current multilateral efforts to develop explicitly accepted cyber norms, has not (and will not) provide middle powers with a solution to the increasing threats they face from malicious cyber activity. Instead, this chapter advances a *voice* strategy for middle powers to participate more actively and effectively in efforts to develop cyber norms by shaping the boundaries of adversarial cyber activity. This strategy draws from research on cyber persistence and the cyberspace strategy of persistent engagement and is tentatively termed "functional engagement."

First, this chapter describes the broad constitutive characteristics of middle powers. This section contextualizes the unique foreign policy interests of middle powers and identifies what types of middle powers would benefit most from a strategy of functional engagement. To illustrate the challenges facing middle powers that seek to pursue a loyalty-based approach, the second section broadly outlines the failures of multilateral efforts to establish explicitly accepted cyber norms. The third section describes the contours of cyber persistence theory and argues that as a complement to ongoing multilateral efforts, the boundaries of tacitly acceptable state behaviour in cyberspace, and potentially even in the wider geopolitical environment, can be cumulatively shaped by employing cyber operations in response to unacceptable behaviour (the voice approach). The fourth section illustrates the point: it draws on traditional middle powers that are vulnerable to exploitation in cyberspace yet have limited resources to respond to formulate the concept of functional engagement as a voice approach tailored to middle powers. As a case study, this section posits functional engagement as an alternative strategy well-suited to Canada's geopolitical identity as a middle power, the threats it faces in cyberspace, and the resources it has at its disposal.

The characteristics of middle powers

Analysts had initially bifurcated the international community into small and great state powers, but it soon became apparent that some small states were more powerful than others. Relative strength was to be recognized in the form of a "scheme of gradation" (Mitrany, 1933), which, in the 1930s, gave rise to the concept of "middle powers." The concept gained momentum thanks to the concerted diplomatic efforts of Canada and Australia to justify and solidify their international influence and core roles in the post-1945 global order (Shin, 2015). In 1947, Canadian diplomat and historian George Glazebrook (1947) asserted that the formation of the United Nations would enable "middle powers" to be "capable of exerting a degree of strength and influence not found in the small powers." A growing number of states have since either self-identified or been described as middle powers, including Argentina, Australia, Canada, Brazil, Denmark, Japan, Malaysia, the Netherlands, Norway, Nigeria, Spain, Sweden, South Korea, and Turkey (Cooper, 2011;

Patience, 2014). Although the question of what constitutes the attributes of a middle power is controversial, international relations scholars generally identify at least three theoretical perspectives: hierarchical, functional, and behavioural (Chapnick, 1999).

First, the hierarchical approach categorizes states by measuring objective capability, asserted position, and recognized status (Chapnick, 1999). It typically ranks states according to economic, military, or social metrics (Holbraad, 1984; Shin, 2015). Their capabilities, international standing, or status rank these states in the "middle" of the international system: greater than those of small states but lesser than great powers. To explain the unique foreign policy behaviour of middle powers, functional and behavioural approaches take the middle power concept beyond the status of a mere tool for ranking real capability.

Second, the functional perspective argues that middle powers may on occasion exert influence in international affairs in specific instances based on their relative capabilities, interests, and degree of involvement (Chapnick, 1999). By contrast, great powers are always capable of exercising international influence, while small states are incapable of exerting any real influence (Chapnick, 1999). At the core of the functional concept is the idea that a state with relatively limited military and economic capacity may nonetheless be successful in accruing "degrees of influence and authority among great powers and its neighbours that even reach into global forums" (Holbraad, 1971). This view holds that middle powers commit to maintaining the status quo, security, and order in the international system through leadership on specific global problems and foreign policy niches of their choosing (Cooper et al., 1993).

Lastly, the behavioural approach is the dominant contemporary paradigm for characterizing foreign policy behaviour by middle powers. Sometimes also referred to as the middle power internationalist approach, the behavioural approach contends that a country is a middle power if it exhibits a certain type of foreign policy behaviour—namely, advocating for compromise and seeking multilateral solutions to international problems (Cooper et al., 1993). Within this understanding, middle powers rely on international law to ensure predictability in global interactions, and on international organizations to provide forums through which they can establish and enforce acceptable conduct. To this end middle powers focus their foreign policy efforts on global normative arrangements promoted through international organizations

(Cooper et al., 1993). Accordingly, the behavioural approach reflects a "particular style of diplomacy, or a strategy backed by a commitment to liberal values and the absence of unilateralism which is a defining trait of a great power" (Lee & Soeya, 2014). The behavioural approach parses into "traditional" and "emerging" middle powers (Jordaan, 2003). Traditional middle powers are "wealthy, stable, egalitarian, social democratic and not regionally influential," exhibit "a weak and ambivalent regional orientation," and offer appeasing concessions to pressures for global reform": Australia, Canada, Norway, and the Netherlands are examples of traditional middle powers (Jordaan, 2003). In contrast, emerging middle powers are semi-peripheral to the core of the global political economy, "materially inegalitarian and recently democratised states that demonstrate much regional influence and self-association" (Jordaan, 2003) and that seek to reform the global order: examples of emerging middle powers include Argentina, South Africa, Malaysia, and Turkey. Traditional and emerging middle powers both benefit from the status quo of the current liberal international order (Jordaan, 2003). Since they lack the real capacity to alter the global balance of power or affect deep change in the international system, both types of middle powers are vulnerable to global instability that threatens to upend the status quo. Traditional middle powers seek to legitimize and stabilize the international order since they already occupy privileged positions at the core of the global political economy. In essence, their interests are best asserted by defending and upholding the status quo of this order. Whereas emerging middle powers may benefit from their regional economic dominance within the international order, they do not occupy privileged positions within the global political economy and thus have an incentive to transform the international order.

Although the constitutive features of middle powers are up for debate, common to all three approaches is an understanding that middle powers have limited economic or military capabilities and are capable of exerting only narrow influence in the international system (the hierarchical approach). To address these challenges and participate in foreign affairs, middle powers focus their resources on specific, relevant issues (the functional approach), or to enhancing their influence through explicit bargaining processes, conflict management, and multilateralism (the behavioural approach). The distinction between traditional and emerging middle powers is a function of divergent interests and incentives. As legitimizers and stabilizers of their privileged role within the current global order, traditional middle powers in particular stand to face the most significant disruption from contemporary threats to the established rules-based international order—including from cyberspace. Owing to their role in the international system, they have a particular incentive to address cyber threats.

The Loyalty Approach and the Issue of Multilateral Effort to Develop "Cyber Norms"

In principle, the deteriorating stability of cyberspace makes the diffusion of transnational norms to regulate the behaviour of state actors in cyberspace appealing to great and middle powers alike. Over the years, these efforts have taken a multilateral shape, touching numerous organizations, including the United Nations, G7, G20, and the Council of Europe (Grigsby, 2017; Maurer, 2020; Tikk-Ringas, 2017). Within more exclusive multilateral security alliances, additional attempts have also sought to codify an understanding of norms in cyberspace and the applicability of international law to cyber operations through NATO's "Tallinn Manual" (Jensen, 2017).

Multilateral efforts to establish cyber norms have been floundering for good reason. First, liberal and illiberal states differ fundamentally in their respective visions of the future of cyberspace and the rules-based international order (Jensen, 2017). Illiberal regimes are working to shape the digital ecosystem in line with authoritarian values, advancing the state-centric concept of "cyber sovereignty" to prioritize the role of regime security and preservation over individual liberty. Russia and China, backed by other member states of Shanghai Cooperation Organisation, have prioritized the concept of "information security" instead of "cyber security." Information security deems uncontrolled information flows dangerous to internal stability and seeks to prevent the dissemination of information incompatible with countries' internal political, economic, and social stability, as well as their spiritual and cultural environment (Stevens, 2012). States that adhere to the concept of information security fundamentally perceive the content of information itself as a threat, which requires them to advocate for deeper state control over online content to preserve regime stability. The fundamental divide between, on the one hand, the United States and its Western allies and, on the other, Russia, China, and other illiberal states, indicates that great power competition and divergent conceptions of cyberspace, particularly regarding the free flow of information, the applicability of international humanitarian law, and the doctrine of state responsibility, permeates multilateral negotiations

(Tikk-Ringas, 2017). Consensus on a normative framework for state behaviour in cyberspace is thus constrained by broader competitive interactions between great powers and perceived threats that the liberal order and the interconnectedness of cyberspace pose to illiberal regimes (Hurwitz, 2014; Maurer, 2020).

At the same time, multilateral efforts have grown increasingly divorced from the operational realities of conducting cyber activities (Grigsby, 2017; Maurer, 2020). Indian diplomat Arun Sukumar argues that multilateral efforts are doomed to fail since states are rapidly scaling up their offensive cyber capabilities and are "buying time" to test the possible effects of new offensive cyber capabilities (Sukumar, 2017). Illiberal states are concerned that any further endorsement of international law will undermine asymmetric advantages they derive from operating in cyberspace (Sukumar, 2017). Even during the most productive years of UN-led efforts to develop cyber norms, the pace, scale, sophistication, and severity of cyber operations of all types conducted by Russia and China have continued unabated. In 2015, as UN diplomats and scholars hailed the recently attained international consensus related to the applicability of international law to cyberspace, Russian cyber actors targeted and disrupted parts of the Ukrainian power grid and nearly destroyed the computer networks of French TV channel TV5 Monde (Corera, 2016; Cyber Law Toolkit, 2015). In 2017—the same year that the Group of Governmental Experts process collapsed over a lack of consensus on the applicability of international humanitarian law to cyberspace—the release and global proliferation of the NotPetya malware, which incurred estimated losses in the tens of billions, was attributed to Russian state actors (Greenberg, 2018). Despite efforts to curb economic espionage and intellectual property theft, an extensive US investigation concluded in 2018 that China has buoyed its economic growth with persistent campaigns of widespread, cyber-enabled technology transfer and intellectual property theft causing estimated losses to the US economy ranging from US$225 billion to US$600 billion annually (United States of America, 2018). By July 2021, the United States and an "unprecedented" number of allies and partners, including the Five Eyes, the European Union, NATO, and Japan jointly condemned widespread cyber espionage campaigns conducted on behalf of the Chinese government (United States of America, 2021). Yet, the boundaries, scope, and scale of malicious state cyber activity have been expanding apace.

After two decades, norms for state behaviour in cyberspace remain "contested, voluntary, unenforceable, vague and weakly internalized" (Maurer, 2020). Some scholars are highly pessimistic, asserting that great power dynamics and fundamental disagreements between liberal and illiberal states over the preferred shape of the international order have so permeated multilateral processes that agreement among cyber powers is unlikely. Traditional middle powers lack the real capabilities necessary to deter or coerce malicious state actors effectively. Yet, they are especially vulnerable to weak normative frameworks for state behaviour in cyberspace. Multilateral efforts alone are insufficient to meet the urgent challenge of setting clear, reasonable, and enforceable international rules for cyberspace. As the development of an explicit normative framework drags on, the empirical record of the past two decades shows that states are increasingly using cyber capabilities as tools of statecraft to achieve strategic advantage in the international environment. Curiously, these activities have largely remained below the threshold of armed conflict, which may indicate that cyberspace norms are actually being shaped tacitly through operations, rather than in the boardrooms of multilateral organizations (Maurer, 2020).

A Voice Approach: Cyber Persistence and Shaping Cyber Norms through Tacit Bargaining

The extensive record of cyberspace competition occurring without escalation to armed conflict signals the emergence of a "new competitive space" wherein explicit agreement over the substantive character of acceptable behaviour remains immature (Goldman, 2022). In essence, state actors appear to acknowledge tacitly that most competitive interactions in cyberspace are "bounded by a strategic objective to advance national interests while avoiding war," and thus are most easily and effectively employed as tools to achieve strategic advantage below the threshold of armed conflict and just short of war (Fischerkeller & Harknett, 2018b). The empirical record of the last decade and scholarship on cyber escalation appears to confirm this assertion (Healey & Jervis, 2020; Kreps & Schneider, 2019).

To characterize the nature of strategic competition between states in cyberspace, scholars have, in recent years, coined the term "cyber persistence," which aims to capture how states employ cyber operations as tools of statecraft to change the relative balance of power and achieve strategic advantage in the international environment (Fischerkeller & Harknett,

2017; Harknett & Goldman, 2016; Harknett & Smeets, 2022). The dynamics of cyber persistence are derived from a fundamental feature of networked computing: interconnectedness, which produces a "structural imperative" for constant contact among all adversaries in the global system (Harknett & Goldman, 2016). Interconnectedness increases the scale at which a state's "core economic, political, social, and military capability and capacity could be undermined" by cyber actors without regard for the constraints of geography and without the degree of control over the global commons on which the projection of conventional force is premised (Harknett & Smeets, 2022). Cyberspace is both offense-dominant insofar as it favours the attacker over the defender and has "very low entry costs for core access," as it offers asymmetric opportunities for attackers to generate cyber operations at scale against larger rivals that are orders of a magnitude greater than would otherwise be possible outside of cyberspace (Fischerkeller & Harknett, 2018a). Together, interconnectedness, offence-dominance, and asymmetry facilitate constant contact among all states, thereby producing a strategic environment that is structurally characterized by persistent (as opposed to episodic) competitive interactions below the threshold of armed conflict (Fischerkeller & Harknett, 2017, 2019; Harknett & Goldman, 2016). The scale of these activities in conjunction with the technical complexity of cyber operations has exceeded the ability of states to understand, manage, and reach consensus on cyber norms to regulate acceptable state behaviour in cyberspace.

Proponents of cyber persistence contend that the consistent employment of cyber operations below the threshold of armed conflict by both liberal and illiberal states demonstrates a process of normalization or agreed competition, whereby tacitly accepted cyber norms have gradually evolved through competitive interaction between states in cyberspace (Fischerkeller & Harknett, 2018b; Goldman, 2020). Through this process (which cyber persistence scholars call a "tacit bargaining" approach), cumulative and robust operational engagement with adversarial actors has the effect of developing mutual understandings of the boundaries of acceptable/unacceptable state behaviour in cyberspace. Ergo, to shape behaviour proactively, states must seize the initiative by actively operating and engaging with adversaries in cyberspace in order to tacitly reach informal agreements about the boundaries of accepted behaviour (Fischerkeller & Harknett, 2018b, 2019; Goldman, 2022). As part of the tacit bargaining process, cyber persistence scholar Michael Fischerkeller suggests that states should coalesce around "focal points," which he defines as "mutual understandings of acceptable/unacceptable behaviour in agreed competition" (Fischerkeller & Harknett, 2019). These focal points, if well-established and continually reinforced, may provide some needed stability in cyberspace by enabling states to use them to predict how other states may interpret or respond to a cyber operation (Farrell & Glaser, 2017). For traditional middle powers, these focal points might include malicious state-sponsored cyber activities that undermine the rules-based international order or that seek to degrade public confidence in democratic institutions, subvert or sabotage critical infrastructure systems, or reduce the effectiveness of international and multilateral organizations.

But is the substantive nature of the "agreed competition" between states in cyberspace beneficial to the interests of traditional middle powers? The "maturity" of these cyber norms remains nascent and "differing perspectives, ambiguity or uncertainty" over the character of acceptable cyber operations short of armed conflict is likely to continue to cause uncertainty and present a risk for inadvertent escalation (Fischerkeller & Harknett, 2019). Essentially this means that the absence of explicitly accepted cyber norms and the current immaturity of tacitly accepted norms leaves room for malicious state actors to legitimize the use of significantly disruptive cyber operations short of armed conflict (Fischerkeller & Harknett, 2019).

In fact, tacit bargaining processes in cyberspace that are antithetical to liberal interest and values may already be occurring. For much of the previous decade, the United States' restraint in responding to the continuous aggression in cyberspace from illiberal state actors such as Russia, China, and Iran has had a destabilizing effect by failing to disincentivize aggressors from operating with impunity. The result has been the gradual shaping and tacit acceptance of norms toward illiberal conceptualizations of cyberspace and the international order (Goldman, 2020). By failing to shape the development of cyber norms in their operational infancy, liberal states risk losing the initiative necessary to manage the emergence of norms that facilitate "massive theft of intellectual property, expanding control of internet content, attacks on data confidentiality and availability, violations of privacy, and interference in democratic debates and processes" (Goldman, 2020).

Shaping the Cyberspace Environment through Persistent Engagement

In 2018 the United States Cyber Command (USCYBERCOM) undertook a series of cyber operations to respond to Russian disinformation efforts targeting US elections and institutions by publicly exposing individuals involved in disinformation efforts and disrupting the functions of the Internet Research Agency—the troll farm at the heart of Russian disinformation operations (Gallagher, 2019; Nakashima, 2019). These activities formed part of the opening salvo of USCYBERCOM's novel cyberspace strategic doctrine of "persistent engagement"—described as the most important development in US cyber doctrine in two decades. These persistent engagement attempts sought to address a perceived strategic deficit in cyberspace on the part of the United States relative to its adversaries by operating as close as possible to the origin of adversarial cyber activity, and persistently contesting adversarial actors to generate continuous tactical, operational, and strategic advantage (United States of America, 2018a). To do so, USCYBERCOM expects to operate "seamlessly, globally and continuously" in cyberspace, using continuous engagement with adversaries to seize and maintain strategic and tactical initiative (United States of America, 2018a). Since 2018, under the banner of persistent engagement and to challenge adversarial activities wherever they operate, USCYBERCOM has deployed at least twenty-seven Cyber National Mission Force teams (called "hunt forward" operations by USCYBERCOM) to fifteen separate countries as part of its efforts to track and disrupt specific nation-state actors in foreign cyberspace (Pomerleau, 2022). Reportedly, USCYBERCOM efforts to defend the 2020 US elections may have involved eleven hunt forward operations across nine different countries (Pomerleau, 2022). More recently, in February 2022, prior to the Russian invasion of Ukraine, hunt forward operations that partnered with Ukrainian network operators were credited with mitigating malware capable of disrupting Ukrainian railway networks, enabling millions of Ukrainians to escape to safety and ensuring the flow of Western assistance remained undisturbed (Srivastava et al., 2022).

Persistent engagement aims to generate "continuous tactical, operational, and strategic advantage in cyberspace," with the ultimate objective of cumulatively shaping the boundaries of acceptable adversarial behaviour in cyberspace (i.e., through the tacit bargaining approach described earlier) (Fischerkeller & Harknett, 2017, 2019; Harknett & Goldman, 2016). Ergo, cyber activities driven by persistent engagement are meant to function as a never-ending series of signals that will coerce adversaries toward a preferred set of cyberspace norms (Healey & Caudill, 2020). In 2018, the USCYBERCOM operationalized a strategy of persistent engagement in its *Command Vision for*

U.S. Cyber Command: Achieve and Maintain Cyberspace Superiority (United States of America, 2018a). Through this strategy, USCYBERCOM aims to "secure US national interests in cyberspace and disrupt the cyber campaigns of US adversaries" by "defend[ing] forward as close as possible to the origin of adversary activity, and persistently contest[ing] malicious cyberspace actors to generate continuous tactical, operational, and strategic advantage" (United States of America, 2018a). The ultimate objective of the strategy is to "influence the calculations of [US] adversaries, deter aggression, and clarify the distinction between acceptable and unacceptable behaviour in cyberspace" (United States of America, 2018a). In essence, the strategic doctrine of persistent engagement necessitates a more active US posture in cyberspace, with the overall strategic objective of inhibiting an adversary's attempts to intensify cyber operations against the United States and allies.

Proponents of persistent engagement contend that previous US approaches to cyberspace were overly reliant on multilateral initiatives to establish cyber norms explicitly, which in turn resulted in a restrained and reactive operational strategy in cyberspace (Fischerkeller & Harknett, 2017). By contrast, the very raison d'être of the persistent engagement strategy is as an operational counterweight to overreliance on multilateral efforts to develop cyber norms, which is believed to have ceded the advantage in cyberspace to adversaries with an incentive to be more aggressive in their use of cyber operations.

Through persistent engagement, the United States aims to "gain strategic advantage" in cyberspace by changing the distribution of power in its favour. This objective is broad, ambitious, and global in scope, with an end state—an altered balance of power—that is challenging to measure. The distinction between what USCYBERCOM defines as acceptable or unacceptable behaviour in cyberspace is also somewhat ambiguous (Smeets, 2019). Critics of persistent engagement are also concerned about the lack of defined objectives and clarity regarding the strategy's actual implementation, proposing that in its current form, persistent engagement appears to proscribe an endless deployment of cyber resources in pursuit of vague strategic objectives (Lin & Smeets, 2018; Lin & Zegart, 2018). Other critics argue that the persistent deployment of US cyber capabilities against rivals is destabilizing and risks unintended consequences through inadvertent escalation, thereby exacerbating instability in cyberspace and accelerating an already hyper-competitive and unstable environment (Haley, 2019). However, concerns about escalation in and through cyberspace have generally been overstated. Recent research suggests that cyber operations are only narrowly escalatory, and only within the context of broader geopolitical crises (Healey & Jervis, 2020).

Functional Engagement for Traditional Middle Powers

Traditional middle powers face significant threats in cyberspace and are vulnerable to adversarial cyber espionage, sabotage, and subversion operations that undermine their national and global interests. Middle powers have largely responded to this growing threat by taking a passive approach: hardening their cyber defence capabilities and participating in multilateral initiatives to develop and diffuse transnational cyber norms. Middle powers may expect that the combination of these efforts will reduce the threats they face from malicious state actors in cyberspace. Since multilateral cyber diplomacy efforts have largely stalled, and given that the threats middle powers face in cyberspace are increasing exponentially, an alternative, or complementary, approach is necessary.

Cyber persistence theory and the concepts of tacit bargaining and normative shaping in cyberspace hold significant strategic utility for middle powers. The problem: cyber persistence theory has been formulated to guide the US approach to countering adversarial behaviour in cyberspace. The only known operationalization of cyber persistence theory—persistent engagement—specifically aims to alter the global balance of cyber power in the United States' favour by continually contesting its adversaries around the clock (United States of America, 2018a). These objectives are unattainable for middle powers, not only by virtue of resources, but also because they are misaligned with the foreign policy ambitions and characteristics of middle powers. In contrast, foreign policy interests more characteristic of middle powers might include maintaining the status quo; ensuring security and order in the international system; upholding the integrity of international organizations and democratic institutions; and protecting economic security and prosperity.

This chapter posits the cyber-strategic concept of functional engagement as a variation on persistent engagement uniquely tailored for operationalization by traditional middle powers. Functional engagement seeks to harness the strategic utility of cyber persistence theory and persistent engagement by adapting it to align more closely with traditional middle powers that strive to influence international affairs selectively as a function of their relative capabilities, interests, and degree of involvement (Chapnick, 1999; Cooper et al., 1993; Holbraad, 1971). The key difference between functional engagement and persistent engagement is the scope and scale of their respective objectives. Functional engagement proscribes a narrower application of tacit bargaining and normative shaping in cyberspace that reflects the limited cyber capabilities and foreign policy ambitions of traditional middle powers. To this end, functional engagement is premised on establishing and reinforcing a limited set of focal points that are communicated unambiguously to set boundaries for acceptable and unacceptable behaviour in cyberspace. Middle powers can then harness their limited cyber capabilities more effectively against adversarial cyber actors that transgress these specific focal points.

An initial set of focal points for unacceptable behaviour could include malicious activities that subvert or degrade the integrity of electoral processes or critical infrastructure systems; actions that undermine economic security or competitiveness; and behaviour that undermine the effective functioning of international institutions. Instead of continuously and globally employing cyber capabilities to change the overall balance of power in the international system, functional engagement calls for middle powers to deploy cyber espionage, subversion, and sabotage operations more narrowly, in specific instances when a malicious actor conducts cyber activity that is antithetical to tacitly accepted focal points. In turn, this strategy enables traditional middle powers to bolster focal points for cyber norms while upholding the rules-based international order.

Canada: A Case Study for Employing Functional Engagement

As a variant of the United States' persistent engagement approach, this chapter contends that functional engagement is better suited to states with limited resources but whose geopolitical ambitions render them targets of, and vulnerable to, adversarial state-sponsored cyber activity. Traditional middle powers provide a critical case study to this effect.

THE FUNCTIONAL PRINCIPLE AND ITS APPLICATION TO CYBERSPACE DOCTRINE

In the post–Second World War period and throughout the Cold War, Canada leveraged the "functional principle" (from which the functional engagement and the functional perspective of middle power identity derive their names) to pursue its interests, justify a disproportionate influence in the international system, and cement its post-1945 status as a leading "non-great power" (Chapnick, 1999, 2000). First articulated by Canadian diplomat Hume

Wrong, the functional principle stipulated that an individual small state's involvement in international affairs should be based on (1) the relevance of the state's interests; (2) the direct contribution of the state to the situation in question, and (3) the capacity of the state to participate (Chapnick, 2000). Practically, the functional perspective holds that middle powers commit to maintaining the status quo, security, and order in the international system through leadership on specific global problems and foreign policy niches of their choosing (Cooper et al., 1993).

Indeed, growing instability and escalating strategic competition between states in cyberspace are both global problems and a foreign policy niche highly relevant to Canada's national security and foreign policy interests. Owing to the resource constraints that characterize middle powers, for the past two decades Canada has been struggling to demonstrate effective international leadership and respond to a highly competitive cyberspace environment. At least three factors continue to coalesce to make Canada a low-risk, high-payoff target for malicious cyber activity. First, Canada has limited soft and hard power resources, which constrains its ability to combine instruments of power or retaliate unilaterally. Second, Canada's economy is highly advanced, with a strong technology sector, high levels of digital connectivity, vast natural resource wealth, and cutting-edge research and development activities (Siebring, 2021). Third, Canada's special relationship with the United States and its membership in an array of coveted security alliances and multilateral institutions provides potential adversaries with an efficient means of targeting both Canada and its great power allies (Canadian Security Intelligence Service, 2021).

Threats to Canada in cyberspace are escalating in sophistication, quantity, and complexity, and the country's core national interests continue to be undermined by malicious state-sponsored cyber actors. Canada's national security and its international interests have long been assured by its geographic location, the security assurances of multilateral institutions, and the legal and normative frameworks of the rules-based international order (Macnamara, 2012). Cyberspace represents a unique departure from these assurances: it allows Canada's adversaries to bypass its geographic advantage entirely, while multilateral approaches to managing state behaviour in cyberspace lack a foundation of stable laws, norms, and incentives to encourage malicious state actors to discipline their activities.

THREATS TO CANADA IN CYBERSPACE AND ITS EVOLVING CYBER STRENGTH

Canada's tradition of liberal internationalism has reflexively inclined it toward supporting multilateral processes that attempt to establish explicitly accepted boundaries for state behaviour in cyberspace. Since 2010, Canada has participated in at least forty-five multilateral statements, communiqués, and initiatives on cyber norms in the G7, G20, NATO, ASEAN, OAS, OSCE, the Commonwealth, and the UN (Carnegie Endowment, 2022). Concerted cyber diplomacy efforts notwithstanding, the Canadian military unambiguously asserts that state actors are increasingly pursuing their agendas using hybrid methods below the threshold of armed conflict (including in cyberspace) to threaten Canada's defence, security, and economic interests (Canada, 2017). Moreover, the director of Canada's domestic security service, the Canadian Security and Intelligence Service, has warned that Russian and Chinese state-sponsored commercial espionage remains the most significant threat to the Canadian economy and future economic growth (Vigneault, 2018). According to Canada's 2020 National Cyber Threat Assessment, cyber operations by China, Russia, Iran, and North Korea posed the most significant threat to Canada's national security and its strategic interests. The assessment further asserts that state cyber actors have carried out cyber operations to influence the Canadian public and conduct espionage against Canadian industry, government, and academia to "advance foreign economic and national security interests while undermining the same within Canada" (Canada, 2020).

Canada also has significant and steadily evolving capabilities that may enable it to play a leadership role in shaping norms in the cyberspace environment. The 2020 Harvard Belfer Center Cyber Power Index (CPI)—ostensibly the most comprehensive effort to evaluate and compare the objectives and capabilities of states in cyberspace—ranks Canada eighth in comprehensive global cyber power (behind the United States, China, the United Kingdom, Russia, the Netherlands, France, and Germany, but ahead of Japan and Australia) (Voo et al., 2020). The CPI characterizes Canada as a high-intent, low-capability cyber power with notable strengths in cyber defence, cyber norms development initiatives, and surveillance (Voo et al., 2020). By contrast, Canada's intent and capability to conduct cyber-enabled foreign intelligence and offensive cyber operations places it in in the middle of the CPI pack: lagging Russia and China and its Five Eyes partners, the United States and the United Kingdom (as well as the Netherlands and Israel) (Voo et al., 2020). On the one hand, the CPI's evaluation of Canada reflects two decades of focus on implementing cyber-security initiatives. On the other, the rankings may indicate a strategic deficit and thus the need for a cyberspace doctrine that can cohesively leverage a range of cyber espionage, subversion, and sabotage capabilities.

In recent years, Canadian policy-makers have made deliberate efforts to develop institutional and legislative mechanisms to support a more assertive cyberspace posture. Canada's 2017 defence policy, *Strong, Secure, Engaged*, recognized that cyberspace is essential for the conduct of modern military operations and complemented a strong defensive cyber posture with more assertive cyber operations (Canada, 2017). In 2019, passage of Bill C-59, *An Act Respecting National Security Matters*, bolstered the prospect for Canadian cyber operations. Bill C-59 expanded the role and impact Canada could have in cyberspace by authorizing the Communications Security Establishment (CSE) to conduct offensive cyber operations, which the legislation parses into "active cyber operations" and "defensive cyber operations"—to supplement CSE's traditional role of ensuring cryptographic security and collecting foreign signals intelligence. The addition of these capabilities to CSE's mandate was hailed as a major step in aligning Canada's cyber operations authorities with its Five Eyes allies (Carvin, 2018). For the first time in its history, the combination of foreign intelligence, active cyber operations, and defensive cyber operations mandates may enable it to conduct the full spectrum of cyber espionage, sabotage, and subversion operations.

In summary, Canada may be an ideal candidate for functional engagement since it (1) has a legacy of restraining its influence on geopolitics to foreign policy niches of particular relevance (the functional principle); (2) faces significant and mounting threats to its national and international interests as a result of malicious state-sponsored cyber activities; and (3) may already have, or is otherwise well on the path toward developing, the requisite cyber capabilities and authorities to begin upholding its interests in the cyberspace environment.

FUNCTIONAL ENGAGEMENT IN THE CANADIAN CONTEXT

Canada may have an opportunity to demonstrate independent international leadership to reduce instability and uncertainty in cyberspace. In doing so, it can uphold and extend its strategic interests. According to cyber persistence theory, helping to establish and strengthen tacitly accepted cyber norms by regularly employing cyber capabilities is the most effective way Canada can reduce uncertainty in cyberspace and limit threats to its national interests. Due to Canada's resource constraints and limited foreign policy ambitions (in comparison to the United States and other great powers), functional engagement prescribes that Canada employ the full range of its cyber capabilities to establish and reinforce a limited set of clearly defined and communicated focal points that define what it deems acceptable and unacceptable behaviour in cyberspace. Instead of continuously and globally employing cyber capabilities to change the overall balance of power in the international system, functional engagement calls for Canada to employ its cyber capabilities more narrowly, in specific instances when a malicious cyber actor conducts activity that is antithetical to those focal points.

An initial set of focal points for unacceptable state-sponsored behaviour in cyberspace could include malicious activities that (1) directly degrade Canada's sovereignty and the security of its people (e.g., cyber operations that target civilian critical infrastructure and ICS/SCADA systems); (2) degrade or subvert international law and the integrity of international, electoral, or democratic institutions (e.g., cyber operations that target electronic voting systems or the functioning of international institutions); and (3) undermine Canada's economic security, competitiveness, and prosperity (e.g., cyber operations that target intellectual property). In turn, this approach remains true to the fundamentals of cyber persistence but is more aligned within the limited resources and unique character of Canada's geopolitical identity as a middle power.

Conclusion

The volume and sophistication of state-sponsored activities in cyberspace has increased apace with deepening global dependence on the Internet and digital technologies. Twenty years of sustained state interactions in cyberspace have demonstrated that cyber conflict is rare and that states prefer to employ cyber operations as tools of statecraft well below the threshold of armed conflict. While the immediate risk of cyber escalation appears to be low, campaigns of cumulative cyber operations aim to generate strategic effects over time, by degrading the integrity of international, democratic, and electoral institutions, undermining economic competitiveness, and/or generating strategic information advantage over an adversary. Meanwhile, multilateral initiatives to reduce instability in cyberspace and develop explicitly accepted cyber norms have failed to deliver significant advances toward regulating the boundaries of state behaviour in cyberspace.

Traditional middle powers, especially those with highly interconnected societies, advanced economies, world-renowned research institutions, and memberships in an array of multilateral and security institutions face threats in cyberspace as acute as those faced by great powers, and possibly even more so given their limited economic and military capabilities and narrow influence in the international system. Traditional middle powers thus present a low-risk, high-payoff target for their adversaries in cyberspace, and consequently are accumulating a strategic deficit vis-à-vis other states that have more readily grasped such threats—and the opportunities of cyber operations as a tool of statecraft. By failing to shape adversarial behaviour in cyberspace around tacitly accepted focal points cumulatively, Canada, the Netherlands, Australia, and other traditional middle powers are ceding the operational initiative to illiberal adversaries such as Russia and China, who will in turn seize that initiative to generate cyber norms that support their strategic interests (Jordaan, 2003).

Faced with the prospects of a deleterious change to their environment as a result of growing instability and malicious activity in cyberspace, middle powers can *exit*, use *voice*, or demonstrate *loyalty*. Traditional middle powers such as Canada had hitherto pursued a *voice* approach that prioritizes multilateral efforts to develop explicitly accepted cyber norms. These efforts have yet to yield significant payoff and have failed to stem the rising tide of adversarial activity that is sweeping traditional middle powers in cyberspace. As a variation on persistent engagement for the United States, *functional engagement* for traditional middle powers is a voice approach that adapts cyber-strategic concepts of cyber persistence theory and persistent engagement to align with the limited resources and foreign policy ambitions of middle powers. Functional engagement in cyberspace seeks to harness the potential of tacit bargaining and normative shaping by focusing the limited cyber capabilities of traditional middle powers in pursuit of narrow strategic objectives. To this end, traditional middle powers need to leverage the full range of cyber capabilities at their disposal deployed to establish and, as required, reinforce a set of focal points that delineate acceptable and unacceptable behaviour by states in cyberspace.

Acknowledgement

Research for this article was supported by the Social Sciences and Humanities Research Council of Canada Partnership Grant 895-2021-1007.

NOTES

1 An earlier version of this chapter appeared in the *US Army Cyber Defense Review.*

REFERENCES

Canada. (2017). *Strong, secure, engaged: Canada's defence policy.* Department of National Defence. https://www.canada.ca/en/department-national-defence/corporate/policies-standards/canada-defence-policy.html

Canada. (2020). *National cyber threat assessment 2020.* Canadian Centre for Cyber Security. https://cyber.gc.ca/sites/default/files/publications/ncta-2020-e-web.pdf;

Canadian Security Intelligence Service. (2021). *CSIS public report 2020.* Government of Canada. https://www.canada.ca/content/dam/csis-scrs/documents/publications/2021/CSIS-Public-Report-2020.pdf

Carnegie Endowment. (2022, 15 July). Cyber norms index and timeline—Canada. *Carnegie Endowment for International Peace.* Retrieved 15 July 2022 from https://carnegieendowment.org/publications/interactive/cybernorms#timeline-section

Carvin, S. (2018, 27 April). Zero D'Eh: Canada takes a bold step towards offensive cyber operations. *Lawfare.* https://www.lawfareblog.com/zero-deh-canada-takes-bold-step-towards-offensive-cyber-operations

Chapnick, A. (1999). The middle power. *Canadian Foreign Policy Journal, 7*(2), 73–82. https://doi.org/10.1080/11926422.1999.9673212

Chapnick, A. (2000). The Canadian middle power myth. *International Journal, 55*(2), 188–206. https://doi.org/10.2307/40203476

Cooper, A., Higgott, R., & Nossal, K. (1993). *Relocating middle powers.* University of British Columbia Press.

Cooper, D. (2011). Challenging contemporary notions of middle power influence: Implications of the proliferation security initiative for middle power theory. *Foreign Policy Analysis, 7*(3), 317–36. https://doi.org/10.1111/j.1743-8594.2011.00140

Corera, G. (2016, 10 October). How France's TV5 was almost destroyed by "Russian hackers." *BBC News.* https://www.bbc.com/news/technology-37590375

Cyber Law Toolkit. (2015, 23 December). Power grid cyberattack in Ukraine (2015). *Cyber Law Toolkit.* https://cyberlaw.ccdcoe.org/wiki/Power_grid_cyberattack_in_Ukraine_(2015)

Farrell, H., Glaser, C. (2017). The role of effects, saliencies and norms in U.S. cyberwar doctrine. *Journal of Cybersecurity, 3*(1), 7–17. https://doi.org/10.1093/cybsec/tyw015

Fischerkeller, M., & Harknett, R. (2017). Deterrence is not a credible strategy for cyberspace. *Orbis, 61*(3), 381–93. https://doi.org/10.1016/j.orbis.2017.05.003

Fischerkeller, M., & Harknett, R. (2018a). *Cyber persistence theory, intelligence contests and strategic competition*. Institute for Defense Analysis. https://apps.dtic.mil/sti/pdfs/AD1118679.pdf

Fischerkeller, M., & Harknett, R. (2018b, 9 November). Persistent engagement and tacit bargaining: A path toward constructing norms in cyberspace. *Lawfare*. https://www.lawfareblog.com/persistent-engagement-and-tacit-bargaining-path-toward-constructing-norms-cyberspace

Fischerkeller, M., & Harknett, R. (2019). Persistent engagement, agreed competition, and cyberspace interaction dynamics and escalation. *Cyber Defense Review–Special Edition*. https://cyberdefensereview.army.mil/Portals/6/CDR-SE_S5-P3-Fischerkeller.pdf

Gallagher, S. (2019, 27 February). Report: US cyber command took Russian trolls offline during midterms. *Ars Technica*. https://arstechnica.com/information-technology/2019/02/report-us-cyber-command-took-russian-trolls-offline-during-midterms/

Glazebrook, G. (1947). The middle powers in the United Nations system. *International Organization, 1*(2), 307–18. https://doi.org/10.1017/S0020818300006081

Goldman, E. (2020). From reaction to action: Adopting a competitive posture in cyber diplomacy. *Texas National Security Review, 3*(4). https://repositories.lib.utexas.edu/bitstream/handle/2152/83957/TNSRVol3Iss4Goldman.pdf?sequence=2

Goldman, E. (2022). Paradigm change requires persistence—a difficult lesson to learn. *Cyber Defense Review, 7*(1), 113–18. https://www.jstor.org/stable/48642031

Greenberg, A. (2018, 22 August). The untold story of NotPetya, the most devastating cyberattack in history. *Wired*. https://www.wired.com/story/notpetya-cyberattack-ukraine-russia-code-crashed-the-world/

Grigsby, A. (2017). The end of cyber norms. *Survival, 59*(6), 109–22. https://doi.org/10.1080/00396338.2017.1399730

Harknett, R., & Goldman, E. (2016). The search for cyber fundamentals. *Journal of Information Warfare, 15*(2), 81–8. https://www.jstor.org/stable/26487534

Harknett, R., & Smeets, M. (2022). Cyber campaigns and strategic outcomes. *Journal of Strategic Studies, 45*(4), 534–67. https://doi.org/10.1080/01402390.2020.1732354

Healey, J. (2019). The implications of persistent (and permanent) engagement in cyberspace. *Journal of Cybersecurity, 5*(1), 1–15. https://doi.org/10.1093/cybsec/tyz008

Healey, J., & Caudill, S. (2020). Success of persistent engagement in cyberspace. *Strategic Studies Quarterly, 14*(1), 9–14. https://www.airuniversity.af.edu/Portals/10/SSQ/documents/Volume-14_Issue-1/Healey.pdf

Healey, J., & Jervis, R. (2020). The escalation inversion and other oddities of situational cyber stability. *Texas National Security Review, 3*(4), 30–53. http://dx.doi.org/10.26153/tsw/10962;

Hirschman, A. (1970). *Exit, voice, and loyalty: Responses to decline in firms, organizations, and states.* Harvard University Press.

Holbraad, C. (1971). The role of middle powers. *Cooperation and Conflict, 6*(1), 77–90. https://doi.org/10.1177/001083677100600108

Holbraad, C. (1984). *Middle powers in international politics.* Macmillan.

Hurwitz, R. (2014). The play of states: Norms and security in cyberspace. *American Foreign Policy Interests, 36*(5), 322–32. https://doi.org/10.1080/10803920.2014.969180

Jensen, E. (2017). The Tallinn manual 2.0: Highlights and insights. *Georgetown Journal of International Law, 48*(1). https://www.law.georgetown.edu/international-law-journal/wp-content/uploads/sites/21/2018/05/48-3-The-Tallinn-Manual-2.0.pdf

Jordaan, E. C. (2003). The concept of a middle power in international relations: Distinguishing between emerging and traditional middle powers. *Politikon South African Journal of Political Studies, 30*(2), 165–81.

Kreps S., & Schneider, J. (2019). Firebreaks in the cyber, conventional, and nuclear domains: Moving beyond effects-based logics. *Journal of Cybersecurity, 5*(1), 1–9. https://doi.org/10.1093/cybsec/tyz007

Lee, G., & Soeya, Y. (2014). The middle-power challenge in East Asia: An opportunity for co-operation between South Korea and Japan. *Global Asia, 9*(2), 85–91.

Leuprecht, C., Szeman, J., & Skillicorn, D. B. (2019). The Damoclean sword of offensive cyber: Policy uncertainty and collective insecurity. *Contemporary Security Policy, 40*(3), 382–407.

Lin, H., & Smeets, M. (2018, 3 May). What is absent from the U.S. cyber command "vision." *Lawfare.* https://www.lawfareblog.com/what-absent-us-cyber-command-vision

Lin, H., & Zegart, A. (2018). *Bytes, bombs, and spies: The strategic dimensions of offensive cyber operations.* Brookings University Press.

Macnamara, D. (2012). Canada's national and international security interests. In D. McDonough (Ed.), *Canada's national security in the post-9/11 world: Strategy, Interests, and threats* (pp. 45–56). University of Toronto Press.

Maness, R. C., Valeriano, B., Jensen, B., Hedgecock, K., & Macias, J. (2022). The dyadic cyber incident and campaign dataset, version 2.0. *Harvard Dataverse.* https://dataverse.harvard.edu/dataset.xhtml?persistentId=doi:10.7910/DVN/CQOMYV

Maurer, T. (2020). A dose of realism: The contestation and politics of cyber norms. *Hague Journal on the Rule of* Law, *12*(2), 227–49. https://doi.org/10.1007/s40803-019-00129-8

Mitrany, D. (1933). *The progress of international government.* Yale University Press.

Nakashima, E. (2019, 27 February). U.S. Cyber Command operation disrupted Internet access of Russian troll factory on day of 2018 midterms. *Washington Post.* https://www.washingtonpost.com/world/national-security/us-cyber-command-operation-disrupted-internet-access-of-russian-troll-factory-on-day-of-2018-midterms/2019/02/26/1827fc9e-36d6-11e9-af5b-b51b7ff322e9_story.html

Patience, A. (2014). Imagining middle powers. *Australian Journal of International Affairs, 68*(2), 210–24. https://doi.org/10.1080/10357718.2013.840557

Pomerleau, M. (2022, 4 March). Cyber Command has deployed to nations 27 times to help partners improve cybersecurity. *Fedscoop.* https://www.fedscoop.com/cyber-command-has-deployed-to-nations-27-times-to-help-partners-improve-cybersecurity/

Shin, Dong-Min. (2015, 4 December). A critical review of the concept of middle power. *E-International Relations.* https://www.e-ir.info/2015/12/04/a-critical-review-of-the-concept-of-middle-power/

Siebring, J. (2021). *Choosing complicated: The Canadian approach to national security in cyberspace* [Master's directed research paper, Royal Military College of Canada]. Canadian Forces Digital Library.

Smeets, M. (2019, 20 March). There are too many red lines in cyberspace. *Lawfare.* https://www.lawfareblog.com/there-are-too-many-red-lines-cyberspace

Srivastava, M., Murgia, M., & Murphy, H. (2022, 9 March). The secret US mission to bolster Ukraine's cyber defences ahead of Russia's invasion. *Financial Times.* https://www.ft.com/content/1fb2f592-4806-42fd-a6d5-735578651471;

Stevens, T. (2012). A cyberwar of ideas? Deterrence and norms in cyberspace. *Contemporary Security Policy, 33*(1), 148–70. https://doi.org/10.1080/13523260.2012.659597

Sukumar, A. (2017). The UN GGE failed. Is international law in cyberspace doomed as well? *Lawfare.* https://www.lawfareblog.com/un-gge-failed-international-law-cyberspace-doomed-well

Tikk-Ringas, E. (2017). International cyber norms dialogue as an exercise of normative power. *Georgetown Journal of International Affairs, 17*(3), 47–59. https://www.jstor.org/stable/26395975

United States of America. (2018a). *Command vision for U.S. Cyber Command: Achieve and maintain cyberspace superiority.* United States Cyber Command.

United States of America. (2018b). *Findings of the investigation into China's acts, policies, and practices related to technology transfer, intellectual property, and innovation under section 301 of the Trade Act of 1974.* Office of the United States Trade Representative Executive Office of the President. https://ustr.gov/sites/default/files/Section%20301%20FINAL.PDF

United States of America. (2021, 19 July). The United States, joined by allies and partners, attributes malicious cyber activity and irresponsible state behavior to the People's Republic of China. *White House.* https://www.whitehouse.gov/briefing-room/statements-releases/2021/07/19/the-united-states-joined-by-allies-and-partners-attributes-malicious-cyber-activity-and-irresponsible-state-behavior-to-the-peoples-republic-of-china/

Valeriano, B., Jensen, B., & Maness, R. (2018). *Cyber strategy: The evolving character of power and coercion*. Oxford University Press.

Vigneault, D. (2018, 8 December). *Remarks by Director David Vigneault at the Economic Club of Canada*. Government of Canada. https://www.canada.ca/en/security-intelligence-service/news/2018/12/remarks-by-director-david-vigneault-at-the-economic-club-of-canada.html?fbclid=IwAR2VWCrD1F4aCznfNfeQrQoyZd_CMxAfCi8ihugtNmzjE_BrjFG4jPD7Pag

Voo, J., Hemani, I., Jones, S., DeSombre, W., Cassidy, D., & Schwarzenbach, A. (2020). *National cyber power index 2020*. Belfer Center for Science and International Affairs. https://www.belfercenter.org/sites/default/files/2020-09/NCPI_2020.pdf

SECTION IV

EMERGING TOOLS AND APPROACHES

10

Digital Tribalism and Ontological Insecurity: Manipulating Identities in the Information Environment

Sarah Jane Meharg

In a world of growing anxiety and fear, new renderings of tribalism emerge to decrease individual anxieties related to belonging. While tribes are relational and emergent in their scope and scale, they are often cast in the same light as *engineered* populist movements that generate hatred and othering to increase fear, resentment, and contestation, in effect increasing individual anxieties and contributing to the production of anxious publics. Organic tribes, on the other hand, are a relational and network-based grouping of like-minded people seeking ontological security to assuage a growing sense of uncertainty in an ever-globalizing, placeless lived experience. "Cultural anxiety and turmoil" are a consequence of the effects of globalization—people are becoming unsettled because they feel they are losing links to their local or national communities (Lieber & Weisberg, 2002). While mainstream media and some scholarly efforts conflate populism with tribalism, this chapter examines digital tribalism as a pathway to reducing ontological insecurity in individuals by focusing on the affective dimensions of belonging and the routinization of such belonging. The chapter examines individual ontological (in) security, rather than international relations scholarship applied at the state level, as the source for the search for belonging that metes itself out in digital materiality. To deter nefarious intentions weaponized through engineered digital tribalism from destabilizing material worlds, the chapter sheds light on ontological security theory (OST) as a theoretical framework to understand the stabilizing effects produced through organic digital tribalism.

The manipulation of ideologies, the molestation of identities, and the era of digital and material *cancel culture* is a hallmark of twenty-first-century public spheres. The deleterious effects on people from the manipulation of narratives of identity and the destruction of places and histories, understood as *identicide* (Meharg, 2001, 2006, 2011) mark uncertain times for peace and stability. What are digital tribes capable of? How quickly can they mobilize against/inside of liberal democracies? How are they being manipulated? To what effect? Are all questions for twenty-first-century deterrence scholars focused on methods for deterring actions? Also, equally important, how do we balance the creation and contestation of powerful competing narratives through private, for-profit social media platforms that simultaneously seal us into our online bubbles while allowing us to see the other in new frames of reference? Understanding ways to take advantage of and manipulate people through ontological- and identity-based means in the information environment may expose how adversaries shape digital tribes to achieve political, economic, religious, and cultural agendas. This chapter examines OST and digital tribalism as a way to understand why and how liberal democracies could be manipulated by adversaries. In reflecting on uncertain identities generated by the breakdown of the liberal democratic rules-based order, there emerge a number of broad deterrence implications in the information domain—namely, information operations undermining ontological security of the people and groups that make up a nation-state. Preliminary considerations are introduced in this chapter, with a focus on the connection between sub-state ontological security, digital tribalism, and identicide.

The ubiquitous social media platforms of the 2000s have contributed to intensified focus on public engagement (Alvares & Dahlgren, 2016) while being less proficient at promoting democratic values, as shown by the results of European and American election results. The intrusion of the Internet into all facets of life has fundamentally changed the spatial aspects of the geospheres experienced by publics. "An individualization of civic cultures has emerged in tandem with the growth of mediated populism through the use of new technologies, with a tendency towards personalization in the public domain." (Alvares & Dahlgren 2016, p. 46). This includes effects on transnational and diasporic identities, as well as hyper-local and new identities. "The innovative affordances of new media technologies, such as social networking sites, podcasts, blogs, open-source software and wikis" (Husain, 2012, p. 1028), pave the path for an individualized civic environment (Gerodimos, 2012), with engagement in the public domain being "subjectively experienced as more a personal rather than a collective question" (Dahlgren, 2013, p. 52). While these engagements can be fair and democratic, emerging organically through processes of informal belonging and identity groups, they can also be hostile and aggressive weaponizations of identity, engineered by nefarious puppeteers intent on manipulating publics to advance agendas. This balance between belonging and manipulation comes to the fore through the examination of tribalism.

Tribalism

Since the 1950s, tribalism has been understood as a distinctive reproductive organizational form based on kinship structures and "social organizations defined by ascribed traditions of common descent, language, culture and ideology, and reliant on the maintenance of territories and boundaries" (St. John, 2018, p. 5). Tribalism was part of an *assemblage* of discourses and practices that contrasted traditional societies and that was synonymous with agrarian, patriarchal societies with modern nation-states. Characteristics of tribalism included Indigeneity, kinship, and bounded territory. Other elements of membership included face-to-face belonging, recognition, and mutuality/reciprocity. Groupings shared cultural symbols, signs, and practices that ranged from the vernacular to the sacred. Western writings on tribalism, and particularly its uses for rationalizing the foreign control or influence of faraway places, cannot be understood outside of constructions of race, class, and gender inherent in (neo)colonialism. Recent contributions by settler colonial writers, including Wolfe (2006) and Grosfoguel (2013), show how colonial discourses rationalized the forcible removal of Indigenous groups from their ancestral lands, thereby allowing them to claim *terra nullis* and ignore the territorial claims of Indigenous peoples (Wolfe, 2006). Colonialists not only controlled this territory with superior military technologies, they also attempted to erase Indigenous knowledge by burning texts, removing Indigenous children from their families, and establishing residential schools. Some have called this cultural genocide, and others epistemicide (Grosfoguel, 2013) and identicide (Meharg, 2001). We will return to identicide understandings later in this chapter.

Tribalism is the production of safety, security, and belonging in concurrence with the strengthening of identity and cohering of autobiographical narratives. These two activities seek to reduce and minimize anxiety, fear, and uncertainty in members of a tribe. The reduction of these emotions strengthens a sense of self, producing certainty of oneself now and in the future. Tribalism, in its digital form, is a conceptual haven creating a sense of togetherness that transcends the superfluous notion of physical connectedness. An alternate theory to explain the drive to enhance in-group identity is *uncertainty reduction* as a social category prototype to define a framework for how group members view each other and how they ought to act and interact, thereby rendering behaviours (including one's own behaviours) predictable (Grimson, 2010; Hogg, 2001). Group members also take comfort from the idea that a social identity has persistence. By contrast, threats to the group's continuity will cause members to feel uncertainty, which in turn can lead to increased conformance to group norms/prototypes, greater levels of intolerance and ethnocentrism, higher in-group solidarity and cohesion, and acts of derogation or retaliation against the out group. Threats that generate such responses include physical threats (harm to group members, group structure, vernacular places, including homes), symbolic threats (damage to values, prestige, symbols, distinctiveness, etc.), physical extinction threats (destruction of the group), and symbolic extinction threats (destruction or permanent loss of prestige, symbols, and sacred and symbolic places) (Meharg, 2001, 2011; Niedbala & Hohman, 2019; Osborne, 2001; Wohl et al., 2010).

With its accessibility, convenience, and popularity, the Internet has enabled tribalism to take on a new form and force. While in-place belonging exists strongly, a new form of belonging has emerged that is both placeless and attractive. "Digital tribalism" refers to the formation of groups in the digital realm centred around commonalities, including ethnic background, nationality, culture, hobbies, and political affiliation. The use of the word "tribe" is intentional, referring to the instinctive need for humans as social animals to recognize and bond with others that are similar; indeed, a "tribal level of organization is the most striking derived feature of human social organization," with "no close analog in other animals" (Richerson & Boyd, 2000). Characteristic of tribalism (as opposed to simple groupings) is a sense of "internal identification and loyalty," which results in a "cohesive extended familyhood" (Plater, 1990). It is the intensity of this affiliation that sometimes causes tribalism to be cast in a negative light, with connotations of exclusion, suspicion, competition, and conflict.

Organic or Engineered Tribes?

Engineered tribes weaponize their membership through securitization, organization, and financing. No longer on a level playing field, these engineered tribes invoke contestation and elimination of alternative opinions: voices viewed as counter to a weaponized agenda are targeted and removed. This elimination is a form of identicide (Meharg, 2001, 2006, 2011) as the spaces, symbols, and people are targeted and destroyed in a form of attack that has moved conflict into the digital realm. Private-sector digital technologies are a weapon system to shape structures and agents in incalculable ways, resulting in intense levels of contestation that can violently erupt back into the material world. Technologies are not tools accessible by the state, but can be conceptualized as available to the highest bidder. Weaponizing tribal identity in the digital information domain using technologies with effects-based operations has brought conflict to the Internet. Online wars are less messy, easier to manipulate, and take place in a relatively plastic environment through which to implement policies, programs, and policing. While it is relatively easy to understand the religious radicalization of people through digital means, it is now not unusual for humanitarian-minded tribes to choose sides and escalate through the early stages of hostilities against their perceived contested "other." Balance, fairness, and free speech are yesterday's ideals—the new game is information control, which leads to control of people, funding, and identities. These new threats to democracy and freedom are advanced through autocratic dictatorships functioning inside states, where they operationalize and weaponize identity narratives producing ontological insecurity at the cost of the many for the gain of a few. Information operations are rarely scrutinized and mostly go unnoticed by people, and this inspires a growing scholarly and practical interest in deterrence. Concurrently, the manipulation of publics is a growing marketing specialization, with companies like Cambridge Analytica being thrust into the limelight.

The Search for Security

People are seekers of neither *routine* nor *certainty*, but of *belonging*. Anxious publics seek belonging, choosing to find a tribe despite the knowledge that they might be manipulated by ads, videos, fake news, deepfakes, and incentives to share and retweet incendiary content. In the face of this, people still choose to belong together online. OST has strong relevance to our understanding of this desire to belong and connect together, highlighting new modalities of deterrence that may contain digital togetherness where it is, online, rather than drawing contestation and violence into the material world.

OST suggests that identities are constructed in an ongoing, continuously constituted process of identification in interlinked processes of agents' identity, narrative constructions, and their performance through practice and action. The need for coherence between identity, narrative, and routinized actions contributes to ontological security (Hom & Steele, 2020). The corollary *insecurity* emerges through incoherence and inconsistencies in state autobiographical narratives, and in the de-routinization of familiar and expected practices (Mitzen, 2006) in places or inside communities. People attempt to preserve predictability and re-establish routines that remind them of previous practices. Analysis of how tribal routines maintain pattern and variety provides insights into how synchronic routine processes are connected to diachronic routine processes (Feldman et al., 2020, p. 508). When routines are changed or broken, people go through a process of building, strengthening, and reassertion, seeking processes of stability. An examination of digital routine-breaking raises questions about *cancel culture*, digital character assassinations, digital hit squads, being jailed by Facebook, or algorithmically induced echo chambers, to name just a few examples, and the effects of contestation between groups/tribes online resulting in concerns about digital tribalism intruding upon the material world and claiming material territory. Digital and social media literature examining online groups is divided between negative discourse and positive discourse. When they are experienced as advancing democracy, globalism, pluralism, or cosmopolitanism, they are *good* and more commonly referred to as communities or social justice movements, yet conversely, when they are experienced as advancing populism, radicalism, and fundamentalism, they are *bad* and referred to as *tribal*. Tribalism is not inherently bad, but it can lead to ideological thinking and sacred values that distort cognitive processing of objective information in ways that affirm and strengthen the views of one's group. Such tribal tendencies lead to ideologically distorted information processing in any group—whether conservative or liberal, left or right (Clark & Winegard, 2020). Questions arise when observing whether organic or engineered digital tribalism is at its core contentious and nefarious or ambivalent and benign.

Individual and State Security in a Digital World

Deterrence theory has been a cornerstone of strategic thinking since the end of the Second World War, when fears of nuclear escalation led Western states to focus on methods of conflict resolution that did not involve direct military confrontation (Freedman, 2020). During the Cold War, deterrence dogma was premised on the aggression of the Soviet Union, creating the dominant paradigm of deterrence as punishment—demonstrating to an aggressor that the cost of an attack would be unbearable due to the retaliation that would follow. However, such an attitude saw the development of scholarship on deterrence theory become trapped in a rigid framework of analysis incompatible with rapidly evolving information, technology, and the benefit of hindsight (McCGwire, 1986). Only in recent decades have other aspects of deterrence been explored, including defensively minded strategies (deterrence by denial), as well as when and how deterrence can be employed (Mazarr, 2018).

The current trend has been to apply deterrence theory beyond the traditional nuclear scope, taking into account the social and technological advancements of the twenty-first century. Scholars have sought to apply varying deterrence theories to new modes of conflict, resulting in a mass of new literature in areas such as counterterrorism (Trager & Zagorcheva, 2006). Most recently, deterrence in cyberspace has captured the attention of researchers, but whether it will last long in the limelight is a matter of much debate (Schulze, 2019). While the literature has largely focused on military networks, government databases, and other state-level digital structures as the prime battlefields of cyberspace, the sub- and supra-state levels have yet to be explored in depth.

"Digital tribalism" describes the creation of socially cohesive groups in an online space. Tribes can be founded from commonalities—for example, shared cultures or hobbies—leading to a strong sense of kinship between tribe members. This can pose a security threat, as platforms for individuals to congregate with like-minded peers may create an environment encouraging radicalization. Tribes can create connections within and/or across borders, and within their closed communities disseminate extremist views; for example, many Islamist and far-right groups who feel that they have lost their identities through globalization resort to using digital tribes to spread their ideologies (Abbas, 2017). Misinformation in such closed communities spreads in a virus-like fashion, misleading members and inciting them to potentially violent action (Cronkhite et al., 2020; Lewandowsky & Smillie, 2020). Thus it is important to understand how to identify the role digital tribes play in cyberspace, when they become dangerous, and how to prevent them from becoming a threat to national security.

Interactions between users on social media mirror those in real life, leading to the formation of communities composed of distinct groups, intermediaries, and follower networks (Przemyslaw et al., 2012). The need for communication and connection through digital means is a growing global trend. In the United States, approximately 75 per cent of households have Internet access, with seven in ten Americans using social media (Pew Research Center, 2021a, 2021b). Studies of African countries, where the number of households with Internet access is below 20 per cent, cite social media as a primary motivator for increasing Internet adoption (Stork et al., 2013). One would assume that with lower Internet access and social media participation compared to other countries, digital tribes would have less influence in such areas. This is not the case: tribes have caused just as much national upheaval in Africa through online congregation and the spreading of misinformation as their counterparts in the United States. For example, fake news sites and troll armies of Twitter users, coordinated by public relations firms, were used to spread narratives about the South African president, with such tweets receiving thousands of interactions through circulation within the troll army. These high engagement numbers imply to outsiders the legitimacy of the information being spread (Wassermann, 2020).

I wish to amplify the apparent asymmetry of tribalism's two spatial imaginaries, the material and imagined processes and outcomes of belonging-seeking, in order to suggest that, in their unlikely compatibility and alignment, something critical about how deterrence operates above and beneath the state is to be gleaned. To comprehend digital tribalism's belonging-making potential and limitations for producing ontological security, we require deeper understandings of how they become meaningful, how they are felt/sensed, and how they are (re)produced in, and as part of, everyday identity narratives of political, economic, and cultural belonging. As we progress through the twenty-first century, how will tribalism continue to evolve and/or be deterred?

Tribalism in the Twenty-First Century

In recent years, the subject of tribalism has had a renaissance of sorts, increasing its cross-disciplinary appeal. Contestation of the other can lead to increased anxiety culminating in degrees of cultural intolerance, and exposure to other groups, world views, cultural objects, routines, and more can be accelerated and appreciated in the intensively interconnected world of the twenty-first century (Karim, 2020). The contemporary variant is neither related to collectivities based on kinship structures nor anchored to a territorially bounded space. Current iterations use tribalism to understand such phenomena as political polarization (Chua, 2018; Hobfoll, 2018; James, 2006; Mason, 2018), nativism, white nationalism, extreme xenophobic intolerance to difference and populism. Chua (2018), for example, contends that American political tribalism as manifest in partisan polarization and political dysfunction in Washington threatens to fragment and weaken the social cohesion of the state—once comprised of a *super group*, one whose narrative, while critical to the coherent autobiographical narrative of the people making up the nation-state, is often ignored, contested, or outright unknown by foreign interveners or the institutions making up the liberal democratic rules-based world order. Chua draws parallels with the Robbers Cave experiment by Harvard social psychologist Muzafer Sherif in 1953, when researchers divided boy campers into two groups and orchestrated situations designed to provoke mutual distrust and animus.

However, the Robbers Cave experiment was preceded by an experiment at Middle Grove, which Sherif chose not to publish because the findings undermined his preferred narrative (Perry, 2018). In this earlier experiment, two groups of boy campers chose to co-operate rather than turn on one another, despite deliberate efforts on the part of Sherif's team to prompt competitive and vengeful inter-group behaviours. Partly because they had come to know and befriend one another prior to the experiment, the boys co-operated to uncover the source of a series of hapless incidents (Perry, 2018). Adding to these dynamics are shared loyalties to persons, whether political or popular chieftains, and concepts evoked and maintained through affects and emotions. Members of digital tribes, unlike the Middle Grove and Robbers Cave subjects, do not typically know each other in person, but shared affects create a strong sense of belonging between and among members, compelling them in contexts of nationalism to bridge the divide between the material and digital worlds to lay claims in both (Duile, 2017, p. 252; Janowitz, 2009). Similarly, those in contexts of leisurely pursuits (sports, for example) have created a safe *belonging* space for participants to escape from society and produce a territory to defend (Baumann, 1996; Delanty, 2011; Hayday et al., 2021; Kauss & Griffiths, 2012). These social, psychological, and political research experiments suggest that organic tribalism itself is neither inherently competitive nor violent; rather, the contextual conditions create a permissive environment for these behaviours and the potential weaponization of people to achieve political, economic, and/or cultural agendas.

An Appeal to Emotion

A tribe's interpellation of political discourse to their publics must resonate within tribe members' affective dimensions of their personal life-world and enhance their autobiographical narratives or suffer rejection. Note that discourses are usually built on simplifications and strong emotional appeals (Alvares & Dahlgren, 2016). All information is potentially politicized and rendered vulnerable to malign intent (Waisbord, 2018). Political discourse embodies rhetorical dimensions that speak to citizens' emotional sides, and populist agendas in Europe are no different; political engagement per se would not take place were it not in part driven by affective dimensions (Alvares & Dahlgren, 2016; Dahlgren, 2006; Papacharissi, 2015), and instant communication between members of digital tribes, facilitated by social media, to incite escalation into real-world mass mobilizations. Emotionally driven narratives describing a trigger event can provoke action in material worlds. Following the death of George Floyd, for example, trending hashtags on Twitter and memorial posts on Instagram were used to quickly coordinate mass protests. Social media allowed users to communicate quickly with each other while also evading detection, as calls to stage protests would be posted and removed in the course of a single day to make developments difficult for authorities to track (Heaney, 2020). Thus it becomes easy for the puppeteers of contrived belonging and engineered tribalism to use social media to turn the Internet into a massive, anonymous, and instant protest organizational body, which is almost impossible to track or prevent by local authorities. Ergo, thousands of online users can band together over an emotionally charged topic and attempt to exact justice in the material world. This is worsened when influential users weigh in on issues, broadcasting calls to action to their large follower bases and increasing the likelihood of action. While this sometimes has positive consequences, such as the firing of an employee for a racist tirade in public, it can escalate into violent attacks and material damage of other identity groups, as with the razing of over two dozen churches in Canada following the discovery of mass graves outside residential schools. Additionally, the 2021 Capitol riot in the United States was orchestrated by groups on Twitter, Facebook, and Parler over the course of months. Prior to the riot, subgroups had already formed to coordinate rallies, plan travel routes, collect funds, and identify targets (Atlantic Council Digital Forensic Research Lab, 2021). Psychological factors influenced the groups' ability to collaborate and carry out an armed attack: followers of political leaders with authoritarian personalities tend to have a preference for aggression, and are more willing to legitimize actions going beyond normative expectations (Petersen, 2020). Later studies showed that there was an enhanced correlation between the participants in the riot and members of Trump-supporting communities that perceived themselves to be socially isolated (Van Dijcke & Wright, 2021). In essence, members of digital tribes that feel threatened may be more motivated to resort to acts of violence as a twisted means of self-defence, especially when the tribe is formed around an extreme political cause. Orchestrators lurking behind engineered tribes can operationalize and harness trigger events for ideological gains.

Ontological (In)Security

Ontological security scholars have been influenced by Gidden's structuration theory (1984, 1991), which draws on the work of R. D. Laing's understanding of security of the self as that which denotes a state of confident autonomy (2010). From this understanding, Giddens defines ontological security as "confidence or trust that the natural and social worlds are as they appear to be, including the basic existential parameters of self and social identity" (Giddens, 1984, p. 375). Giddens contends that, through social interaction, individuals learn the rules and codes of conduct, which guide predictable and routinized behaviours, and render fear and anxiety manageable and constitute self-identity. Routinized practices make life knowable. However, when conditions change to the extent that the future is no longer knowable and predictable, whether due to forces beyond an individual's control, or the result of decisions and actions by an individual, a person experiences ontological insecurity. Since persons exercise agency, they are not totally under the whim of forces outside their control or of their own making. They may act in ways that attempt to restore the status quo, or to create routinized behaviour and practices. Both courses of action are designed to restore a knowable, predictable future in which reassurance emerges, and anxiety is mitigated.

In their study on ontological insecurities and the politics of populism, Steele and Homolar (2019) expand on Giddens's ideas by describing the psychological need for continuity as the gateway for populist politics that leverages promises to regenerate and reinforce past notions of spatialized belonging and inclusion, in particular when agents experience trauma and anxiety. Self-identity consists of the development of a consistent feeling of *who one is* in relation to others, offering biographical continuity in which an individual is able to sustain a narrative about oneself and answer questions about doing, acting, and being, informed from a bifurcated reality of *us* and *others*.

International relations (IR) scholars have drawn on this concept of ontological security from the fields of psychology and sociology to understand state and interstate relations and to scale up the analytical level from the individual to the state and interstate relations. While traditional realist approaches focus on the politics of fear under conditions of anarchy, ontological security scholars are careful to differentiate fear from anxiety. They define fear as an emotion that is directed at a specific object, such as the death of one's child, or business closures enforced through COVID-19 pandemic politics or the threat of violence from a transnational terrorist group such as al Qaeda or ISIS, which elicits a fight, freeze, or flight response. In contrast, anxiety is a psychic condition or mood associated with uncertainty that can trigger a range of emotions and responses not limited to fight/freeze/flight. Attention to anxiety derives from the view that anxiety is increasing in the context of human displacement and migration, employment precariousness, and global inequality linked with globalization, climate change, pandemics, and digital technologies (Kinnvall, 2004; Kinnvall & Mitzen, 2018).

States defend against ontological insecurity with a range of behaviours. These include a turn toward authoritarianism and populism, as evidenced by the electoral victory of the Law and Justice Party in Poland and slogans like "Take Britain back again" and "Make America great again" by Brexiteers and Trump supporters, respectively (Browning, 2019; Kinnvall, 2018). Anxiety is also linked with othering and scapegoating, in which groups are named as a threat to the nation's imagined identity, prompting hard-line foreign affairs and security policies with regard to immigration and border control. Examples of extreme security policies include the so-called Muslim travel ban in the United States, the construction of border walls and fences in Israel-Palestine, the US-Mexico border, and Hungary's fence in the context of the migration to Europe. Scapegoating is not limited to groups like migrants and refugees but extends to philanthropists like George Soros and Bill Gates through anti-Semitic or conspiratorial campaigns. Anxiety is also linked with the concept of a *risk society* (Beck et al., 1992) and efforts to identify and manage national and transnational risks.

The second-generation scholarship attempts to overcome the reliance on Giddens's ideas about ontological security, particularly his emphasis on the need to maintain psychological well-being and avoid existential anxieties, which centre on stasis and cannot fully account for change. Kinnvall (2018) moves away from Giddens's approach of ontological security as a security of being in favour of a focus on ontological security as a process of becoming (2018). Connecting to process relational philosophy, we can understand tribes, their members, and the geoscape in which tribes are (re)produced and maintained as being in various states of subjectivity and digital materiality.

Current examinations of ontological security through an IR lens are pushing the boundaries in a number of directions relevant to this chapter. Looking at the first boundary—the under-specification of unconscious processes—Cash (2020) employs a psychoanalytic approach to explore unconscious defences against anxiety. Cash makes reference to Isabel Menzies Lyth's 1960 case study of the norms and rules of behaviour governing nurse conduct in a UK hospital to defend against the anxieties evoked in the process of executing their care duties to ill and terminal patients. Menzies Lyth argued that nurse trainees adopted routines and practices to socialize themselves to manage such anxieties. These included minimizing patient contact, maintaining strict hierarchies and deference to superiors, restricting independent judgment and discretion, and limiting any sharing of feelings about their work with experienced staff. Cash sees this as "a cultural repertoire, predominantly encoded with psychic mechanisms of splitting and projection, organized role-identities, practices, emotions, and social relations in order to support the ontological security of nurses who regularly have to deal with anxiety-provoking situations" (2020, p. 315).

Another boundary is the tendency of proponents like Mitzen (2006) and Steele (2008) to focus on the actions of actors to preserve their self-identity and restore or protect ontological security. Browning and Joenniemi (2017) argue ontological security scholarship is prone to collapsing notions of self, identity, and ontological security. By focusing on how perceived threats to an actor's established identity undermine their ontological security and rationalize security moves to defend and reinforce self-identity, securitization is equated with moves to enhance stability, and de-securitization is linked with instability. But since identities are always in flux and "never fully stable, settled and complete, the promise of stability in securitization practices is illusory" (Browning & Joenniemi, 2016, p. 34). Browning and Joenniemi argue that it may be more productive to understand how actors come to self-identify and articulate identity claims instead of emphasizing identity stability. Instead, they argue that "more focus is needed on how reflexivity towards identity is also central to ontological security . . . [and that] desecuritization—and not just securitization—may be central to re-stabilization processes" (Browning & Joenniemi, 2016, p. 34).

An overview of related arguments (Kinnvall & Mitzen, 2020, pp. 251–2) suggests that when ontological insecurity is experienced, there are options for the anxious and fearful, producing a reflexive opportunity to engage uncertainty and dwell in ambivalence (Cash, 2016; Kinnvall, 2018; Solomon, 2015). "The amorphous, ambivalent character of politics, while often frustrating for analysts, is also a long-term strength for democracy, allowing citizens to engage, participate and ally themselves in ever-new constellations" (Alvares & Dahlgren, 2016, p. 51).

Lastly, ontological security studies in IR have scaled up the work to the state level but have not adequately addressed the international level (Rumelili, 2020). For this chapter in particular, understanding the production of anxiety and belonging-seeking at the supra-state level will be an area of further research relevant to engineered digital tribalism and the deterrence of negative effects of such belonging.

The need for ontological security, a sense of continuity and order, is deep, and attachment to routines is profound and universal. Change to an individual's established routines can be disruptive, ranging from something as simple as a highway detour to something more complex like the arrival of a new baby, loss of employment, or homeschooling during the COVID-19 pandemic. Empirical research in various areas of social psychology confirms that uncertainty generates identity insecurity, which is resolved through routines. The basic insight of anxiety/uncertainty management (AUM) theory, for example, supported by experimental work, is that uncertainty is both a cognitive and affective problem (Grinson, 2010; Hogg, 2001). Humans need to *make sense of their world*, and when there is insufficient information or meanings are unsettled, individuals suffer anxiety. "When 'normal' expectations are not met . . . reactions are anomic and demonstrate confusion. Ontological security is the mechanism individuals employ to get on with their daily lives" (Steele & Homolar, 2019, p. 215). Ontological insecurity produces existential anxiety.

Identicide

When identities and autobiographical narratives are disrupted, various forms of insecurity emerge. This can be intentionally induced through identicide: the deliberate, systematic, and targeted destruction of one's established places, symbols, objects, and routines, including ideas, values, and aesthetica, and other cultural property that represent the identity of a people, with the intent to erase the cultural narrative and memory of that people, demoralize a population, absorb it into another cultural/political verity, or to rid an area of that people altogether (Meharg, 2001, 2006, 2011).

Identicide can include the calculated targeting of the places and objects that hold identity for a contested group, but also the intentional targeting of places and objects in cyberspace—namely, elements of digital materiality that generate meaning for people online. Identicide is more easily observed in the destruction of physical buildings and symbolic objects, limiting the ability of an identity group to carry out well-established and important rites and practices, and arresting and harming individuals who are responsible for maintaining and passing down crucial societal information, oral histories, and customs. It is less easily detected, while no less harmful to people, in the destruction of intangible digital-material aspects of modern life that generate life-worlds and contribute to ontological security. The destruction, suspension, and manipulation of online content, digital assassinations, bullying and vilification of ideological views and sacred values, disappearance of truth and the generation of deepfakes produces levels of anxiety in people, and the results of such destruction can trigger ontological insecurity in individuals, groups, and entire nations and states. Identicide is a precursor stage of genocide but does not necessarily result in genocide. As a conflict strategy it deliberately targets and destroys the cultural elements of a people through a variety of means in order to contribute to the eventual acculturation, removal, and/or total destruction of a particular identity group, including its contested signs, symbols, behaviours, values, heritages, places, and performances. Identicide is the intentional killing of the relatedness between people and place that eliminates the bond underpinning individuals, communities, and national identities. Identicide takes many forms but serves a single function: to negatively affect the relationships between people and their places (Meharg, 2011), whether these places exist in the physical world, the imagined world, or the digital world. The resulting condition of anomie destabilizes one's sense of the future, and this leads to inconsistencies in actions, attitudes, and social behaviours. When important places and symbols, as well as their digital-material counterparts online, have deep cultural meaning and are intentionally targeted and destroyed during periods of contestation as a strategy to rid an area of a marginalized people and to reduce their cohesion, ontological security becomes a useful framework for understanding strategies that secure identity and offer a certain future for affected peoples and their tribes.

Yet the implications of human behaviour and identity on stability and the wider security dimension have frequently been disregarded by those seeking to assess a situation and to potentially intervene. By making alternative perspectives, identities, histories, and narratives invisible, identicide effectively negates the presence and value of others, and allows for their reconstruction in a manner that is untethered from existing structural and socio-cultural realities. Negation is a necessary precondition for reconstructing identities in specific ways. It is through routines and relationships and narratives that identities are constructed (Mitzen, 2006; Subotić, 2016). Identity has two instrumental aspects—in other words, it has a form expressing agency. This agency can then turn into action when there is a threat or a perceived notion of a threat. Therefore, it is critical that the discussion-to-action transition is deterred.

Deterrence and Digital Tribes

Attempting to provide oven-ready policy prescriptions that represent effective deterrence in the context of all "digital tribes" is far from a fruitful approach. The complexity of these tribes and the threats that they may pose is such that one cannot hope to cover the necessary degree of tailoring strategies in a single chapter. Nevertheless, this section will use some of the core principles of deterrence theory to explore the broad contours of key considerations in shaping a deterrence posture in direct reference to digital tribes.

The definition of deterrence has been given in too much detail elsewhere to reiterate here, but it is worth noting that the "fourth wave" of deterrence research has led to "new constructivist and interpretive scholarship that explores the practices of deterrence" and that acknowledges the social construction of deterrent strategies (Lupovici, 2010). This acknowledgement of identity and ideology as a point of serious consideration in relation to deterrence is of particular importance in this case. It is also crucial to note that deterrence is inherently relational. That is, deterrence posture is connected to place, actors, and action. What deters in one relationship between adversaries cannot be assumed to deter in another, and an action that one actor perceives to be necessary to deter may not be mirrored by another actor. It is also unavoidably connected to the concept of costs and cost imposition. Even if a necessarily broad understanding of "costs" is used, deterrence is predicated on one actor deciding that the costs associated with accomplishing a certain action are either greater than the anticipated benefit, or that the response to that action, even if the action were to be accomplished, would impose such costs as to render the initial action unwise (Gray, 2000). The nature of these costs may be diverse, and what is considered "costly" can differ spectacularly, but it is here that the confluence of perceptions of belonging, digital tribalism, and the mitigation of threat occurs.

It is evident that digital tribalism and its psychological effects on identity building can be highly influential in pre-emptively dissuading an aggressor from taking action. Interference with a group's sense of self can pacify aggression, interrupt communication, or (de)construct identities. Such consequences reflect deterrence attributes such as fear (fear that digital tribes will be disrupted and coordination made impossible), denial measures (creating a stronger digital tribe that is a repository of information and seems futile to attack), and cost-benefit analysis (having a digital tribe disrupted in retaliation for an attack) (McKenzie, 2017).

There are, therefore, three key questions associated with deterrence and digital tribalism. While they may seem straightforward, their articulation is central to understanding an appropriate deterrent posture: (1) Who is to be deterred? (2) What actions are we intending to deter? And (3) what costs can be leveraged on a digital tribe?

The action to be deterred is not simply stand-alone behaviour, but part of a continuum (Mazarr et al., 2018). The behaviours leading to this point may not be desirable or considered reasonable, but they are nevertheless (at worst) tolerated, and it is a particular action that is the focus of deterrence. This provides an opportunity to make a warning signal to turn a digital tribe from continuing their route toward physical violence prior to the threats central to the deterrence posture being carried out, but also necessitates a conversation about the extent of action or conversation that is allowed to occur. Thus, one could posit a posture that attempts to deter the formation of any or all digital tribes. This would be challenging, but in theory it is an arguably robust approach to preventing existing social orders from being broken down. Perhaps more reasonably, one could seek to deter digital tribes from considering or discussing the use of violence in the physical realm. While it would undoubtedly be to the benefit if no one within a digital tribe realistically conceived to use violence to advance their aims, in practical (and clichéd) terms, talk is cheap. The real harm of the discussion of violence in itself is, in short, limited. Setting aside the potential requirement that violent action requires discussion prior to its use, where the discussion of violence becomes actually problematic for digital tribes, and therefore the key focus of deterrence, is the potential crossover from the discussion of violence to its manifestation in a material environment. As such, we must conceive of the costs that a digital tribe can impose as an amalgam of drawing individuals into the tribe to the extent that they consider themselves in opposition to the identity narrative of the state, and radicalizing such individuals to the extent that they take physical and violent action against the state. The recruitment and development of the digital tribe may be problematic in eroding what unity exists within a state, but it is the violent action that is the absolute focus of the deterrence.

Similarly, we must think of the threatened imposition of costs that comprise deterrence as actions that would disrupt a member of the digital tribe, or the tribe as a whole. The costs to be imposed on a digital tribe can therefore fall into three categories: (1) those that affect an individual member; (2) those that affect intra-tribe bonds; and (3) those that affect the material ability of the tribe to effect its desired goals. The influence of all three of these in certain scenarios is discussed in more detail below.

Deterrence and deterrence theory encompasses a multitude of facets and approaches, but it is two core (and interlinked) pairs of precepts that must remain the focus of consideration here. The first pair relates to the form of deterrence that is to be leveraged—deterrence by punishment, or deterrence by denial (Mazarr, 2018). In practice, of course, it is rare for one to occur without the other, but in dictating a deterrent posture one may lean more heavily on the communication of an ability to defend oneself, or the ability to counter-attack. Parsing these two approaches in isolation is helpful in illuminating the nature of the threat posed by digital tribes and the most efficient deterrent posture in this context. The second pair underpins the way in which deterrence is successful. Returning to the decisional basis of the theory, the deterree (in this case, the digital tribe) must decide that their adversary has the capability and resolve to carry through the threats signalled by their deterrent posture (Jarvis, 1976). Obviously, if these threats are actually carried out, then deterrence has failed, but successful deterrence requires a belief that the deterred action would be carried out, and impose significant costs if done so. Thus, whatever strategy or posture is adopted to deter digital tribes, it must be feasible and realistic.

Deterring Digital Tribes by Denial

Deterring by denial, that is, demonstrating that the costs incurred in conducting a particular action would outweigh the benefit (either because the target is resilient and the action would not produce the intended psychological or strategic outcome, or because the targeted actor would not allow the action to occur at all), inherently provides the more normatively acceptable policy approach—since, in principle, wielding a shield against which an adversary's attacks will founder has fewer negative connotations than the use of the sword to impose direct costs on an adversary, even if this is in response to their attack (Snyder, 1960; Wilner & Wagner, 2021). Similarly, it is preferable to deter through the ability to prevent an attack, rather than rely on the retaliatory imposition of costs—in the case of deterrence failure (that is, the adversary takes the action that one has attempted to deter), denying the adversary the ability to accomplish their goals would, in all likelihood, mean that one has not had to weather significant costs.

However, deterrence by denial brings with it some particular challenges. First, there is a universal inability to accurately ascertain whether the defences that one has in place are, in fact, sufficient to deter, let alone defeat, an adversary's attack. Second, violence does not generally occur with absolute suddenness, but is a product of a longer arc of behaviour that culminates in such action. This raises questions about identifying the moment at which deterrence has failed and pre-emptive action is required. In this case, the challenge is about knowing when violent online discourse will be turned into violent action, or how long the deterrent posture will hold such action at bay.

That said, deterrence by denial in the context of digital tribalism may be worthwhile. The resiliency approach may not, however, be efficacious. The act of physical violence in itself can have a meaning beyond the damage that it causes, delineating even more clearly the "other." Thus, even if a digital tribe conducted an action that caused significant destruction, merely demonstrating that the destruction made no meaningful difference to the routines of the attacked party may not deter similar future actions, regardless of the response.

In deterring by denial, we must therefore look to the threat of pre-emptive action. In this case, such a posture relies on the ability to monitor the communications of digital tribes and successfully identify the key moment at which the threat is bound to become realized. As noted, this is a difficult task. Nevertheless, by threatening the disruption of groups through the removal of key individuals (permanently or temporarily) from engagement with others within the tribe, or removing equipment if there is an expectation of imminent violence, it is possible to ensure that potentially dangerous digital tribes steer clear of violent action in the material world. The individualized effects of violence in the digital world is thus far not fully understood by sociologists, cultural geographers, and ethnographers, to name but a few, and therefore will have to await future diagnosis with regard to deterrence. For now, we can rely on understandings of violent action in the material world. In an example, the challenge of disrupting groups in the United States through the removal of guns is, of course, rendered more difficult due to Second Amendment rights, but the belief of the deterree that the deterrer has an ability to impose costs through actively pre-empting an attack can be a powerful disincentive to commence preparation.

Considering the possible success of such actions requires turning to the potential ability to signal capability and resolve to effectively pre-empt the transition to physical violence. Such capability must be demonstrated across three levels. The first is in the ability to monitor the communications of the digital tribe in order to ascertain the shift in likelihood of physical violence. The second is the ability to take action against individuals within the tribe. The third, more broadly, is the ability to effectively coordinate knowledge and action across what have traditionally been understood to be intelligence boundaries. Part of the distinction of digital tribes is their potentially cross-national structure. This is not totally unique—the emergence of terrorist groups and other non-state military actors has followed a similar trajectory in recent years—but digital tribes represent a slightly new challenge. While, at least in the West, terrorist organizations have been universally condemned, or at minimum understood to be dangerous actors, understandings of the actual goals of, and threats posed by, a digital tribe may differ between the various state actors that play a role in deterring their transition to violence. As such, coordination is likely to be not only a matter of security and logistics, but also of delicate negotiation that must take into account distinctions in political, economic, religious, and social cultures.

It is also worth considering the normative and practical challenge of monitoring the communications of a digital tribe. The well-acknowledged labyrinth of secure digital communications and complexity of symbolism can make the identification of centres and trajectory of discourse difficult (Parker et al., 2019), exacerbated by the disruption of platforms that forces groups into different online locations.

Capability is demonstrated by indicating an ability to intercept communications before they reach a critical or dangerous stage. This raises a further challenge in "tipping one's hand" to potentially dangerous actors. By indicating that a particular channel of communication is monitored, rather than convincing them of the futility of planning an attack, it may simply cause a shift to another, unknown, channel of communication. Similarly, overt monitoring of communications could further strengthen the bonds between digital tribe members, even if no further action is taken, creating a more dominant framing of the tribe as outsiders who are viewed with suspicion, if not hostility.

Signalling the capability to take action against individuals within the digital tribe and/or digital objects owned by the tribe can only occur through demonstrated action. This is a challenge for deterrence, which is fundamentally about not performing the threatened action. Nevertheless, if the potentially dangerous digital tribes are viewed as discrete units, then the successful interdiction of one tribe (and thus the failure of deterrence in that case) could potentially deter others from taking similar steps. Such action would also be a key demonstration of resolve, signalling that a state is willing to take pre-emptive action despite the legal and normative justifications that such action would require in the post-event environment.

Deterring Digital Tribes by Punishment

Perhaps the more traditional understanding of deterrence, particularly with regard to strategic nuclear weapons, rests on the concept of punishing an actor for taking the action that was the focus of deterrence, such that the costs imposed vastly outweigh the benefits of the action. Punishment in the context of digital tribes could focus on individuals, but unlike the "denial" approach, it may also target the digital tribe more broadly. That is, the punishment for translating violent discourse into violent action would be the obliteration of that tribe or the erosion of its identity such that it no longer exists as a meaningful actor.

This is, however, a simplistic response, paralleling the attempted deterrence of terrorist groups (or other non-state violent actors) whose existence has been characterized by physical violence through selectively punishment of particular individuals and/or the group as a whole. The literature on leadership decapitation indicates that this is not universally helpful (Jordan, 2009). Although the threatened punishment of leaders for violent actions should not be discounted as a potential deterrent, this does not appear to be a particularly straightforward or effective mode of punishment. Particularly on the understanding that a digital tribe has developed organically, punishing leadership is rendered more challenging by a potential lack of an identifiable hierarchy or leadership. While ideas and symbols may be communicated, this does not necessarily occur within the forms of structures that have emerged in governments or among non-state actors. One current example of this is the incel movement, a roughly aligned digital tribe whose members have conducted a number of violent actions, but for whom there does appear to be a central hub of coordination (Brzuszkiewicz, 2020). Punishment is therefore meted out only to those who conduct violent actions. However, in the context of digital tribes who share a common understanding that their cause transcends individuals, or in the context of a digital tribe who believes that the costs they impose on another group, regardless of a member's own destruction, may create a martyr, rather than a deterrent.

As such, the solution would appear to be the punishment of the digital tribe as a whole, the forcible dissolution of bonds that link members of the tribe, thereby preventing their reconnection so as to undermine the reinforcement of beliefs. Such an act would be, to all intents and purposes, a form of identicide. In some cases, such action may not appear to represent a particular problem, but these seemingly clear cases veil the true normative challenge: At what point does the violent actions of one individual within a digital tribe necessitate the entire tribe's complete destruction? The forcible removal or alteration of identity is an action that should not be entered into lightly. The destruction of a digital tribe is also given a further level of complexity due to the speed with which everyday or common symbols can be co-opted and internalized as part of a particular identity, without necessarily requiring conversion into physical objects. Preventing connection between members is therefore a significant challenge, and when achieved, may induce higher levels of anxiety in members, contributing to insecurity writ large.

In addition, once again the threat of punishment, if not communicated effectively, may be counterproductive. The uniqueness of the digital tribes in relation to the way in which they create or develop a sense of belonging that transcends physical space allows for the carving out of a distinct sphere of influence and tight bonds of belonging between members. Once created, this bond's potential destruction is an act of considerable violence, and may further inculcate a perception of shared otherness. In combination with the perception that the tribe to which they belong holds a unique position of normative or social rightness, its threatened destruction can provide further confirmation of members' position within existing social frameworks, and the threat may further strengthen bonds or result in pre-emptive attack.

Consequently, demonstrating capability and resolve to destroy such tribes is a considerable challenge. Again, it may be helpful to view digital tribes in distinct silos, and to understand that the destruction of one may deter others, but measuring the likely effectiveness of this is extremely difficult. Despite these challenges, deterrence is critical, particularly given the disconnect between certain digital tribes and Western society, and the possibility of the spillover into physical violence in the material world.

However, the nature of tribalism and the acceptance in the West of the value of, and right to, alternative viewpoints also necessitates the consideration of parallel approaches. Deterrence must always be seen on the spectrum of (inter)action that spans persuasion and compellence. If we can accept an understanding of the basis of these tribes that stems from a perception of a lack of belonging, it is also possible to conceive of an approach that involves persuasion whereby the group is not perceived to be an *other* and an understanding their networks of belonging are at least tangentially connected to those of the state.

Of course, we cannot condone the existence of groups that advocate violence against us, nor should this involve even a tacit acceptance of the values of a digital tribe deemed fundamentally at odds with our own. Nevertheless, without going so far as to promote a fully global community (which indeed is a cause of some concern to certain digital tribes) it is only through creating a sense of unity in diversity that the possibility of violence can be reduced. The threatened imposition of costs alone can provide only limited comfort that the transition from violent discourse to violent action will not occur.

Conclusion

People experiencing globalization (especially in the West) as a negative experience are seeking connection and belonging because of unconscious anxieties caused by ontological insecurity. This is more than the ubiquitous call to "find your tribe!" Rather, it exists as the existential experience of belonging to a group that reinforces autobiographical narratives of identity. Evidence of this activity is seen with the rise of powerful leftist and rightist digital tribes like QAnon, European and American populist political groups, and COVID-19 pro-vaccination warriors, as well as social justice groups like Black Lives Matter, Stop AAPI Hate, and benign groups with hugely supportive fan bases such as YNABers (You Need a Budget, ynab.com). This type of belonging-seeking with groups of like-minded people ensures the reduction—even the elimination—of specific threats of globalism—namely, threats against the hierarchy of needs expressed by Maslow, most particularly individualized security, esteem, and belonging. A never *truly belonging* state of mind can become chronic. Belonging-seeking is a pathway to reinforcing a coherent sense of one's autonomy and ontological security. Uncertainty of one's future leads one to cling to the familiar and continue to recreate the familiar through material acts aimed at the *routinization of belonging*. In this time of social networking, popular social media sites are the place to find one's tribe and to satisfy the need to belong.

These connections are forged through social media networks in ways that mirror the forging of connections in places, and they contribute profoundly salient elements to one's identity narratives. Routinization of belonging to a digital tribe takes place online through specific, culturally contextualized action(s). This produces the effect of belonging. While contrived and weaponized digital tribalism can advance counter-democratic processes, organic digital tribalism is an activity enjoyed by people who are mostly doing nothing more than assuaging their deep psychological-biological need to belong.

The connection between OST and deterrence is belonging. To reduce existential anxieties in fringe or marginalized groups, we must focus on reducing anxieties (encouraging belonging) rather than building on fear (removal of Facebook pages, cancel culture, pulling down web content). These are essentially undemocratic activities that lean toward identicide, and as such democratic stakeholders should abstain from these actions if their purpose is the deterrence of non-aligned ideologues. If marginalized, or even nefarious, engineered digital tribes are targeted and contested, their organizers may reorganize, disappear, appear. This itself is a cause of uncertainty in tribe members and can be at the root of belonging-seeking, and such uncertainty can artificially suspend—perhaps indefinitely—the satisfaction of the most basic of human needs. Online tribalism reduces the traditional conflict/war effects within the geoscape, therefore, with regard to deterrence, encouraging digital *tribing* may reduce the movement between digital and material worlds. While our security apparatuses are set up for conflicts in the physical world, much work must still be done to recalibrate these apparatuses to confront conflicts in the digital world, and to contain them where they derive from.

There is no singular narrative or super group, as Chua (2018) claims, but rather multiple complementary, conflicting struggles over identity coexisting in the media terrain of the geoscape. Reducing existential anxiety through belonging—particularly in the form of routines—is a pathway to deterring behaviours that, if actioned, could confine violence to discourse rather than action inside democratic states. Coupling material and digital environments creates a more permanent certainty for people. Kinnvall and Mitzen (2018) offer a prescription for such anxiety: "To hold existential anxiety at bay, focus on practices of the 'everyday,' such as routines and maintaining a coherent autobiographical narrative" (p. 245). Minimizing belonging to engineered tribes by exposing the nefarious intentions of orchestrators may reduce anxieties related to political, economic, and cultural identity in participating publics, who in a manipulation process of information operations advance anti-democratic and anti-humanitarian agendas.

Therefore, deterrence strategists do not need to allocate resources and assets to understand broadly defined identities and autobiographical narratives of a state, an adversary, or a digital tribe to gain an advantage. Rather, strategists could allocate resources to analyze the routines of tribes representing identities. In situations in which identity routines have been disrupted, OST offers a lens through which to understand modalities of identity, narratives, and digital materiality. New renderings of tribalism as anxiety-reducing mechanisms produce a psychological sense of certainty in an otherwise uncertain state of anxiety.

Acknowledgements

This chapter benefited, directly and indirectly, from the many enlightening conversations and collaborations that I have had over the years with my esteemed colleague Brian Osborne, who knows a lot more than I do about people, identity, and belonging. I would also like to thank the editors for their helpful and insightful comments. Any mistakes and omissions are entirely my own. For research guidance on deterrence, many thanks to A. Thomas Hughes. For research assistance on this chapter, thank you to Mona Ghali, Hailey Ng, and Nick Ramsay.

REFERENCES

Abbas, T. (2017). Understanding the nature of online extremist narratives. In *The Challenge of Jihadist Radicalisation in Europe and Beyond* (pp. 90–9). European Policy Centre. https://www.epc.eu/content/PDF/2017/The_Challenge_of_Jihadist_Radicalisation.pdf

Alvares, C., & Dahlgren, P. (2016). Populism, extremism, and media: Mapping an uncertain terrain. *European Journal of Communication, 31*(1), 46–57. https://doi.org/10.1177%2F0267323115614485

Atlantic Council Digital Forensic Research Lab. (2021, 10 February). "#Stopthesteal: Timeline of social media and extremist activities leading to 1/6 insurrection. *Jest Security*. https://www.justsecurity.org/74622/stopthesteal-timeline-of-social-media-and-extremist-activities-leading-to-1-6-insurrection/

Baumann, G. (1996). *Contesting culture: Discourses of identity in multi-ethnic London*. Cambridge University Press.

Beck, U. (1992). *Risk society: Towards a new modernity*. University of Munich Press.

Browning, C. S. (2019). Brexit populism and fantasies of fulfilment. *Cambridge Review of International Affairs, 32*(3), 222–44. https://doi.org/10.1080/09557571.2019.1567461

Browning, C. S., & Joenniemi, P. (2016). Ontological security, self-articulation and the securitization of identity. *Cooperation and Conflict, 52*(1), 31–47. https://doi.org/10.1177%2F0010836716653161

Brzuszkiewicz, S. (2020). *Incel radical milieu and external locus of control*. International Centre for Counter-Terrorism. https://www.icct.nl/sites/default/files/import/publication/Special-Edition-2-1.pdf

Clark, C., & Winegard, B. M. (2020). Tribalism in war and peace: The nature and evolution of ideological epistemology and its significance for modern social science. *Psychological Inquiry, 31*(1), 1–22. DOI: 10.1080/1047840X.2020.1721233

Cash, J. (2020). Psychoanalysis, cultures of anarchy, and ontological insecurity. *International Theory, 12*(2), 306–21. https://doi.org/10.1017/S1752971920000147

Chua, A. (2019). *Political tribes: Group instinct and the fate of nations*. Penguin Books.

Cronkhite, A. B., Zhang, W., & Caughell, L. (2020). Special commentary: #Fakenews in #natsec. *US Army War College Quarterly, 50*(1), 5–22.

Dahlgren, P. (2006). Doing citizenship: The cultural origins of civic agency in the public sphere. *European Journal of Cultural Studies, 9*(3), 267–86. https://doi.org/10.1177%2F1367549406066073.

Dahlgren, P. (2013). Force-fields of the web environment. *The political web: Media, participation and alternative democracy* (pp. 36–64). Palgrave Macmillan.

Delanty, G. (2011). Cultural diversity, democracy and the prospects of cosmopolitanism: A theory of cultural encounters. *British Journal of Sociology, 62*(4), 633–56. https://doi.org/10.1111/j.1468-4446.2011.01384.x

Duile, T. (2017). Islam, politics, and cyber tribalism in Indonesia: A case study on the Front Pembela Islam. *International Quarterly for Asian Studies, 48*(3/4), 249–72. https://doi.org/10.11588/iqas.2017.3-4.7443

Freedman, L. (2020). *The revolution in strategic affairs*. Routledge.

Freedman, L. (2021). Introduction: The evolution of deterrence strategy and research. In F. Osinga, & T. Sweijs (Eds.), *NL ARMS Netherlands annual review of military studies* (pp. 1–10). Asser Press. https://doi.org/10.1007/978-94-6265-419-8

Gerodimos, R. (2012). Online youth attitudes and the limits of civic consumerism: The emerging challenge to the Internet's democratic potential. *Information, Communication & Society, 15*(2), 217–45. https://psycnet.apa.org/doi/10.1080/1369118X.2011.572983

Giddens, A. (1984). *The constitution of society*. University of California Press.

Gray, C. S. (2000). Deterrence in the 21st century. *Comparative Strategy, 19*(3), 255–61. https://doi.org/10.1080/01495930008403211

Grimson, A. (2010). Culture and identity: Two different notions. *Journal for the Study of Race, Nation and Culture, 16*(1), 61–77. https://doi.org/10.1080/13504630903465894

Grosfoguel, R. (2013). The structure of knowledge in westernized universities: Epistemic racism/sexism and the four genocides/epistemicides of the long 16th century. *Human Architecture: Journal of the Sociology of Self-Knowledge, 11*(1), 73–90.

Hayday, E. J., Collison, H., & Kohe, G. Z. (2021). Landscapes of tension, tribalism, and toxicity: Configuring a spatial politics of esport communities. *Leisure Studies, 40*(2), 139–53. https://doi.org/10.1080/02614367.2020.1808049

Heaney, M. T. (2020). Protest at the center of American politics. *Journal of International Affairs, 73*(2), 195–208. https://jia.sipa.columbia.edu/protest-center-american-politics

Hobfoll, S. E. (2018). *Tribalism: The evolutionary origins of fear politics*. Palgrave Macmillan.

Hogg, M. A. (2001). A social identity theory of leadership. *Personality and Social Psychology Review, 5*(3), 184–200. https://doi.org/10.1207%2FS15327957PSPR0503_1

Hom, A. R., & Steele, B. J. (2020). Anxiety, time, and ontological security's third-image potential. *International Theory, 12*(2), 322–36.

James, P. (2006). *Globalism, nationalism, tribalism: Bringing theory back in.* SAGE.

Janowitz, K. M. (2009). Netnographie—Ethnographische Methoden im Internet und posttraditionelle Vergemeinschaftungen. In P. Ohly (Ed.), *Tagungsband zur Wissensorganisation '09 "Wissen—Wissenschaft—Organisation," 12. Tagung der Deutschen* (pp. 1–9). https://nbn-resolving.org/urn:nbn:de:0168-ssoar-65241

Jarvis, R. (1976). *Perception and misperception.* Princeton University Press.

Jordan, J. (2009). When heads roll. *Security Studies, 18*(4). https://doi.org/10.1080/09636410903369068

Kinnvall, C. (2004). Globalization and religious nationalism: Self, identity, and the search for ontological security. *Political Psychology, 25*(5), 741–67. https://www.jstor.org/stable/3792342

Kinnvall, C. (2018). Ontological insecurities and postcolonial imaginaries: The emotional appeal of populism. *Humanity & Society, 42*(4), 523–43. https://doi.org/10.1177%2F0160597618802646

Kinnvall, C., Manners, I., & Mitzen, J. (2018). Introduction to 2018 special issue of *European Security*: "Ontological (in)security in the European Union." *European Security, 27*(3), 249–65. https://doi.org/10.1080/09662839.2018.1497977

Lewandowsky, S., & Smillie, L. (Eds.). (2020). *Technology and democracy: Understanding the influence of online technologies on political behaviour and decision-making.* Publications Office of the European Union. https://data.europa.eu/doi/10.2760/709177

Lieber, R. J., & Weisberg, R. E. (2002). Globalization, culture, and identities in crisis. *International Journal of Politics, Culture, and Society, 16*(2), 273–96. https://www.jstor.org/stable/20020163

Lupovici, A. (2010). The emerging fourth wave of deterrence theory. *International Studies Quarterly, 54*(3), 705–32. https://www.jstor.org/stable/40931133

Mason, L. (2018). *Uncivil agreement: How politics became our identity.* University of Chicago Press.

Mazarr, M.J. (2018). *Understanding deterrence.* RAND Corporation. https://www.rand.org/content/dam/rand/pubs/perspectives/PE200/PE295/RAND_PE295.pdf.

Mazarr, M. J., Chan, A., Dmus, A., Frederick, B., Nader, A., Pezard, S., Thompson, J. A., & Treyger, E. (2018). *What deters and why.* RAND Corporation.

MccGwire, M. (1986). Deterrence: The problem—not the solution. *International Affairs, 62*(1), 55–70. https://doi.org/10.2307/2618067

McKenzie, T. M. (2017). *Is cyber deterrence possible?* Air University Press.

Meharg, S. J. (2001). Identicide and cultural cannibalism: Warfare's appetite for symbolic place. *Peace Research, 33*(2), 89–98. https://www.jstor.org/stable/23608075

Meharg, S. J. (2004). *Identicide in Bosnia and Croatia: The destruction, reconstruction, and construction of landscapes of identity* [Unpublished PhD dissertation, Queen's University]. Library and Archives Canada.

Meharg, S. J. (2006). Identicide: Precursor to genocide. Working Paper 5. *Centre for Security and Defense Studies.*

Meharg, S. J. (2011). Restoration and reconstruction for environmental security. In G. E. Machlis, T. Hanson, Z. Spiric, & J. E. McKendry (Eds.), *Warfare ecology: A new synthesis for peace and security* (pp. 117–88). Springer.

Mitzen, J. (2006). Ontological security in world politics: State identity and the security dilemma. *European Journal of International Relations, 12*(3), 341–70. https://doi.org/10.1177%2F1354066106067346

Niedbala, E.M., & Hohman, Z. P. (2019). Retaliation against the outgroup: The role of self-uncertainty. *Group Processes & Intergroup Relations, 22*(5), 708–23. https://doi.org/10.1177%2F1368430218767027

Osborne, B. S. (2001). Landscapes, memory, monuments, and commemoration: Putting identity in its place. *Canadian Ethnic Studies, 33*(3), 39–77.

Papacharissi, Z. (2015). We have always been social. *Social Media + Society, 1*(1). https://doi.org/10.1177%2F2056305115581185

Parker, D., Pearce, J. M., Lindekilde, L., & Rogers, M. B. (2019). Challenges for effective counterterrorism communication. *Studies in Conflict and Terrorism, 42*(3), 264–91. https://doi.org/10.1080/1057610X.2017.1373427

Perry, G. (2018). *The lost boys: Inside Muzafer Sherif's Robbers Cave experiment.* Scribe.

Petersen, M. B. (2020). The evolutionary psychology of mass mobilization: How disinformation and demagogues coordinate rather than manipulate. *Current Opinion in Psychology, 35*, 71–5. https://doi.org/10.1016/j.copsyc.2020.02.003

Pew Research Center. (2021a, 7 April). Internet/broadband fact sheet. *Pew Research Center.* https://www.pewresearch.org/internet/fact-sheet/internet-broadband/

Pew Research Center. (2021b, 7 April). Social media fact sheet. *Pew Research Center.* https://www.pewresearch.org/internet/fact-sheet/social-media/

Plater, Z. J. B. (1990). Keynote essay: A modern political tribalism in natural resources management. *Public Land Law Review*, 11, 1–17.

Richerson, P. J., & Boyd, R. (2001). The evolution of subjective commitment to groups: A tribal instincts hypothesis. In R. M. Nesse (Ed.), *Evolution and the capacity for commitment* (pp. 184–220). Russell Sage Foundation.

Rumelili, B. (2020). Integrating anxiety into international relations theory: Hobbes, existentialism, and ontological security. *International Theory, 12*(2), 257–72. https://doi.org/10.1017/S1752971920000093

Schulze, M. (2019, 21 August). Cyber deterrence is overrated. *Stiftung Wissenschaft und Politik*. https://www.swp-berlin.org/10.18449/2019C34/

Snyder, G. H. (1960). Deterrence and power. *Journal of Conflict Resolution, 4*(2), 163–78. https://doi.org/10.1177%2F002200276000400201

Steele, B. J. (2008). *Ontological security in international relations: Self-Identity and the IR state*. Taylor and Francis.

Steele, B. J., & Homolar, A. (2019). Ontological insecurities and the politics of contemporary populism. *Cambridge Review of International Affairs, 32*(3), 214–21. https://doi.org/10.1080/09557571.2019.1596612

St. John, G. (2017). Civilised tribalism: Burning Man, event-tribes and maker culture. *Cultural Sociology, 12*(1), 1–19. https://doi.org/10.1177%2F1749975517733162

Stork, C., Calandro, E., & Gillwald, A. (2013). Internet going mobile: Internet access and use in 11 African countries. *Info, 15*(5), 34–51. https://doi.org/10.1108/info-05-2013-0026

Subotić, J. (2016). Narrative, ontological security, and foreign policy change. *Foreign Policy Analysis, 12*(4), 610–27. https://doi.org/10.1111/fpa.12089

Trager, R. F., & Zagorcheva, D. P. (2006). Deterring terrorism: It can be done. *International Security, 30*(3). 87–123. https://www.jstor.org/stable/4137488

Van Dijcke, D., & Wright, A. L. (2021). *Profiling insurrection: Characterizing collective action using mobile device data*. Becker Friedman Institute.

Waisbord, S. (2018). The elective affinity between post-truth communication and populist politics. *Communication Research and Practice, 4*(1), 17–34. https://doi.org/10.1080/22041451.2018.1428928

Wassermann, H. 2020. Fake news from Africa: Panics, politics, and paradigms. *Journalism*, 21(1), 3–16. https://doi.org/10.1177%2F1464884917746861.

Wilner, A., & Wagner, A. (Eds.). (2021). *Deterrence by denial: Theory and practice*. Cambria.

Wohl, M. J. A., Branscombe, N. R., & Reysen, S. (2010). Perceiving your group's future to be in jeopardy: Extinction threat induces collective angst and the desire to strengthen the ingroup. *Personality and Social Psychology Bulletin, 36*(7), 898–910. https://doi.org/10.1177%2F0146167210372505

Wolfe, P. (2006). Settler colonialism and the elimination of the native. *Journal of Genocide Research, 8*(4), 387–409. https://doi.org/10.1080/14623520601056240

11

Deterrence for Online Radicalization and Recruitment in the Twenty-First Century

Anne Speckhard and Molly Ellenberg

In comparison with other Western countries, Canada may be considered relatively lucky in terms of its history of violent extremism. The Canadian Incidents Database identified 1,405 terrorist or extremist incidents occurring in Canada between 1960 and 2014, in addition to 410 Canadian-affiliated (perpetrator or target) terrorist or extremist incidents occurring outside of Canada during the same period. These incidents include bombings (46 per cent), facility or infrastructure attacks (24 per cent), threats (18 per cent), thefts (3 per cent), armed assaults (2 per cent), unarmed assaults (2 per cent), and others (5 per cent), and were linked to groups representing or claiming to represent a myriad of ideologies (Canadian Network for Research on Terrorism, Security and Society, n.d.).

Canadian Militant Jihadists

Canadian militant jihadists became a focus in the twenty-first century, especially after the events of 11 September 2001. Indeed, Canada had its own landmark terrorist event inspired by al Qaeda that thankfully was thwarted before being carried out by the so-called Toronto 18. The global "war on terror" consumed counterterrorism experts in the West, including in Canada, though, aside from the thwarted Toronto attacks, which would have been of the same magnitude of those of 9/11, there have been only 6 militant jihadist-inspired attacks perpetrated in Canada over the past two decades, with all of them inspired by ISIS and committed during ISIS's heyday between 2014 and 2018. All were committed by so-called lone actors as well; these individuals did not have direct contact with ISIS members but were inspired to commit violence after engaging with the group's content online. Prior to September 2014, there were no successful jihadist-inspired attacks on Canadian soil, though 5 plots were foiled, and 25 people were arrested in connection to those plots, including the Toronto 18. Another 3 jihadist-inspired plots were thwarted between 2014 and 2020, with 4 people arrested. Harris-Hogan, Dawson, and Amarasingam (2020), whose research on violent extremism in Canada is paramount to any relevant literature review, note that only 3 of the 14 executed or planned jihadist attacks in Canada over the past twenty years targeted civilians, with the majority targeting police, the military, or the government. They also note that all of the attacks involving a single actor using an edged weapon or firearm were successfully executed; Canadian security services were able to thwart planned attacks using explosives, but not smaller-scale attacks that did not require as much preparation. These plots, successful and thwarted, involved 36 individuals who were arrested or killed in the course of the attacks. Another 14 Canadian domestic jihadists have been arrested since 2000 on other terrorism charges, including financing or assisting international attacks. In total, Harris-Hogan, Dawson, and Amarasingam identified 50 Canadian domestic jihadists active over the past twenty years (Harris-Hogan et al., 2020). This number pales in comparison to the approximately 185 Canadian citizens and residents who left Canada to join ISIS in Iraq and Syria as foreign terrorist fighters (FTF), including one who returned and infuriated Canadians by his claims made in the *New York Times' Caliphate* podcast series.

In many ways, Canadian FTFs are similar to those of other Western countries, though a far greater number left from western Europe than from North America and their reasons for travel differ in important ways. Western Europe has also faced attacks perpetrated by people who trained with ISIS in Syria before returning home, while Canada and the United States have not. This is despite the fact that somewhere between 10 and 60 Canadian FTFs have returned home since 2017 (Wickson, 2019). Both European and North American ISIS members were also recruited by the ISIS *emni* (intelligence) to train in Syria and then later return to carry out attacks at home. Interviews with Canadian FTFs, family members, friends, and other connected parties conducted by Dawson, Amarasingam, and Bain (2016) found that many Canadian FTFs were radicalizing and travelling to join ISIS in clusters of friends, primarily from larger cities. They also found that Canadian FTFs seemed to cite more "pull" than "push" factors in their decisions to travel to join ISIS. That is, they did not feel marginalized or discriminated against in Canada, as many Muslims do in the West, but rather joined because they believed that it was their religious duty to make *hijrah* and fight jihad (Dawson et al., 2016). Indeed, many left at a time when ISIS was advertising itself as a functioning state. ISIS cadres were sending around pictures of themselves hanging out in villas with pools and eating well, while claiming that Canadians holed up in snow needed to come help their Muslim brothers and sisters suffering under Assad's atrocities.

Canadian White Supremacists

Of course, militant jihadists are not the only terrorists who have posed a threat to Canada in the past, nor are they the only terrorists who will pose a threat to Canada in the coming decade. White supremacists and other far-right violent extremists are a growing threat in Canada, and indeed throughout the Western world. These groups have been active in Canada for decades but have long been underestimated. As a case in point, a study in the *Canadian Review of Sociology* (conducted in 1993 and published in 1997) concluded that "the political consciousness of skinheads is rooted in extreme violence and lacks coherence: this, combined with the structure of their groups and their histories of [personal] oppression, serves to inhibit long-term political activity" (Baron, 1997, p. 125). Even in 2015, another study concluded that the Extreme Right was a "negligible" force in Canada (Ambrose & Mudde, 2015).

More recent research, and the testimony presented in this chapter, demonstrate that these predictions were wrong. There is evidence that increased anti-immigrant and Islamophobic rhetoric in Canadian local and national politics may have contributed to a "climate of hate" that empowered some far-right extremists, and that police and security services in Canada, as in other Western countries, have underestimated the threat of far-right extremists in comparison to militant jihadists (Perry & Scrivens, 2018). Likewise, with their neighbour having a president seemingly encouraging white supremacists and groups like the Proud Boys, vulnerable Canadians were undoubtedly also influenced to have a less dim view of such groups. Indeed, one study attributes the rise of white supremacist violence and hate crimes in Canada, which paralleled trends in the United States, to the rhetoric and election of former president Donald Trump, with a flyer posted on the McGill University campus reading, "Tired of anti-white propaganda? It's time to MAKE CANADA GREAT AGAIN!" The article acknowledged, however, that Canada has an insidious far-right history, specifically the neo-Nazi skinhead movement that began to arise in the 1970s, influenced by the British white power music scene (Perry et al., 2018). Perry and Scrivens (2015) note that far-right violent extremists in Canada, who include more traditional white supremacist groups (including Canadian chapters and offshoots of American groups) as well as sovereign citizens and some single-issue groups, often engage in non-ideological criminality, such as drug dealing and fighting (Perry & Scrivens, 2015). This is a key difference between white supremacist violent extremists and militant jihadists who may have histories of non-ideological crime. Whereas the former continue their criminality, the latter often refrain from drug use and criminality that is not related to the militant jihadist cause. However, there are plenty of non-ideological criminals who have been recruited into militant jihad and whose recruiters encouraged them to continue their criminal activities against the *kuffar* (unbelievers), giving a share of the proceeds to the jihadist cause. It is also critical to note that not all white supremacy in Canada is imported. The Proud Boys, a far-right group that has recently gained a great deal of media attention, is typically identified as an American group, yet its founder, Gavin McInnes, is Canadian (Leichnitz, 2020). Finally, involuntary celibates, or incels, are often identified as part of the Far Right, given their misogynistic views and the overlap between participation on incel and white supremacist web forums. However, the incel ideology, the "blackpill," does not have any white supremacist connotations (Speckhard et al., 2021). Canada has experienced a few incel-related attacks, including Alek Minassian's 2018 Toronto van attack, which killed ten people, and the government deciding in 2020 to charge a minor with a terrorism offence after he fatally stabbed a woman (Hoffman et al., 2020).

Online Radicalization and Recruitment

ONLINE VIOLENT EXTREMIST ACTIVITY IN CANADA

Unsurprisingly, given the ubiquity of social media in people's daily lives and the increasing evidence of terrorists' adept use of social media for radicalization and recruitment, social media has played a role in Canadian radicalization and recruitment. A 2018 study of Canadians involved in militant jihadist terrorism since 2012 found that for at least twenty-one of the thirty-two individuals for whom information on radicalization was available, the Internet played a role in the radicalization process. The authors found that at least half of the subjects who were converts to Islam became radicalized online, and that at least twenty-six individuals in the sample used the Internet to post support for terrorism or to communicate with other violent extremists after they became radicalized. Combining these data, they concluded that "the Internet played a role either during or after the radicalization process of at least 76 percent ($n = 39$) of the sample" (Bastug et al., 2018, p. 631).

Scrivens and Amarasingam (2020) examined far-right extremism on Facebook, finding that those individuals whom they identified could be categorized as members of either anti-Islam or "white Canadian pride" groups. Both groups targeted Islam and shared Islamophobic posts, but the latter was more focused on condemning the Canadian government for its stance on immigration more generally, which were supposedly destroying traditional Canadian values. The study also found that these groups were not growing in popularity at any meaningful rate, but that they do not appear to be taken down by Facebook at the same rate as jihadist groups. The authors noted, however, that the more extreme far-right groups may not be using Facebook at all, and are instead promoting their ideology on platforms such as Reddit, 4chan, 8chan, and Gab (Scrivens & Amarasingam, 2020). Likewise, it is notable that immediately following the 6 January Capitol Hill riots, Facebook and other mainstream social media platforms took a more aggressive stance against such accounts.

THE IMPACT OF COVID-19

There is extensive evidence that the COVID-19 pandemic has been linked to increased violent extremist radicalization and recruitment online. Not only are people simply spending more time online during lockdowns, especially young people who might otherwise be in school, but the anxiety regarding public health and the economy has led many to search for some sense of certainty online. Indeed, there is evidence that feelings of personal uncertainty, related to one's health or financial security, for instance, can increase people's tendency to identify with a group that provides them with a sense of certainty (Hogg & Blaylock, 2011). This certainty may be provided by conspiracy theories such as those spread by militant jihadist and white supremacist groups alike. Such conspiracy theories and disinformation were accompanied by a slew of hate crimes, especially against Asian Americans during the early months of the pandemic (Kruglanski et al., 2020). The danger of conspiracy theories morphing from online communities to groups of violent actors was put on full display on 6 January 2021 on Capitol Hill in Washington, DC, where adherents of the QAnon conspiracy were among the rioters attempting to stop the peaceful transfer of power in the United States (Paresky et al., 2021).

In Canada specifically, a large study (n = 644) found that COVID-19 risk perception was similar to that in the United States in that it was highly politically polarized. Despite the fact that no members of the Canadian Parliament were found to be downplaying the seriousness of the virus, as many American legislators did, Canadian conservatives nevertheless viewed the virus as less severe than liberals did. Misperceptions related to a reduced risk perception included conspiracy theories believed by small minorities of Canadians. These included claims that the coronavirus was created in a lab (6.99 per cent), that the coronavirus was created as a bio-weapon (5.66 per cent), that a cure for the coronavirus had already been discovered at the time of the study but was being suppressed by people who wanted the pandemic to continue (3.57 per cent), and that the coronavirus was probably a hoax (0.62 per cent) (Pennycook et al., 2020). Interestingly, while the QAnon conspiracy is largely centred around the United States government, it also has followers in other countries, including Canada. One such adherent was arrested in July 2020 for attempting to assassinate Prime Minister Justin Trudeau, whom the perpetrator believed was trying to "turn Canada into a communist dictatorship." One Canadian QAnon social media channel alleged that Hillary Clinton and former Canadian prime minister Paul Martin were working together to sell children, and that Trudeau was aware of their criminal behaviour (Ling, 2020).

Beyond QAnon, the researchers at Moonshot CVE (2020) found that there was a marked increase in engagement with online extremist content in Canada's largest cities since the onset of COVID-19 restrictions. Specifically, weekly searches for violent far-right content increased by an average of 18.5 per cent. Such content included podcasts by purveyors of misinformation and conspiracies such as Alex Jones, a Nazi-glorifying documentary entitled *The Greatest Story Never Told*, forums and social networks favoured by white supremacists, and high-risk searches such as "how to make a Molotov cocktail" and "how to join Ku Klux Klan" (Moonshot CVE, 2020).

The Present Study

It is clear from recent research that both Canadian militant jihadists and white supremacist violent extremists pose a risk that has yet to be fully understood. Over the next decade, online recruitment and radicalization are likely to become even more of a threat than they have been previously, and such online behaviour could translate into violent, in-person crime. Moreover, while the primary militant jihadist threat in Canada, Canadians joining ISIS abroad, appears to have abated with the territorial defeat of the Caliphate, the risk of an ISIS resurgence remains and is in fact growing. Thus, preventing future waves of Canadian domestic attacks as well as FTFs is paramount. The present study examines all of these risks. First, we examine the prevalence of online radicalization and recruitment among a sample of 261 ISIS returnees, defectors, and imprisoned cadres. We then explore the modes by which Canadian FTFs specifically were recruited to join ISIS abroad, and their motivations for doing so. We then provide in-depth case studies of three Canadian FTFs and three Canadian former white supremacists, focusing on what can be learned for future counterterrorism efforts aimed at preventing and countering violent extremism. Finally, we discuss strategies for deterring violent extremist radicalization. We argue that in the twenty-first century, with people more connected than ever through social media, efforts at deterrence must be widespread and well publicized, including through online campaigns. In Canada specifically, deterrence by denial—reducing the perceived benefits of joining a violent extremist group—may be a prudent course of action given that many Canadian violent extremists appear to be pulled toward violent extremist groups by the opportunity to gain a sense of meaning, significance, and purpose, rather than pushed out of mainstream society via discrimination or marginalization.

METHOD

The present study utilizes interview data from two larger projects aimed at understanding the vulnerabilities, motivations, influences, roles, experiences, and sources of disillusionment of male and female ISIS and far-right violent extremist group members. The study sought to gain access to any member of ISIS or a far-right violent extremist group, male or female, whether a defector, returnee from the battleground, or imprisoned ISIS cadre, and to then conduct a semi-structured, video-recorded, in-depth psychological interview with that person. The lead researcher worked with prison officials, fixers, translators, and research associates, who arranged access to, video recorded, and translated the interviews. Moreover, in six cases, these individuals carried out the interview in the researcher's absence, in one case due to the ISIS cadre arriving unannounced, in the second due to the interviewee refusing to talk to a woman, and in the last four due to the COVID-19 pandemic and technical difficulties of achieving a stable video link-up.

The sample for this study is by necessity a convenience sample, as it is extremely difficult to gain safe access to ISIS cadres and to obtain their informed consent for an in-depth interview; thus, random sampling is not possible. The first author, who served as interviewer, attempted to obtain a representative sample in terms of requesting access to women as well as men and attempting to talk to a wide range of nationalities and ethnicities, age groups, and roles fulfilled within ISIS.

Interview Procedure and Ethical Considerations

The authors of this study are associated with an independent, non-profit think tank with its own internal institutional review board (IRB) modelled after the first author's previous experience with the RAND Corporation's IRB. In all cases, the semi-structured interview started with an informed consent process followed by a brief history of the interviewee focusing on early childhood and upbringing and covering life experiences prior to becoming interested in ISIS or their far-right group. Demographic details were gleaned during this portion of the interview, as were vulnerabilities that may have impacted the individual's decision to join their group. In the case of ISIS cadres, questions then turned to how the individual learned about the conflicts in Syria, and about ISIS, and became interested in travelling and/or joining, as not all of the interviewees actually travelled to live under ISIS; a few acted as recruiters at home. Similarly, members of far-right groups were asked how they first learned about their group and its ideology. Questions explored the various motivations for joining in order to obtain a detailed recruitment history: how the individual interacted with their group prior to joining; whether recruitment took place in person or over the Internet, or both; how travel was arranged and occurred; intake procedures and experiences with other militant or terrorist groups prior to joining their group; and training and indoctrination. The interview then turned to the interviewee's experiences in their group: family, living, and work experiences, including fighting and job history; the positive and negative aspects of the individual's experience in their group; possible disillusionment and doubts; traumatic experiences; experience and/or knowledge about one's own or others' attempts to escape; being, or witnessing others, being punished or tortured; imprisonment; the owning of slaves; treatment of women and the prevalence of marriages. The interview covered where the individual worked and lived during his or her time in their group and changes over time in orientation to the group and its ideology, which often ranged from strongly endorsing it to wanting to leave. The semi-structured nature of the interview ensured that participants were asked the same questions about their emotional states throughout their trajectories into and out of terrorism, regardless of gender. Moreover, the interviewer found that all interviewees, including men, found it easy to express themselves emotionally when in the presence of a non-judgmental female psychologist.

In accordance with American Psychological Association guidelines and United States legal standards, a strict human-subjects protocol was followed in which the researchers introduced themselves and the project, explained the goals of learning about ISIS and/or the Far Right, and noted that the interview would be video recorded with the additional goal of using video-recorded material of anyone willing to denounce the group to later create short counter-narrative videos. These videos use insider testimonies denouncing ISIS and white supremacist groups in order to disrupt these groups' online and face-to-face recruitment and to de-legitimize the groups and their ideologies. The subjects were warned not to incriminate themselves and to refrain from speaking about crimes they had not already confessed to the authorities, but rather to speak about what they had witnessed inside their groups. Likewise, subjects were told they could refuse to answer any questions, end the interview at any point, and could have their faces blurred and names changed on the counter-narrative video if they agreed to it. Subjects' real names are used in both the counter-narrative videos and the present study only for those individuals who gave explicit consent to do so. Subjects who did not explicitly agree to use their real names in counter-narrative videos and in research papers were given pseudonyms. Prisoners are considered a vulnerable population of research subjects, so careful precautions were taken to ensure that prisoners were not coerced into participating in the research and that there were no repercussions for not participating. The interviewer also made clear to the participants that she was not an attorney or country government official and could not provide them with legal advice or assistance regarding their situation.

Risks to the subjects included being harmed by members of their respective groups for denouncing the group, although for those who judged such punishment to be a significant risk, the researchers agreed to change their names and blur their faces and leave out identifying details. Likewise, there were risks of becoming emotionally distraught during the interview, but this was mitigated by ensuring that interviews were conducted by an experienced psychologist who slowed things down and offered support when discussing emotionally fraught subjects. The rewards of participating for the subjects were primarily to protect others from undergoing a similar negative experience with their respective groups and having the opportunity to sort through many of their motivations, vulnerabilities, and experiences in the group with a compassionate psychologist over the course of an hour or more. The majority of interviewees thanked the researcher for the interview.

Statistical Analyses

The data presented in this chapter are both qualitative and quantitative. The researchers used the interviewer's notes, transcribed interviews, and video-recorded interviews to perform a comprehensive thematic analysis, which, along with the interview questions, decided a priori, was then used to create 342 variables on which the semi-structured interviews were coded. The 342 variables related to the participants' demographic information, life experiences, motivations and influences for joining their groups, travel to Syria or Iraq if applicable, roles and experiences in the group, sources of disillusionment with the group, and present feelings about the group and each participant's actions within the group. The second author coded the interviews on 342 variables and conducted the data analysis for this chapter in the SPSS data-analysis software.

Quantitative Results

ONLINE RECRUITMENT

The full sample. Of the 263 ISIS returnees, defectors, and imprisoned cadres interviewed by the first author, 260 are analyzed herein. This number includes 211 men and 49 women. Of those, 50.8 per cent were influenced or recruited to join ISIS, at least in part, over the Internet. This includes watching videos produced by ISIS, other groups, or by Syrian civilians online, communicating over social media with friends or family who had already joined the group, or communicating directly with ISIS recruiters. Of the entire sample, 20.0 per cent were *solely* influenced or recruited to join ISIS via these online methods. Even if their online communication was with people they already knew, they had never spoken to these friends or family members in person about ISIS or its ideology. Of course, such recruitment does not occur in a vacuum, but rather in the psychosocial context of push and pull factors motivating individuals' decisions to join.

Foreign terrorist fighters. When people living in Iraq and Syria ("locals") were excluded from the sample, the prevalence of online recruitment and radicalization grew. Of the 260 analyzed interviews, 162 were with foreigners, though not all actually travelled to join ISIS—they either became recruiters at home or were thwarted before making it to Syria. Of the 162, 122 were men and 40 were women. Any online recruitment or influence was reported by 74.1 per cent of the foreigners, and 29.0 per cent reported being influenced and recruited to join ISIS solely over the Internet.

Westerners. In approaching the specific numbers of Canadians influenced or recruited to join ISIS over the Internet, we may first narrow the sample down to Westerners. This sample includes those from the United States, Canada, Australia, and Europe, including Turkey and the Balkan countries, which are aspiring or candidate European Union members. Non-EU European countries, including the United Kingdom and Switzerland, are also included. This sample includes 114 people (86 men and 28 women). Once again, this narrowing of the sample increased the prevalence of online influence and recruitment, with 77.2 per cent reporting any Internet influence or recruitment and 29.8 per cent reporting sole Internet influence and recruitment.

Canadians. The final sample includes only those who were living in Canada at the time that they joined ISIS (one man was a dual British-Canadian citizen and is not included because he did not live in Canada). Three men and 1 woman were therefore included. Of those, 3 reported any online influence or recruitment (75 per cent) and 1 (25 per cent) reported sole Internet influence and recruitment. Two of the men and the woman's stories are explored in depth in a later section of this chapter. The third man's story is not reported out of respect for his privacy.

MOTIVATIONS

The full sample. Regardless of how they were influenced and recruited to join ISIS, the ISIS defectors, returnees, and imprisoned cadres varied in terms of their reasons for actually joining. Of the full sample of 260, the most commonly reported motivations were the desire to pursue or solidify their Islamic identity (31.5 per cent), the desire to help the Syrian people, whom ISIS claimed to be defending (30.8 per cent), and the desire to build and live under a true Islamic Caliphate (23.1 per cent).

Foreign terrorist fighters. Among the 162 foreigners, the most commonly reported motivations were also the desire to help the Syrian people (48.1 per cent), the desire to pursue or solidify their Islamic identity (43.2 per cent), and the desire to build and live under the Caliphate (29.0 per cent). The higher prevalence of these motivations among foreigners as compared to the entire sample can be attributed to fewer foreigners being motivated by ISIS's promise to fulfill their basic needs (15.0 per cent in the entire sample versus 4.9 per cent for foreigners) and to give them employment (17.3 per cent for the entire sample versus 4.3 per cent for foreigners).

Westerners. Narrowed down even further, the 111 Westerners were primarily motivated by the desire to help the Syrian people (52.6 per cent), pursue or solidify their Islamic identity (48.2 per cent), and the desire to build and live under the Caliphate (30.7 per cent). Once again, the proportion of people motivated by basic needs and employment shrunk, though other motivations were more common among Westerners than foreigners in general and the entire sample—namely, the "push" factor of discrimination in their home countries (10.0 per cent for the whole sample versus 15.4 per cent for foreigners and 20.2 per cent for Westerners).

Canadians. None of the Canadians were motivated by basic needs or employment. Two of the 4 were motivated by the desire to pursue or solidify their Islamic identity, and 3 of the 4 were motivated by the desire to feel personally significant. Three were also motivated by the desire to help the Syrian people. One Canadian each was motivated by the prospect of adventure, the prospect of romance, the desire to pursue or solidify their masculine identity, the desire to pursue or solidify their feminine identity, anger at the Assad regime, the desire to build and live under the Caliphate, the desire to engage in jihad, belief in the *takfir* ideology, and the belief that they would be redeemed or forgiven in God's eyes by joining ISIS. Notably, none of the Canadians were motivated by any societal push factors: discrimination, harassment by the police, or arrests related to their ideology.

Qualitative Narratives

The above-mentioned data regarding Canadian ISIS members cannot be considered representative, and the authors' current sample of white supremacists remains too small to glean meaningful quantitative data. However, a great deal can be learned from case studies of Canadian violent extremists of different genders, ages, religious and ethnic backgrounds, socio-economic statuses, and ideologies. What follows are the personal narratives describing the trajectories into and out of violent extremism of three Canadian ISIS members and three Canadian white supremacists.

PROFILES OF CANADIAN ISIS MEMBERS

Mohammed Khalifa was thirty-six years old at the time of his interview in an SDF (or Syrian Democratic Forces) prison. Born in Saudi Arabia to an Ethiopian family, he moved to Canada at age five. He describes his family as happy, and he has a college degree in computer systems. At eighteen, he became more religious, and at twenty-three he intently watched the arrests of the "Toronto 18," fourteen adults and four minors who were plotting to enact al Qaeda–inspired attacks in southern Ontario. A few years later, he says, "I was listening to lectures by Anwar al Awlaki." He was inspired by "the fact that he was approaching the life of the Prophet Mohammed and bringing it into a modern context and interspersing it with a jihad narrative." At the same time, in 2013, "I started following Ahrar al Sham on [a] website and [watched] videos . . . of going out to battle, shooting a tank, firing off a tank artillery, stuff like that. I knew what was going on [in Syria]; I supported the cause." The combination of his support for the Syrian cause and believing the jihad narrative as being the authentic interpretation of Islam inspired by al Awlaki's lectures drove Khalifa to decide to travel to Syria.

He reached out to different sources online and finally found an article describing a hotel in Reyhanli, Turkey, where men with long beards who looked like jihadis were gathering before crossing the border into Syria. Khalifa saved his money, and, in the spring of 2013, he boarded a flight to Cairo. From there, he says, "I took a flight to Hatay. From Hatay, it was close to the border, I thought I'd look around and I took a taxi to Reyhanli. I talked to the driver, he made it seem easy to cross, so I went straight to the border gate." From there, he was taken by bus to the Syrian side, where he told someone that he wanted to join Jaish alMuhajireen walAnsar, a group consisting of foreigners, most from the North Caucasus, that in 2015 pledged allegiance in Syria to Jabhat alNusra. As he explains, "I was there to fight the Syrian regime, ISIS was not even on my mind until it actually came up itself. They had already expanded into Syria, but even then, it was not on my mind." His unit within Jaish alMuhajireen walAnsar pledged itself to ISIS in November 2013, and Khalifa did the same.

In the early days of ISIS, the group was less organized. Khalifa did not undergo any weapons training or ideological indoctrination, though he says, "In Raqqa, I attended a [shariah] course out of my own volition." In January of 2014, "the whole conflict kicked off," and Khalifa served as a fighter and a guard but subsequently decided he wanted to focus on his religious studies. Later, "the ISIS media heard I knew English and Arabic and they took me to Raqqa." In ISIS's media department, Khalifa translated the group's propaganda material and did voiceovers for videos to be posted on Telegram. Around the same time, in the summer of 2014, he got married to a woman from Kenya who was studying medicine in Sudan. Explaining how he met her, Khalifa says, "There was a friend in Muhajireen walAnsar, he was Portuguese, he knew my wife online. . . . We were talking online, and I helped her with the process, setting it all up. She was happy when she came." Khalifa and his wife had two children, the first in a hospital in Raqqa and the second at home, assisted by a midwife. Their life was happy, and Khalifa's wife hoped to finish her medical training at an ISIS-run school in Mayadeen. She was not able to do so, as she and her family fled from village to village trying to avoid bombings by the Syrian regime. Still, Khalifa admits that he did not become disillusioned with ISIS until after he was captured, and that he and his family were some of the last to remain in ISIS's last stronghold of Baghouz, where Khalifa left his media job to fight until the end. He recalls, "Basically, during the last offensive from Hajin to Baghouz . . . I decided to go out and fight instead of staying with media. [I was] in a gun battle [and was] taken by [the] SDF. Basically, they called us to surrender. I was out of ammo, so I came out."

Working in the media department, it was his job to make ISIS look good, but Khalifa states that when he met men in prison who had actually experienced the atrocities he had previously dismissed as "baseless rumours," he began to think more critically about ISIS, though he still appears to deny many of ISIS's atrocities. Khalifa explains, "That ISIS was committing a lot of injustice and oppression behind the scenes [I was] not aware of. To a certain degree, based on what I've heard, the way they operated in their prison is not Islamic." He goes on, "Even though I don't support them anymore, I don't want to speak out against them. . . . Maybe there is the hope that they would realize what they were doing and change for the better." The remorse he feels now relates to the fact that "I ignored what was going on. I ignored the warning signals. I dismissed prematurely." Seemingly failing to grasp the power and influence of ISIS's propaganda in fomenting violence both in Syria and Iraq and worldwide, he says, "I hope I didn't take part in [the atrocities]."

Henricki is another Canadian man in his late thirties. Born in Vancouver, Henricki is of Trinidadian-Indian descent. Henricki's parents separated when he was a baby, and after his mother remarried a strict prison officer, Henricki spent much of his time with his grandparents in Trinidad. Henricki graduated from college with a degree in business and civil engineering and was briefly married, though he and his wife divorced before he left for Syria. Henricki describes his process of deciding to travel to Syria for what he says were purely humanitarian purposes. He recalls that a work colleague knew he was Muslim and asked him about Syria:

> She was telling me about the news she was hearing. [I thought] let me take a look and see what it's about. I watched the news to keep tabs on it. [In] 2012 or 2013, I saw a [video on] YouTube of a little girl bombed and she was crying and her whole family [had been] killed. It affected me. My older brother, he was working in Africa with kids, we are all humanitarian.

In December of 2014, Henricki saw a video in which Syrians were calling out for the Muslims of the world to come and help them, that the regime was killing their sons, fathers, daughters. In March of 2015, Henricki flew to Turkey with a group of friends. By 2015, ISIS's actions were well-known, and Henricki therefore kept his travels a secret. When his mother found out about his plans a few days before he left, Henricki told her, "You see what's going on there, we can't sit and not help the people. I told her I'll be back. I'll be there for a short while." This statement, along with the way he claimed to have used his money in the first five months he was in Syria, suggest that Henricki did intend to offer humanitarian aid in Syria. He says that before he was "taken" by ISIS, he spent $6,000 paying a man he met in Aleppo to procure "medication for the kids, Pampers, baby food, milk, rice, flour, . . . tablets to treat the water."

Henricki's later experience with ISIS was highly disillusioning: "In 2016, I was accused of being a spy and put in prison." In prison, he was tortured by being beaten while suspended such that he was forced to stand on his toes. He was starved and waterboarded before being released after "they found nothing on me." It was during this time that the ISIS *emni* approached Henricki and tried to recruit him to return home to enter the United States to conduct an attack. Henricki claims he refused the offer. Later, he and his wife (who is profiled later in this chapter) tried to escape. They were caught and put in prison. His wife was tortured in prison and suffered a miscarriage after being released. The pair could not afford to pay a smuggler to take them out of ISIS territory, and they remained in the Caliphate until Baghouz. It was there that Henricki's hatred for ISIS grew stronger:

> People were sleeping in the street, no food. If there was food, you couldn't afford it. The ISIS fighters had food. I was angry, I actually developed a hate for this organization, for the people on top. They don't know the religion. I'm not a scholar; I can't read a book in Arabic, but they interpret Islam as they want to suit their ways, which is extremism, and . . . if you are against them, you will be killed. I believe [the ISIS leadership] escaped. They were generating $100,000 a day by oil; they could afford to feed the people, and it was not happening. Women were asking for money to buy milk for their kids, women whose husbands have passed away, and they are supposed to be taking care of them, but they are begging on the street.

Eventually, Henricki, his wife, and a group of other disillusioned people found an abandoned van and drove to an American checkpoint, where they surrendered. He insists that if he had known the truth about ISIS, he never would have joined, and he encourages others to "seek knowledge that will give you the best of advice and the truthful knowledge, not how this organization made propaganda." He says that the only positive aspect of his time with ISIS was that he met his wife during this period, "who I really love," and that he wants to go back to Canada with her. When told by the interviewer that she would try to talk to his wife, Henricki responded, "Tell her every day I pray for her."

Kimberly Pullman married Henricki after travelling to Syria. Her life was fraught with trauma prior to joining ISIS. Her father was addicted to amphetamines and died of leukemia when Kimberly was nineteen. She has three children, some of whom were the result of rape. After having her children, Kimberly converted to Islam in 2004, when she was thirty. She married a Kuwaiti man and moved to the Middle East with her children, but her new husband mistreated her children and threatened her with violence. She returned to Canada, where she met an Egyptian imam who counselled her and her children, even taking them on picnics with his wife, but he raped her as well. During his trial for a series of rapes, in which Kimberly did not testify, Kimberly experienced deeply distressing PTSD symptoms and had to stop taking university classes. Her children moved out and she was about to lose her home when she came across a man on Twitter. He asked her why she had gotten divorced, and she told him what happened in Kuwait. He responded that when Kuwait is "back in actual Muslim hands, we will go and restore you and your children's honour." Kimberly recalls, "That is something I haven't had. Giving back a purity that was taken away was something I wanted so badly, that is something that he didn't hold against me, and then that pulled me in."

Kimberly was deeply suicidal at the time she married this man over the Internet; during this time, he continued to recruit her, telling her she should come join in ISIS's Caliphate, and threatening divorce if she didn't travel. She remembers, "We are taught in Islam that your husband is the emir of your life." He husband continued to lure her in: "Come where you are loved, your children don't even see you, you have skills, you shouldn't be alone." Kimberly was suicidal at the time and was taking medication to help with her insomnia. She says that she could not afford therapy. Seeing videos of suffering Syrian civilians, she thought, "If I was going to die, at least I could die helping children. . . . I felt if I did something good, it would overwrite the bad that had happened." In 2015, Kimberly flew to Antalya, Turkey, and was brought to Raqqa. Shortly after she left Canada, a letter arrived indicating that she had qualified for disability benefits due to her severe mental illness. Kimberly now states she would never have left Canada had she known she would be adjudicated as mentally disabled and provided for.

Kimberly's new husband was emotionally abusive, although she claimed that he did not need to hit her because she was so weak and vulnerable. He later *takfired* her (declared her an apostate) and left her in a *madhafa*. To leave the *madhafa*, Kimberly remarried, this time to Henricki, in 2016. True to her desire to do humanitarian work, Kimberly worked in a hospital in Raqqa as a nurse but was horrified by the injuries she saw from bombings and was also becoming deeply disillusioned by ISIS's un-Islamic actions. Henricki and Pullman tried once to escape and were thrown in prison. In the ISIS prison, Kimberly was raped yet again. She recounts, "They accused me of being a spy. The first night, they pulled me out and you could hear the screams down the hallway, and they made me watch. They said if I didn't start giving [them] information, this was going to happen to me too." Before being released from prison with "a massive concussion," Kimberly was forced to sign her name in blood on a statement saying that she would be killed if she tried to escape again. She did not tell Henricki exactly what happened to her in prison, as she did not trust him to not react violently to the fact that she had been raped.

By the time they got to Baghouz, Kimberly had completely lost her will to live. She claims that she kept going in order to save the lives of the orphaned children for whom she was caring. Eventually, they made it to SDF territory. Sick with lupus and hepatitis, she yearns to go home and feels "abandoned by the Canadian government." She says that ISIS never established a true Caliphate, and that she has turned away from the group completely. Indeed, Pullman's case is of a severely mentally disturbed individual suffering from repeated rapes and violence prior to her travel to Syria in a suicidal state, with her mental condition continuing to worsen over time as the traumas continued to pile up. She has many times expressed suicidal ideation to the first author and requires medication for her mental suffering and emotional anguish, if not immediate psychiatric hospitalization, none of which are possible while she remains in SDF detention.

PROFILES OF CANADIAN MEMBERS OF THE FAR RIGHT

Brad Galloway, aged forty, is a prominent former white supremacist from Toronto who is now active in trying to pull others out of the world of violent extremism. Adopted as a baby, Brad never felt as though he had a solid identity or secure attachment to his adopted family, where he didn't feel that he fit in. Early in his high school years, he began selling drugs and fighting, landing in the juvenile justice system, which, he says, was not yet focused on harm reduction and prevention. Brad says his risk-taking behaviours stemmed in large part from the traumatic experience of hearing about a friend dying in a car accident when he was twelve years old. He recounts, "I got into risky behaviour because I didn't care. If she could be killed, maybe I'll die, maybe I won't." He recognizes now that this "was my way of processing sadness. She was a very good person. I thought death was for bad or old people." Brad was also into the rave and punk music scene of the 1990s. Though Brad had friends of different races growing up, he had also grown up hearing his grandparents make racist comments and jokes. He had been inured to racism and was attracted to the culture of white power music after being introduced to it be a friend he met in a bar. He trusted this man and instantly accepted the white supremacist ideology of the group he was invited to join so that he could fit in. Brad claims that he didn't become a Holocaust denier, but "I thought we should stop immigration and create a white enclave." He thought random acts like vandalism of synagogues did not advance the white cause, and yet he admits that he was wearing a shirt with a swastika on it on the day he got into a violent fight and was subsequently treated by a Jewish doctor, an event on which he later reflected when he decided to leave the movement. Looking back, Brad describes his continued involvement with the group as an addiction to a peer group that gave him a sense of freedom, belonging, and empowerment.

Brad became a major recruiter for the white supremacist cause, utilizing early Internet chatrooms and web forums like Stormfront. In 1995, he established a Canadian chapter of Volksfront, originally started in Portland, Oregon. Volksfront's mission was to buy land in the United States and Canada in order to create a white ethno-state. They also raised money for and wrote letters to imprisoned hate crime offenders, people they called "prisoners of war." Brad was a leader in his group but found it stressful and depressing to try to manage violent and unstable people who were always fighting, even with each other. He found it exhausting to wake up with hate in his heart. The cause was about saving the white race, he thought, and yet most of its adherents were simply "getting arrested and doing horrific things." There was also a lot of in-fighting between different groups, and Brad was afraid for his life and his family's safety. Likewise, he began realizing all of the counter-examples to the hatred of minorities he was preaching, including looking back at the kind Jewish doctor who treated him without saying a word while he was wearing a swastika-adorned T-shirt.

When Brad left the movement, he was cut off from all of his friends and once again felt lost. Soon after, he was "doxed," meaning that his personal information was revealed in order to identify him as a white supremacist, and he lost his job as a result. Brad struggled trying to keep his family afloat for two to three years afterward. In 2015, however, he met a representative of a group called Life After Hate. He recalls, "That was a real turning point for me. Now I've met another person who left these groups, and we can talk about it." While Brad had also tried therapy, he felt alienated by the fact that professionals were uncomfortable hearing about his struggle to overcome the traumas and reasons behind his white supremacism. "I couldn't talk in therapy because they were too uncomfortable hearing about the violence," Brad recalls. He has now started telling his story to practitioners and academics, leading to a job as a research assistant, which has given him a new sense of purpose.

Despite all of the progress he has made, Brad still recognizes the journey from disengagement to de-radicalization is a lengthy process. For him, it took four years of work, including intense study of other races and religions. About the newer hate groups prevalent now, Brad says, "People think these groups evolve. I don't think they do. They change their look, their name. We see militia groups, Proud Boys, it's all about the way I got in. . . . They are not really using anything brand new to recruit people, [just] using differences, us and them." He thinks about all of the different aspects that contribute to people joining white supremacist groups: trauma, identity crises, insecure attachment, toxic masculinity. Brad wants the public to understand that even though they have involved themselves in hate groups, these people are human, and that with compassionate interventions, they can change.

Josh Chernofsky is thirty-six years old, born to a Jewish family in Toronto. A tall, skinny child with respiratory problems, Josh was bullied in school for his inability to succeed in gym class. With no friends with whom to bond, he spent most of his time playing video games. Josh went to university for a year and a half before dropping out due to mental health challenges. He then started working as a security guard. As a plainclothes private investigator, Josh was pursuing a shoplifter when he lost his balance and fell. His head was injured, and he experienced post-traumatic stress disorder.

After a few years of moving from job to job, Josh was working as a process server when he heard about a protest from a friend. As he recalls it, "Saturday morning, I was bored and antsy, so I decided to check it out." Josh arrived at the protest area and saw members of a variety of different groups carrying

Canadian flags. They were Proud Boys, Josh learned, and they were being surrounded by people in black masks, whom Josh identified as Antifa. He recalls that he "didn't understand why they were attacking these people with the flags. Why were they preventing people from expressing themselves; I was always a really strong proponent of that." After leaving the protest, Josh followed the Proud Boys on YouTube and contacted them in order to find out about future events.

Josh remembers that the second Proud Boys event he attended ended in a violent brawl with Antifa. Josh had never been in a fight before, and after the altercation with Antifa, he explains, "I wanted to get them even more." At the time, Josh claims, the Proud Boys were not talking about their ideology, though he also admits adhering to some of their core beliefs: "I felt like I was standing up for Canada. There were some [members] who weren't white. One guy was Asian." The values they professed, says Josh, were "Judeo-Christian values. They were upset about 'creeping shariah,' that our prime minister is allowing it," Josh explained, referring to fears that some non-Muslims express about Muslims potentially imposing shariah law where they live. Soon after joining, Josh became a sort of intelligence agent for the Proud Boys, helping to dox the group's enemies.

Slowly, however, Josh started to become disillusioned with the Proud Boys, in part through interactions with the organizer of counter-protests against his own group. The catalyst to his decision to leave came when "an activist in Toronto killed herself." The activist had fled to Canada from Egypt after being jailed and tortured for flying a rainbow flag at a concert. Josh had never interacted with her personally but had seen her at events where his group opposed her. His fellow members called her a terrorist, and after she killed herself, they sent messages to her friends suggesting they also should commit suicide. Josh thought those messages were "disgusting," so he reached out to his acquaintance from the other side in order to send the activist's family an anonymous condolence letter. Soon enough he was reaching out to exit organizations.

Josh's story of leaving his group demonstrates the danger of doing so, and the reason why many who are disillusioned may still be hesitant to leave. Josh recounts, "recently I was attacked by someone in my own group, then they all turned on me. It started online. He was attacking [online] and wanted to meet up for coffee to make amends. I believed he was sincere. [In person,] it escalated, and he punched me in the face." The same man spread a rumour online that Josh had been hired by Antifa to spy on the Proud Boys, which caused Josh so much anxiety that he checked into a hospital. Josh, who was born Jewish but converted to Christianity, was threatened by Proud Boys quoting the far-right extremist Rabbi Kahane, saying, "we have to kill the fake Jews." As Josh explains, "When I first started doubting things, I wanted to gradually exit out, but then I got attacked and it was sudden."

Now that Josh has left the group, he has found it difficult to find a job, since he was doxed. Still, he recognizes, "If you were to search my name online, you'll see all this stuff. You'll see my name. Now that I'm out, I'm fully responsible for what I wrote. . . . I'm ashamed now." Looking back, he has gained a profound insight into why he joined: "I was bullied and alone as a kid. I found these groups of people that welcomed me. [It] felt almost like a family. I got so absorbed into that, but after a while, it gets really dark, really quick, nothing like a family." He continues, "Hate is so consuming. It consumes every bit of your life. It is so much easier not to hate people than to hate people. It takes so much out of you, fighting other people for simply existing or lifestyle choice."

Tony McAleer, who is fifty-three years old, is another well-known "former." Born in England, he moved to Vancouver as a toddler. Tony grew up in a troubled family marked, and the experience left him with feelings of rejection. Tony was physically abused by priests at his Catholic school and developed "a healthy mistrust of all authority figures" as a result. He was sent to boarding school in England, where he felt rejected and humiliated once again. It was in England that he got involved in the punk skinhead scene, which was also flourishing back home in Vancouver. He says of the skinheads, "They became my best friends. My coping [mechanism] was to befriend the bully, become the bully, because I was not big. They had one thing I didn't have, that people feared them. They were tough. I was with them to feel safe, [to gain] attention, acceptance." He explains that after the humiliation he suffered in school, "coming from that void of powerlessness, that false sense of power, the notoriety and fear that created was intoxicating."

Tony also got involved in the white power music culture, but in this period—the late 1980s and early 1990s—the movement was undergoing a shift. The Aryan Nations in Idaho was uniting hate groups under the banner of "The Order." Tony explains, "In 1989, I was dressed as a skinhead, and in 1991, I was in a suit and tie. Mainstreaming myself, I took over an existing Aryan group in Vancouver. . . . [I] started a phone line, Canadian Liberty Net, versus Aryan [Liberty Net], saying extreme things in a very pleasant way." Eventually, Tony became the leader of the Aryan Resistance Movement. The group's aim was to create a whites-only homeland. He explains the ideology he subscribed to at the time, admitting that he referred to people of colour as "mud people," and said that "Jews were the ones who were engineering the downfall of the white race."

Tony explains, "I don't know if I bought it, but that's how I sold it. . . . Ideology was the pill I had to swallow to get attention, approval, power, but I did swallow it willingly." Looking back, he realizes that his feelings of powerlessness and shame made him vulnerable to the desire wanting to belong, even at such a high cost, and that the violent fights gave him an addictive rush of adrenaline.

In 1998, after over a decade in the movement, Tony began to disengage, choosing to focus instead on raising his children. He admits that he was still dysfunctional at that time: "[I] didn't deal with the issues that made it attractive in the first place. Even though I didn't get in fights, I was still an asshole." Then, he started making more money from his new career as a financial adviser, building relationships, and taking part in personal-growth workshops. Tony went to therapy for the first time and confided to his therapist his previously held beliefs. Tony remembers, "He leans in with a big, huge grin, 'You know I'm Jewish, right?'" This man, for whose annihilation Tony had once advocated, told him, "That's what you did, not who you are. I see you. I see little Tony." Tony realized, "If he could love me, [there's] no reason why I couldn't love myself." Tony went on to help start the exit organization Life After Hate, through which he focused on helping people deal with their internal struggles and histories of trauma.

Lauren Manning, thirty-one, was born just outside of Toronto. Although she has happy memories of her family, she also remembers being "shamed" by her maternal grandfather for her weight and poor grades. According to Lauren, her grandfather had "never wanted a girl. He made that clear to [my mom]." When Lauren was seven, her father was diagnosed with leukemia; he died when she was sixteen. Over time, Lauren saw her strong, police officer father become "weak and dependent." To deal with her grief and loneliness at home and at school, she "started binge drinking and getting in trouble at school. Originally petty things, fighting." From the ages of sixteen to twenty-two, she got drunk daily, sometimes mixing alcohol with opioids. At seventeen, Lauren was exposed to National Socialist black metal music on Facebook, where she also started communicating with a recruiter. When she turned eighteen, her mother and brother "couldn't take my drinking and newfound belief system, [and] I was given an ultimatum: give this up or find somewhere else to live." Lauren moved in with the recruiter.

Recalling her ideological indoctrination, Lauren admits, "I bought into the anti-Semitic part right away. [I thought Jews] are in control, at fault for everything wrong in your life. I also bought into the white replacement narrative—these people are taking over, we will be wiped out." Lauren relished her new identity as a white supremacist. A loner in high school, "I liked having this taboo label. I was always an outsider. . . . It was also a good feeling to think you have all this secret knowledge that no one else knows or understands." Soon enough, Lauren had shaved part of her head and gotten racist tattoos on her neck and back, all of which have since been removed and covered. Still, she felt alone. The Hammerskins enforced hyper-gendered roles, and Lauren "didn't fit in with the rest of these guys' wives and girlfriends; I'm not feminine, not subservient." She was expected to have children, but the group would not allow her to fight or give her patches to symbolize her membership. Looking back on the relationship she had with her father, who taught her self-defence, she says, "If my dad would come back from the dead, [he] would come back to beat my ass for putting up with this."

Lauren recounts that her group made an effort to recruit people with military experience. She explains, "There were a few guys that were in the Canadian Forces. One got discharged for his severe PTSD from Iraq; he was out when he joined us. Ex-military have that very tribalist mindset, [so it is] very easy to go to a group like this. There were others who had been in Iraq as well as him. They were valuable." She continues, "They can bring their former combat training and impart those skills."

Lauren began her disengagement and de-radicalization process in 2012, when her friend in the group was murdered in self-defence while "doing collections for bikers." As Lauren describes, "The group was trying to appropriate his death, spin doctor the story into a hate crime against our people, saying he was targeted for being in the group. But he really walked into it himself." Lauren tried to leave the group immediately but was violently attacked by her former comrades. She then took a more gradual approach, getting sober and seeking treatment for post-traumatic stress disorder. She used her sobriety and her break-up with her partner as an excuse to distance herself from the group. Despite continued attempts by the group to pull her back in, Lauren was finally able to cut all ties, and she continues to work every day to control some of the ideological indoctrination that sneaks into her thoughts.

Elisa Hategan was born in Bucharest, Romania, the only child of parents with a thirty-year age gap between them. When she was nine, Elisa's mother defected to Canada and left her with her emotionally and physically abusive father. At eleven, Elisa and her father joined her mother in Canada, but her father returned to Bucharest to be with his mistress; he died soon after. Elisa's relationship with her mother was no better than that with her father: "She wanted to tell me what to do, wanted me to translate. I was backwards, not fitting into Canadian society. She would be angry, hit me, very physically abusive. I ran away at fourteen." Elisa was bullied at school and in the group home where she lived after running away, including by some of the Black residents, whom her mother had already told her were "troublemakers." Skipping school and counting down the days until she could get a job, Elisa saw a clean-cut man on TV: "He was saying what's wrong with being proud of your white heritage?" She wrote to the Church of the Creator in the United States, inquiring as to whether there were any similar groups in Canada. Soon enough, she was meeting a recruiter from Heritage Front at a mall. She recalls, "I was just happy that someone was asking questions about me' [before that] nobody cared. Asking questions [like,] 'What do you want for your future?' He said I was so smart at such a young age to be racially conscious." The recruiter told Elisa that she could become a journalist for their new magazine, and "within a month I was recording messages for the hotline. They cast me as the face of this organization. I was the only female representing the Heritage Front."

Elisa used her young age to "slip into high schools and put flyers in lockers." She gave speeches at rallies, and "really believed there would be a revolution, . . . [that] we are being exterminated." Cracks started to appear in the ideology when the group asked Elisa to terrorize women who were involved in anti-racist groups. Heritage Front leadership wanted her to impersonate the women and to call sex lines, saying, "I want Black men to come to my house and rape me," and then to give them these women's addresses. Elisa recounts, "This was no longer defending our rights." When she asked the leadership why all of the people they were terrorizing were women, she was told that "women are more emotional, easier to break." She realized that Heritage Front thought the same about her. The group's leaders also used anti-gay slurs when describing the anti-racist women, which hit Elisa, who had been denying her own sexuality, to her core.

At eighteen, Elisa was arrested for distributing racist flyers. Heritage Front wanted her to take the fall for the entire group, even though Elisa had not made the flyers, and in fact had actually been using them to warn women to be careful. Feeling that she had no way out of the group, she decided to take her own life by overdosing on pills from her mother's medicine cabinet. Before she died, someone called an ambulance, which brought her to the hospital. Elisa did not know whom to call when the hospital staff told her that she could not leave alone. "I didn't have a mother, couldn't call the Heritage Front." One phone number Elisa remembered was that of the anti-racist woman whom she had once terrorized. When Elisa called, "She thought it was a sting, some sort of set-up. She came with a partner and picked me up. For the next three weeks we met in secret. She did de-programming, [asking] 'Why do you believe this?' She gave me stats that answered each thing. In talking to her, I realized I had no sense of myself anymore."

On 23 November 1993, Elisa went "underground, ran away to this [anti-racist] network," after providing the police with information that they could use to charge Heritage Front members. She eventually needed to return to Toronto to testify but was not given witness protection despite feeling that she was truly in danger: "Through the grace of strangers, I was able to make it through that time. In my short eighteen years, I could count on one hand the people who were kind to me. . . . I stayed on an Indian reservation, with a Black pastor. I used to hate these people, but if it wasn't for them, I don't know what I would have done."

Future Risk

Moving forward into a new decade, it is imperative that researchers, practitioners, and policy-makers take into account past lessons as they make decisions. Much has changed over the past decade, with five lessons from the data and narratives presented here standing out. First, while earlier extremists also used the Internet to recruit and send around their hate propaganda, social media is an increasingly potent tool for violent extremists and terrorists. Nowadays, individuals can build trusting, intimate relationships without ever meeting in person, and global connectivity and awareness can make them sympathize with the plight of victims thousands of miles away. Used strategically, social media can also be a tool for counterterrorism and preventing and countering violent extremism, but it is clear that the field is years behind the terrorists. Second, security services and other professionals' underestimation of the violent Far Right is apparent and must be remedied. Third, we know that experiences of discrimination and marginalization increase the risks of recruitment into violent extremism, and this effect is amplified as reciprocal radicalization occurs when opposing groups violently fight and attack one another, accelerating polarities and acts of violence. Fourth, culture can be used for good or for bad. In the case of the Far Right, hate music coupled with drinking has been used to draw new recruits in, conferring a sense of belonging that comes at a price. In the case of ISIS and al Qaeda, hijacked and twisted scriptures and revised interpretations of Sunni Islam have been used to draw in new recruits. To adequately counter either of these and redirect potential recruits, one needs to understand the aspects of culture being used to manipulate and draw in new recruits. Fifth, people's desire for a sense of belonging, a feeling of significance, purpose, and dignity are often important vulnerabilities, and they are needs that are met by these groups with promises of family, belonging, purpose, and dignity conferred upon joining. These also lend credence to the Three N model posited by Arie Kruglanski, which holds that needs, network, and narrative are essential to someone becoming a violent extremist (Kruglanski et al., 2019).

ISIS RESURGENCE

With regard to militant jihadist violent extremism, the primary risk for Canada appears to be future waves of FTFs participating in conflicts abroad, and so-called lone wolf attacks called for by these groups and enacted on Canadian territory. Returning FTFs currently held by the SDF may pose some risk, either in radicalizing others in prisons or in carrying out acts of violence if these individuals go free, and they should have access to proper rehabilitation and reintegration services to preclude either happening, though Canada has not yet been the target of any attacks committed by returnees. Rather, it appears more likely that returnees are disillusioned and want to simply return home, face justice if necessary, and pursue normal, low-profile lives. However, ISIS is currently undergoing a resurgence in Syria and Iraq, as well as in other areas where they have established *wilaya* (provinces). They continue to post high-quality propaganda content, encouraging their followers to help them rebuild their once-great Caliphate and telling them to enact revenge at home for its downfall.

There is extensive documentation of diehard ISIS women continuing to enforce ISIS rules, especially surrounding proper dress, in SDF camps, primarily Camp al Hol. The women have violently attacked and even killed other women who have become disillusioned with ISIS, as well as the guards in the camp. They are indoctrinating their children, teaching them to throw rocks at the guards. Moreover, these women run social media pages through which they fundraise to be smuggled out of the camps. Some women simply wish to escape their dire circumstances and return home, but others aspire to help rebuild the Caliphate. They have also encouraged male followers to commit attacks in SDF territory on their behalf (de Azevedo, 2020). These efforts do not, however, appear to involve Canadian women.

In Syria and their various provinces, ISIS has been continually conducting assassinations, kidnappings, and suicide bombings since the loss of their last stronghold, Baghouz, and the death of Abu Bakr al Baghdadi in 2019. As of 2020, ISIS's remaining war chest was estimated at over US$400 million, a far cry from the US$2 billion they were once estimated to possess, but nevertheless enough to finance attacks with lethal consequences. These attacks and proof of wealth are also useful in showing supporters and potential recruits that ISIS is thriving. The group's propaganda emphasizes the narrative of the "long war" and pushes followers to engage in "digital jihad," thus keeping them engaged even without a territorial Caliphate or iconic caliph (Azman, 2020).

FAR-RIGHT GROWTH

Canada has recently taken a number of steps that indicated that the government takes the threat from far-right violent extremists seriously. In 2019, neo-Nazi groups Blood and Honour and Combat 18 were added to Canada's list of terrorist organizations, which had never before included white supremacist groups. Around the same time, the Canadian Security Intelligence Service also identified far-right violent extremism as a national security threat (Kaur, 2019). In 2021, following the Capitol Hill riot, Canada added the Proud Boys to its terrorist list, along with a slew of other white supremacist groups. Designating these groups does not simply symbolize a strong stance against white supremacist violent extremism, however, as Canada's *Anti-terrorism Act* allows the government to seize the property and monitor the finances of individuals or entities on the list of terrorist organizations (Li, 2021).

Scholars suggest that the surge in far-right violent extremism in Canada can be attributed to white supremacists having been empowered and emboldened by the far-right rhetoric of politicians all over the world. This empowerment has led to a greater number of rallies and demonstrations, an increase in the frequency and severity of hate crimes, and the establishment of a number of new groups, including the Proud Boys. As these scholars have explained, a focus on white supremacist violent extremism does not negate the threat of militant jihadism. Rather, we must shift our focus because the understanding of white supremacist violent extremism is far less developed than that of militant jihadism. Likewise, it is important to understand how these groups radicalize in a reciprocal fashion. Especially unexamined is the prevalence of far-right violent extremist activity in rural areas of Canada, which may be more culturally conducive to far-right ideology than urban areas, despite generally higher levels of crime in urban areas. Indeed, a study of far-right violent extremist incidents in Atlantic Canada (which is more rural than the rest of Canada) between 2000 and 2019 identified 156 such incidents. The same study also showed that the frequency of incidents was increasing, with 60 per cent of the identified incidents occurring after 2016. This finding is consistent with previously cited studies positing that 2016 was a turning point for white supremacists in Canada, as it was in the United States (Hofmann et al., 2021). Other studies have found that the number of far-right violent extremist groups active in Canada grew by 30 per cent between 2015 and 2019, and that the number of reported hate crimes increased by more than 60 per cent between 2014 and 2017 (Habib, 2019).

Policy and Practice Recommendations

The quantitative and qualitative data presented in this chapter provide a road map for preventing and countering violent extremism as we move into the new decade. As previously noted, two primary implications of the last decade of research in this field, including that described in this chapter, are the potential for radicalization and recruitment to terrorism to occur solely online, and the increased risk posed by far-right violent extremist groups. The qualitative narratives from Canadian violent extremist themselves, coupled with a meticulous review of the literature, can inform future practice and enable us to counteract both of these threats.

With regard to online radicalization and recruitment, broadly speaking, government and non-governmental efforts at deterrence by denial and counter-speech must parallel the quality and quantity of violent extremist propaganda, which advertises the benefits, both material and existential, of joining violent extremist groups. Essentially, in this case deterrence refers to denying violent extremist recruiters the opportunity to radicalize potential followers, in addition to denying potential followers the supposed benefits of becoming radicalized. Narratives aiming to counter these messages must be just as emotionally engaging and credible. In many cases, counter-narratives produced by government entities are not trusted by vulnerable audiences. The Breaking the ISIS Brand Counter Narrative Project is perhaps an exception. It was created by a non-profit organization and uses actual ISIS insiders to speak out against the group, and it has been found to be credible and emotionally evocative (Speckhard & Ellenberg, 2020a; Speckhard et al., 2018, 2020). Likewise, the Escape Hate Counter Narrative Project encourages former white supremacists to denounce their groups and their ideologies. These counter-narrative projects, as well as others, also produce videos, and then provide resources to help viewers understand the content they've just consumed, including resources for counselling and off-ramping. These resources and action items are key, as violent extremist groups are successful in radicalizing and recruiting online because they immediately provide potential recruits with concrete steps that allow them to act on whatever they have learned from their online content. This could range from attending a rally or protest, to conducting an attack at home, to travelling to Syria to join the Caliphate or help to rebuild it. It also behooves organizations to deploy skilled professionals who can reach out to vulnerable individuals online to answer questions and suggest alternative paths that meet their needs for acceptance, belonging, meaning, and significance.

In Canada specifically, the qualitative testimony from former ISIS members emphasizes the impact of pull, rather than push, factors in their decisions to join the group. Therefore, especially effective counter-narratives for Canadians might emphasize ISIS's lies and the reality of its actions and life under the Caliphate, utilizing the testimony of former ISIS members. Additionally, alternative narratives may be more effective in Canada than they have been elsewhere. A primary criticism of alternative narratives has been that they do not resonate with their target audiences. For example, a video extolling the virtues of a liberal democracy may not be convincing to a Muslim woman in western Europe who has been harassed or discriminated against because she wears a niqab. She will not be convinced that she can practise her religion freely if her daily experience is inconsistent with such claims. While this is not to say that Muslims and people with immigrant backgrounds do not experience discrimination in Canada (the rise of white supremacism is evidence to the contrary), the research presented in this chapter and elsewhere suggests that Canadian ISIS members were not driven to join the group because they felt alienated and marginalized in Canada. Moreover, the few militant jihadist attacks on Canadian soil have been aimed at hard targets representing the Canadian government and military, not at civilians. These attacks, both successful and thwarted, were horrific and exemplify the militant jihadist view that the West is at war with Islam, but they also demonstrate a lack of anger at Canadian society more broadly on the part of the perpetrators. Thus, exposing adherents to the reality of ISIS and encouraging them to find a sense of purpose outside of militant jihad may be effective in countering such groups' online content. Likewise, the government could take greater care in explaining its foreign policies in ways that ensure that Muslims are not affronted, or, for those already convinced by jihadist narratives, that make clear the West is not at war with Islam.

With regard to the Far Right, the steps that the Canadian government has taken over the past year are in the correct direction, but policy-makers must be judicious in their decisions to designate various groups as terrorist entities. The advantages of doing so, such as the ability to seize property and monitor finances, are great, but such designations also pose a risk of further alienating already marginalized communities. Early counterterrorism efforts in the wake of 9/11 led to the unfair and unwarranted securitization of Muslim communities, thus pushing them out of the mainstream and making some individuals more vulnerable to terrorist narratives. Efforts going forward must be cognizant of these unintended consequences. For instance, the decision to charge a seventeen-year-old incel with terrorism offences, in the absence of a full terrorist designation for the incel movement writ large, risks isolating an already isolated community that is largely non-violent and has yet to be fully investigated with regard to whether it can truly be considered a violent extremist movement (Speckhard et al., 2021).

Other efforts must be made to approach white supremacist violent extremism with the same seriousness as militant jihadist violent extremism. Further research and investigation are needed to fully understand the scope of white supremacist violent extremism in Canada, specifically the risk factors for joining such groups and the best practices for disengagement and de-radicalization. Strategies for countering online radicalization and recruitment must also be pursued with regard to white supremacist violent extremism. There is a great deal of debate as to the utility and efficacy of removing content from social media, but Scrivens and Amarasingam (2020) found that posts by and on violent far-right groups on Facebook were less likely to be taken down than militant jihadist posts. Regardless of whether governments and social media companies use this as a mechanism for countering radicalization and recruitment online, white supremacist radicalization and recruitment must be considered just as grave a threat to Canadian national security as militant jihadist radicalization and recruitment are.

Lastly, it is important in trying to thwart any type of violent extremism to look at push and pull factors with an awareness that violent extremist recruiters promise a sense of belonging, significance, purpose, and dignity alongside adventure and even perhaps a paid job and housing, as well as an outlet for internal rage. When society is failing to offer all its citizens pathways to success, a sense of significance, belonging, purpose, and dignity, we can be sure that violent extremists will step in to fill that gap. Of course, good governance is the better answer. Deterrence by denial, therefore, can include the provision of benefits that would otherwise be offered by a violent extremist group, thus denying violent extremist radicalizers and recruiters the opportunity to prey on vulnerable people and propagate their heinous views.

REFERENCES

Ambrose, E., & Mudde, C. (2015). Canadian multiculturalism and the absence of the far right. *Nationalism and Ethnic Politics, 21*(2), 213–36. https://doi.org/10.1080/13537113.2015.1032033

Azman, N. A. (2020). Islamic State's narratives of resilience and endurance. *Counter Terrorist Trends and Analyses, 12*(1), 82–6. https://www.jstor.org/stable/26865755

Baron, S. W. (1997). Canadian male street skinheads: Street gang or street terrorists? *Canadian Review of Sociology/Revue canadienne de sociologie, 34*(2), 125–54. https://doi.org/10.1111/j.1755 618X.1997.tb00204.x

Bastug, M. F., Douai, A., & Akca, D. (2020). Exploring the "demand side" of online radicalization: Evidence from the Canadian context. *Studies in Conflict & Terrorism, 43*(7), 616–37. https://doi.org/10.1080/1057610X.2018.1494409

Canadian Network for Research on Terrorism, Security and Society. (n.d.). *Canadian Incident Database.* Retrieved 3 August 2023 from https://www.tsas.ca/canadian-incident-database/

Dawson, L. L., Amarasingam, A., & Bain, A. (2016). *Talking to foreign fighters: Socio-economic push versus existential pull factors.* Canadian Network for Research on Terrorism, Security, and Society. https://www.tsas.ca/publications/talking-to-foreign-fighters/

de Azevedo, C. V. (2020). ISIS resurgence in Al Hawl camp and human smuggling enterprises in Syria. *Perspectives on Terrorism, 14*(4), 43–63. https://www.jstor.org/stable/26927663

Habib, J. (2019). Far-right extremist groups and hate crime rates are growing in Canada. *CBC News*. https://www.cbc.ca/passionateeye/features/right-wing-extremist-groups-and-hate-crimes-are growing-in-canada

Harris-Hogan, S., Dawson, L. L., & Amarasingam, A. (2020). A comparative analysis of the nature and evolution of the domestic jihadist threat to Australia and Canada (2000–2020). *Perspectives on Terrorism, 14*(5), 77–102. https://www.jstor.org/stable/26940040

Hoffman, B., Ware, J., & Shapiro, E. (2020). Assessing the threat of incel violence. *Studies in Conflict & Terrorism, 43*(7), 565–87. https://doi.org/10.1080/1057610X.2020.1751459

Hofmann, D. C., Trofimuk, B., Perry, S., & Hyslop-Margison, C. (2021). An exploration of right-wing extremist incidents in Atlantic Canada. *Dynamics of Asymmetric Conflict, 14*(3), 1–23. https://doi.org/10.1080/17467586.2021.1876900

Hogg, M. A., & Blaylock, D. L. (Eds.). (2011). *Extremism and the psychology of uncertainty* (Vol. 3). John Wiley & Sons.

Kaur, H. (2019, 28 June). For the first time, Canada adds white supremacists and neo-Nazi groups to its terror organization list. *CNN*. https://www.cnn.com/2019/06/27/americas/canada-neo-nazi-terror organization-list-trnd/index.html

Kruglanski, A. W., Bélanger, J. J., & Gunaratna, R. (2019). *The three pillars of radicalization: Needs, narratives, and networks*. Oxford University Press.

Kruglanski, A. W., Gunaratna, R., Ellenberg, M., & Speckhard, A. (2020). Terrorism in time of the pandemic: Exploiting mayhem. *Global Security: Health, Science and Policy, 5*(1), 121–32. https://doi.org/10.1080/23779497.2020.1832903

Leichnitz, J. (2020, 30 October). Canada has a white supremacist problem. *International Politics and Society*. https://www.ips-journal.eu/topics/foreign-and-security-policy/canada-has-a-white-supremacist-problem-4757/

Li, D. (2021, 3 February). Canada labels far-right Proud Boys a terrorist entity. *NBC News*. https://www.nbcnews.com/news/us-news/canada-labels-far-right-proud-boys-terrorist-entity n1256615

Ling, J. (2020, 13 July). QAnon's madness is turning Canadians into potential assassins. *Foreign Policy*. https://foreignpolicy.com/2020/07/13/qanon-canada-trudeau-conspiracy-theory/

Moonshot CVE. (2020). The impact of COVID-19 on Canadian search traffic. *Moonshot CVE*. https://moonshotteam.com/resource/covid-19-increase-in-far-right-searches-in-canada/

Paresky, A., Goldenberg, A., Riggleman, D., Shapiro, J., & Farmer, J. (2021). How to respond to the QAnon threat. *Brookings*. https://www.brookings.edu/articles/how-to-respond-to-the-qanon-threat/

Pennycook, G., McPhetres, J., Bago, B., & Rand, D. G. (2020). Predictors of attitudes and misperceptions about COVID-19 in Canada, the UK, and the USA. *PsyArXiv, 10*, 1–25. https://files.osf.io/v1/resources/zhjkp/providers/osfstorage/5e9629a5f135350453d57d00?action=download&direct&version=3

Perry, B., Mirrlees, T., & Scrivens, R. (2018). The dangers of porous borders: The "Trump effect" in Canada. *Journal of Hate Studies, 14*(1), 53–75. https://jhs.press.gonzaga.edu/articles/10.33972/jhs.124

Perry, B., & Scrivens, R. (2015). *Right-wing extremism in Canada: An environmental scan.* Public Safety Canada. https://www.researchgate.net/profile/Ryan Scrivens/publication/307971749_Right_Wing_Extremism_in_Canada_An_Environmental_Scan_215/links/593aa39a0f7e9b3317f41358/Right-Wing-Extremism-in-Canada-An-Environmental-Scan2015.pdf

Perry, B., & Scrivens, R. (2018). A climate for hate? An exploration of the right-wing extremist landscape in Canada. *Critical Criminology, 26*(2), 169–87. https://doi.org/10.1007/s10612-018-9394-y

Scrivens, R., & Amarasingam, A. (2020). Haters gonna "like": Exploring Canadian far-right extremism on Facebook. In Littler, M., & Lee, B. (Eds.), *Digital extremisms.* Palgrave Macmillan. https://doi.org/10.1007/978-3-030-30138-5_4

Speckhard, A., & Ellenberg, M. (2020a). Breaking the ISIS brand counter narrative Facebook campaigns in Europe. *Journal of Strategic Security, 13*(3), 120–48. https://www.jstor.org/stable/26936548

Speckhard, A., & Ellenberg, M. D. (2020b). ISIS in their own words. *Journal of Strategic Security, 13*(1), 82–127. https://www.jstor.org/stable/26907414

Speckhard, A., Ellenberg, M., Morton, J., & Ash, A. (2021). Involuntary celibates' experiences of and grievance over sexual exclusion and the potential threat of violence among those active in an online incel forum. *Journal of Strategic Security, 14*(2), 89–121. https://www.jstor.org/stable/27026635

Speckhard, A., Ellenberg, M., Shaghati, H., & Izadi, N. (2020). Hypertargeting Facebook profiles vulnerable to ISIS recruitment with "Breaking the ISIS Brand Counter Narrative video clips" in multiple Facebook campaigns. *Journal of Human Security, 16*(1), 16–29. https://doi.org/10.12924/johs2020.16010016

Speckhard, A., Shajkovci, A., Wooster, C., & Izadi, N. (2018). Mounting a Facebook brand awareness and safety ad campaign to break the ISIS brand in Iraq. *Perspectives on Terrorism, 12*(3), 50–66. http://www.jstor.org/stable/26453135

Wickson, M. (2019). Legal implications of Canadian foreign fighters. *Canadian Military Journal, 20*(1), 58–64. http://www.journal.forces.gc.ca/Vol20/No1/page58-eng.asp

12

Assessing Influence in Target Audiences that Won't Say or Don't Know How Much They Have Been Influenced

Ronald D. Porter, Minqian Shen, Leandre R. Fabrigar, and Anthony Seaboyer

Introduction: The Challenge of Measuring Influence

Defending against and conducting influence operations has always been an important challenge facing the Canadian Armed Forces (CAF) and other national security organizations responsible for protecting Canadian citizens. For example, the CAF has long recognized the value of having a capability to influence the attitudes and behaviours of enemy forces in support of its military operations conducted abroad. Such a recognition by the CAF has resulted in the training of military personnel specifically tasked with conducting influence operations (i.e., psychological operations, or "PSYOPS," personnel).

However, with the increasing centrality of the Internet in every facet of citizens' lives and the prominence of social media platforms as a means of communication, the potential "battlefield" for social influence operations has expanded far beyond what might have been imagined by national security organizations even twenty-five years ago. In the online information environment of contemporary liberal democracies, both state and non-state adversaries are routinely targeting audiences with persuasive appeals designed to shape their attitudes and behaviours (e.g., see Kim et al., 2018)—though the degree of persuasiveness varies significantly depending on the adversary, the level of effort, and other mitigating factors (e.g., corruption in the implementation of influence operations). For instance, the intelligence services of adversaries might be expected to conduct social influence operations in an effort to undermine support for a nation's leaders, policies, and institutions. Likewise, armed non-state groups and other radical organizations conduct influence campaigns in an effort to recruit new members or incite lone individuals to undertake violent or destructive actions. In response to such efforts, government organizations in some liberal democracies sometimes attempt to counteract the persuasive efforts of adversaries with their own influence operations.

At least since 2016, governments have understood the power non-kinetic influence campaigns can have compared to the more traditional measures of security organizations. The election of Donald Trump was, at the very least, supported by massive adversarial influence campaigns that were launched through micro-targeted, hyper-personalized influence campaigns (Lewis & Hilder, 2018). Many—but not all—subject-matter experts claim that the Russian influence campaign was effective enough to sway the election by 2–3 per cent, a margin that may well have been crucial to the outcome. Long before 2016, adversaries focused the larger part of their operations against the West in the non-kinetic environment. In a 2013 article, Russian general Valery Gerasimov famously described his perception that the way war is conducted has fundamentally changed and that non-kinetic means exceed kinetic means in a ratio of 4:1 (Gerasimov, 2016). China, other actors such as Iran and North Korea, as well as armed non-state actors, have certainly implemented similar strategies. Additionally, digitalization and the increasing use of social media are making influence operations more effective, easier, less risky for the actor, cheaper, and more efficient (Seaboyer, 2016, 2018; Singer, 2018). Finally, the need to understand which adversarial influence operations are actually effective derives from the fact that our information space in democratic societies is much easier to target than the information space of our adversaries—in which the Internet is heavily censored and (and at least somewhat) contained by firewalls and other measures to reduce foreign influence. Therefore, in order to defend our open democratic societies, it is essential to understand which adversarial influence campaigns are effective so that defence resources can be directed to where they are likely to be the most effective.

For these and other reasons, Western governments are increasingly seeing the importance of understanding which influence campaigns are effective, and are therefore focussing efforts on increasing their abilities to measure the impact of influence campaigns.

Regardless of whether influence operations are being conducted on the traditional battlefield or in an online environment, key to evaluating the impact of an adversary's attempts at influence, as well as the efficacy of one's own efforts at influence, is the ability to measure attitudes in the target audiences of interest—as a first step to identifying the effectiveness of campaigns. More specifically, the impact of influence can only begin to be empirically evaluated when we are able to measure a target audience's attitudes both before and after exposure to that attempt. Alternatively, we must be able to measure attitudes in a subgroup of the target audience that has been exposed to an influence attempt, and then compare those attitudes to the attitudes of a comparable subgroup of the target audience that has not been exposed to the influence attempt. In either case, in the absence of an effective method for measuring attitudes, it is impossible to know which of an adversary's messages is proving especially effective, and thus to prioritize counteracting it. Likewise, it is difficult to know which of one's own influence operations are successful, and then accord them further resources.[1]

Unfortunately, the target audiences of adversaries' social influence operations are often not amenable to traditional methods of assessing public opinion (e.g., telephone or online surveys). For instance, members of radicalized audiences that are likely to be targets for recruitment by armed non-state actors might be expected to be unwilling to participate in a telephone survey on their views of political violence, and if they did participate, they might not be expected to give honest answers. Likewise, the target audiences of Canadian national security organizations' influence operations abroad are also unlikely to be audiences whose attitudes can be assessed using traditional approaches. For example, the soldiers of an adversary targeted by the CAF with PSYOPS leaflets urging surrender are unlikely to be in position to complete a survey indicating how seriously they are contemplating surrender. Thus, in many (perhaps most) cases in which national security organizations such as the CAF might wish to evaluate the efficacy of their own influence operations or those of their adversaries, the ability to measure the attitudes of target audiences is a major challenge.

The importance of measuring attitudes in such contexts, as well of the practical challenges of accomplishing this objective, have long been recognized by national security organizations such as the CAF. For example, in a comprehensive review of military PSYOPS training manuals from the United States, United Kingdom, Canada, and NATO, Fabrigar and Porter (2008) noted that such materials routinely acknowledged the importance of assessing the impact of social influence attempts and the need to develop non-traditional measures for doing so. However, their review also noted the absence of concrete standardized procedures for constructing such measures in these training materials.

Chapter Overview and Objectives

The central goal of the present chapter is to discuss some of the challenges of assessing attitudes in the sort of environments and among the target audiences for which social influence must be evaluated by the CAF and other national security organizations. As it turns out, some of these challenges parallel those faced by social scientists in other contexts. In an effort to overcome these challenges, social scientists have developed a number of indirect measures of attitudes (e.g., see Gawronski & De Houwer, 2014; Kidder & Campbell, 1970; Petty et al., 2009; Webb et al., 1966). We begin by reviewing the reasons why social scientists have sometimes used indirect attitude measures before providing an overview of traditional indirect measures and more contemporary indirect measures of attitudes that have been proposed to overcome these problems. In discussing these traditional and contemporary approaches, we describe the procedural features of these measures, discuss their strengths and weaknesses, and evaluate their potential utility for use by the CAF and other national security organizations. In the next section, we propose potential adaptations to existing indirect measurement approaches that might enhance their utility for national security applications. We also discuss more novel procedural innovations that build on the principles of prior indirect measures that could potentially lead to other indirect measures with practical utility for national security contexts. In the final section, we present a set of key unresolved issues that must be addressed in order to develop an enhanced capability to assess the impact of social influence operations in national security settings.

Traditional and Contemporary Indirect Measures of Attitudes: The Origins of Indirect Attitude Measurement

Beginning in the 1920s, researchers in psychology and related disciplines began to develop formal procedures for assessing people's attitudes (e.g., see Guttman, 1944; Likert, 1932; Osgood et al., 1957; Thurstone, 1928). These various procedures all involved what have been traditionally called "direct measures" of attitudes and are now more commonly termed "explicit measures" of attitudes. Essentially, direct measures assess people's attitudes in overt ways by specifically prompting people to report their likes and dislikes (e.g., "Do you favour or oppose the death penalty for serious crimes?"). Such direct measures, when carefully constructed, have substantial utility, and they continue to be the most common form of attitude measures used in both research and application. However, even at a fairly early phase in the history of the research literature on attitude measurement, social scientists recognized that direct measures were not without their limitations (e.g., see Hammond, 1948; Proshansky, 1943). Concerns regarding direct measures arose from two potential problems.

First, because direct measures are so overt, the intent of what they are designed to assess is readily apparent. For many issues (e.g., "To what extent do you have a negative versus positive opinion of Crest toothpaste?," "To what extent do you dislike versus like spaghetti?"), this property of direct measures is unlikely to be a problem as people might be entirely comfortable reporting their attitudes. In other cases, issues might be more sensitive, but placing people in a sufficiently comfortable context (e.g., in a situation where their answers are anonymous) might be sufficient for people to respond accurately. However, in other cases, the issues might be so sensitive, or mistrust on the part of respondents might be so pronounced, that people are unlikely to respond honestly even when their responses are anonymous. In these cases, people might be expected to refuse to answer questions, or, if they do answer, to provide answers they believe the questioner wishes to hear rather than their true views (i.e., to engage socially desirable responding; see Paulhus, 1991).

A second potential limitation with direct measures that was recognized early on in the attitude measurement literature, and which has been even more prominently featured in contemporary discussions of attitude measurement, is that direct measures are to some degree based on the assumption that people can accurately access their own attitudes. That is, in order for a person to directly report their attitudes, they must know what their attitude is. However, what if people have positive or negative reactions to something of which they are not consciously aware? Or alternatively, what if people have instant positive or negative "gut" reactions of which they are consciously aware, but whose accuracy they might doubt upon careful reflection? Despite their more considered doubts regarding these instant reactions, might these people's responses influence them when they are not actively monitoring these reactions? One might expect that direct measures of attitudes would do a poor job capturing such unconscious and/or spontaneously activated positive or negative reactions.

To overcome these potential problems, a number of "indirect measures" of attitudes (now more commonly termed "implicit measures" of attitudes) have been suggested.[2] Indirect measures involve a procedure for assessing attitudes that does not require overtly asking people their likes and dislikes. Rather, attitudes are inferred on the basis of some behavioural response or set of behavioural responses presumed to be related to the attitude of interest, or on the basis of how people perform some judgmental task presumed to be related to the target attitude of interest. Initial interest in indirect measures began in the 1940s and continued to grow through the 1950s and '60s (see Kidder & Campbell, 1970; Webb et al., 1966). While interest in indirect measures never entirely disappeared, it waned somewhat over the next thirty years, and then exploded in the early 2000s under the rubric of "implicit measures" (Porter, 2010). This interest has continued for the past twenty years, and the study of implicit measures remains a major topic of inquiry in contemporary social psychology and related disciplines (Gawronski & De Houwer, 2014; Petty et al., 2009).

Traditional Indirect Measures

Early attempts to indirectly measure attitudes were based on projective approaches (e.g., the thematic appreciation test; see Proshansky, 1943), but indirect measures soon evolved into more structured judgmental tasks (e.g., error choice; see Hammond, 1948) or behavioural observation procedures (e.g., lost letter; see Milgram et al., 1965).[3] Here, we discuss some of the better-known traditional indirect measures to illustrate the logic underlying these procedures and comment on their strengths and limitations.

BEHAVIOURAL OBSERVATIONS

One general approach to indirectly measuring attitudes is through the examination of a person's demonstrable behaviour. The underlying premise of this approach is that, if someone has a favourable or unfavourable attitude toward an attitude object, then it would presumably be reflected in their behaviour toward that attitude object. One of the best-known early examples of this approach is the lost letter technique (LLT) (Milgram et al., 1965). In this technique, a specific attitude object is identified (e.g., legalized abortion). A large number of pre-addressed and stamped envelopes are then randomly left in a variety of public locations. Half of the envelopes are addressed to an organization (fictitious but plausibly real) that someone could clearly identify as being positive toward the specific attitude object (e.g., "The Citizen Pro-Choice Coalition") and the other half addressed to an organization that could be clearly identified as negative toward the attitude object (e.g., "The Pro-Life Citizen Alliance"). The researcher then tracks how many letters are delivered to each addressee. The underlying assumption of this technique is that when a letter is found, people assume it has been accidentally dropped and are more likely to place it in a mailbox if it is addressed to an organization that is consistent with their own attitude, thereby providing a rough estimate of the popularity of each position. In this way, the people are not affected by social desirability because no one, other than themselves, are aware of their actions. Research has indicated that the LLT provides a reasonable overall estimate of the popularity of a given attitudinal position in a group of people (i.e., the group of people represented by the physical local in which the letters were initially distributed; Milgram et al., 1965), and can even function adequately in settings where people might fear for their physical safety were they to openly express their opinions (Kremer et al., 1986). However, one limitation of the approach is that although it can be used to infer the general distribution of two opposing views in a group of people, it does not provide individual-level information regarding the opinions of specific people (i.e., one has no way of deducing who specifically returned letters and thus what their opinions might be).

More recently, the LLT has been adapted to work in a more current technologically oriented environment focusing on emails rather than letters (Stern & Faber, 1997; Vaughan-Johnston et al., 2021). As a result, the name has been changed to the lost email technique (LET). The underlying premise of this technique is similar to the LLT, except emails are sent "in error," with the rates of return assessed (Stern & Faber, 1997). In the LLT the participant has two options (mail or ignore the letter), whereas in the LET the recipient of the email can ignore or delete (interfere with the communication), send the message to the intended recipient, or return the email to the originator (letting them know that they made an error). The discrepancies in return rates in the LET can then be interpreted as either approval or disapproval of the contents (i.e., message) of the email (Bushman & Bonacci, 2004; Stern & Faber, 1997). In the case of the LET, one would often be able to infer the identity of individuals who received emails and whether they returned/forwarded the email or ignored/deleted them. Thus, one could infer individual-level attitudes, although such inferences would provide only a crude dichotomous assessment of attitudes (i.e., whether people are positive or negative in their evaluations, but not the extremity of those evaluations) and would likely reflect a substantial amount of error (e.g., some people might inadvertently miss the email or be very busy at the time the email arrives or regard the email as spam).

There are a number of other behavioural observation methods that have demonstrated validity in applied settings (Webb et al., 1966). Behavioural observation is the systematic recording of behaviour (usually surreptitiously) by an observer. The underlying premise of this approach is that, if someone has a favourable or unfavourable attitude toward an attitude object, then it would presumably be reflected in their behaviours toward that attitude object. Additionally, because evidence of people's attitudes is gathered from unobtrusive observation, attitudes can be assessed without affecting the behaviour of the people whose attitudes are being assessed (Webb et al., 1966). A number of general categories of behaviour have been suggested as reflective of attitudes. For example, Webb et al. (1966) noted that the physical distance people place between themselves in environments in which they can control their physical location can be used to infer interpersonal attitudes. Likewise, the tone of a person's voice when discussing a particular attitudinal position or when interacting with another person can be reflective of their attitudes toward that attitudinal position or that person. Obviously, any single behaviour will be determined by multiple factors and as such provides a very imperfect measure of attitudes. However, if a variety of behavioural responses can be aggregated, this aggregate score is likely to provide a more accurate assessment of attitudes.

Such observational behaviour approaches have often been advocated for use in military settings such as the assessment of PSYOPS activities (Goldstein & Findley, 1996). In theatre, for example, this could be the number of opposition soldiers that surrender following an information operation, or the number of posters torn down advocating a particular group or stand on a policy. However, discussions of behavioural observation measures have generally been highly specific and illustrative rather than leading to the development of standardized behavioural assessment procedures that might be applied broadly such as the LLT.

As with the LLT, in many cases it will not be possible to track the identity of specific people who have performed the target behaviours (e.g., the specific people who tore down posters). Thus, such observational measures will generally not permit the collection of individual-level information regarding people's attitudes as much as group-level information regarding the popularity of a particular position within a specified region or target group.

JUDGMENTAL BIAS APPROACHES

An early indirect approach to attitude measurement involved the use of a modified self-report measure called structured objective questionnaires. In this method, respondents are given what they believed to be an objective information test that assesses their knowledge on a particular subject; however, some of the questions are not objective and have no correct response. Rather, these questions have responses intentionally weighted for or against an attitude object and randomly dispersed within the information test (Coffin, 1941; Hammond, 1948; Kubany, 1953; Newcomb, 1940, 1946; Smith, 1947; Weschler, 1950a, 1950b). The underlying premise of this approach is that there is a relationship between a person's attitudes and how they interpret information presented as fact. That is, this method assumes that when people are presented with a question for which they do not know the correct response, their guessing reflects the respondents' attitudes (Coffin, 1941; Hammond, 1948; Newcomb, 1946).

Probably the best exemplar of this general approach is the error choice (EC) technique (Hammond, 1948). The EC technique involves presenting a set of objective knowledge questions that are in principle knowable but unlikely to be known and whose response options imply something either positive or negative about the attitude object. This procedure rests on two basic premises. First, when people are faced with a knowledge-based question for which they do not know the answer, their guess will not be random; and one factor that they might rely upon in such guessing is their attitude. For example, when faced with a question where there are two factual possible answers, they will tend to pick the answer that best fits with their attitude. Thus, across a series of objective knowledge questions that are in principle knowable, but to which respondents are very unlikely to know the true answers, one might expect to find a systematic guess pattern that is consistent with people's attitudes. The second premise of the measure is that, because each of the items is presented as a factual question, people will not be aware that their attitude is being assessed. Early research suggested that the EC technique had promise, but its performance was never fully evaluated in subsequent research. More recent examinations of EC have provided further encouraging evidence (see Porter, 2010). Specifically, answers to EC questions do appear to reflect a single systematic response pattern that is comparatively reliable and at least in part represents the respondent's attitude. These studies also suggest that (as intended) this response pattern to the EC questions is highly resistant to socially desirable responding. Importantly, completion of measures allows for the collection of individual-level information about peoples' attitudes, just as completion of direct measures provides such information.

Contemporary Indirect Measures

Beginning in the late 1990s, interest in indirect measures of attitudes underwent a renaissance with the emergence of a new generation of indirect measures (e.g., Fazio et al., 1995; Greenwald et al., 1998), now more commonly referred to as implicit measures. These new methods built on methodological procedures used and phenomena documented in the research literatures within cognitive psychology and social cognition. These new implicit measures required the use of computers, which allowed for very precise timing in the presentation of stimuli and high-resolution recording of reaction times in responding to stimuli. Although different implicit measures vary in their specifics, all of these procedures involve presenting people with stimuli related to the topic of interest (i.e., the attitude object), usually in the form of words and/or images, and then asking people to perform some sort of judgmental task related to the stimuli. Some aspect of how these judgments are performed (e.g., the speed with which judgments are made) is assessed. This task performance criterion is, on the basis of some theoretical logic, presumed to be influenced by the attitude of interest. Importantly, these measures are all indirect in that they never specifically ask people to report their attitudes. A number of such measures have been proposed (see Gawronski & De Houwer, 2014; Petty et al., 2009). For purposes of illustration, we will just briefly discuss three of the better-known of these contemporary indirect measures.

Implicit Association Task

The implicit association task (or IAT; see Greenwald et al., 1998) is a measure that, in its original form, assesses attitudes toward two competing persons, objects, or concepts. The technique has most famously been used to assess prejudice toward social groups (e.g., racial groups), but can be adapted to assess attitudes toward virtually anything. Participants complete rapid judgment tasks in which they are instructed to sort words (or images) into one of two categories as quickly as possible using one of two designated computer keys to indicate the group to which the word belongs.

For example, an IAT designed to measure attitudes toward Canada versus the United States would first present respondents with words either associated with Canada (maple leaf, Ottawa) or America (Washington, DC, bald eagle). Respondents indicate for each word presented whether it is a word related to Canada or America by pressing one of the two designated keys. They are then presented with a new list of words (e.g., death, love, vomit, peace) with a second categorization task of indicating whether the words are positive or negative, once again using the two designated response keys.

In the critical later phases, these two categorization tasks are combined so that words are randomly presented from either list (Canada/America and positive/negative), but only two response keys are used, which mean the keys must be shared for both categorization tasks. For example, if the classifying categories are Canada/America and positive/negative, one of the two keys might be designated for words that are related to Canada or positive, and the other key for words that are related to America or bad. In a later phase, this sorting task is repeated for the reverse combination of shared keys (i.e., if the first round used Canada/positive and America/negative, the next phase would use America/positive and Canada/negative as the shared response keys). The time it takes for participants to sort each word after presentation is recorded.

The theory behind the IAT is that strong congruent associations between concepts should lead to fast responses when they share a response key, and that strong incongruent associations between concepts should lead to slow responses when they share a response key. In other words, if people have very positive attitudes toward Canada, they should be relatively fast at performing the task when Canada/positive share the same response key compared to when Canada/negative share the same response key. Likewise, very positive attitudes toward America should produce a response pattern in which people are much faster when America/positive share the same response key than when America/bad share the same response key. Thus, the difference in time it takes for people to perform the task when Canada/positive and America/negative share keys compared to when America/positive and Canada/negative share response keys provides a measure of whether people's attitudes toward Canada are more positive versus negative than their attitudes toward America. Revised versions of the IAT have been developed that can be used to assess attitudes toward a single group, concept, or person (Karpinski & Steinman, 2006).

The strengths of the IAT mainly revolve around its implicit nature; by assessing implicit evaluations through quick reaction time–based tasks, respondents do not have time to consider whether their responses are socially appropriate. Similarly, word sorting does not have very intuitive connections to attitude assessment, and thus respondents will be less likely to ascertain the intent of the measure, further shielding them from socially desirable modified responses. Another strength of the IAT is its versatility; it can be formatted to measure associations between any classification/concept (e.g., black/white, fat/thin, America/Iraq) and virtually any attribute (good/bad, strong/weak). Thus, the core procedure of the IAT can be adapted to study a wide range of judgments.

Of course, the practical weaknesses of the IAT include its resource demand and the vulnerability of its accuracy to outside interference. The IAT is a computer task that requires limited distractions for an extended period of time (often fifteen to twenty minutes) in order to gather high-resolution data based on reaction times. Thus, participants in uncontrolled settings might be unwilling or unable to complete the IAT appropriately, although reasonably good data can be collected in online settings if respondents are sufficiently motivated and have a location where they can perform the task that is not too distracting (e.g., Xu et al., 2014).

Evaluative Priming

Evaluative priming (or EP, also sometimes referred to as affective priming; see Fazio et al., 1995) involves presenting target words (or images) representing the topic of interest for which one wants to measure attitudes along with words (or images) representing positive or negative evaluation. The words representing the topic of interest serve as the "primes," and the words representing positive or negative evaluation serve as the targets of judgment. In this task, respondents are told that they will first be presented with an orientation word to help focus their gaze on the appropriate location on the computer screen (the prime) and that this word will appear only briefly, rapidly followed by the target word. They must then judge as quickly as possible if the target word is either positive or negative. For each judgment, the speed with which the target word is judged is recorded by the computer.

For example, if EP was being used to measure attitudes toward Canada, the prime words used for each trial would be words strongly related to Canada (e.g., maple leaf, Ottawa). The target words would be words almost universally seen as positive or negative (e.g., love, vomit). The EP procedure is based on a well-documented phenomenon that when evaluative responses are evoked, they will tend to facilitate the ease with which people can make judgments about things congruent with that evaluation and will interfere with judgments about things incongruent with the evaluation. Thus, if people have very positive attitudes toward Canada, the Canada-related prime words should evoke positive evaluative responses in people, which will in turn make them very fast at categorizing positive target words (e.g., love) and very slow at categorizing negative target words (e.g., vomit). People with negative attitudes toward Canada should have negative evaluative responses evoked by the Canada-related prime words, thus showing a reverse pattern (i.e., fast at judging negative words and slow at judging positive words). The difference in the average speed of judging positive target words versus negative target words that are preceded by Canada-related prime words provides the measure of people's attitudes.

Evaluative priming shares some of the same practical strengths and weaknesses of the IAT. The task itself largely bypasses any effortful modification of responses due to the primed words being presented very briefly and the need to categorize target words very quickly. Importantly, people are never asked to make any judgments of the word primes themselves (which are the words actually related to the topic of interest), and thus the intent of the task is not readily apparent. However, like the IAT, it requires a reasonably large number of judgment trials to be valid, and thus requires some extended time and effort on the part of respondents. Likewise, the high-resolution concerning reaction times required for the measure are vulnerable to outside distractions.

AFFECT-MISATTRIBUTION PROCEDURE

Similar to evaluative priming, the affect-misattribution procedure (or AMP; see Payne et al., 2005) uses words (or images) related to the topic of interest as "primes" in a judgmental task. However, the specific targets of judgment in the task are somewhat different in that they are stimuli that would not be expected to evoke a negative or positive evaluation (e.g., an abstract shape, symbol, or ideograph). Participants are then asked to judge target neutral stimuli as either positive or negative.

For instance, continuing with our attitudes toward Canada example, the primes could once again be words related to Canada (e.g., maple leaf, Ottawa). The neutral stimuli could be letters from an ancient language unknown to the respondents. For each trial, the prime word (e.g., maple leaf, Ottawa) would very briefly appear, rapidly followed by a letter from the ancient language, which itself is presented only briefly. Respondents are then queried to judge if they feel more positive or negative toward the letter that was just presented.

The logic behind the AMP is simple; the primed word will trigger an evaluative response within the respondent, which, because of the very brief presentations of both the prime and the target of judgment, will subsequently be misattributed to the neutral stimulus. Hence, the task works via affect misattribution, as the evaluation of the ambiguous stimulus is directly influenced by an individual's evaluation of the primes representing the topic of interest (e.g., Canada). Thus, in the case of our example, positive attitudes toward Canada would be expected to produce a response pattern in which people tend to report being positive toward most of the letters that are preceded by Canada-related words. In contrast, negative attitudes toward Canada would be expected to produce a response pattern in which most of the letters preceded by Canada-related words would be judged negative.

Like the IAT and EP, the AMP is opaque in its intent in that people are never asked to judge the primes (i.e., the stimuli directly related to the topic of interest). Additionally, because of the very rapid presentation of stimuli, it is very difficult for people to exert intentional control over their responses. Indeed, instructing respondents to not allow the primes to have any effect on their judgments of targets has little actual impact on their judgments of the neutral stimuli (e.g., ancient letters). Because the procedure involves very precise timing in presenting stimuli, it requires computers in order to be administered. However, the procedure makes no use of the reaction time of the respondents, but instead simply the proportion of positive versus negative responses to the letters or other neutral stimuli. Thus, it is likely less sensitive to distractions. Additionally, the measure can be used with comparatively few trials and thus can be completed in just a few minutes. Hence, the simpler nature of the AMP makes it a potential candidate for wider adoption in a variety of circumstances.

Concluding Thoughts on Existing Indirect Measures of Attitudes

As illustrated in our review, the use of indirect measures has a long history in social psychology and related disciplines. In some respects, the reasons for developing these measures arose in response to challenges that parallel the sort of issues faced by the CAF and other national security organizations when they attempt to gauge the efficacy of their own influence operations or those of their adversaries (e.g., concerns that target audiences might be unwilling to honestly report their attitudes). Specifically, these existing measures were designed to assess attitudes in audiences and/or contexts where people might be unwilling or unable to respond to overt attitude measures.

That being said, there are important practical differences in how these existing measures have been applied in social science research and the likely contexts and audiences for which they would need to be used in national security settings. In many situations, the contexts and audiences in national security settings present far more challenging practical constraints, and thus one cannot assume that respondents will have either the ability or the motivation to undertake lengthy measurement procedures, even when they are unaware of the intent of these procedures. For instance, soldiers of an adversary are unlikely to have the opportunity or inclination to complete a twenty-minute IAT procedure assessing their attitudes toward surrender. Thus, comparatively few of these indirect measures are likely to be suitable in their current form for use in national security settings. That being said, many of the core concepts and procedures underlying these existing indirect measures could provide a foundation for developing indirect measures that might be suitable for these more demanding contexts and audiences (e.g., enemy soldiers on a battlefield). It is this possibility to which we turn our attention in the next section of this chapter.

Developing Indirect Measures for National Security Settings

Conceptually, indirect attitude measures share a number of features. Most notably, people are never directly asked to report their attitude, making it difficult to deduce what exactly these techniques are measuring. In addition, many of these procedures are designed to assess attitudes without giving people a chance to intentionally adjust or consider their responses, which can be important for gathering information in areas where expressing one's true attitude may carry negative consequences and/or when one wants to assess people's instant "gut" reactions. That said, the contemporary techniques that are particularly salient here are computer-based assessments that require attention and time, which can often not be guaranteed in field settings. In some cases, it might be possible to overcome these practical challenges simply by presenting these tasks in creative ways that might be likely to engage people to expend the effort to complete the procedures. Thus, with some minor adaptations, existing measures could be rendered suitable in some circumstances. In other cases, more fundamental changes might be necessary that ultimately involve creating new indirect measures. However, even in these cases, the existing measures might provide a conceptual and/or procedural starting point upon which to base these new measures.

Potential Adaptations of Existing Indirect Measures

Even if the exact procedures for the techniques previously discussed cannot be precisely replicated for use in some field settings, the core procedural features could be utilized in many settings where online-based administration of measures is feasible. As we have noted, with the explosion of social media platforms for communication, much of the social influence conducted by adversaries and the government organizations tasked with countering them is likely to occur in online settings or via other forms of digital communication. Many of the methods previously discussed could be administered in these settings, and indeed social scientists have been collecting data using indirect measures in online settings for many years (e.g., the Project Implicit Website at https://implicit.harvard.edu/implicit/; see also Xu et al., 2014). The primary challenge is finding ways to "frame" the purpose of these tasks such that they are at best likely to encourage people to devote time to completing them, and at worst do not cause the target audience to actively avoid responding to these measures. That is, these measures must be opaque not only in terms of what they are measuring, but also who is sponsoring them and the purpose for which the information is being used.

In considering existing measures for adaptation, perhaps the easiest might be the error-choice technique (EC) and the affect-misattribution procedure (AMP), because neither measure requires high-resolution response-time data and both are comparatively short in duration. These procedures could be administered in online environments and likely completed even in contexts where people have some outside auditory distractions. However, plausible cover stories would need to be provided for the purposes of such measures. For example, the AMP could be presented under the guise of a game that informs the respondent of a certain skill based on their evaluation of neutral stimulus. Judging unknown letters might be framed as a measure of people's ability to learn or intuit new languages or symbol systems. In the case of the EC, it could be framed as a test of people's knowledge of certain topics or general trivia knowledge. Importantly, just as such Internet games often include prizes for performance, similar prizes could be offered to induce people to undertake these tasks. Such games could be advertised on social media, where they would be exposed to many people within a specified geographical area, interest group, or other designation to allow for widespread but precise data collection.

Similarly, if the target group of interest is likely to be accessing measures in contexts where distractions are comparatively modest and they might have time to complete lengthier measures (e.g., a home or a workplace setting), reaction time–based measures such as EP and IAT could be feasible. These tasks could be advertised as "reaction time" or "brain age" tests for participants to assess their cognitive speed. Once again, incentives could be offered and advertisements on social media outlets could be targeted at designated groups.

Potential New Indirect Attitude Measures

In other cases, it might not be feasible to adapt existing measures, or it might be useful to develop new measures to supplement existing ones. In these cases, following the general logic of traditional indirect measures based on behavioural observations could be an avenue for developing new measures. However, the opportunities for collecting behavioural data are far richer now than was the case in the 1950s and '60s, when these approaches were originally developed. The vast majority of countries now either have widespread Internet access or are approaching that point; using this medium to gather behavioural information could be invaluable due to the unprecedented reach it enjoys among the potential audience.

Researchers could construct websites focusing on a central topic of interest and advertise them via social media. A target audience's engagement with the content of these websites could be measured by counting the number of visits to a site, average time spent on a website, and registered email subscriptions. Additionally, activity can be monitored for various pages of the website covering different types of content to compare which content is engaged with more and can therefore be interpreted as reflective of attitudes. In addition to advertising the website through social media, flyers with QR codes could be posted or distributed to a target audience.

In addition to websites, social media could be directly engaged to assess user attitudes. Many social media outlets have built-in measures of community engagement (e.g., Facebook "likes," Twitter "likes" and "retweets," YouTube views and subscriptions, and Reddit "upvotes") where the degree of community engagement and valenced evaluations of content can be directly ascertained. For example, Facebook is one of the most used social media outlets worldwide and has many different methods with which users can engage with people. Creating and advertising a "Facebook page" that represents a certain belief or idea would allow a researcher to assess a target audience's engagement with said beliefs by measuring the number of people who follow that page and "like" its posts. Similarly, comments on said posts can be coded for valence and intensity to assess attitudes toward them (see Rockledge et al., 2018). Overall, Facebook has the potential to be a versatile and far-reaching tool for data and information collection.

Twitter is another highly popular social media outlet that measures an online community's engagement with short messages or images via "likes," which indicate approval of a message, and "retweets," where a user reposts another user's message to their own social network. Both of these responses can be gauged to assess the degree of exposure and agreement with the associated public posts. Like Facebook, Twitter users can reply to posts while simultaneously spreading them to their own social network. Thus, engagement allows the message to be more visible to more people, creating a snowball effect for data collection.

In addition to the previous outlets, researchers can use YouTube to upload videos containing certain messages or arguments and track engagement through view count, subscriptions to the channel that posts the video (indicating that the user wishes to see more content of the same nature), and monitoring the like/dislike ratio and comments on the video itself. Videos also allow for richer stimuli to be tested on social media users for assessing attitudinal responses.

In summary, the Internet offers a vast array of options for presenting members of a target audience with opportunities for engaging in behaviours related to a given topic of interest that might be used to reliably infer those people's attitudes. However, recent developments in data analytics might permit this method to achieve even higher levels of accuracy than was possible with earlier behavioural observation techniques. More specifically, an emerging literature in the social sciences has focused on developing computational algorithms that can be used to infer specific attributes of people from their "digital footprints" (i.e., their online activities). Thus, large of arrays of online behavioural responses can be combined using formal computational algorithms optimized for accuracy of prediction.

For example, inferences regarding personality traits on the basis of social media content can be made using computer-based algorithms that outperform the judgments of laypeople examining the same social media content (see meta-analytic summaries by Azucar et al., 2018, and Hinds & Joison, 2019; see also Park et al., 2015). However, inferences are not confined to personality traits. Research suggests that prediction algorithms can be used to infer a variety of other characteristics such as sexual orientation, ethnicity, religious and political views, intelligence, happiness, age, and gender (e.g., Kern et al., 2016; Kosinski et al., 2013; Settanni et al., 2018). It is also possible to infer more specific features of people's attitudes such as their emotionality and extremity (e.g., Rockledge et al., 2018). Thus, it might be possible to construct websites and/or create social media content to elicit behavioural responses in a target audience and then develop specific computational algorithms to optimize the value of this information for inferring attitudes on the topic of interest.

Of course, not all situations in which social influence is assessed will be amenable to Internet-based data collection. For example, the CAF will still find itself confronting situations in which the efficacy of its influence operations or those of its adversaries must be assessed in places such as a physical battlefield. In these contexts, adapting traditional behavioural observation measures might still be possible. Following the general logic of procedures such as the LLT, it might be possible to develop tangible physical communications (e.g., leaflets, posters) or other actions that imply a certain attitudinal position and then create contexts where people have the possibility to engage in behavioural response that either facilitate or inhibit these efforts. One might then infer the prevalence of attitudinal positions at an aggregate level, or, if precise behavioural data can be collected on individuals, perhaps even at an individual level. Importantly, one could in principle develop computational algorithms that combine responses to a variety of these focal behavioural actions so as to enhance the accuracy of inferring attitudes from such behaviours, just as they are used to more accurately infer attributes on the basis of online behaviours. Developing "standardized behavioural opportunity" protocols that mimic essential features of techniques such as the LLT and that can be applied with only modest modification across a range of situations constitutes one of the great challenges and potential opportunities for enhancing the ability to evaluate social influence operations. Equally important and promising is the effort to developing more sophisticated and efficient data analytic procedures for inferring information from this behavioural observation data.

Concluding Thoughts

While many promising methods of indirect attitude assessment have been developed over the years, the research focusing on the application of these methods to field settings, particularly of the sort often faced by militaries and other national security organizations, has been relatively sparse. Indeed, some of these techniques are dependent on controlled environments to minimize distractions and involve relatively lengthy procedures that can become tedious. Given these facts, many of the current indirect measures of attitudes are likely to be more suitable to relatively controlled environments, and particularly to audiences that are at least reasonably motivated to be co-operative.

That being said, these challenges are by no means insurmountable, and this research literature has the potential to provide valuable contributions to the efforts of government security organizations seeking to better assess the impact of their own social influence operations and those of their adversaries. A few of these procedures might, with only modest adaptations, be employed in some relevant field settings. Likewise, established indirect attitude assessment techniques employ general principles that can be retained and transferred to new mediums and designs that could be suitable for an even wider range of naturalistic environments. Of course, the potential adaptations and innovations we have discussed are at this point speculative. Future research would need to be conducted to fully develop the procedural details of these adaptations and new approaches and to evaluate their validity. Thus, if a robust capability in assessing the impact of social influence operations is to be developed by the CAF and other Canadian government organizations tasked with conducting and countering such activities, a sustained commitment to empirically investigating indirect measures will need to be undertaken. Such challenges are unlikely to be addressed by the academic community on its own.

Equally important, the CAF and other relevant organizations will also need to make a sustained commitment to carefully consider the doctrinal issues that arise from utilizing such measures. For example, our speculations regarding the alternative ways in which existing measures such as the EC and AMP might be presented involve the active deception of respondents. Indirect measures necessarily involve some level of deception and/or ambiguity, the cost of which will have to be weighed against the potential benefits of obtaining such information.

Additionally, there are important operational considerations that must be addressed. If such techniques are employed, there is the distinct possibility that adversary governments and organizations will condemn such techniques of information gathering. As such, they may intervene to stop or corrupt data collection. This can be done directly by having websites taken down, engaging in cyber-attacks, or feeding fake/useless information through the data-collection streams. Indirect methods of shutting down such research can also be employed (e.g., disabling Internet access in areas of interest, or warning people to be suspicious of new surveys and pages on their social media pages). These practical challenges will need to considered and tactics for coping with them developed accordingly.

In summary, because these techniques are novel to the CAF and other security organizations, many implications, as well as the potential challenges of indirectly assessing attitudes in national security applications, remain unknown. More empirical research and doctrinal development are required if the potential of these techniques is to be fully realized and the related risks fully appreciated. Ultimately, it is important to grapple with not only the questions of if and how these measures can be used, but also whether they should be used at all, and if so, for whom and under what circumstances.

Authors' Note

Preparation of this chapter was supported in part by an Insight Development Grant (430-2019-00099) from the Social Science and Humanities Research Council of Canada (SSHRC) of Canada to the first and third authors and Insight Grants (435-2015-0114, 435-2022-0034) from SSHRC to the third author.

NOTES

1 It should be noted that in most influence operations in national security settings (as well as other applied settings), the ultimate goal of operations is some form of behavioural outcome, be it a very specific target behaviour or a broad pattern of behavioural responses across an array of relevant behaviours. Generally, attitude change is a necessary but not sufficient condition for achieving broad and enduring behavioural change. Thus, the assessment of attitude change can provide a preliminary evaluation of the likelihood of success of an influence operation, but not a definitive verdict on its ultimate efficacy. The topic of when and why attitudes predict behaviour and how to assess the likelihood that attitude change might be expected to translate into changes in behaviour is itself the subject of a large research literature that goes beyond the scope of this chapter (see Fabrigar et al., 2019; Fabrigar et al., 2010).

2 Throughout this chapter, we primarily use the terms "direct/indirect attitude measures" to differentiate between traditional attitude measures that overtly ask people to report their attitudes and more subtle forms of attitude measurement that never overtly ask people to report their attitudes. This terminology has been the traditional set of labels for differentiating between overt and subtle attitude measures, but it is less commonly used in contemporary discussions of attitude measurement. Instead, the terms "explicit/implicit" have become more popular. In many discussions, the manner in which these two sets of terms have been used can be considered interchangeable. However, in some contemporary discussions (e.g., Gawronski & De Houwer, 2014), the term "implicit measure" has been used in a somewhat more restrictive manner to refer to indirect measures that are presumed to reflect comparatively automatic psychological processes that operate outside people's intentional control. For this reason, we use the "direct/indirect" terms, which refer to the overtness of the measure and convey no formal assumptions regarding the nature of the psychological process it reflects.

3 Another alternative approach to direct measures of attitudes is the use of physiological responses. A number of physiological measures of attitudes have been proposed (Blascovich, 2014), some of which have been found to function reasonably well. Because such measures are unlikely to be feasible in the field settings in which one might expect to use attitude measures for the purposes we discuss, we do not analyze these measures in this chapter.

REFERENCES

Azucar, D., Maregndo, D., & Settanni, M. (2018). Predicting Big 5 personality traits from digital footprints on social media: A meta-analysis. *Personality and Individual Differences, 124*, 150–9. https://doi.org/10.1016/j.paid.2017.12.018

Blascovich, J. (2014). Using physiological indexes in social psychological research. In H. T. Reis & C. M. Judd (Eds.), *Handbook of research methods in social and personality psychology* (2nd ed., pp. 101–22). Cambridge University Press.

Bushman, B. J., & Bonacci, A. M. (2004). You've got mail: Using e-mail to examine the effect of prejudiced attitudes on discrimination against Arabs. *Journal of Experimental Social Psychology, 40*(6), 753–9. https://doi.org/10.1016/j.jesp.2004.02.001

Coffin, T. E. (1941). Some conditions of suggestion and suggestibility: A study of certain attitudinal and situational factors influencing the process of suggestion. *Psychological Monographs, 53*(4), 125–7. https://doi.org/10.1037/h0093490

Fabrigar, L. R., MacDonald, T. K., & Wegener, D. T. (2019). The origins and structure of attitudes. In D. Albarracin & B. T. Johnson (Eds.), *Handbook of attitudes and attitude change*, vol. 1 (2nd ed., pp. 109–57). Routledge.

Fabrigar, L. R. & Porter, R. D. (2008). *Evaluating the psychology in psychological operations: An assessment of the state of psychological knowledge in Canadian Forces' PSYOPS training* (Research Report 2008-01). Royal Military College of Canada.

Fabrigar, L. R., Wegener, D. T., & MacDonald, T. K. (2010). Distinguishing between prediction and influence: Multiple processes underlying attitude-behavior consistency. In C. R. Agnew, D. E. Carlston, W. G. Graziano, & J. R. Kelly (Eds.), *Then a miracle occurs: Focusing on behavior in social psychological theory and research* (pp. 162–85). Oxford University Press.

Fazio, R. H., Jackson, J. R., Dunton, B. C., & Williams, C. J. (1995). Variability in automatic activation as an unobtrusive measure of racial attitudes: A bone fide pipeline? *Journal of Personality and Social Psychology, 69*(6),1013–27. https://doi.org/10.1037/0022-3514.69.6.1013

Gawronski, B. & De Houwer, J. (2014). Implicit measures in social and personality psychology. In H. T. Reis & C. M. Judd (Eds.), *Handbook of research methods in social and personality psychology* (2nd ed., pp. 283–310). Cambridge University Press.

Gerasimov, V. (2016). The value of science is in the foresight: New challenges demand rethinking the forms and methods of carrying out combat operations. *Military Review*, January–February, pp. 23–9.

Goldstein, F. L., & Findley, B. F. (1996). *Psychological operations: Principles and case studies*. Air University Press.

Greenwald, A. G., McGhee, D. E., & Schwartz, J. L. K. (1998). Measuring individual differences in implicit cognition: The implicit association test. *Journal of*

Personality and Social Psychology, 74(6), 1464–80. https://doi.org/10.1037/0022-3514.74.6.1464

Guttman, L. (1944). A basis for scaling qualitative data. *American Sociological Review, 9*(2), 139–50. https://doi.org/10.2307/2086306

Hammond, K. R. (1948). Measuring attitudes by error-choice: An indirect method. *Journal of Abnormal and Social Psychology, 43*(1), 38–48. https://doi.org/10.1037/h0059576

Hinds, J., & Joinson, A. (2019). Human and computer personality prediction from digital footprints. *Current Directions in Psychological Science, 28*(2), 204–11. https://doi.org/10.1177/0963721419827849

Karpinski, A. & Steinman, R. B. (2006). A single category implicit association test as a measure of implicit cognition. *Journal of Personality and Social Psychology, 91*(1), 16–32. https://doi.org/10.1037/0022-3514.91.1.16

Kern, M. L., Park, G., Eichstaedt, J. C., Schwartz, H. A., Sap, M., Smith, L. K., & Ungar, L. H. (2016). Gaining insights from social media language: Methodologies and challenges. *Psychological Methods, 21*(4), 507–25. https://doi.org/10.1037/met0000091

Kidder, L. H., & Campbell, D. T. (1970). The indirect testing of social attitudes. In G. F. Summers (Ed.), *Attitude measurement* (pp. 333–85). Rand McNally & Co.

Kim, Y. M., Hsu J., Neiman D., et al. (2018). The stealth media? Groups and targets behind divisive issue campaigns on Facebook. *Political Communication, 35*(4), 515–41. https://doi.org/10.1080/10584609.2018.1476425

Kosinski, M., Stillwell, D., & Graepel, T. (2013). Private traits and attributes are predictable from digital records of human behavior. *Proceedings of the National Academy of Sciences, 110*(15), 5802–5. https://doi.org/10.1073/pnas.1218772110

Kremer, J., Barry, R., & McNally, A. (1986). The misdirected letter and the quasi-questionnaire: Unobtrusive measures of prejudice in Northern Ireland. *Journal of Applied Social Psychology, 16*(4), 303–9. https://doi.org/10.1111/j.1559-1816.1986.tb01142.x

Kubany, A. J. (1953). A validation study of the error-choice technique using attitudes on national health insurance. *Educational and Psychological Measurement, 13*(2), 157–63. https://journals.sagepub.com/doi/pdf/10.1177/001316445301300201?casa_token=CMyHev5uD3MAAAAA:A9fppFAINUwxlaVfTVe9KrY2WCx5Z70mkLoZtpX9NxOoxrWtVeiuIcDmg1U5EfgdUezVtXkOmGp-Lw

Lewis, P., Hilder, P. (2018, 23 March). Leaked: Cambridge Analytica's blueprint for Trump victory. *The Guardian*. https://www.theguardian.com/uk-news/2018/mar/23/leaked-cambridge-analyticas-blueprint-for-trump-victory

Likert, R. (1932). A technique for the measurement of attitudes. *Archives of Psychology, 22*(140), 5–55.

Milgram, S., Mann, L., & Harter., S. (1965). The lost-letter technique: A tool of social research. *Public Opinion Quarterly, 29*, 436–7. http://www.communicationcache.

com/uploads/1/0/8/8/10887248/the_lost-letter_technique-_a_tool_of_social_research.pdf

Newcomb, T. M. (1940). Labor unions as seen by their members: An attempt to measure attitudes. In G. W. Hartmann, & T. M. Newcomb (Eds.), *Industrial conflict* (pp. 313–38). Cordon.

Newcomb, T. M. (1946). The influence of attitude climate upon some determinants of information. *Journal of Abnormal and Social Psychology, 41*(3), 291–302. https://doi.org/10.1037/h0058824

Osgood, C. E., Suci, G. J., & Tannenbaum, P. H. (1957). *The measurement of meaning.* University of Illinois Press.

Park, G., Schwartz, H. A., Eichstaedt, J. C., Kern, M. L., Kosinski, M., Stillwell, D. J., Ungar, L. H., & Seligman, M. E. P. (2015). Automatic personality assessment through social media language. *Journal of Personality and Social Psychology, 108*, 934–52.

Payne, B. K., Cheng, C. M., Govorun, O., & Stewart, B. D. (2005). An inkblot for attitudes: Affect misattribution as implicit measurement. *Journal of Personality and Social Psychology, 89*, 277–93. https://doi.org/10.1037/0022-3514.89.3.277

Petty, R. E., Fazio, R. H., & Briñol, P. (Eds.). (2009). *Attitudes: Insights from the new implicit measures.* Psychology Press.

Paulhus, D. L. (1991). Measurement and control of response bias. In Robinson, J. P., Shaver, P. R., Wrightsman, L. S. (Ed.), *Measures of personality and social psychological attitudes*, vol. 1 (pp. 17–51). Academic Press.

Porter, R. D. (2010). *Resurrecting the error choice technique: The premature demise of an indirect measure of attitude?* [Unpublished PhD dissertation]. Queen's University.

Proshansky, H., & Murphy, G. (1942). The effects of reward and punishment on perception. *Journal of Psychology, 13*(2), 295–305. https://doi.org/10.1080/00223980.1942.9917097

Rockledge, M. D., Rucker, D. D., & Nordgren, L. F. (2018). The evaluative lexicon 2.0: The measurement of emotionality, extremity, and valence in language. *Behavioral Research Methods, 50*, 1327–44. https://link.springer.com/article/10.3758/s13428-017-0975-6

Seaboyer, A. (2016). *Social media messaging for influence in national security.* Defence Research & Development Canada. Report number DRDC-RDDC-2016-C257. https://www.researchgate.net/publication/331071944_Social_Media_Messaging_for_Influence_in_National_Security.

Seaboyer, A. (2018). *Influencing techniques using social media.* Defence Research & Development Canada. Report number DRDC-RDDC-2018-C177. https://www.researchgate.net/publication/331069575_Influence_Techniques_Using_Social_Media.

Settanni, M., Azucar, D., & Marengo, D. (2018). Predicting individual characteristics from digital traces on social media: A meta-analysis. *Cyberpsychology, Behavior, and Social Networking, 21*(4), 217–28. https://doi.org/10.1089/cyber.2017.0384

Singer, P. W., Brooking, E. T., (2018). *LikeWar: The weaponization of social media.* Eamon Dolan/Houghton Mifflin Harcourt.

Smith, G. H. (1947). Beliefs in statements labelled Fact and Rumor. *Journal of Abnormal & Social Psychology, 42*(1), 80–90. https://doi.org/10.1037/h0057845

Stern, S. E., & Faber, J. E. (1997). The lost e-mail method: Milgram's lost-letter technique in the age of the Internet. *Behavior Research Methods, Instruments, & Computers, 29*(2), 260–3. https://link.springer.com/article/10.3758/BF03204823

Thurstone, L. L. (1928). Attitudes can be measured. *American Journal of Sociology, 33*(4), 529–54.

Vaughan-Johnston, T. I., Fowlie, D. I., & Jacobson, J. A. (2021). *Facilitating scientific communication between strangers: A preregistered lost email experiment* [Unpublished manuscript]. Queen's University.

Webb, E. J., Campbell, D. T., Schwartz, R. D., & Sechrest, L. (1966). *Unobtrusive measures: Nonreactive research in the social sciences.* Rand McNally.

Weschler, I. R. (1950a). An investigation of attitudes toward labour and management by means of the error-choice method. *Journal of Social Psychology, 32*(1), 51–62. https://www.tandfonline.com/doi/pdf/10.1080/00224545.1950.9919030?casa_token=vE9GWsxIqOYAAAAA:gGl7XiEr1wFKNoL3Lil7F2Ef-0E0e-1-TqsCUZ_0Ry-UDVlohuLQe5a8uNUImNnDn6nrspCm--OMNQ

Weschler, I. R. (1950b). A follow-up study on the measurement of attitudes toward labour and management by means of the error-choice method. *Journal of Social Psychology, 32*(1), 63–9. https://www.tandfonline.com/doi/pdf/10.1080/00224545.1950.9919031?casa_token=IWdQMntASEgAAAAA:wFLCZ1Jze77ddK7CjT0md7IDB8eDFgNzgO3gSNgntupiy1-PfkagtYQUczWF3Sw0M5VtUwDZ9Pvvuw

Xu, K., Nosek, B., & Greenwald, A. G. (2014). Psychology data from the race implicit association test on the Project Implicit demo website. *Journal of Open Psychology Data, 2*(1), e3. https://doi.org/10.5334/jopd.ac

Conclusion

Keith Stewart and Madeleine D'Agata

Eric Ouellet's introduction to this volume set out a series of essential questions. The chapters that followed provided expert insights that offer a starting point for addressing the critical issues faced. However, we are far from having clear solutions at this point. In soliciting contributions, the net was cast wide, as befits a problem set as challenging as this. The aim was to examine the implications of the changing information environment (IE) for security at all levels, including national security and the security of individuals and organizations. The major theme of the book has been the harnessing of information to achieve strategic influence internationally by a range of actors, both state and non-state, most recently in the context of renewed and overt great power competition, but equally during the period since the fall of the Berlin Wall and particularly in the wake of September 2001. In modern times, the perennial problem of disinformation has resurfaced, promulgated widely using novel media, especially since the development of social media and Web 2.0, and this has been highlighted in the material presented by many of the authors. However, this is not the only challenge posed by the constantly changing nature of the IE, and other critical concerns have been discussed here—for example, the opportunities afforded malign actors to harness cyber means to threaten critical infrastructure and military capability.

Perhaps the most basic question we face is how to achieve security in the face of the challenges posed by adversary action that exploits the IE. This can be considered at a number of levels of analysis; for example, the personal security of individuals and their assets, operations security for military, police, and other security services that must guard essential information, and, ultimately, national security. The diversity of material in this book reflects this. At the national strategic level, our security has rested, since the end of the Second World War, on the achievement of mutual deterrence based on the threat of massive retaliation with nuclear weapons. Thus, paraphrasing the challenge laid down by Dr. Ouellet in the introductory chapter, it is important to ask to what extent a deterrence-based posture has the potential to maintain security given information-based challenges and threats, and if so, how do deterrence theory and practice need to adapt to this new reality? This line of inquiry led Ouellet to a number of supplementary questions, including the following: Given the salience of the threat posed by adversarial disinformation, to what extent can it be deterred? If so, is it possible to deter disinformation or other information-based threats through the threat of punishment, or is a different approach required? If deterrence is found to be a viable approach, then what do we need to understand about our adversaries in terms of their perception of costs and benefits that might enable us to achieve a deterrence stance? How should Canada and its allies face up to these challenges, and are there any ways in which the West might begin to fight back? Importantly, how can we achieve all of the foregoing and still conform to our own legal and ethical standards without being brought to the level of our adversaries? This volume has provided a diverse set of insights from leading international experts that have a bearing on all of these problems and more. This final chapter presents reflections on some of the above questions based on a selective distillation of some information from the preceding chapters combined with material from other sources with the aim of offering a series of concluding thoughts.

Perspectives on the Challenge of Deterrence in the IE

We have seen that the spread of misinformation and disinformation in the IE has increased dramatically in the past few years around the world, often severely impacting individuals and organizations and causing confusion, panic, and, on occasion, distrust in government (Bennett & Livingston, 2018; Liu & Huang, 2020). Geography offers little protection against this scourge, and Canada and Canadians, among other polities, have been increasingly targeted in recent years. Certain nations have been, and continue to be, at the forefront of the spread of disinformation, impacting elections in the United States as well as more recently propagating falsehoods surrounding COVID-19 (US Department of State, 2020). Not only does such disinformation lead to financial losses—for example, at the time of writing, $7.75 million has been lost to COVID-19 fraud in Canada according to the Canadian Anti-Fraud

Centre (2021)—it also discourages susceptible individuals from following public health guidelines and promotes vaccine hesitancy, potentially, in the end, contributing to the further spread of COVID-19. Moreover, whether we are discussing cyberspace, or the IE more broadly, it is recognized that it is extremely difficult to defend against adversarial activity. In their chapter Leuprecht and Szeman identified several attributes of the IE that present significant challenges. These include its interconnectedness, which enables adversaries to generate effect without concern for geography or political borders, the relatively low costs of entry, and the possibility of engagement in continuous offensive operations. Adaptation of deterrence for the challenges of the IE must take account of these characteristics.

As noted in the chapter by Jackson, despite the importance being placed on deterring the spread of disinformation in Canada from a security and safety standpoint, there is actually little consensus from academia or policy-makers on how exactly Canada should defend itself. As that author points out, part of the problem is a lack of consensus on defining disinformation, which Jackson and others approach as a societal and cultural issue as much as one of security. Disinformation is typically understood to imply the intentional spreading of deliberately false information. This contrasts with misinformation, which implies the unintentional dissemination of similarly false or inaccurate information. Thus, by many definitions, disinformation is meant to intentionally and maliciously mislead others. And yet, it is not always possible to ascertain intention. Jackson stresses that government efforts aimed at attenuating the spread of disinformation need to proceed with caution to ensure they are not perceived as interfering with freedom of speech.

A consistent theme in this book has been the observation that the IE, and specifically the Internet and social media, have substantially increased the potential for adversaries to engage in information operations (IO) against competitor nations, effectively overcoming geographical and territorial boundaries to a variety of ends, including the spreading of false narratives and propaganda, enabling clandestine access to information and networks, and interference with control systems for civilian and military infrastructure. Chapters in this volume have examined the activities of specific competitor nations. For example, the chapters by Heide and by Seaboyer and Jolicoeur focus on Russia and China, respectively, while Bar-Gil examines information activities directed against Israel by Iran and its proxies, as well as examples of Russian IE tactics. This work demonstrates that, in addition to seeking to catch up with the West in terms of IE capability, the adversary powers considered here have taken the opportunity to adapt technologies to their own preferred methods. For example, Seaboyer and Jolicoeur describe China's policy of "informationalization," which has, in part, enabled the Chinese Communist Party (CCP) to exploit tools, originally conceived of as enabling the free exchange of information, to bound and manipulate the narratives to which Chinese citizens have access.

In a similar vein to Seaboyer and Jolicoeur's comments on China, Heide reminds us that Russia also engages extensively in the IE internally, as well as externally. Heide points out that this contrasts with democratic nations that only conduct IO on operations (in almost all cases abroad). Domestically, both have a specific focus on maintaining the mood and morale of their populations and armed forces by controlling the information and ideas that they can access with a view to avoiding any threat to the authority of the ruling regimes through dissent or uprisings. After a degree of thawing in the late 1980s and '90s, Chinese and Russian authorities are again exerting a high degree of control over the IE of their citizens. While the technologies have changed, the intention is reminiscent of earlier attempts to block access to information from the outside world—for example, Soviet radio jamming operations against Radio Free Europe and Radio Liberty, which broadcast from Munich during the Cold War to provide domestic news to audiences behind the Iron Curtain.[1] Today's equivalent is manifest in the complex system of technological control and enforced censorship that has been dubbed the "Great Firewall of China."[2] Stittmatter (2018) describes the techniques of "intimidation, censorship, and propaganda" that enabled the CCP to take back control of the Internet after a period of relative freedom before 2012. Deletion of social media accounts, blocking of websites, restrictions on the numbers of persons with whom a social media user can share information, and the introduction of fake information, among others, are all cited as techniques through which the CCP was able to fulfil the leader's command to "win back the commanding heights of the internet" (Stittmatter, 2018, p. 70). Similar to the point made by Leuprecht and Szeman regarding the possibilities provided by the IE for engagement in persistent operations, these authors observe that, in their external affairs, both Russia and China appear to adopt a posture of constant conflict, notably in the IE, where they are able, in Lindsay and Gartzke's (2019) terms, to inflict some harm "through cyber exploitation, covert infiltration, and other 'gray zone' provocations that fall below clear thresholds of . . . retaliation" (p. 15).

Russian operations in the IE are constant and are aimed widely at all sections of the targeted nations, including the military, civil society, and policy-makers. Bar-Gil's chapter describes a struggle for "the global mindset." That author also observes that, compared to some of its adversaries, Israel is at a relative disadvantage owing to the breadth and sophistication of its information infrastructure and, by extension, its dependence on such technology-enabled systems, which leaves it exposed to information and cyber-attacks. This echoes Lindsay and Gartzke's (2019) observation that "It is possible and much feared in some circles, that weaker states and nonstate actors might exploit the technologies of globalization to undermine the conventional military advantages of great powers" (p. 3). In this regard, it is interesting that Bar-Gil notes that access to the IE means that malicious activity that "what was formerly a gradual, professional psychological impact is now a high-speed action that even the least competent, remote, and disassembled forces may conduct due to technological improvements." As Leuprecht and Szeman observed, in the modern IE, the costs of entry are low.

Several authors in this volume point to the use of proxies as part of operations in the IE. Bar-Gil describes how Iran provides capability to its allies Hezbollah and Hamas to enable operations against Israel, and in some cases directs specific cyber operations, thus achieving the benefits of deniability while overcoming the disadvantages of physical dislocation from its target. Heide provides a very comprehensive description of the multitude of proxy channels adopted by Russia in its IO, noting the overt use of third-party organizations such as state media as well as a range of "grey" and "black" means that again confer plausible deniability. Seaboyer and Jolicoeur describe how the CCP exploits various levels of the Chinese and foreign media domestically and externally with a view to controlling its message. In addition, they outline how China is able to expand its technical capability for IO via manipulation of academic and industrial relationships, blurring the lines between civil and military research and development and industrial capacity.

As mentioned previously, the challenges addressed by this volume require consideration at several different levels of analysis. While the foregoing comments relate exclusively to the national strategic level, it would be wrong to ignore the fact that engagement with the IE occurs at the individual level, and thus effort must be expended in understanding the risks associated with individual actions and the contexts in which individual actors operate. Although the IE can serve as an environment that facilitates positive human interaction, as observed by Ducol et al. (2016), deviant behaviours, attitudes, and beliefs are of great concern and can lead to serious consequences for individuals such as cyber-bullying, cyber-stalking (Hango, 2016), and fraud (Canadian Anti-Fraud Centre, 2021; Johnson, 2019), among others. Research suggests that certain types of individuals are particularly susceptible to being influenced in the IE. For instance, D'Agata and colleague found links between lowered Honesty-Humility (one of the six factors of personality) and greater online disinhibition, engagement in risky online behaviours (D'Agata & Kwantes, 2020), and engagement with strangers online (D'Agata, Kwantes, & Holden, 2021). These are examples of behaviours that can increase not only one's exposure to adversaries and criminals, but also one's susceptibility to oversharing or behaving in unsafe ways online. Peter et al. (2021) found certain individuals, such as younger adults, to be more susceptible to belief in disinformation or conspiracy theories. Furthermore, psychological tendencies or needs seem to be influential in the IE; for instance, as noted in the chapters by Meharg and by Speckhard and Ellenberg, the need to belong or connect with others or establish one's identity can promote engagement with strangers online. Moreover, for some, these needs may be met in the IE more so than in real-world settings. For instance, research has found a link between heightened real-life social isolation as well as social anxiety and increased comfort with or reliance on online communication (e.g., Whaite et al., 2018; Prizant-Passal et al., 2016). Speckhard and Ellenberg found that in extreme cases, such a need can result in individuals being radicalized, leading to even more serious outcomes such as engaging in illegal activity. More concerning, these authors also note that the sophistication extremists and extremist organizations display in the IE is particularly challenging to effectively counter or dispel.

How Should Deterrence Theory Change to Match the Challenges of the IE?

A number of the contributors to this volume have observed that classical models of deterrence require revision to address the realities of the early twenty-first century. As Jackson and Leuprecht and Szeman have all pointed out, to effectively deter in the IE, Canada and its allies must update their deterrence theory and practice. The changes necessitating such a rethink are in large part bound up, as Cimbala and Lowther and Ankersen, for example, have pointed out, with changes within the IE itself. Ankersen chapter includes the observation that "what has changed are the "operant media through which and with which opponents" communicate, while Cimbala and Lowther note in theirs that "the nuclear-cyber relationship . . . makes deterrence a much more complex task." Nevertheless, material presented in this volume provides some grounds for optimism that the fundamental aspects of deterrence, such as communication, credibility, and risk calculation, are broadly similar today when compared with the immediate post-1945 period, and are likely to remain so with the consequence that deterrence continues as a possibility in the modern era. Stressing the importance of the non-physical elements of deterrence such as credibility and communication, Ankersen states that a "material bias" focused on, for example, weapons systems, has directed attention from the fact that "deterrence actually operates—has always operated—in the information environment." Thus, Ankersen sees contextual change in terms of the means, that is to say the information technology that enables communication between the deterring parties.

Self-knowledge of vulnerability to threat is essential to building preparedness and resilience in anticipation of likely future attacks, as was stressed by Robinson in a paper that emphasized the requirement for "synchronised and systemic" (2019, p. 8) responses to adversary hybrid tactics. Similar to Ankersen, Robinson notes that while many of the threats facing NATO nations are not new, the means that an adversary might employ, such as cyber, are. Thus, Robinson emphasizes the need for deterrence theory and strategies to address such change, and notes that new approaches, including non-kinetic options, have developed with a view to deterring hybrid threats.

Lastly, Ankersen's comments align well with many of the other authors in this volume with regard to the likely benefits of dissuasion through defence in a "deterrence by denial" approach. The framework of cyber threats presented by Ankersen provides a useful means for structuring an integrated defensive posture across all domains and environments, based on an understanding of the various threat categories. Many authors in this volume have stressed the importance of promoting resilience in order to be positioned to engage in deterrence by denial. Jackson's chapter includes the observation that doing so "not only mitigates harmful effects of hostile influence, but also changes adversaries' cost-benefit analyses by denying them (technical or strategic/political) benefits." Jackson adds that such efforts may need to be carried out in coordination with governments, private actors, and civilians.

Deterrence is a form of influence operation in that it seeks to achieve psychological effects in a decision maker with a view to guiding that individual to behave in a certain way. Smith (2005) summed up the basis for all deterrence in noting that, "In short, the real target of someone wishing to deter is the mind of the opposing decision maker" (p. 190). Deterrence theory has seen regular revision in the light of real-world contextual changes, for example, the end of the Cold War. It has also adapted to take account of research that used observational studies to examine the fundamental assumptions of the theory. For example, Jervis (1985) lamented the fact that an examination of case studies demonstrated that "participants almost never have a good understanding of each other's perspective, goals or specific actions. Signals that seem clear to the sender are missed or misinterpreted by the receiver, actions meant to convey one impression often leave quite a different one" (p. 1). Jervis further stated that classical deterrence theory was flawed to the extent that it relied on deductive logic rather than an examination of real-world experience, and that it was "based on the premise that people are highly rational" (p. 1). The aim of Jervis and colleagues (1985) was to strengthen the theory and its application with an improved understanding of, among other things, how, in the real-world, officials and institutions of state process information, how humans make decisions, and the cognitive and other biases that may undermine those processes. Thus, it is to be hoped that adaptation to the realities of the modern IE should represent a continuation of a process of evolution rather than a major transformation.

A very good example of an adaptation of deterrence theory that appears well-suited to the challenges of IE-mediated deterrence was described in Wilner's chapter in the context of counterterrorism. Wilner describes the development of a novel theoretical approach based upon deterrence by de-legitimization that "weighs on an adversary's normative or ideological perspective" with a view to undermining the logic upon which their use of terror tactics is based by "targeting and degrading the ideological motivation that guides support for and participation in terrorism." This raises an important issue—namely, the development of a sound understanding of an adversary (as well as that adversary's supporters and potential supporters) to see how justification for their actions is achieved, and consequently how it might be undermined. Wilner's chapter extends the application of the notion of deterrence by de-legitimization by applying it to the issue of deterrence in the IE, advocating specifically for the establishment of international norms for actors' behaviour within the IE, for more publicity for breaches of acceptable behaviour, and, lastly, for proactive efforts within society to strengthen shared basic principles with a view to achieving collective resilience. Citing Doorn and Brinkel, Wilner stresses the importance of building and enabling trust and credibility within our societies in order to establish "societal counterweights to malicious propaganda and disinformation campaigns." As noted in Jackson's chapter, Canada's responses to disinformation are broad, and future research is needed to better understand how these responses could be better refined as well as tailored to different situations.

Understanding Adversaries in Order to Deter Them

In their chapter, Cimbala and Lowther note that part of the process of adapting deterrence to the modern strategic environment is a recognition that there is a requirement for "tailored" approaches, based on an in-depth understanding of the specific adversary to be deterred. Ankersen likewise stresses the importance of the development of an improved appreciation of the adversary and, citing Jervis, notes the importance of understanding how potential adversaries view the world in order to understand their behaviour and, ultimately, their intentions. Moreover, Ankersen emphasizes the fundamental psychological nature of deterrence, quoting Filipidou (2020) and Jervis et al. (1985), who refer to it, respectively, as "a state of mind" and "a psychological relationship." Perhaps the essential point in Ankersen's chapter is that, by focusing on the intended effects of adversary action, it should be possible to discern these actors' goals and therefore how they would perceive the likely costs and benefits of their actions. The contention is that the apparent "uniqueness" of cyber, which Ankersen argues is "overstated" and is based on a focus on means and capability, can be bypassed, thereby allowing a more integrated perspective of the threat and enabling a comprehensive view of deterrence that includes cyber. This, according to Ankersen, is essential to deterrence via threat of reprisal, since "without an appreciation for what the intended effects or benefits of an attack are, it is difficult to calibrate the costs necessary to dissuade an opponent from carrying it out."

Cimbala and Lowther point out that nuclear crisis management is "both a competitive and a co-operative endeavour" and emphasize that communication is essential to enable each party to demonstrate its appreciation of a situation to the other. Seen in this way, deterrence is reliant on the development and maintenance of an effective relationship between the parties based on clear communication. In addition, they underline the importance of each side developing a clear and accurate understanding of their adversary's intentions and capabilities upon which to base risk assessment and course-of-action decision making. These observations align with early iterations of deterrence theory. For example, Schelling (1966) pointed out that "a hot line can help to improvise arms control in a crisis: but there is a more pervasive dialogue about arms control all the time between the US and the Soviet Union. . . . I have in mind . . . the continuous process by which the USSR and the US interpret each other's intentions and convey their own" (p. 264). Cimbala and Lowther's focus is on nuclear crisis management, but these elements are central to all deterrence relationships, whether in a crisis or in a steady state.

In their chapter, Schleifer and Ansbacher provide their perspective on the deterrent relationship between Israel and Hamas. They judge that Hamas has achieved an appropriate appreciation of Israeli decision makers' perception of risk and is therefore managing to deter them by shaping public opinion with respect to the acceptability or otherwise of the probable costs of specific military action. Their chapter provides a series of examples of how, in their opinion, a combination of terror tactics, disinformation, and influencing international opinion has enabled Hamas to achieve this deterrence despite Israel's military advantages.

Importantly, the chapters in section 1 of this volume emphasize the critical element of credibility in deterrence communication. This comprises, at least, the extent to which the party receiving the deterrent message believes that their adversary has both the capability claimed and the intention and will to use that capability in the circumstances specified. This is, in turn, dependent on issues such as the credibility of the source of the deterrent message and the effectiveness of the transmission of that message, neither of which can be assumed. Even heads of state can fall foul of this basic requirement. For example, as Keegan (2005) reminds us, by 2002 Saddam Hussein was "a victim of his own fictions and evasions. Because of his systematic mendacity, he had lost the capacity to persuade anyone that he was telling the truth" (p. 113).

Understanding Situations

More than one author in this volume touched on the critical issue of protagonists' ability to achieve and maintain what Endsley (e.g., 1995) and others have called "situation awareness" and, particularly in the case of Cimbala and Lowther's chapter, the dangers of protagonists not being able to maintain such an appreciation. The implication is that the increasing speed and complexity of situations mediated in the IE renders the achievement and maintenance of situation awareness extremely difficult and thus increases risk of misdiagnosis, miscalculation, and human error. In particular, they provide several examples of how cyber operations have the potential, deliberately or inadvertently, to skew or undermine an opponent's understanding, as may be the case, for example, through the manipulation of information within an adversary's C4ISR systems, or through disruption of their internal communications, or perhaps through direct interference with the systems controlling the weapons themselves. A critical element of Cimbala and Lowther's argument is that having lost situational awareness, participants could feel increased pressure to take pre-emptive action.

Many of the situational characteristics described by the authors in this volume, and in particular the crisis-management situations discussed by Cimbala and Lowther, such as limited time, situational ambiguity, and changing conditions, are in line with applied settings studied by psychologists interested in "naturalistic decision making" (NDM), notably Klein (e.g., 2008). Their studies of fire commanders, process control operators, surgical teams, and military commanders, to name a few, demonstrated, much as Jervis observed, that, placed in such situations, people tend not to conform to best practices predicted by rational decision theory. Rather, in time-compressed emergency environments, the experts reported using prior experience and knowledge rapidly to categorize the situation and generate as adequate a response as possible in terms of a course of action. Cimbala and Lowther make a similar observation citing the work of March and Simon. Indeed, Simon (e.g., 1978) had, as part of the development of a theory of bounded rationality in the 1950s, dubbed such decision making "satisficing," that is, finding a solution that is satisfactory and sufficient relative to the decision maker's level of aspiration. Cimbala and Lowther quite rightly make the chilling observation that in the context of nuclear crisis management, there is simply no margin for error. In view of the foregoing, there is no suggestion that what has been described is the "best" way to make decisions; rather the implication is that under extreme time pressure, with a need to respond to stay ahead of a dynamic situation, it may be the only possible way to respond within the capacity of human decision makers. One useful conclusion of the NDM work is that in order to promote good decision making, we should focus on optimizing, as much as possible, the conditions under which decision makers make decisions. Their work strongly suggests that a focus on achievement and maintenance of situational awareness, a high-functioning command team and organization to support the decision maker, and efficient communications and coordination are key. Cimbala and Lowther's work shows us a variety of ways in which cyber means might be used by an adversary to undermine these critical structures and processes. The implication of the NDM research is that, as well as hardening against cyber intrusion, organizations should seek to optimize the decision-making context, for example, through training, improved organizational design, and, if available, decision-support systems.

Cimbala and Lowther point out that currently we can only "speculate about the impact of cyber-attacks and efforts to inject technical disinformation into systems responsible for nuclear crisis management." Nevertheless, their chapter provides a range of scenarios that could be used in modelling, experimentation, and simulation with a view to achieving an improved appreciation of the demands of such situations. Such work could provide the basis for improved preparation and potentially training and education for decision makers and their teams. In addition, such an approach offers some hope that we might achieve some degree of deterrence by denial, hardening our critical systems and augmenting the resilience of our people and organizations with a view to avoiding crisis escalation.

How Can Canada and Its Allies Achieve Increased Resilience?

A number of the chapters in this volume have implications for how states might achieve increased resilience. The IE has been leveraged by criminals and adversaries now for many years in an effort to influence, intimidate, manipulate, and radicalize individuals. Multiple streams of research exist in this domain to better understand what makes individuals vulnerable to others' manipulations in the IE, as well as strategies or techniques that can be employed to reduce the effects of such efforts. Furthermore, understanding the motivations and techniques employed by our adversaries can help in the development of methods to deter such actions in the IE. In addition, as discussed in the chapter by Porter, an examination of the online influence campaigns employed by our adversaries is needed in order to better understand how to build resilience in our own personnel and citizens and to engage in deterrence by denial.

The authors in this volume provide several recommendations for specific interventions to promote resilience, including technological developments to aid identification of adversary IO and hardening of critical civilian and military systems. Bar-Gil and Heide both favour augmenting such tools with a range of non-technical interventions, for example, training and education. Heide proposes that both the general public and the media would benefit from the ability to identify malicious IO more effectively, and Bar-Gil advocates for training military and civilian audiences alike in critical thinking about information, especially that which is presented in social media. In fact, there is a great deal of research, particularly in the field of psychology, that highlights the benefits of critical thinking, such that analytical thinking is associated with lowered belief in disinformation (e.g., Bronstein et al., 2019; D'Agata, Kwantes, Peter, & Vallikanthan, 2021). Heide points out that adversaries benefit from ordinary persons unintentionally spreading their falsehoods as misinformation, and consequently invest time and energy in its creation and dissemination through a broad range of media, both state-sponsored and commercial, for example, TV, radio, and fake accounts on social media platforms. Bar-Gil stresses the potential for limiting the success of such tactics through promotion of "digital literacy," efforts that have been shown to be successful in limiting the spread of false messages. In addition, both authors address the controversial topic of governments restricting access to specific media within their own nations, with Bar-Gil discussing the potential use of specific instruments under Israeli law, and Heide advocating the blocking of access to Western audiences for news outlets spreading propaganda and disinformation and the cutting of funding sources for organizations involved in malicious IO.

With respect to the challenge of developing strong counter-narratives to challenge adversary influence operations and disinformation, we need to address the question of when our strategic communications might be considered equivalent to an adversary's propaganda. Some authors even seem to have attempted to rehabilitate the term "propaganda." Cull (2015) argues that most propaganda is, at base, an attempt to hinder the advance of an opposing idea, and as such could conceivably be considered defensive "counter propaganda." Employing the same term, Taylor (2002) expressed the view that "propaganda"[3] is required "on behalf of . . . peace" (p. 439).

At the tactical level, Cull describes actions to counter a specific message and cites the work of the US Information Agency in identifying and debunking Soviet disinformation rumours in the 1980s. At the strategic level Cull sees "a communications policy" (2015, p. 3) aimed at adversary propaganda, for example, the US information campaign during the Cold War and British foreign-language broadcasts aimed to counter totalitarian propaganda in the 1930s. Interestingly, Cull also notes that, "In our own time China's large scale spending on cultural outreach and international broadcasting is seen by Beijing as a corrective to the western bias of global media outlets" (p. 3), and as such is, in their eyes, essentially a counter-propaganda exercise. To this we could doubtless add their construction of a "golden shield" containing and protecting "an internet with Chinese characteristics" (Strittmatter, 2018, p. 79) and enabling their near total control of the information that Chinese citizens can access.

How Might Canada and Its Allies Respond?

The chapters by Bar-Gil and Heide present proposals for solutions to achieve deterrence in the face of the threats they describe. As a general point, it is possible to conclude that both authors advocate an approach that can be characterised as "deterrence by denial" based on the achievement of high levels of resilience in the states, institutions, and systems discussed. Moreover, we should also note that in advocating an approach based on proactive strategic communications, Heide is, in parallel, proposing a form of pre-emption in the IE. This, it is suggested, is important to ensure that audiences are presented with "truthful accounts" before being exposed to the adversary's disinformation, which Heide notes may be harder for individuals to discount once internalized.

In order to begin to achieve the necessary resilience, Heide stresses that Canada needs to develop strong narratives tailored to specific audiences that explain "what defines Canada, its beliefs, and its actions." In order to achieve this, Heide proposes that Canada needs a strategic communications capability that is always active in order to deter adversary IO in a pre-emptive fashion. In addition, Heide suggests monitoring and analysis of adversary messaging combined with the development and dissemination of Canadian narratives.

The proposed developments outlined above, as well as others described in detail in the individual chapters, may have the potential to both bolster resilience and harden Western societies against the malign information activities of adversary powers. Nevertheless, in formulating policy and doctrine for such a capability there would be many questions that would need to be addressed, not least those in the moral and ethical spheres. Indeed, it will be essential to be prepared to address any suggestion that in responding within the IE Western nations could risk constructing a mirror image of the structures and tactics they are seeking to counter. Certainly, the development of information-related capability by government and military in the West is sometimes treated with suspicion by domestic audiences. For example, Galeotti (2017) suggests that strategic communications "could perhaps be glibly described as 'propaganda we like'" (p. 1). Taylor (2002) similarly points out that there is "an entire range of euphemisms" (p. 437) within which we can assume "strategic communications" would figure. Taylor expressed the view that democracies "tend to delude themselves that they are not in the business of propaganda" (p. 437), arguing that it is assessed to consist of untruths and to be conducted only by undemocratic parties. The crux of Taylor's paper was that at that time, as now, "when certain value systems are under attack . . . they . . . need to be defended . . . by a reaffirmation of the values that were being challenged" (p. 440–1). Moreover, Taylor stated the opinion that this should be a job for governments owing to a concern that "the free, democratic media of any country have become an unreliable mirror of the true nature of that society by virtue of the increasingly commercialised environment in which they now operate" (p. 439).

Both Heide and Bar-Gil recommend the development of analytic capability aimed at understanding adversary IO aims and approaches with a view to identifying domestic capability gaps and developing countermeasures. For example, Bar-Gil notes that Internet and social media present opportunities for the collection of relevant open-source intelligence (OSINT), and that such information has the potential to be used to underpin proactive responses. Bar-Gil provides the example of the Bellingcat investigations into the shooting down of Malaysian Airlines Flight 17 over Ukraine. Moreover, Bar-Gil describes how OSINT, based on an adversary's social media presence, has provided the foundations for responses both within the IE and, in a cross-domain response, in physical action.

One area that perhaps received less attention is the notion of cross-domain operations or cross-domain deterrence as a means to respond to, or get ahead of, hostile information activities. Cull, for example, emphasizes that "not all propaganda is best countered in the communications sphere . . . [and that] addressing the source of the propaganda can prove an effective strategy for counter propaganda" (2015, p. 14). Illustrating that, when conducted by unscrupulous state actors, this can involve drastic and illegal measures, Cull provides the example of the assassination of a Bulgarian journalist by Romanian operatives. Bar-Gil provides examples of the use of physical attack in response to cyber activities noting that these were intended to degrade the adversary's IE capability and simultaneously deliver a deterrent message. Such examples highlight the need for governments to engage in an examination of ethics and proportionality in adopting cross-domain tactics.

With this in mind, democratic nations might do well to ask about the extent to which the proposals put forward by Bar-Gil and Heide require the establishment of completely new capability, or whether what is needed is, in part, the re-establishment of capability that has seen under-investment in recent times. Taylor noted that reductions in US public diplomacy in the 1990s, such as cuts to Voice of America broadcasts to the Middle East, had led to "an information vacuum which was then vacated by the morass of lies, rumours and disinformation generated by its adversaries" (p. 439). In a similar vein, in a 2005 article published on the BBC website announcing cuts to World Service broadcasts in eight languages, including Polish and Hungarian, the head of its Polish-language service was quoted as saying that, while they found the BBC's position on Europe "somewhat optimistic," they acknowledged that central Europe "is not the greatest geopolitical need at the moment" ("BBC East Europe voices silenced," 2005). Clearly, we have the benefit of hindsight in having seen the increasing tensions in central and eastern Europe in recent years and the rise of quasi-authoritarianism in some quarters. The conclusion must be that over time the specific focus of counter-adversary IO will shift, and the capability that we build to support such operations must possess the flexibility needed to address new requirements from time to time. It would seem reasonable to suggest that the chapters in this book have demonstrated enough basic similarities in the techniques employed by a range of potential adversaries that such a capability could be created, although this does not necessarily address the problem that area expertise cannot be created in short order.

The chapters in this book have provided a range of useful recommendations for the enhancement of democratic nations' capacity to operate in the IE that might broadly be characterized as falling into developments in the areas of analytic capability and proactive information capabilities. It should be advantageous to such efforts that similar capability has existed in the past and that lessons learned from the experience of the twentieth century are available. The exception might well be, as Ankersen notes, the substantial changes in the media, systems, and organizations that constitute the modern IE. The arms race in communications and information technology is unlikely to slow soon, and it is clearly the case that it will be those nations that can adapt to the new environment and harness the opportunities presented to achieve their strategic goals that will come out on top in the information battle.

Leuprecht and Szeman propose that Canada may not have sufficient resources to carry out "persistent engagement" and should instead look to partner with the United States. Jackson notes that Canada's "attempts to deter strategic disinformation have included accelerated efforts to strengthen cyber defence and resilience and to develop legislation and norms to hamper disinformation efforts, especially during elections. More generally, there have been efforts to increase co-operation and to share more information (about disinformation) to 'deny' actors (further) access at the domestic and international levels."

Final Thoughts

This volume has covered a very wide range of topics in an attempt to conduct a preliminary examination of the risk presented by adversary activities in the IE and methods through which democratic nations might respond. We have seen a general consensus that the IE has rendered geographic boundaries less relevant to malign actors who are able to exploit connectivity to conduct operations against the West. Our networked environment also affords these adversaries the opportunity to achieve their strategic intentions incrementally and without crossing the threshold that would trigger a more robust response. The implication is that there is also asymmetry in acceptability of methods. The West is rightly much less ready to use methods that would be considered illegal and unethical to achieve its aims. Thus, we are assailed by a constant barrage of disinformation that has the potential to decay the credibility and trust citizens have in the essential institutions of state and society. Meanwhile the same capabilities are targeted internally at the populations of nations like China and North Korea by governments who simultaneously exert near total control over the information their people can access.

A challenge facing defence departments in the IE is ensuring that operations are targeted toward our adversaries as well ensuring no harm comes to domestic populations in the process. The IE allows for individuals and groups to disguise their true identities when operating online, making it more difficult to identify who they are, and to prevent them from continuing to engage in nefarious activities against our armed forces and citizens. In addition, it is extremely difficult to fully measure the scope and depth of targeted online campaigns. As discussed by Porter and colleagues, techniques aimed at assessing attitudes indirectly offer one approach to help quantify the scope and depth, however, more sophisticated techniques, perhaps based on cutting-edge technologies such as machine learning, may be needed. A challenge facing defence analysts and researchers in particular is an inability to directly study and understand our adversaries. As discussed in the chapter by Speckhard and Ellenberg, work on defectors can be enlightening, but it is not sufficient in its own right. Continued work in this area focused on creative ways to assess and understand adversaries and their campaigns is needed.

Research aimed at identifying vulnerabilities in individuals to being influenced and/or radicalized online can be key to the development of strategies and techniques to help reduce such vulnerabilities. Moreover, such work can help promote resilience in our own personnel and citizens by identifying approaches to help individuals more thoroughly consider and examine information online before behaving hastily. In addition, research in this domain has the potential to inform areas such as public affairs as to the types of messaging that could be effective at promoting resilience against influence and disinformation in the IE. Finally, as mentioned, evaluating the effectiveness of adversary online campaigns might help identify means to deter similar campaigns in the future. More research in the area of deterrence in the IE is needed. Moreover, a move toward a more integrated approach with other areas of government may be needed in order to better capture the effects, scope, and depth of our adversaries' actions in the IE, in an effort to deter attacks in the future.

A repeated theme in this volume has been a recognition that if potential adversaries are able to sidestep our attempts to deter their activities through threat of reprisal, then we need to expand our repertoire of deterrence methods to achieve deterrence by denial. A variety of proposals have been made throughout the book that, when taken in aggregate, amount to the beginnings of a recipe for how Canada and its allies can begin to reinforce the essential resilience of our societies and state institutions built up over hundreds of years, and in so doing, face up to the new authoritarian regimes that seek to undermine us. For example, training of military personnel and education for the general population is required to enable them to navigate the IE safely and securely; training and simulation will help our civil and military crisis responders and decision makers respond in the face of adversary escalation; increased understanding of adversaries will offer the capacity to anticipate their stratagems, achieve early warning, and counter their propaganda; and an improved understanding of the structure of their ideology will enable de-legitimization in the eyes of their own populations and the wider world. Perhaps most importantly, there is the undercurrent of a confidence that the West has prevailed in the past in the face of opposing narratives and that it can do so again by building an information infrastructure to counter adversary narrative and present a strong alternative.

NOTES

1 These stations were particularly threatening to the Soviet authorities since they attempted to provide news about events in the targeted nations based on local sources (e.g., Kind-Kovács, 2013).

2 For example, Strittmatter (2018) observes that "China's attempt to censor the web, as the former US president Bill Clinton joked, was like 'trying to nail Jell-O to the wall.' That was in the year 2000. The Chinese listened to the prophecy, and swiftly built a new great wall: the Great Firewall" (p. 61).

3 It might be argued that, in part, Taylor's paper is an attempt to rehabilitate the term "propaganda," which, it is argued, is essential in defence of democratic values—in Taylor's terms, "democratic propaganda."

REFERENCES

BBC East Europe voices silenced. (2005, 21 December). *BBC News*. http://news.bbc.co.uk/2/hi/europe/4550102.stm

Bennett, W. L., & Livingston, S. (2018). The disinformation order: Disruptive communication and the decline of democratic institutions. *European Journal of Communication, 33*(2), 122–39. https://doi.org/10.1177/0267323118760317

Bronstein, M. V., Pennycook, G., Bear, A., Rand, D. G., & Cannon, T. D. (2019). Belief in fake news is associated with delusionality, dogmatism, religious fundamentalism, and reduced analytic thinking. *Journal of Applied Research in Memory and Cognition, 8*(1), 108–17.

Canadian Anti-Fraud Centre. (2021). Homepage. https://www.antifraudcentre-centreantifraude.ca/index-eng.htm

Cull, N. J. (2015). *Counter propaganda: Cases from US Public diplomacy and beyond.* Legatum Institute.

D'Agata, M. T., & Kwantes, P. J. (2020). Personality factors predicting disinhibited and risky online behaviors. *Journal of Individual Differences, 41*(4), 199–206. https://doi.org/10.1027/1614-0001/a000321

D'Agata, M. T., Kwantes, P. J., & Holden, R. R. (2021). Psychological factors related to self-disclosure and relationship formation in the online environment. *Personal Relationships, 28*(2), 230–50. https://doi.org/10.1111/pere.12361

D'Agata, M., Kwantes, P., Peter, E., & Vallikanthan, J. (2021). Testing tactics to reduce belief in fake news in a North American sample. Defence Research and Development Canada, Scientific Letter, DRDC-RDDC-2021-L338.

Ducol, B., Bouchard, M., Davies, G., Ouellet, M., & Neudecker, C. (2016). *Assessment of the state of knowledge: Connections between research on the social psychology of the Internet and violent extremism.* TSAS: The Canadian Network for Research on Terrorism, Security, and Society.

Endsley, M.R. (1995). Toward a theory of situation awareness in dynamic systems. *Human Factors,* 37(1), 32–64. https://doi.org/10.1518/001872095779049543

Hango, D. W. (2016). Cyberbullying and cyberstalking among Internet users aged 15 to 29 in Canada. *Insights on Canadian Society.* Statistics Canada. https://www150.statcan.gc.ca/n1/pub/75-006-x/2016001/article/14693-eng.htm

Galeotti, M. (2017, 22 February). "Propaganda needs to be clever, smart and efficient," but Russian army's "information troops" are not just propagandists. *In Moscow's Shadows.* https://inmoscowsshadows.wordpress.com/2017/02/22/propaganda-needs-to-be-clever-smart-and-efficient-but-russian-armys-information-troops-are-not-just-propagandists/

Jervis, R. (1985). Introduction: Approach and assumptions. In Jervis, R., Lebow, R., & Stein, J. (Eds.), *Psychology and deterrence* (pp. 1–12). Johns Hopkins University Press.

Jervis, R., Lebow, R., & Stein, J. (1985). *Psychology and deterrence.* Johns Hopkins University Press.

Johnson, E. (2019, 20 January). TD Bank should have seen "red flags" as senior lost $732 K in romance scam, son says. *CBC News.* https://www.cbc.ca/news/canada/toronto/senior-wires-life-savings-through-td-bank-in-romance-scam-1.4980649

Keegan, J. (2005). *The Iraq War.* Vintage.

Kind-Kovács, F. (2013). Voices, letters, and literature through the Iron Curtain: exiles and the (trans)mission of radio in the Cold War. *Cold War History,* 13(2), 193–219. https://doi.org/10.1080/14682745.2012.746666

Klein, G. (2008). Naturalistic decision making. *Human Factors, 50*(3), 456–60. https://journals.sagepub.com/doi/pdf/10.1518/001872008X288385?casa_token=RHLPXO5oURYAAAAA:f5s9qqlfAsbEmNT9_VD33eWJIXiQGvQjqm2wHeQyTDBorN_yqFCtKRvAFwOf_ywzzs00pB5mm8q4iw

Lindsay, J. R. & Gartske, E. (2019). Introduction: Cross-domain deterrence, from practice to theory. In E. Gartzke & J. R. Lindsay (Eds.), *Cross-domain deterrence: Strategy in an era of complexity* (pp. 1–25). Oxford University Press.

Liu, P. L., & Huang, L. V. (2020). Digital disinformation about COVID-19 and the third-person effect: Examining the channel differences and negative emotional outcomes. *Cyberpsychology, Behavior, and Social Networking, 23*(11), 789–93. https://doi.org/10.1089/cyber.2020.0363

March, J. G., & Simon, H. A. (1958). *Organizations.* John Wiley and Sons.

Peter, E., D'Agata, M., Kwantes, P., & Vallikanthan, J. (2021). *Individual differences in susceptibility to disinformation.* Scientific Report, DRDC-RDDC-2021-R114. Defence Research and Development Canada.

Prizant-Passal, S., Shechner, T., & Aderka, I. M. (2016). Social anxiety and Internet use—a meta-analysis: What do we know? What are we missing? *Computers in Human Behavior, 62*, 221–9. https://doi.org/10.1016/j.chb.2016.04.003

Robinson, E. (2019). *Hybrid warfare and modern deterrence theory.* Scientific Letter, DRDC-RDDC-2019-L184. Defence Research and Development Canada.

Schelling, T. C. (1966). *Arms and influence.* Yale University Press.

Simon, H. A. (1978, 8 December). *Rational decision-making in business organizations.* Nobel Memorial Lecture. http://www.nobelprize.org/uploads/2018/06/simon-lecture

Smith, R. (2005). *The utility of force: The art of war in the modern world.* Allen Lane.

Strittmatter, K (2018). *We have been harmonized: Life in China's surveillance state.* Custom House.

Taylor, P.M. (2002). Strategic communications or democratic propaganda? *Journalism Studies, 3*(3), 437–41. https://doi.org/10.1080/14616700220145641

US Department of State. (2020). *GEC special report: Pillars of Russia's disinformation and propaganda ecosystem.* https://www.state.gov/wp-content/uploads/2020/08/Pillars-of-Russia%E2%80%99s-Disinformation-and-Propaganda-Ecosystem_08-04-20.pdf

Whaite, E. O., Shensa, A., Sidani, J. E., Colditz, J. B., & Primack, B. A. (2018). Social media use, personality characteristics, and social isolation among young adults in the United States. *Personality and Individual Differences, 124*, 45–50. https://doi.org/10.1016/j.paid.2017.10.030

Afterword

What does the future hold for us as it relates to deterrence and disinformation? Surely not clarity and certainty. The world shall continue to be VUCA (volatile, uncertain, chaotic, and ambiguous) as it has always been since humans have started to organize themselves in social groups. One could argue that the world is VUCA because it describes the human condition, i.e., our capacity and need to "gossip" as the most social animal on earth, as well as our predispositions to perceive threats coming from others we don't necessarily know or understand. I'm sure that in the year 166, Marcus Aurelius would have found the world very VUCA while battling a pandemic, insurgencies, constant wars, and instability on the borders of the Roman Empire. The world is VUCA because we can't predict the future nor control or predict human behaviour.

One could think that highly sophisticated modern communication systems could dissipate these frictions and ambiguities. As many experts rightly pointed out, the advances in communication technologies and social media have added additional layers of complexity to human interactions where anyone can reach wide audiences instantaneously without having the correct information at the source. In other words, *anything goes*, and it goes fast. In the international security environment and international relations disciplines we should therefore expect a real challenge in terms of deterring threats and disinformation. And this will not go away anytime soon.

I could offer that framing disinformation in the context of others (adversaries, competitors, and allies) may be useful in the sense that disinformation to us may represent the reality or the truth for others. In my view, this scenario is even more dangerous, as fighting deeply engrained beliefs is more complex than merely associating disinformation with spreading lies. As such, we could argue that the invasion of Ukraine has been in the works for many years as the West consistently ignored Putin's sense of threat coming from a NATO on its continued expansion course to the East since 1999. And the same could be said for China. To qualify Russia's action as barbaric and unnecessary in the twenty-first century is not helpful. In a VUCA world, we should expect the unexpected. Although we know we have no ill intent or plans to threaten Russia and China, these state leaders *feel* threatened and their rhetoric, behaviours, and information campaigns reflect just that.

Although deterrence consists in a wide range and combination of different scalable means, maybe it starts with establishing trust, one conversation at a time in the back rooms of diplomacy walking in with our eyes wide open. Establishing trust could mean taking seriously others' sense of feeling threatened. Simply put, maybe deterrence starts by proactively treating our adversaries, competitors, and allies with respect. Especially when we disagree. We should not underestimate the disarming long-term effects of honesty, transparency, and coherent comprehensive approaches.

LIEUTENANT-GENERAL JENNIE CARIGNAN,
Chief of Professional Conduct and Culture
7 June 2022

Postface

In the early hours of 7 October 2023, the terrorist organization Hamas launched a massive and surprise multi-pronged attack against Israel, resulting in the murder of more than 1,200 Israeli citizens, most of them civilians. This attack was also marked by numerous acts of extreme brutality by the Hamas attackers, including the murder of children and babies, rape, torture, body desecration, and burning captives alive. The Hamas terrorists' exactions were very similar in scope and cruelty to those of the Islamic State. As of this writing, Israel has launched a massive air and land operation to defeat Hamas into Gaza and has mobilized an unprecedented number of reservists. Hamas-related agencies are claiming that there have been over 11,000 casualties among the Palestinians. It is not yet known if the conflict between Israel and Hamas will escalate to involve other actors, nor how long the military operations in Gaza will last.

The chapter by Ron Schleifer and Yair Ansbacher was written before these horrible and tragic events, but it was to some degree predictive. There is no doubt that Israel was deceived by its adversary and indeed self-deterred in taking decisive actions against Hamas prior to 7 October 2023. This weaker self-imposed deterrence posture may have also, at a more unconscious level, contributed to the Israeli intelligence failures and Israel's political authorities' lack of attention to warning signs received. Furthermore, as Schleifer and Ansbacher noted, Hamas had developed a quasi-air force and navy, and it made the most of them in its murderous rampage.

On the more specific topic of disinformation, although Hamas did try to muddy the waters about the cruelty of its actions, it does not seem to have worked. Many supporters of Hamas and critics of Israel in the Western world have either changed their views or remained silent. Most Arab states have taken a moderate tone, and only a handful have celebrated Hamas' exactions, mostly Iran and its proxies such as Syria and Hezbollah. Israel has been quite effective in showing the world the actual cruelty of Hamas and in preventing Hamas disinformation to flourish. As it has been the case in all conflicts involving Israel since military operations in Lebanon in the 1980s, international public pressures and contested press coverage are now influencing the potential scope of Israeli operations. However, in a most cynical way, Hamas, by copying the example of the Islamic State, has changed the disinformation and deterrence context against itself. As the authors noted, "So far, Hamas has been successful in maintaining the psychological and informational notion that invading and permanently occupying the Gaza Strip is an unthinkable option." This is no more the case.

—Eric Ouellet

LIST OF ABBREVIATIONS

AAA	Actor and audience analysis
AIDS	Acquired immunodeficiency syndrome
AMP	Affect-misattribution procedure
APA	American Psychological Association
ASEAN	Association of Southeast Asian Nations
AUM	Anxiety/uncertainty management theory
BBC	British Broadcasting Corporation
BMD	Ballistic missile defense
CAF	Canadian Armed Forces
CCP	Chinese Communist Party
CDC	Centers for Disease Control and Prevention
C4ISR	Command, control, communications, computers, intelligence, surveillance, and reconnaissance
CIA	Central Intelligence Agency
CIDB	Canadian Incidents Database
CNO	Computer network operations
COGAT	Coordinator of Government Activities in the Territories (Israel)
COTS	Commercial off-the-shelf
CPD	Central Propaganda Department (People's Republic of China)
CPI	Cyber Power Index
CSE	Communications Security Establishment
CSIS	Canadian Security Intelligence Service
DCCC	Democratic Congressional Campaign Committee
DDOS	Distributed denial of service
D5	Degrade, deny, disrupt, destroy, deceive
DND	Department of National Defence
DOD	Department of Defense
DRDC	Defence Research and Development Canada

EC	Error choice
EFP	Enhanced Forward Presence (NATO)
EP	Evaluative priming
EU	European Union
EW	Electronic warfare
FBI	Federal Bureau of Investigation
5G	Fifth-generation telecommunications network
FSB	Federal'naya sluzhba bezopasnosti Rossiyskoy Federatsii (Federal Security Service; Russian internal security agency)
FTF	Foreign terrorist fighters
G7	Group of Seven
G20	Group of Twenty
GAC	Global Affairs Canada
GGE	Group of Governmental Experts
GRM	Gaza Reconstruction Mechanism
GRU	Glavnoye Razvedyvatelnoye Upravlenie (Main Intelligence Directorate; Soviet and Russian military intelligence)
HIV	Human immunodeficiency virus
IAF	Israeli Air Force
IAT	Implicit association task
ICC	International Criminal Court
ICS/SCADA	Industrial control systems/supervisory control and data acquisition
IDF	Israel Defense Forces
IE	Information environment
IHL	International humanitarian law
Incel	Involuntary celibate
IO	Information operation
IR	International relations
IRA	Internet Research Agency
IRB	Institutional Review Board
ISIS	Islamic State of Iraq and Syria
IT	Information technology
ITW/AA	Integrated tactical warning and attack assessment
IW	Information warfare

KGB	Komitet Gosudarstvennoy Bezopasnosti (Committee for State Security; Soviet internal security and foreign intelligence agency)
LET	Lost email technique
LLT	Lost letter technique
LW	Legal warfare
MAD	Mutually assured destruction
MIIT	Ministry of Industry and Information Technology (People's Republic of China)
NATO	North Atlantic Treaty Organization
NCSA	National Cyber Security Authority (Israel)
NC3	Nuclear command, control, and communication
NDM	Naturalistic decision making
NIS	New Israeli shekel
NIST	National Institute of Standards
OAS	Organization of American States
ODNI	Office of the Director of National Intelligence
OSCE	Organization for Security and Cooperation in Europe
OSINT	Open-source intelligence
OST	Ontological security theory
PGS	Prompt global strike
PLA	People's Liberation Army (People's Republic of China)
PRC	People's Republic of China
PRC	Popular Resistance Committees (Gaza)
PSYOPS	Psychological operations
QR	Quick response
R&D	Research and development
RCMP	Royal Canadian Mounted Police
RPG	Rocket-propelled grenade
RRM	Rapid response mechanism
RT	Russian state-controlled media organization (formerly known as Russia Today)
SCO	Shanghai Cooperation Organisation
SDF	Syrian Democratic Forces
SIOP	Single integrated operational plan

SITE	Security and Intelligence Threats to Elections
SSF	Strategic Support Force
SSHRC	Social Science and Humanities Research Council
START	Strategic Arms Reduction Treaty
UN	United Nations
UNHCR	United Nations High Commissioner for Refugees
USCYBERCOM	United States Cyber Command
VPN	Virtual private network
VTS	Voice of the Strait
VTSM	Violent transnational social movements
VUCA	Volatile, uncertain, chaotic, and ambiguous
WHO	World Health Organization
WMD	Weapons of mass destruction

About the Authors

Christopher Ankersen is a clinical professor of global affairs at New York University's Center for Global Affairs, where he leads the global risk specialization. Prior to joining NYU in 2017, Dr. Ankersen worked at the United Nations; was a consultant to businesses, governments, and militaries; and served as an officer in the Canadian Armed Forces with Princess Patricia's Canadian Light Infantry, deploying on missions with the UN and NATO. Christopher Ankersen holds a BA (hons) in international politics and history from Royal Roads Military College (Canada) and an MSc and PhD in international relations from the London School of Economics and Political Science.

Yair Ansbacher has been serving in the IDF's Special Operations Forces for two decades. He is a senior research associate for defence at the Kohelet Policy Forum in Israel. A postgraduate student at Bar-Ilan University, Mr. Ansbacher's doctoral thesis is on the impact of SOF on the modern battlefield.

Stephen J. Cimbala is distinguished professor of political science, Penn State Brandywine, an American Studies Faculty member, and is the author of numerous books and articles in the fields of international security studies, defence policy, nuclear weapons and arms control, and intelligence. He received bis BA in journalism from Penn State University in 1965. Steve received an MA and PhD (1969) in political science from the University of Wisconsin, Madison. He serves on the editorial boards of various professional journals, has consulted for a number of government agencies and defence contractors, and is frequently quoted in the media on national security topics.

Maddie D'Agata received her PhD in social-personality psychology from Queen's University in 2017 and has been employed by the Department of National Defence since 2016. From 2017 to 2022, she was a defence scientist in the Intelligence, Influence, and Collaboration Section at Defence Research and Development Canada's Toronto Research Centre. She conducted research in two main areas: mental health and influence activities. Her work on influence activities was focused on identifying what makes individuals susceptible to being influenced within the cyber context. She is now responsible for leading a team that enables the broadened awareness and communication of DND/CAF's evidence-based research findings on conduct and culture such that they are actionable by decision makers and senior leadership.

Molly Ellenberg is a research fellow at the International Center for the Study of Violent Extremism. Molly is a doctoral student in social psychology at the University of Maryland. She holds an MA in forensic psychology from the George Washington University and a BS in psychology with a specialization in clinical psychology from UC San Diego. Her research focuses on radicalization to and de-radicalization from militant jihadist and white supremacist violent extremism, the quest for significance, and intolerance of uncertainty. Molly has presented original research at NATO Advanced Research Workshops and Advanced Training Courses, the International Summit on Violence, Abuse, and Trauma, the GCTC International Counter Terrorism Conference, UC San Diego Research Conferences, and for security professionals in the European Union.

Leandre R. Fabrigar is a professor of psychology at Queen's University in Kingston, Ontario. He has co-authored more than 110 publications. Most of his publications fall within the domain of the psychology of attitudes and persuasion or within the domain of research methodology. Dr. Fabrigar's research has appeared in a number of journals, including the *Journal of Personality and Social Psychology*, the *Personality and Social Psychology Bulletin*, the *Journal of Experimental Social Psychology*, the *Personality and Social Psychology Review*, *Psychological Science*, the *Psychological Bulletin*, and *Psychological Methods*. He has been elected to membership in the Society of Multivariate Experimental Psychology and is a fellow of the Society for Experimental Social Psychology, the Society for Personality and Social Psychology, the Association for Psychological Science, and the Midwestern Psychological Association. Dr. Fabrigar has served as an associate editor for the *Journal of Experimental Social Psychology* and as co-editor for the *Personality and Social Psychology Bulletin*.

Rachel Lea Heide works for Canada's Department of National Defence as a defence scientist/strategic analyst in Defence Research and Development Canada's Centre for Operational Research and Analysis. Foci include space, pilot shortages, peace support operations, capacity building, information operations, humanitarian assistance and disaster relief, future security trends, concept development, war gaming, terrorism and counter-insurgency, and war diary research. Dr. Heide is also an air force historian, specializing in the period from 1916 to 1946. She has researched air force organization, training, leadership, morale, professionalization, mutinies, accident investigation, and government policy. She has also instructed distance learning courses in Canadian history and Canadian military history for Algonquin College, the Canadian Forces College, and the Royal Military College.

Nicole J. Jackson is associate professor at the School for International Studies, Simon Fraser University, Vancouver. She teaches and researches in the areas of security studies and foreign policy analysis, concentrating in particular on Russia and Central Asia. Her first book, *Russian Foreign Policy and the CIS: Theories, Debates and Actions*, examined Russian ideas and debates over military involvement in Georgia, Moldova, and Tajikistan. Most of her research focuses on Russia's involvement in the post-Soviet space, including the securitization of trafficking in Central Asia, Russia's policies toward Central Asia, and Russia's involvement in regional organizations. More recently she has written on Russia's approach to outer space and NATO and Canadian approaches to hybrid threats and disinformation. She is currently writing on countering disinformation in the context of the Russia-Ukraine war, as well as a comparative analysis of Russia's military involvement in the former Soviet space.

Pierre Jolicoeur is full professor in the Department of Political Science at Royal Military College of Canada. Specialist of the former Soviet Union and southeastern Europe, his research focuses on secessionist movements, foreign policy, federalism, and cyber security. At RMCC, he teaches international relations and comparative politics. Through NATO programs, he also taught in Moldova and in the former Yugoslav Republic of Macedonia. Author or co-author of 2 books, 10 articles in peer-reviewed journals, 23 book chapters, his publications, in both French and English, have appeared in *Études internationales*, the *Journal of Borderland Studies*, the *Canadian Journal of*

Foreign Policy, and *Connections*. He has also contributed to the public debate, notably by publishing 29 articles in the *Point de mire* series, which he edited between 2000 and 2006, contributing 20 op-eds (*Le Devoir*, *La Presse*, *Whig Standard*), and giving numerous interviews. He has been the RMCC representative to the Canadian Federation for the Humanities and Social Sciences since 2011.

Christian Leuprecht is a Class of 1965 Distinguished Professor in Leadership, Department of Political Science and Economics, Royal Military College, editor-in-chief of the *Canadian Military Journal*, director of the Institute of Intergovernmental Relations in the School of Policy Studies at Queen's University, senior fellow at the Macdonald Laurier Institute, and adjunct research professor in the Australian Graduate School of Policing and Security, Charles Sturt University.

Adam Lowther is director of Strategic Deterrence Programs at the National Strategic Research Institute at the University of Nebraska, US Strategic Command's university-affiliated research centre. He holds a PhD in political science from the University of Alabama. Adam previously taught at the US Army's School of Advanced Military Studies. He also served as the founding director of the School of Advanced Nuclear Deterrence Studies, Kirtland AFB. Dr. Lowther was also the director of the Center for Academic and Professional Journals at the Air Force Research Institute (AFRI), Maxwell AFB. Prior to assuming this position, Adam was a research professor at AFRI, where he led and participated in a number of studies directed by the chief of staff of the air force. Early in his career, Dr. Lowther served in the US Navy aboard the USS *Ramage* (DDG-61). He also served at CINCUSNAVEUR-London and with NMCB 17.

Sara Meharg is a global authority on the economic, cultural, and security reconstruction of post-disaster and post-conflict environments. Dr. Meharg is assistant professor at the Canadian Forces College and is the recent recipient of the prestigious Top Women in Defence and Security 2020 award. She is a recognized expert in managing the competing interests of defence, diplomacy, and development stakeholders in post-disaster and post-conflict planning. Dr. Meharg has extensive teaching experience at the undergraduate and graduate levels, and of note, with more than 1,100 senior military officers and civil servants, in institutional, operational, and cross-cultural contexts across national and international settings. She holds a bachelor of landscape architecture from the University of Guelph, a master of arts in war studies from the Royal Military College of Canada, and a PhD in cultural geography from Queen's University, where she studied the intentional destruction of cultural heritage sites during contemporary armed warfare. Dr. Meharg has served as a research fellow with organizations such as the Centre for Security and Defence Studies, the Canadian Global Affairs Institute, and the Security and Defence Forum.

Eric Ouellet is full professor of leadership, command, and management with the Department of Defence Studies at the Royal Military College of Canada as well as the Canadian Forces College (CFC). He is currently the academic lead for the Centre for National Security Studies, located at CFC. He holds bachelor's and master's degrees from Université Laval, Quebec City, and a PhD from York University, Toronto. His academic research and publications cover issues such as disinformation, institutional analysis and theory, organizational theory, counter-insurgency, military adaptation to irregular warfare, post-heroic warfare, special operation forces, defence planning, terrorist organizations, military sociology, and anomalous aerial phenomena. He is member of the international board of the Inter-University Seminar on Armed Forces and Society.

Ronald D. Porter (Major, Ret.) has developed expertise in attitude measurement and personnel selection in both academic and applied collaborations. He has published in the areas of attitude measurement, exploratory factor analysis, and personnel selection. Presently, Dr. Porter is an adjunct professor at Queen's University. Previously, he served in the Canadian Forces, where he developed an officer-selection process and validated several selection instruments as a member of the CF Human Resources research unit before being posted to the Royal Military College (RMC) as an assistant professor. At RMC, Dr. Porter conducted research in army culture, instrument psychometric assessment, and psychological operations. His academic experience also includes appointments as an associate professor at St. Mary's University and a senior lecturer at York St. John University in the United Kingdom.

Ron Schleifer is a senior lecturer at the School of Communication of Ariel University of Samaria, Israel, and is a renowned authority on psychological warfare. His books and articles deal with psychological warfare and the Arab-Israeli Conflict. He taught at the IDF Command College, and lectures and trains defence organizations on issues of information warfare both in Israel and abroad.

Anthony Seaboyer is director of the Centre for Security, Armed Forces and Society at the Royal Military College of Canada, where he teaches political science, political philosophy, and political geography. He is a senior lecturer at the Peace Support Training Centre teaching adversary information exploitation and information weaponization. At the Centre for Philosophy and AI Research of the Friedrich-Alexander Universität, he researches the effects of government AI exploitation for influence operations. He is a regular guest commentator on national security for CTV News Channel and a contracted national security commentator for the CBC News Network. His research focuses on national security regarding information warfare, AI for influence operations, social influence, psychological warfare, persuasion, social media exploitation, armed non-state actors, as well as the effects of the weaponization of information and AI on democracies.

Minqian Shen is a PhD candidate at Queen's University. He works in the Attitudes and Persuasion Lab under Dr. Leandre Fabrigar. His research focuses on attitude structure, the role of vocal properties in persuasion, and attitude measurement. Minqian holds a bachelor of science with a specialization in psychology from the University of Toronto and a master's of science in social psychology from Queen's University. His master's thesis focused on the structure and sequencing of information and its effects on persuasion. He is interested in the application of social psychology theory to practical domains of society and industry. Minqian's other interests include teaching, having taught statistics courses at Saint Lawrence College.

Anne Speckhard, PhD, is director of the International Center for the Study of Violent Extremism. She serves as adjunct associate professor of psychiatry at Georgetown University School of Medicine and an affiliate in the Center for Security Studies, Georgetown University. She has interviewed over 800 terrorists and violent extremists, as well as their family members and supporters around the world, including in western Europe, the Balkans, Central

Asia, the former Soviet Union, and the Middle East. Over the past five years, she has conducted in-depth psychological interviews with 273 ISIS defectors, returnees, and prisoners, and 16 al Shabaab cadres (as well as family members and ideologues,) studying their trajectories into and out of terrorism, and their experiences inside ISIS and al Shabaab.

Keith Stewart works at Defence Research and Development Canada's Toronto Research Centre. In a thirty-year career that has included periods in private industry and government service, he has focused on human-centric research issues, including influence operations, human elements of military command, and human error in high-hazard environments. He has worked previously on theoretical analysis of command approach, an examination of non-technical interoperability in the command and control of multinational forces, and an investigation of organizational structures in net-enabled organizations.

Joseph Szeman is a political studies and history graduate of Queen's University at Kingston, where he has conducted research on the strategic culture of middle powers, cyber operations, and deterrence and coercion in cyberspace.

Alex Wilner is an associate professor at the Norman Paterson School of International Affairs, Carleton University, Canada. His research explores the nexus between deterrence and emerging security considerations and domains. His books include *Deterrence by Denial* (co-edited with Andreas Wenger, Cambria Press, 2021), *Deterring Rational Fanatics* (University of Pennsylvania Press, 2015), and *Deterring Terrorism* (co-edited with Andreas Wenger, Stanford University Press, 2012). His articles have been published in top-ranked journals, including *International Security*, the *Journal of Strategic Studies*, and *Security Studies*. His scholarship has been awarded nearly $2 million in funding, including a SSHRC Insight Development Grant (2016–17), a SSHRC Insight Grant (2020–5), and a Government of Ontario Early Researcher Award (2021–6) for his cyber-deterrence project; two IDEaS grants (2018–21) and several Department of National Defence MINDS grants (2019, 2020) in support of his AI-deterrence project; and a major Mitacs grant (2020–2) and MINDS Collaborative Network grant to explore Canadian defence and emerging technology.

INDEX

www.ingramcontent.com/pod-product-compliance
Ingram Content Group UK Ltd.
Pitfield, Milton Keynes, MK11 3LW, UK
UKHW051915310125
454510UK00010B/142

9 781773 85403